To

Kelvin and Marisol,

Enjoy the read.

regards

Parnesh

07/6/2013

"Whilst industrialised countries continue to struggle with the aftermath of the global financial crisis, others face a much greater catastrophe of the effects of the global food crisis. This wide ranging and insightful book thoroughly explores the nature, dimensions and causes of the global food crisis. It provides policy options which can address the food crisis. A must read book on this major crisis for the world." --- **Malcolm C. Sawyer,** Emeritus Professor of Economics, University of Leeds, Leeds, UK.

"This is an important book taking a holistic and systems modelling approach to one of the most critical issues facing humanity: food security. It offers a multivariate measurement system to analyze and manage famine, hunger, malnutrition within a framework of GAFS: global agricultural and food system. Starting with the Bangladesh famine of 1972-3 and examining landmark contributions at the first World Food Conference in Rome in 1972 which led to the creation of the World Food Council, this book provides in eight chapters a path-breaking systems approach to ensure global food security. It is essential reading to specialists and informed public alike". --- **Ozay Mehmet,** Professor Emeritus, International Affairs and Economics, Carleton University, Ottawa, Ontario, Canada.

"Dr. Chopra's book is a fascinating study of global food crisis and brings many fresh ideas. It encapsulates different crucial dimensions of global food crisis, and perhaps the most critical is the attempt to measure the extent of the crisis. This is conspicuous by its absence in the existing literature. It is a real contribution for which Dr. Chopra's work will be remembered for a long time by analysts, economists and policy-makers. It will be relevant not only to those who eat to live but also to those who live to eat as well." --- **B.N. Ghosh,** Visiting Professor, Institute of Management and Technology, Government of Kerala, Alleppey, India.

"Dr Chopra's work can be deemed to be the first advanced reference book for studying and assessing the outcomes of the global food crisis in the framework of the world agricultural and food system. The model developed by Chopra with the contribution of Kanji allow to study and clarify within a comprehensive theoretical approach the multiple interactions of manifold factors affecting the main social effects of the present global agricultural system, with the help of a measuring metrics and a list of possible food policy options. We have here a precious working tool for both scholars and policy makers interested in reducing negative impacts of recent food crises on emerging countries and populations". --- **Franco Praussello,** Professor and Jean Monnet ad personam Chairholder in EU Economic Studies, Universities of Genoa and of Parma, Italy.

"To understand a food crisis it is necessary to identify the whole range of factors and obstacles linked with the way food is priced and internationally traded. Dr Chopra applies a scientific approach to measure the severity of food crisis. And this is where he makes an important contribution to the understanding, prevention and management of food crises in his book". --- **Ahmet Aker,** Professor & Dean, Faculty of Agriculture and Technology, Cyprus International University, N.Cyprus.

Through a focussed exploratory, descriptive, and causal, multi-layered approach, Parvesh Chopra, significantly contributes to addressing the global food crisis. He perceptively analyses a series of complex and challenging concepts clearly establishing a case for a holistic conceptualisation as a process to addressing the worsening global food security. Dr. Chopra argues through rigorous and elegant prose the necessity of understanding the global food crisis from a "complexity perspective". He challenges the claim that the true magnitude of the food crisis in its totality is not measureable. We are able to measure the food crisis at world level "not only by hard measures but by soft measures". With hard-edged intellect, Dr. Chopra explores decades of literature usually regarded as separate knowledge. An astonishing range of information is explored to expose complex interdependent and interconnected factors that model the international economy. Chopra defines the kind of information needed in order to make instruments suitable for immediate application to food policy options leading to greater food security, social welfare, environmental sustainability and ecological security. This seminal, ambitious book is clearly written from Professor Chopra's conviction that economists have a responsibility to make a better world. It deserves to be read by anyone interested in justice in the world they inhabit. Dr Chopra's book is essential to understand the food crisis and tragedy of famine during in the 21st century what AK Sen's work did in the 20th century. --- **Nancy Hudson-Rodd** PhD, Human Geographer, Honorary Research Associate in the School of Geography and Environmental Studies, University of Tasmania, Hobart, Australia.

"The global food crisis is a burning problem that has not been addressed with the urgency it deserves. The global economy faces imminent collapse, in a way that is unimaginable, if economists, policy makers and governments turn their heads the other way, instead of squarely facing the issue. Dr Chopra grabs the problem by its horns, and is unfazed by the myriad factors that are involved. Instead, he adopts a holistic approach and takes recourse to ideas that emerge from complexity theory. This is essential reading for anyone seriously interested in the global food crisis. --- **Shankaran Nambiar,** Professor, Manipal International University, Malaysia, and Associate Research Fellow, Malaysian Institute of Economic Research, Malaysia.

'The Global Food Crisis is indeed a 'silent tsunami', which demands much more considered and sustained attention. The acute problem of food security in the world is often overshadowed by the linked financial, energy and environmental crises, but the food crisis is more immediate and more deadly. Detailed analysis such as this one by Dr Parvesh K. Chopra is critical to deeper understandings and more effective action. The book goes beyond the simple, failed explanations of the past.' --- **Tim Anderson** PhD, Senior Lecturer in Political Economy, University of Sydney, Australia.

On Measuring Global Food Crisis

A Multivariate Modelling Approach

ALSO BY PARVESH K. CHOPRA

- *Essential Emotional Intelligence: Pathways to Success in Work and Life (Under Preparation)*

- *Corporate Social Responsibility in a New Global Economy*

- *Development Macroeconomics, Global Issues and Human Development: Essays in Honour of Professor B.N. Ghosh*

- *Measuring Country Risk*

- *Poverty as Human Contestability Failure*

- *Gender and Development (2 Volumes) (with B.N. Ghosh)*

- *Logic, Scientific Method and Economic Analysis*

- *Management with Measurement: Can't Measure Can't Manage (with Gopal K. Kanji)*

- *Existing but Not Living: Studies in Poverty and Inequality (with B.N. Ghosh)*

- *Political Economy of Rural Poverty Alleviation Measures in India*

- *Globalisation, Human Degradation and Unequal Competition (with B.N. Ghosh)*

- *A Dictionary of Research Methods (with B.N. Ghosh)*

- *A Dictionary of Statistics*

- *A Dictionary of Demography and Human Development (with B.N. Ghosh)*

- *Economics: Basics and Beyond*

On Measuring Global Food Crisis

A Multivariate Modelling Approach

Parvesh K. Chopra

2012

Wisdom House

On Measuring Global Food Crisis
A Multivariate Modelling Approach

First published in 2012 by

Wisdom House Publications Ltd.
Unique House, 1 Dolly Lane, Leeds LS9 7NN, England (United Kingdom)
Tel: +44 (0)113 2420555 Fax: +44 (0) 113 2420963
Email: editor@wisdomhousepublications.co.uk
Internet: www.wisdomhousepublications.co.uk

Simultaneously published in India by

Wisdom House Academic Publishers Pvt. Ltd.
126, Housing Board Colony,
Ambala Cantt. – 133 001, Haryana, India.
Tel: +91 (171) 2821237, 2821299, Fax: +91 (171) 2821282
E-mail: Wisdom_hap@yahoo.co.in
Internet: www.wisdomhousepublications.co.uk

Wisdom House is a registered trade mark of Wisdom House Publications Ltd.
Our distribution links across the world.
First edition 2012
British library cataloguing in publication data
Chopra, Parvesh K.
On Measuring Global Food Crisis: A Multivariate Modelling Approach
ISBN 978-1-84290-240-0 Paperback
ISBN 978-1-84290-241-7 Hardbound

The book is printed on acid free paper in England (United Kingdom)

Cover and Design by
Sergio Sanchez Martinez

To my mother
Mrs. Shanti Rani Chopra
for her care, upbringing and motherly love,
and my sons
Sameer** and **Nikhil
for their patience and profound understanding

Contents

List of Tables

List of Figures

Acronyms and Abbreviations

AMOS	Analysis of Moment Structures
ANCOVA	Analysis of Covariance
ANOVA	Analysis of Variance
ASF	Animal Source Foods
BMI	Body Mass Index
BoP	Balance of Payment
CARD	Center for Agricultural Research and Development
CBOT	Chicago Board of Trade
CFS	FAO Committee on World Food Security
CFCFs	Critical Food Crisis Factors
CPI	Consumer Price Index
DAGs	Directed Acyclic Graphs
EU	European Union
FAC	Food Aid Convention
FAO	Food and Agriculture Organization of the United Nations
FAPRI	Food and Agricultural Policy Research Institute
FDSRs	Food Demand Side Restrictions
FEWSNET	Famine Early Warning Systems Network
FSSRs	Food Supply Side Restrictions
GAFC	Global Agricultural and Food System
GAMFs	Global Agricultural Markets Failures
GDP	Gross domestic product
GFC	Global Food Crisis
GHGs	Greenhouse Gases
GIEWS	Global Information and Early Warning System
GMOs	Genetically-modified Organisms
HDN	Human Development Network
IAASTD	International Assessment of Agricultural Knowledge, Science and Technology for Development
IEA	International Energy Agency
IFAD	International Fund for Agricultural Development
IFPRI	International Food Policy Research Institute

IMF	International Monetary Fund
IPCFS	International Planning Committee for Food Sovereignty
IRRI	International Rice Research Institute
KCGFCMS	Kanji- Chopra Global Food Crisis Measurement System
LVSM	Latent Variable Structural Model
LDC	Least-developed Country
LFS	Local Food Systems
LISREL	Linear Structural Relations
MANOVA	Multivariate Analysis of Variance
MENA	Middle Eastern and North African
MNCs	Multinational Corporations
MRE	Meal Ready to Eat
NIEO	New International Economic Order
NGOs	Non-governmental Organizations
NPP	Neoliberal and Productionist Paradigm
OECD	Organization for Economic Cooperation and Development
OFS	Organic Food Systems
OPEC	Organization of Petroleum Exporting Countries
OSFPs	Organizations of Smallholder Food Producers
PLS	Partial Least Squares
PREM	Poverty Reduction and Economic Management
PSICA	Public Sector Intervention and Collective Action
R & D	Research and Development
SAS	Statistical Analysis System
SEM	Structural Equation Modelling
TFP	Total Factor Productivity
TNC	Transnational Corporations
UNCTAD	United Nations Conference on Trade and Development
UN HLTF	United Nations High-Level Task Force
USA	United States of America
USAID	United States Agency for International Development
USD	United States Dollar
USDA	United States Department of Agriculture
WB	World Bank
WFP	World Food Programme
WTO	World Trade Organization

Acknowledgements

"There are people in the world so hungry, that God cannot appear to them except in the form of bread............"
Mohandas Karamchand (Mahatma) Gandhi, 1869-1948, Spiritual Leader and Father of India.

In acknowledgement of the everlasting influences of intellectual legacies of the pioneers of different intellectual streams of agricultural and food economics research, I would like to express my sincere gratitude to Francois Quesnay, Adam Smith, Arthur Young, David Ricardo, Von Thünen, Antoine Augustin Cournot, Alfred Marshall, Thorstein Bunde Veblen, J.R. Hicks, John Wynn Baker, Henry Charles Taylor, John D. Black, Frederick V. Waugh, Mordecai Joseph Brill Ezekiel, Wassily Wassilyovich Leontief, Theodore W. Schultz, Willard Cochrane, Paul A. Samuelson, Kenneth E. Boulding, George Stigler, D. Gale Johnson, Earl O. Heady, Nicholas Georgescu-Roegen, R. J. "Jim" Hildreth, Zvi Grilliches, Karl Brandt, J. Wayne Reitz, J. K. Galbraith, Milton Friedman, Amartya K. Sen, James M. Buchanan, Manmohan Singh (renowned economist and 13th and current Prime Minister of India), Albert Hirschman, William G. Murray, Norman Borlaug (Father of the Green Revolution), Paul Streeten, Mark Blaug, B. Swerling, A. Martin, R.L. Cohen, B.H. Hibbard, G.W. Forster, Simon Kuznets, Joseph Eugene Stiglitz, P. S. Dasgupta, W.H. Nicholls, A.M. Khusro, J. W. Mellor, V.M. Dandekar, Keith Griffin, Charles Peter Timmer, Michael Lipton, M. S. Ahluwalia, Kaushik Basu, T.J. Byres, D.G. Johnson, T.N. Krishna, E. Boserup, Krishna Raj, M. Ravallion, C.H. Hanumantha Rao, A. Vaidyanathan, V.K.R.V. Rao, G. Parthasarathy, B.S. Minhas, Wallace C. Olsen, N.A. Mujumdar, E.O. Heady, A. Rudra, P. K. Bardhan, Krishna Bharadwaj, *inter alia.*

A research work on such a tropical issue as global food crisis required the expertise of many scholars, researchers and authorities who munificently offered their insights across a wide range of issues. I have immeasurably benefited from the candid observations and constructive suggestions of the pioneer in the field of Statistics *Professor Kanti V. Mardia,* Senior Research Professor, Department of Statistics, School of Mathematics, The University of Leeds, Leeds, England, who also kindly gave me a free signed copy of his world-renowned book on Multivariate Analysis. I have overtly or covertly learnt a lot from his superb acumen, treasure of knowledge and never-ending dedication to innovative research works. I would like to take this opportunity to express my sincere gratitude to Professor B.N. Ghosh for his suggestions and fruitful comments particularly in connection with discussions on economics and meta-economics of food. His critical suggestions and advice will always stay with me.

Right from the genesis of the idea up to the completion of this study, I have received immense benefits from the numerous comments, analytical advice and informative emails from Emeritus Professor Malcolm C. Sawyer, Leeds University Business School, The University of Leeds, U.K. who was also my teacher, guide and source of inspiration during my research at The University of Leeds. I shall remain grateful to Emeritus Professor Ozay Mehmet, Carleton University, Ottawa, Ontario, Canada, for his critical advice and insightful suggestions especially on global governance for world food security. In particular, I would like to express my sincere thanks to Professor Mark Cleary, Vice-Chancellor, University of Bradford, England, for his various remarks and valuable suggestions on the smouldering humanitarian issue of worldwide food crisis. I feel grateful to Professor Cleary for inviting me to meet and attend the lecture of Nobel Peace Prize winner Adolfo Pérez Esquivel, a former Professor of Architecture from Argentina, on the challenges to human rights in the 21st century. I am highly grateful to my sister-in-law Professor Dr. Monica Lakhanpaul, Integrated Community Child Health, University College London (Institute of Child Health), and brother-in-law Dr. Sandeep Lakhanpaul (Dentist, Nottingham) for their constant goading and encouragements.

I will remain grateful to my brother-in-law Mr. Sanjay Dhir (Partner, Long Grin Cambodia, www.lgrcambodia.com) and sister-in-law Mrs. Caroline Dhir (Partner, Human Capital, Ernst Young, London), who directly or indirectly gave me necessary impetus for studying the phenomenon of global food crisis. I would like to especially mention here that Mr. Sanjay Dhir and his associates through their venture of rice plant founded in Cambodia in 2011 would modernise and expand Cambodia's indigenous rice milling industry to process the country's high quality rice paddy produce. This will certainly contribute to a certain extent to resolve the food problems especially for Cambodia and its neighbouring countries in Asia via processing and distribution of rice and generating employment opportunities. It gives me immense pleasure to express my thankfulness to my brother-in-law, Dr.

Neil Sikka, founder Barbican Dental Care, Canary Wharf, London, who via his charity works has been contributing and making difference so that the rural poor communities in Gwalior (India) and around Kampong Cham (Cambodia) can have free access to much needed dental care. Many thanks to my uncle Professor H.R. Chopra, Department of Library and Information Services, Panjab University, Chandigarh, India, for his highly appreciated support. I am also thankful to my nephew Dr. Sunil Malhotra (Dentist, London, Canada) and his wife Dr. Anuka Malhotra (Dentist, London, Canada) for their valuable conversations over food problems. I express my thanks to my dear friend Dr. Rajeev Gupta, Consultant Paediatrician, Barnsley Foundation Hospital, NHS, England and Visiting Professor to many international universities, for various insightful and profound discussions we had on understanding human behaviour and decision-making processes by exploring human relationships, communications and emotional intelligence.

It was my great privilege to have academic association and friendship with my co-author late Emeritus Professor Gopal K. Kanji, University of Sheffield, England. We worked together on many projects involving thoughtful statistical thinking and advanced statistical modelling in economics, management, health, and other areas of research. We jointly developed robust measurement models namely Kanji-Chopra Multivariate Poverty Model, Kanji-Chopra Corporate Social Responsibility Model, Kanji-Chopra Work Stress Model, Kanji-Chopra Environmental Health Model, Kanji-Chopra Country Risk Model, Kanji-Chopra Emotional Intelligence Model, Kanji-Chopra Social Capital Model, Kanji-Chopra Value Generation Model, Kanji-Chopra Performance Excellence Model, and so on. Our most recent model entitled *A Kanji-Chopra Model of Global Food Crisis* was published in *Journal of Human Development* in 2011 (Chopra, Parvesh K., 3(2), 197-230). Even though Professor Kanji is no more with us physically, his vision and thoughts in the fields of statistics, quality, performance and business excellence shall always remain with us as a guiding light and continue to lead us in our pursuit of imparting value based research and education to the society. My sincere thanks are also due to Mrs. Valerie Kanji for her enormous support for the completion of this book.

I very sincerely thank my teachers Professors H.S. Shergill, A.C. Julka, V.K. Gupta, M. R. Aggarwal, B.R. Kandoi, Pritam Singh (currently working at Business School, Oxford Brookes University, England), Shyama Bhardwaj among others for their academic teachings and guidance during my student days in 1980's at Department of Economics, Panjab University, Chandigarh,

India. The author is grateful to Mr. Merlin Treymaine (ECO, Chiltern Mills, Leeds, England), Mr. Vineet Choudhary (ECO, Climax Brushes, New Delhi, India), Mr. Ashwani Handa (ECO, Sunrise Freight Forwarders, New Delhi and member of Governing Body, *Institute for Development and Communication,* Chandigarh, India), Mr. Vipin R. Sardana (Partner, Fashion Group International, Panipat, India), Mr. Kamaljit Singh Bhogal (Project Architect, Leeds, England), Jacqui Sykes (Leeds) and Mr. Bryan Kelly (Dublin, Ireland) who provided feedback, background materials, or other supports at various stages in the preparation of this research work.

I will always remain grateful to my father late Dr. Mulkh Raj Chopra, my mother Mrs. Shanti Rani Chopra and father-in law late Mr. Satya Prakash Dhir who taught me to place education and soft skills formation above all other worldly desires. The unfailing encouragements and constant support from my mother-in-law Mrs. Santosh Dhir provided me sufficient momentous to complete this research work on time while she helped me immensely in my various domestic responsibilities. I am profoundly thankful to my wife Anita, and sons Sameer and Nikhil, for encouraging, supporting and standing by me during the course of my hectic engagements as a reviewer of the *Total Quality Management & Business Excellence* journal (SSCI indexed), academic and non-academic works and this research and even by sacrificing many moments of humdrum moorings simply to see this work a success and whose painful pleasure lying underneath throughout has inspired me all the more with agility, ado and ambrosia. My sincere thanks to Mr. Dayal Sharma (MBE) ECO, *Centre for Politics and Public Participation,* Bradford, England, for his help and support at many a critical junctures of this work. I will remain grateful to my brother in law Mr. Rajinder Kumar Malhotra, Food Corporation of India, Ludhiana, India and my elder sister Mrs. Jai Malhotra, Principal, Government School, Ludhiana, India. It is matter of massive contentment to acknowledge here that Mr. Rishi Baveja (MSc Economics, Cambridge and MMS, London Business School) currently working at Oliver Wyeman, London, who chose his MSc Dissertation topic on *Global Food Crisis* at Cambridge University and successfully completed it.

Special thanks are due to my uncle, Dr. Om Prakash Sikka, Consultant Opthalmology (retired) and auntie, Dr. Swadesh Sikka, currently working as NHS locum and in family planning clinic, Grimbsy, UK, for their help and blessings. I will be failing in my duty if I do not acknowledge my indebtedness to Ionela Cristina Nicolae (M.A. in TESOL, The University of Leeds, England) for her immense help at many stages of this research work without which this work would have not completed on time. I express my sincere gratitude to all the reviewers of this work for their various positive externalities. Comments on the book by all the reviewers are gratefully acknowledged with the usual disclaimer that the author alone bears responsibility for all possible errors that might be muffling around this research work.

Dr Parvesh K. Chopra
Leeds, United Kingdom
drparveshchopra@gmail.com
World Food Day, 16th October 2012.

Prolegomena

"Eating is a need. Knowing how to eat is an art".
Francois de La Rochefoucauld (1613-1680), An Eminenet French Writer

Food[i] is the first necessity as it satisfies a basic human instinct – hunger. Everyone requires food and all creatures must eat to live. Access to adequate, quality, safe and nutritious food is a fundamental human right. Food remains a necessary ingredient in sustaining and maintaining human life besides water and air. After breathing, eating is what we do most regularly during our lifetime. For rich and poor alike a certain amount of food is indispensable to keep the body in good condition, to maintain efficiency and normal human health. It has been argued that plant-based food is better than animal-based food for good health, balanced growth and longevity (Pollan, 2008). The phenomenon of *body capital*, an essential dimension of *human contestability*[ii], also subsumes the issue of *utilisation of food* which remains critically dependent upon the availability, accessibility and affordability of quality food consisting of different components of variable nutritional value called nutrients[iii]. A balanced diet in small portion sizes should include foods from different natural food groups instead of processed foods, ensuring adequate nutrients intake without exceeding the energy requirements.

As early as in 1857, Statistician Ernst Engel observed that "all poor spend large proportion of their household income on food"[iv]. An increase in Engel's coefficient (the percentage of food consumption to total spending and a quantitative measure of the misery of the working class) indicates the deteriorating living standards of low-income families. Therefore, the living conditions and quality of life of poor households are adversely affected by exorbitant basic food prices. Recently, millions of people across the world have been hit very hard as they struggle to make ends meet due to the rocketed basic food prices between 2008 and 2012 (FAO, 2008a, 2010, 2012a). According to the United Nations report, the world's poorest countries could pay 40 percent more for food in 2008 than they did last year because of rising prices[v]. The Food Price Index, a measure of the cost of a basket of food commodities, for July 2012 surged to 213 points (United Nations, 2012). Moreover, the food prices hike in July 2012 has passed the level that sparked food roots from Haiti to Bangladesh to Egypt and to Mexico in

2008. The price of corn (maize) has rocketed two thirds since mid-June 2012 (Fraser and Rimas, 2011; Fortson, 2012), a 30% surge in the price of soya and similar price increase in wheat and rice. The surging food prices have brought the issue to a boiling point. Further food price surges are likely to spark similar roots and social unrest when people who are living on a dollar a day spend majority of their money on basic food products and they feel dramatically worse off when food prices go up. The recent 'biblical events' similar to the dust bowl years of 1930s have given rebirth to a disastrous situation termed as global food crisis (GFC).

However, by no means the present GFC is a *new phenomenon* as it also occurred many times before including during 1970s and 1990s. The factors like the US dollar depreciation during 1971-74, the USSR procurement of food grains, increase in food demand during 1972, cut in government food stocks, devastating famine in Bangladesh during 1972-74 and so on, contributed to the increase in international grain prices that led to the first World Food Conference in 1974 and the establishment of many international organisations such as International Food Policy Research Institute (IFPRI)[vi] and others. From their peak during 1970s crisis, real food prices steadily declined during the 1980s. The food price crisis of mid-90s was an outgrowth of factors like East-Asian financial crisis, adoption of protectionist policies, depreciation in US dollar, cut in food reserves, reduction in the area under cultivation[vii] and so on (Deaton and Laroque, 1990). Thereafter the real food prices reached an all-time low during the end of last century and beginning of the present century. However, the global prices of major food cereals surged upward from 2006 onwards and the predictions were that real food prices would remain high until at least the end of the next decade. The policy to achieve national food security[viii] in both developed and developing world was relied on food import instead of investing in domestic agricultural sector. Nevertheless, this acuity quickly collapsed with the re-emergence of contemporary global food crisis. During the period 2007-12, many countries around the globe became repeat-offenders when they continued to implement conflicting, controversial and lopsided food policies such as farmer subsidies[ix], food export restrictions[x] and food import bans[xi].

The origin of the contemporary global food crisis can be traced back around the beginning of the 21st century. During the year 2002 US dollar further devaluated, oil prices started rising since the year 2003 and the year 2004 witnessed a momentous use of food for bio-fuels production[xii]. During the year 2005 Russia and Ukraine experienced severe droughts and Australia was hit by dry spell in a century (Bradsher, 2007). The year 2006 observed a diversification of investors and hedge funds into agricultural commodities, floods hit Northern Europe, droughts dried Southern Europe, Turkey, northwest Africa and Argentina during 2007. Russia, India, China and other countries imposed export restrictions in 2007. The year 2008 experienced severe economic downturn, recession, banking crisis and food prices also peaked. During 2009 the food prices stayed high and even rose due to structural factors such as increased prosperity in emerging economies, low cereal stock, bio-fuel production and climate change[xiii]. The year of 2010 was a landmark year for food inflation (food prices rose by 32%) as local food prices returned to their inflation peak levels across the globe. Wheat prices doubled between July and August 2010 due to natural calamities such as severe drought, floods in Pakistan, loss of harvest in Russia and so on. In August 2010, Russia, one of the world's biggest producers of wheat, barley and rye, imposed a ban on grain exports after a severe drought and a spate of wildfires devastated crops[xiv]. During 2011 the severe drought across Kenya, Ethiopia, Somalia, Uganda and Djibouti had left an estimated 11.5 million people on the brink of starvation. In 2012 millions of people were displaced in Syria, Africa, Bangladesh, and other countries due to political conflicts and natural disasters. For the third time in ten years drought (lack of rainfall and the intense heat) is wreaking havoc in the Sahel region of West Africa and this time, the resulting famine could be the worst humanitarian crisis in history. In July 2012 the United States Department of Agriculture declared natural disaster areas in more than 1,000 counties and 26 drought-stricken states, making it the largest natural disaster in America ever. A sharp acceleration in the price of basic foods is of major and special concern to the world's poor[xv]. There would be less corn coming onto global markets over the next year because of a sharp drop in US exports (Goldenberg, 2012). Iran is seeing a chicken crisis, Mexicans are seeing a rise in the price of their corn tortillas, and Indonesia is experiencing protests from tofu industry (Robinson, 2012). The United Nations says North Korea has requested immediate 'food aid' after devastating floods in July 2012 as about 5 million people face food shortages[xvi]. More than 18 million people in the African region which covers parts of Senegal, Mauritania, Mali, Algeria, Niger, Chad, Sudan and Eritrea are facing a food crisis and more than a million children under the age of five risk severe acute malnutrition during August 2012. A very serious situation worldwide is that global grain stocks have reached a new low with the US and other countries running down their reserves. This affects the poorest of the poor the most in food-scarce developing countries through price transmission (Dawe, 2008;

Cudjoe et al., 2010).

On the one hand, lifestyle choices, lack of physical exercise and medical reasons[xvii] have given birth to the problem of obesity. Another seriously neglected insight in the dynamics of food related human behaviour reveals two interwoven issues: first, 'from farm to plate' and second, 'from brain to mouth'. The economics and meta-economics of food have given birth to a paradoxical situation of co-existence of global hunger[xviii] and global obesity[xix] (globesity). When people consume more calories than they burn, they put on weight and vice-versa. The main reasons for obesity are lack of willpower, genes, culture of junk and fast food, drinking too much alcohol, eating habits (declining trend of sit-down traditional meals), food addiction in children and adults, cognitive demanding lifestyle, more food variety encouraging overeating, intense food marketing and advertising, physical inactivity, comfort eating, eating out a lot, medical reasons, and so on. People with higher body mass index (BMI) tend to partner with those of similar BMI and have heavier offsprings. Thus, we have a group of millions of people across globe that is much heavier than ever before (overweight and obese). On the other hand, there is another group of millions of people who are suffering from hunger[xx] and acute malnutrition. The intertwined dynamics of food, obesity, and hunger have produced both severe hunger and obesity epidemic, i.e., out of 7 billion global population there are one billion people without enough food to eat (suffering from hunger) and 1.6 billion overweight or obese at present[xxi]. This is intensifying the worldwide health crisis and putting stresses on global resources. Popkin (2003) observed that nutrition concerns relate to malnutrition in some places or group of people and obesity in others, as there is inequitable distribution of the quality as well as quantity of food, and negative consequences arise from multiple eating patterns. Thus, this prevailing huge paradox of global obesity and chronic hunger is simply another manifestation of the complex multidimensional phenomenon of global food crisis.

Global food crisis is perhaps one of the hottest topics in the modern day world. As a subject of study, it has lately become a major concern for the international community, organisations and political leaders. There are quite a few research studies and books published on food problems (food crisis, security, hunger, malnutrition, famine and so on). Just to quote a few serious books on world food crisis available in the market: *Food "Crisis"* (Hendrickson, 1943); *Food Enough* (Black, 1943); *The World Food Crisis* (Marx, 1975); *Fast Food Nation* (Schlosser, 2001); *The End of Food* (Roberts, 2008); *Assessing the Global Food Crisis* (Buchanan, 2008); *The Global*

Food Crisis: Governance Challenges and Opportunities (Cohen and Clapp, 2009); *The Food Wars* (Bello, 2009); *Stuffed and Starved: The Hidden Battle for the World Food System* (Patel, 2009); *The Environmental Food Crisis* (Nellemann, 2009); *The Coming Famine: The Global Food Crisis and What We Can Do to Avoid it* (Cribb, 2010); *The Global Food Crisis: New Insights into an Age-old Problem* (Himmelgreen and Kedia, 2010); *Global Food Crisis: Contemporary Issues and Policy Options* (Ghosh, 2011); *Accounting for Hunger: The Right to Food in the Era of Globalisation* (De Schutter and Cordes, 2011); *Economics of Food Prices and Crises* (Lagi et al., 2012); and many more. These works are either collection of articles by experts from different fields or highlights of the contemporary controversies on the food issues or comprehensive story-type narration on how world food crisis happened. Most of the recent work on GFC has been non-academic commentary in terms of internet blogs, articles in newspapers, magazines and internet sites or rushed books either story telling or collection of articles or intuitive, astute, rigorous and resourceful, but deal with one or few aspects of the world food crisis. Much of the work has been necessarily 'quick and patchy' just to feed hasty information to policy makers rather than undertaking comprehensive, rigorous, profound and scientific research (Chopra, 2011). Some of the studies have taken into consideration the same food crisis factors. The science and art of *management with measurement* of global food crisis in a systematic and scientific way is missing in previous works. Despite its astonishing severity, no major previous study has been undertaken to conceptualise the phenomenon of GFC as a holistic syndrome, to quantify its magnitude, intensity and severity, identify and analyse its critical crisis factors (sources), comprehend its consequences, and offer food policy options to manage it effectively on Planet Earth. The profound statistical, economic and meta-economic thinking behind the present research work can be elaborated as follows:

Food problems have haunted mankind since the dawn of history. However, an intellectual history of scientific research in agricultural and food economics reveals the paradigm shifts in its focus. Ancient thought gave agriculture an important place in society. The pre-classical and classical school of economic thought regarded it as a source of wealth. From 1798 to 1826, Malthus analysed the food-to-population ratio and argued that population would grow at a geometric rate while the food supply grows at an arithmetic rate[xxii] and resulting overpopulation would be checked sooner or later by positive and preventive measures[xxiii]. Throughout the 20th century the domain of agricultural research was expanded by application of various mathematical, statistical and econometrics methods and models such as Marshallian demand and supply tools, Marginalism, correlation analysis, regression pricing, Cobweb model, input-output analysis, linear programming, optimization, subjective probability, recursive programming models, project evaluations, and so on. During the period 1940s and 1970s, a series of research, development and technology transfer initiatives (Green Revolution[xxiv]) resulted in phenomenal growth in agriculture that saved over a billion people from starvation. The decade of 1970s also witnessed a debate on *trickle-down hypothesis,* i.e., relationship between agricultural development and rural poverty reduction. Thereafter, the factors such as agricultural income levels per head, food prices and so on were included in this analysis. Amartya Sen (Sen, 1981, 1982; Dreze and Sen, 1995) introduced a major paradigm shift and established the *access to food*[xxv] as opposed to *availability* only at individual level as a critical factor to food security. This view asserted that hunger and food insecurity are not just a matter of food scarcity, food shortage or high food prices[xxvi], but are critically linked with poverty and inequality in access to food[xxvii]. To quote Sen (1999), "a tendency to concentrate on food production only, neglecting *food entitlement,* can be deeply counterproductive.... People suffer from hunger when they cannot establish their entitlement over an adequate amount of food". This entitlement is determined by endowment (ownership over productive resources as well as wealth that commands a price in the market), production possibilities and their use and exchange conditions (ability to sell and buy goods and food prices vis-à-vis wage rate)[xxviii]. As more and more people do not grow the food they eat, the emerging view on food security strongly emphasises inequity in food distribution and allocation and purchasing power of households (disposable income) along with *consumption patterns and preferences.* The domain of food security was amplified by focusing on the issues of *utilisation of food* [xxix], *nutritionally adequate and safe food, right to food* [xxx] and food insecurity resulting from *human contestability failure* [xxxi]. Food security research framework has been further enlarged by the insights from the *livelihoods approach to poverty and vulnerability.* Over the last five decades, there are ten major areas of contributions made in agricultural and food research (see, Chapter 2 for further details).

Food security (availability, accessibility, acceptability, adequacy and agency of food) is an important policy issue for every economy. At a lower level of complexity, global food security is linked with a sharp rise in basic food prices due to food shortage (decline in the size of food output) or rising global food demand or a mixture of both. The supply side of national food security, however, involves the size of food output plus food imports. Food security at individual/household level is determined by either growing own food, bartering for food or purchasing it in the market place. Such a manifestation of food crisis conceals more than it reveals since it is a highly complex phenomenon. In fact, food security at a household, community, national, regional and global level depends upon the factors and forces ranging from domestic to global level in this new globalised world. For example, large farmers love the bio-fuel programme because the crops production provides incentives in terms of guarantee of a market and a good price. From another perspective, it does not make any sense to put crops into cars rather than feeding hungry people. It is also true that the lack of demand and falling food prices will keep the size of food output down which in turn generate poverty of the poorest farmers and landless rural labourers. At any level, food security is a dynamic socioeconomic condition which involves multiple layers of causation (web of causal relations) resulting from the interplay of diverse complex critical factors related to dynamics of global agricultural and food system[xxxii]. Thus, the dynamics of food security are closely linked with the rapidly changing global agricultural and food system[xxxiii]. This system has many inherent food paradoxes such as 'paradox of plenty' that generate food inequalities[xxxiv]. The question is: What drives changes in this system? These changes are produced by natural and man-made socioeconomic, political, institutional, technological, ecological and environmental driving forces that have backward and forward linkages with the production, demand, supply, distribution, processing, consumption and utilisation of food. The changes these driving forces produce are posing serious unprecedented stresses within world food systems and hence on food security[xxxv]. The mechanism of underlying interactions among driving forces, resources, processes and activities of world food system produce rapid changes in outputs, outcomes and impacts contributing to food security, social welfare, development sustainability and ecological security. The phenomenon of global food crisis, therefore, is an outcome of and lies within the domain of the prevailing global agricultural and food system.

The phenomenon of GFC cannot be explained by the normal food demand and supply dynamics alone. There are many visible and invisible factors involved. The causes of contemporary GFC are complex, diverse and interwoven. It is, therefore, pertinent to identify various critical food crisis factors and establish their causal mechanisms and pathways. Some of the critical factors that have been identified as new entrants in the prevailing global food crisis are: use of plants to grow bio-fuels, biopharmaceuticals, bio-plastics, and pharmaceuticals; food demand from fast growing economies such as China, India[xxxvi] etc, diverse food demand[xxxvii], emerged global financial crisis during 2007-08, high costs of inputs like fertilisers, oil, etc., emergence of oligopolistic and oligopsonistic structures (multinational agribusiness and food giants), neo-liberal globalisation, role of speculators, growth in global meat consumption, climate change (Backlund et al., 2008) and so on. However, the present study has taken into consideration simultaneously all possible critical food crisis factors into its analytic umbrella. GFC is not only a *financial* come but also a *real* phenomenon since its repercussions reach the real sector via its linkages to systematic causes and heavily distorted food system that favoured the large rich farmers and food multinationals at the cost of billions of poor consumers and producers. Thus, the GFC is not only connected with the financial and economic forces, but also with the climatic/environmental disasters, socio-ecological interactions, socio-political forces and institutional mechanisms.

This work outlines an integrated analysis of environmental, social, cultural, political, economic and technological activities, involving their interconnections and contributions in generating and perpetuating global food crisis. The present book, however, introduces *a new approach* to study, analyse, measure and manage GFC that is based on holistic conceptualisation, systems thinking, multivariate analysis and structural equation modelling. The concept of global food crisis is holistic, multidimensional and multidisciplinary. This work identifies the critical food crisis factors and constructs the dimensional structure that subsumes global agricultural and food system, food demand-side forces, food supply-side restrictions, agricultural market failures (malfunctioning) and public sector interventions and collective actions failures. A new generic robust *research methodological structure* has been introduced that develops conceptual, operational, latent variable structural equation and measurement model that is consistent with the ideas and thoughts of major agricultural research contributors and satisfy the suggested modelling criteria and incorporates critical food crisis factors. It can be used as a tool to analyse, measure and manage the phenomenon of global food crisis from complexity perspective in order to drill through the multiple complex layers of causation and to construct causal pathways leading the global food crisis. It determines the structural relationships and strengths of causal connections among critical food crisis factors and global food crisis. Such a *new multivariate analysis* is indispensable to construct an index to measure the depth, intensity and severity of global food crisis within certain boundaries of global agricultural and food system. It validates the

Kanji Chopra Global Food Crisis Model with relevant data and testing with suitable statistical methods. It provides a measure or index of food crisis at global level, country level or regional level. Strengths and weaknesses of various components of the model will also indicate the characteristics at certain level in order to pinpoint what exactly is required from the national governments, policy makers and international organisations to manage the food crisis effectively. The model produces a more accurate reflection of the degree to which different dimensions of GFC have been contributing to the overall world food crisis. Given the vital need for such a work that deals with GFC in its full depth and range, the present work endeavours to fill an important knowledge gap in literature on economics and meta-economics of food.

Considering the internationalised nature of the food crisis and increasing economic and non-economic interconnectivity of the different regions of the globe, there is a greater need for global governance for world food security now than it has ever been. Undoubtedly, the ultimate aim of every economy is to achieve 'zero hunger and obesity' by fulfilling its commitment of right to nutritious food for its citizens. The *sine qua non* is: all countries must endeavour to achieve self-sufficiency in food production, equal distribution of food at affordable prices, maintain food security by all means, and ensure the proper utilisation of quality nutritious food by ways of suitable measures. However, the need for a multivariate approach can hardly be exaggerated in the context of the contemporary world food crisis. I have arranged the book in eight chapters for clarity and simplicity purpose and to make it a systemic study that can analyse and explore the underlying interactions within and among economy, society, ecology and polity at various levels. I have provided as many endnotes as possible to explain the technical concepts in each chapter so that this work is more accessible to non-experts readers. Such an interactive, integrative and discursive framework of global food crisis measurement, albeit missing in the existing literature, brings under its analytic umbrella all possible dimensions and manifest variables affecting the GFC. This book explores the greatest issue of our age and provides practical suggestions and policy options in order to manage the phenomenon with its measurement. *Can't measure, can't manage.* Hence there is a need for an analytical volume on global food crisis. I hope this first full-length study of global food crisis based on analytical treatment, profound statistical thinking, multivariate modelling technique and systems approach, would generate further academic and public interest in the prevailing vital and critical food crisis factors. Needless to say that national governments, agricultural scientists, policy makers, researchers, teachers, informed students and laymen readers with an interest in agricultural economics, food policy, food prices and food security will find this book to be a timely, up-to-date and informative volume for their personal book collection.

Dr Parvesh K. Chopra
Leeds, United Kingdom
drparveshchopra@gmail.com
World Food Day, 16th October 2012.

Notes

i.   Food is any substance that, when taken into the body, serves to nourish, build and repair tissues, supply energy or regulate body processes. Beside its nutritional function, food is valued for its palatability and satiety effect as well as for varied meanings attached to it (emotional, social, religious, cultural, etc) by different individuals, groups or races.

ii.   The notion of 'human contestability' was first coined and discussed by Parvesh K. Chopra (2003 and 2007) in relation to a new perspective and approach of poverty as human contestability failure.

iii.   These are carbohydrates, proteins, fats and oil, minerals, vitamins and water. Carbohydrates, proteins and fats and oil are referred to as macro-nutrients because they are needed in large quantity while vitamins and minerals are referred to as micro-nutrients (needed in small quantity).

iv.   Engel's law is an observation in Economics stating that as income rises, the proportion of income spent on food falls, even if actual expenditure on food rises. In other words, the income elasticity of demand of food is between 0 and 1. The law was named after the statistician Ernst Engel (1821–1896). Engel's Law doesn't imply that food spending remains unchanged as income increases: It suggests that consumers increase their expenditures for food products (in % terms) less than their increases in income (Timmer, Falcon and Pearson, 1983). One application of this statistic is treating it as a reflection of the living standard of a country. As this proportion or "Engel coefficient" increases, the country is by nature poorer, conversely a low Engel coefficient indicates a higher standard of living.

v.   "U.N.: Poor Countries Could Pay 40 percent More for Food". http://edition.cnn.com/2008/US/05/22/food.crisis.

vi.   The International Food Policy Research Institute was established in 1975 in Washington, D.C., U.S.A. to identify and analyze alternative national and international strategies and policies for meeting food needs of the developing world on a sustainable basis, with particular emphasis on low-income countries and on the poorer groups in those countries. Its research effort is geared to the precise objective of contributing to the reduction of hunger and malnutrition, the factors involved are many and wide-ranging, requiring analysis of underlying processes and extending beyond a narrowly defined food sector. The Institute's research program reflects worldwide collaboration with governments and private and public institutions interested in increasing food production and improving the equity of its distribution. Research results are disseminated to policymakers, opinion formers, administrators, policy analysts, researchers, and others concerned with national and international food and agricultural policy.

vii. Relatively speaking the price hike in the mid-90s was lesser than the 1970s price hike.

viii. Food security is defined as when all people, at all times, have physical and economic access to sufficient, safe and nutritious food to meet their dietary needs and food preferences for an active and healthy life (World Food Summit, 1996).

ix. Subsidies distort free market forces, hide the true cost of food to consumers, and often encourage wasteful production practices. Agricultural subsidies in the Western world allow the farmers to undercut the prices of food supplied by the farmers of developing countries. It is generally agreed by economists in the World Trade Organization that agricultural subsidies are not a good thing, do not encourage sustainable and efficient agriculture, and should be ultimately abolished.

x. During this period, many countries instinctively closed their borders upon threat of a food shortage. These actions have proven to have detrimental effects both domestically and globally due to market distortions. Export restrictions on grains were one of the key drivers of the food crisis and price spikes.

xi. South Korea imposed beef import ban from USA in 2003.

xii. Bio-fuels production has diverted crops away from human consumption into the energy sector.

xiii. This discussion has been imbibed from "http://www.wfp.org/photos/gallery/food-crisis-timeline"http://www.wfp.org/photos/gallery/food-crisis-timeline. See this website for detailed discussion on the timeline and pathway to global food crisis.

xiv. "Russia ban on grain export begins" http://www.bbc.co.uk/news/business-10977955.

xv. Corn prices reached an all-time high trading at $8.24 a bushel on the Chicago exchange on 20th of July, 2012. America is the world's largest producer of corn, dominating the market. Corn is also connected to many food items – as feed for dairy cows or for hogs and beef cattle, as a component in processed food – expanding the impact of those price rises.

xvi. http://www.bbc.co.uk/news/world-asia-19107049.

xvii. Medical conditions that can cause weight gain include: Cushing's syndrome - a rare disorder that causes an over-production of steroid hormones (chemicals produced by the body), an under-active thyroid gland (hypothyroidism) - when your thyroid gland does not produce enough thyroid hormone (called thyroxine, or T4), and polycystic ovary syndrome (PCOS) - when women have a large number of cysts in their ovaries. Certain medicines, including some corticosteroids and antidepressants, can also contribute to weight gain. Weight gain can also be a side effect of taking the combined contraceptive pill, and from quitting smoking. http://www.nhs.uk/Conditions/Obesity/Pages/Causes.aspx.

xviii. This group of people, who is willing and requires to consume sufficient amount of food but have no ability or availability to consume, struggles to find ways to afford to purchase and consume food on daily basis.

xix. This obesity epidemic is not limited to America and Western Europe: it is visible in East Asia, Central and South America, and even in Africa. In South Africa, 30.5% of black women are obese. In China, the prevalence of childhood obesity rose from 1.5% in 1989 to 12.6% in 1997.

xx. There are more than 13 million people live below the poverty line in the UK in the year 2011. There are more than 100 food banks in the UK run by various charities like the trusts e.g., Trussell Trust. The food banks provide a minimum of three days emergency food and support to people experiencing crisis in the UK. Last year our UK food bank network fed over 60,000 people. Today many people across the Western world will struggle to feed themselves and their families. Redundancy, illness, benefit payments delays, domestic violence, debt, family breakdown and paying for heating during winter are just some of the reasons why people go hungry.

xxi. See, Otter, Chris (March, 2010), Feast and Famine: The Global Food Crisis, Origins-ehistory, "http://ehistory.osu.edu/osu/origins/article.cfm?articleid=38"http://ehistory.osu.edu/osu/origins/article.cfm?articleid=38.

xxii. To quote Malthus (1798), "The constant effort towards population increases the number of people before means of subsistence are increased. The food therefore which before supported seven millions must now be divided among seven millions and a half or eight millions. The poor consequently must live much worse, and many of them be reduced to severe distress. The number of labourers also being above the proportion of the work in the market, the price of labour must tend toward a decrease, while the price of provisions would at the same time tend to rise. The labourer therefore must work harder to earn the same as he did before. During this season of distress, the discouragements to marriage, and the difficulty of rearing a family are so great that population is at a stand. In the mean time the cheapness of labour, the plenty of labourers, and the necessity of an increased industry amongst them, encourage cultivators to employ more labour upon their land, to turn up fresh soil, and to manure and improve more completely what is already in tillage, till ultimately the means of subsistence become in the same proportion to the population as at the period from which we set out."

xxiii. Sen (1999) argued against Malthusian theory of food-population relation. 'Malthusian pessimism' may be misleading as a predictor of the food situation in the world, what may be called 'Malthusian optimism' can kill millions when the administrators get entrapped by the wrong perspective of food-output per head and ignore early signs of disaster and famine.

xxiv. In 1968, U.S. Agency for International Development (USAID) Administrator William S. Gaud coined the term "Green Revolution" to describe this phenomenal growth in agriculture.

xxv. Amartya K. Sen (1981, 1982) is universally credited with establishing the importance of access to food, as opposed to only availability, as critical to food security. He developed the "entitlements approach" to analyze food problems, in order to better explain how a person could starve even during periods of high abundance of food. In a market economy, entitlements refer to the different commodity bundles that a person can acquire in society given his original bundle of ownership, or his endowment. A person could thus starve (even under conditions of abundant food supplies) through such events as a fall in his or her endowment (e.g. loss of assets such as land and livestock), or detrimental changes in the conditions of exchange (e.g. unemployment, wage cuts, food price increases, etc.). For a discussion of some of the critiques and counter-critiques to Sen's entitlements approach, see also Devereux (2001).

xxvi. When one takes a long-term perspective, food scarcity and high food prices are only some of the immediate symptoms of hunger and food insecurity.

xxvii. Access to food is determined by how well people can convert their various financial, political, and other assets into food, whether produced or purchased.

xxviii. For further discussion on these issues, see Chapter 7 in Development as Freedom by Sen (1999).

xxix.   Recently research works (Young, 2001; Haddad and Gillespie, 2001; Pelletier, 2002; Popkin, 2003; World Bank, 2006; Ericksen, 2007) with an interest in the health outcomes of food utilization have enlarged the food security framework by adding food utilization. The influence of age, health and disease on how the human body utilizes food and its needs for different nutrients, calories and protein were studied. Utilization is affected by poor hygiene, food preferences and the physiological condition affecting food absorption.

xxx.   See, De Schutter and Cordes (2011).

xxxi.   The perspective of human contestability failure approach describes a situation where an individual or household fails to compete in establishing ownership over food. This failure can arise either due to lack of body capital, human capital, emotional capital, command over productive resources or a mixture of two or all dimensions of human contestability failure framework (Chopra, 2007).

xxxii. The global agricultural and food system has been interchangeably used with world food system or food regime.

xxxiii. The growth of non-western economies like China almost invariably generates a shift to a more "western" style diet, which involves rising meat consumption, which in turn necessitates diverting vast quantities of cereals from humans to cattle. This is a high-status but inefficient way to consume protein and calories. See, chapter 5 for further details.

xxxiv. There are six main food paradoxes: First paradox is that the farmers and landless rural farm labourers (mainly women in many regions) who spend their lives producing food for others remain poor and go hungry themselves. The second paradox is the co-existence of obesity and under-nutritious and hungry people. The third paradox is that the nations who face food shortages are forced to export food to other food rich countries. The changing diet has triggered the co-existence of food for the animals as well as for humans giving rise to the fourth paradox as more and more food grains are needed to feed animals. The fashion and trend of bio-fuels originated from the policies on biofuels in Europe and the US have led to the food-fuel paradox. Last but not the least paradox is the co-existence of massive food wastage and food shortage in both Western world and developing world.

xxxv.   A quick look at Chapter 2 of this book reveals that poverty, chronic hunger and food insecurity are closely linked with each other. There might be a decline of people in hunger and malnutrition in percentage terms but the total number of people in hunger and malnutrition has gone up considerably over the years.

xxxvi. Overall growth in net incomes has caused a world-wide dietary transition to more meat (with a concomitant rise in demand for grain production), dairy, sugars and oils. This is exacerbated by the growth of middle-class urban populations mainly in developing countries like China and India who rely almost completely on purchasing food (Kennedy et al., 2004).

xxxvii. More people consuming more beef, pork, poultry, eggs and dairy products. This led to increase in more grain demand since livestock and poultry are fed on grain.

Chapter 1   Introduction

There is a wise old saying that 'Eat to live, not live to eat'
Socrates (469-399 BC), a Classical Greek Athenian Philosopher.

Introduction

The present book introduces, constructs, develops and validates a reliable robust structural multivariate measurement system to conceptualise, analyse, measure, and manage the magnitude and severity of the phenomenon of GFC, paying particular attention to critical food crisis factors and underlying complex driving forces within certain boundaries of the prevailing *global agricultural and food system* (GAFS). This new measurement system is based on a holistic, multidisciplinary and systems modelling approach rather than preliminary evidence, isolated or piecemeal approaches. It adopts complexity perspective for understanding and analysing GFC where its genesis has been explored in the well-established systematised theories and approaches in the economics and meta-economics of agriculture and food, food insecurity, hunger, starvation, and food vulnerability including the behaviour and environment of GAFS. The present measurement system subsumes a *conceptual model,* an *operational model,* a *latent variable structural model* and a *measurement model* under its analytical umbrella.

The present work analyses the system dimensional structure of GFC and applies the *causal pathways approach* in causal context (causal modelling) to examine *structural causal connections* (web of relations) among its various latent variables. It provides us with a measurement or *index* of GFC at world level. Being highly versatile measurement system, it can also be applied to any economy, region or households to compare different areas of food problems. The index will indicate the extent to which the worldwide economy, region, economy or a group of households is facing food crisis and its dimensional decomposition will indicate the extent of contribution of each construct to the food crisis problems. Strengths and weaknesses of various components and their manifest variables will point out characteristics at a

Introduction

certain level in order to reveal what exactly the global economy or country requires from food policy makers, national governments and international organisations to improve global food security, development and opportunity, social welfare, ecological security and environmental sustainability. Thus, this specially designed research methodology also aims to identify the food crisis management strategies that may help to manage the crisis most effectively by reducing its severity or negative consequences.

The shattering famine in Bangladesh during 1972-73 led to first *World Food Conference* held in Rome in 1974 by the United Nations under the auspices of the UN Food and Agricultural Organisation (FAO). All governments attending the Conference declared that *"every man, woman and child has the inalienable right to be free from hunger and malnutrition in order to develop their physical and mental faculties".* The eradication of chronic hunger, food insecurity and malnutrition within a decade was the main goal set by the Conference. Sadly, even after four decades this goal is still to be achieved. Nevertheless, the Conference put in place a World Food Council (subsequently disbanded) and led to follow-up World Food Conferences.

In its fortieth session the *UN Committee on Economic, Social and Cultural Rights* (28 April-16 May 2008) passed a statement recognising the existence of contemporary GFC along with highlighting the need for increased investment in rural areas, small scale agriculture, and achieving the equitable distribution of food aid internationally. It broadly detailed the GFC in the context of soaring energy and staple food (wheat, rice, soybeans, and maize) prices given that households in underdeveloped countries spent 60-80% of their income on foodstuffs compared to 20% in the developed world. The *UN Economic and Social Council* (2008) further stated that, "... the world food crisis severely affects the full realization of the human right to adequate food and to be free from hunger, and therefore calls upon all States to fulfil their basic human rights obligations under the Covenant". Many observers predicted that the food price volatility would melt away soon. This did not happen. On the contrary, prices of major commodities soared during 2012 and the FAO Food Price Index for September 2012 was the highest (in both real and nominal terms) since the index began in 1990[i]. The basic food prices dynamics witnessed three sharp peaks in 2007/2008, 2010/2011 and August-October 2012 severely impacting vulnerable populations worldwide.

The theme of World Food Day 2012, held on the 16th October, was agricultural cooperatives: key to feeding the world. However, the same day kicked off in Rome (Italy) with a series of meetings of United Nations to try and get ahead of the third GFC in four years since 2008. Disgracefully, on World Food Day, an emergency meeting of the newly formed G-20 Rapid Response Forum, a crisis prevention group of global agricultural policymakers, was cancelled because it was felt that it was not necessary at this time. For G-20 group of economically powerful nations it represented an inconvenience, but in poor households it means a threat to life and livelihood. Yet on the same day, BBC1 breakfast news reported that food prices were too volatile and dangerously high ever recorded in human history and expected to climb by 15 per cent in 2013. GFC is getting worse due to wet weather in Britain, summer droughts and severe heat waves in the United States, India and poor planting conditions and crop failures in Russia. It is extremely devastating that poor people's food basket cost even four times higher than the average weekly salary in some developing countries.

Poverty, climate change, and the world food crisis were also at the forefront of the G8 Summit held in Hokkaido, Japan during July 2008. Although these three global issues are closely interlinked, worldwide food crisis has hit the world's poor people the most as they can no longer afford the nutritious food because prices have soared beyond their reach. Food prices are rising (some have more than tripled) hampering those in need of humanitarian assistance and making them suffer further through increased hunger and malnutrition. This was a new face of hunger. High food prices were believed to remain high by historical standards and were predicted to stay high in many years to come, intensifying concerns about food security[ii] and risking a "major setback" in the accomplishment of the UN Millennium Development Goals. A study by the World Bank (2011) stated that since June 2010, the number of extreme poor people has increased by 44 million in low and middle-income countries as a result of food price hike[iii]. Presently there are more than 35 countries that do not produce enough food to provide 2400 calories per day to its population, even if the food is distributed equally.

The contemporary GFC has been considered as a silent tsunami which knows no borders sweeping the planet with slight warning plunging hundreds of millions of people in abject poverty, hunger, misery and malnutrition

3

Introduction

(Buchanan, 2008). The role of GFC in social unrest and political instability can be identified from the triggered food riots. In 2008 more than 60 food riots occurred worldwide in 30 different countries such as Mozambique, Haiti, Cameroon, Indonesia, Egypt, Tunisia, Algeria, Madagascar, Niger, Senegal, Burkina Faso, so on and 10 of which resulted in multiple deaths (Berazneva and Lee, 2011). The end of 2010 and beginning of 2011 witnessed additional food riots in Mauritania and Uganda. During 2011 and 2012 larger food related protests and government changes and other events took place in North Africa and Middle East (Arab Spring) due to exorbitant food prices. Food riots will replace the religious, political and race riots as unending cycles of famines (droughts), floods, hunger, environmental degradation, and food insecurity sweep across the world. "Just like the collapse of large banks, widespread hunger entails systemic risks. Less wholesome and less nutritious diets create an economic liability for the development of future generations in terms of risks in health, productivity and performance. If the coping strategies adopted by vulnerable households cause reductions in the quantity and/or quality of diets at critical stages of child growth or during pregnancy, this may have long-lasting consequences on physical and mental growth" (De Schutter and Cordes, 2011). Food shortages force many of the poorest families to distress sales, including sales of productive assets such as land, tools or live-stocks, thereby making recovery less likely. Thus, food insecurity is deemed as a dangerous threat to economic, social and political stability as well as economic growth and welfare.

Food security involves the physical availability of food and the capability of people to pay for the food they need. Global food requirements will continue to increase in coming years due to global population growth in world's most food insecure regions, bio-fuel initiatives, growing incomes, changing pattern of food consumption, and the like. The ultimate food security challenge is not about producing enough to feed the world, but rather ensuring the poorest of the poor have physical access to food, equitable distribution of food and proper utilization of food to avoid malnutrition and obesity. However, various studies have identified varied factors responsible for GFC (Timmer, 2008; Abbott et al., 2008; Lagi et al., 2012)[iv]. Some of the identified factors are change of diet in developing countries, bio-fuels conversion, financial speculation in the commodity futures market, the price of crude oil, variation in currency exchange rates, trade policies, panic, thin markets, fiscal expansion, climate change, inventories and R&D decline, population increase, income growth, financial crisis, recession, monetary policy, land degradation, income growth, globalization, urbanization, and so on. Some studies have considered food policy measures (export restrictions, taxes or subsidies) detrimental in the contemporary global food crisis. Export restrictions on grains were one of the key drivers of the food crisis and price spikes during the period 2007-12. The dominant causes of price increases are investor speculation and ethanol conversion (Lagi et al., 2012). A study by the Organisation for Economic Cooperation and Development (2010) showed that given a surge of 70 percent in world prices of wheat and rice due to natural disasters were hiked to 98 percent and 134 percent respectively when the countries implemented export restrictions[v].

There have been welfare losses for the global economy as a whole since both exporting and importing countries highlight the overall negative global effect of export restrictions. The June 2011 Joint Policy Report of FAO, IFAD, IMF, OECD, UNCTAD, WFP, the World Bank, the WTO, IFPRI and the UN HLTF stated that "During the 2007-2008 period, some policy measures put in place by a number of governments contributed directly and indirectly to the crisis (export restrictions, hoarding), increasing the amplitude of price movements and in some cases provoking price increases that were otherwise inexplicable in terms of the market fundamentals. Inappropriate policy responses also contributed to volatility and could continue to do so unless the international community is able to take steps to avoid such actions."[vi]

Many other important studies have argued that "more important than the net economic welfare loss, however, is the large decline in consumer welfare; this is in fact what makes export restrictions so detrimental. Price increases caused by export restrictions have the greatest impact on the world's poorest consumers and pose a serious threat to their food security. As such, export restrictions on staples have contributed to unrest in different parts of the world threatened by food insecurity."[vii] Another major concern for policy makers and international community is the decline in agricultural productivity and agricultural production in coming years due to climate change and other factors that are expected to convert many of today's food sufficient countries as net food importers (Kavi and Parikh, 2001; Fischer et al., 2002; Fuglie, 2008).

Introduction

From an initial food price crisis, there have been seven different transmission mechanisms that make this food crisis truly 'global' in nature. First, food products (e.g. maize, rice, wheat, vegetables, fruits, spices, tea, sugar, poultry, etc.) travel long distances across borders due to vertical and horizontal concentration of supermarkets, reliance on heavy food imports rather than domestic production and diverse food demand. International trade in food products is intensifying as markets have globalised with backward and forward linkages, networks and forces of globalisation and transportation routes have improved and extended. Second, trade in agricultural inputs (e.g. oil, fertilisers, seeds, etc.) to produce food has become essentially a global phenomenon with the emergence of multinational giants which acquired monopoly power. Third, the effects of climate change or environmental degradation on agricultural productivity do not restrict to one country or continent only. Conversely, agriculture also has its negative consequences on global environmental degradation. The fourth mechanism is related to the policies of governments and international food organisations that have undermined the very incentives that could boost food production and distribution putting an end to the present crisis as well as possibly helping to prevent future ones. The fifth mechanism gives insight into the global availability and affordability of fast foods and meat products which are changing the eating habits of people across the globe. Sixth is the acknowledgement of food problems as global by various countries which led to the establishment of different international food organisations. Last but not the least, it is the global demand for bio-fuels and livestock revolution. During the period 2008-2012, food crisis became a real global phenomenon when many developing and developed countries were less self-sufficient in food and dangerously had to rely on food imports to feed their growing, urban and more prosperous population at higher costs.

What is Global Food Crisis?

Concentrating on a single or few dimensions of GFC such as rising food prices (food price crisis) or food shortages (food availability crisis) or food demand hike (food demand crisis) and neglecting all other important dimensions can be profoundly counterproductive. Moreover, the phenomenon of GFC should not be confused with food-price inflation[viii]

•

as it represents simply a single manifestation of the world food crisis. It is also different from incidences of hunger, starvation, undernourishment, famine, food shortages[ix] or food insecurity[x] that is either the sources or the ramifications of GFC. As a holistic phenomenon, GFC lies within the domain of much broader and complex world agriculture and food system that not only includes food demand, food production, or food supply, but also more broadly relates to the functioning of the entire global economy as well as the behaviour and environment of GAFS. Due to the complex and dynamic nature of the functioning of the global economy, the behaviour of GAFS is governed by the operations, processes and interdependencies of economic, social, political, institutional, environmental and ecological forces, their mutual interactions and causal connections. These dynamic and complex driving forces affect the agricultural and food activities that give birth to food demand versus supply, availability versus ability to command adequate amount of food[xi] and global population versus food growth imbalances. Moreover, food acquirement is determined by either growing own food, buying in the market or food sharing within the family or through food aid. Food crisis affects individuals when they fail to get the same amount of quality food either due to personal human contestability failures (unemployment, lack of income, low wages, lack of assets, illiteracy, etc) or country's social, economic, political, and institutional circumstances and arrangements (economic slowdown, absence of social security system, unequal distribution of off, lack of political will or natural disasters such as floods, famines and so on). Therefore, there is a need to subsume and integrate the whole range of factors influencing GFC in order to have a fuller and clearer understanding of this phenomenon.

In relation to food problems, the term 'crisis' refers to a perception or experience of an extreme situation or a series of events revealing an unendurable difficulty that exceeds households' current resources for food insecurity coping mechanisms. It is a critical turning point leading to have worse situation and varies substantially in type and severity. As a holistic syndrome, GFC can be conceptualised as a process of continuous worsening of food security situation that people enjoy worldwide. Being a complex multidimensional and multifaceted phenomenon in its manifestation, GFC is the outcome and outgrowth of a combination of various complex interconnected, interwoven and interdependent critical factors and driving forces within GAFS that place the overall well-being (physical, emotional, environmental and socio-economic) of human beings at risk. In other words, it is an aggregate exposure or disaster borne out of the functioning, behaviour and interdependence of a range of underlying processes and mechanisms within GAFS that, directly or indirectly, influence food security situation worldwide. This involves three aspects: (a) crisis as an *outcome*; (b) a variety of *critical food crisis factors*; and (c) *inability* to manage those critical food crisis factors leads to calamity and catastrophe of food crisis at global scale.

The functioning of GAFS is shaped by the interwoven six sets of critical food crisis factors. The first set of factors is rooted in the GAFS while the second set contains critical factors on food demand side. The critical factors on food supply side constitute the third set and global food market failures in contrast with the free competition conditions among global market players result from the fourth set of factors. Factors contributing to public sector interventions in terms of government failures in food markets and collective actions failures are subsumed in the fifth set of factors. The factors signifying the impact of GFC are included in the construct of global food crisis. Thus, the overall GFC is composed of the constructs containing multiple manifest variables that are often a combination of subjective evaluations and more objective agricultural related statistics. To sum up, GFC is a disaster comprising the likelihood and frequency of occurrence, severity and strength of impact, vulnerability of change and degree of complexity and interdependency among all dimensions, factors or situations associated with GAFS causing exorbitant food prices, hunger, malnutrition, food insecurity, political and economic instability, and social unrest in both poor and developed nations.

Why Measure Global Food Crisis?

Now the question that rises is why we need to measure the phenomenon of GFC. Measurement is all about precision and assigning numbers to objects, ideas, views or answers. To quote Stover (1987), "If it can't be expressed in figures, it is not science; it is opinion". In general, individuals, organisations, economies including global economy have a need to manage all of their activities which imply that there is nothing which should not be measured. However, one must be sure of what one wants to measure. It has to be recognised that measuring every activity of an economy is not desirable because it would be costly and counterproductive in terms of the resistance to the control process and the loss of creativity and innovation which it engendered. In a realistic sense, the positions between no measurements at all and measuring everything, there are a range of measurement opportunities which can be recognised and utilised by those who set the measures and those who do the measuring. Through measuring, valid and meaningful insights into the behaviour of the GAFS and GFC are obtained which inform the need for and pattern of the corrective and preventive actions that are to be undertaken in pursuit of effective management of such phenomenon.

There are a number of reasons to support a case for measuring GFC. To begin with, GAFS has many inherent contradictions and paradoxes, and like every other system it has a tendency to fail in achieving its desired goals such as erradication of food insecurity, hunger and obesity due to failing mechanisms (Chopra and Kanji, 2010). The free market system fails to deliver the goods and the government also fails to provide the desired results due to various imperfections (Ghosh, 2001). The fundamental question is: Why do crises like the global financial crisis, banking crisis, economic crisis or GFC occur? These crises encounter a situation of systemic failures or collapse wherein the activities and processes of the system are not managed properly and effectively. Both the agents and the mechanisms of the system produce greater complexity that increases its costs and reduces benefits, creating a cyclical pattern that later becomes unsustainable and the system eventually collapses. The Stuart Kauffman's (1995) 'order for free' hypothesis that the free interplay of agents of a system[xii] is self-organising does not work in the case of GAFS and GFC. Hence, we cannot do without food management because worldwide food system needs managing systematically and regularly which can only be achieved by measuring it holistically. *If we cannot measure, we cannot manage* (Kanji and Chopra, 2010).

Secondly, a valid measure is indispensable for effective decision-making and improved global governance for world food security and hunger mitigation/eradication. Thirdly, an agricultural scientist has to fight the battle of measurement on three fronts. The *first* is the conceptual definition of the phenomenon of GFC in order to be absolutely clear what is being measured. One will first want to know how it is defined. The *second* is how the phenomenon of GFC is measured in an accurate representation of the construct which means creating different items in a measurement system. This is the battle of interpreting or converting the conceptual definition into an operational definition very vigilantly and precisely. This challenge involves establishing casual connections, specifying the measurement model, estimating of the model, model identification and assessment of model fit, including validating the reliability of the measurement model. The *third* is of course related to the capability and knowledge of an individual researcher regarding how to use a measurement system and how to interpret the results or values. The measurement system introduced, developed and validated in this book acts as a one-stop shop solution to all the above adumbrated fronts of the measurement battle.

Fourthly, agriculturalists and food economists need to understand the various critical food crisis factors with their varying significance. One may want to know the various dimensions and different structural causal pathways leading to GFC. Fifthly, food policy makers also need to know the scale of the food problems vis-à-vis the current level of global agricultural performance as indicated by input, throughput, output and outcomes levels, and the impact, positive or negative, even minor changes in processes that are generating and are capable of generating. An understanding of self-protection of farmers is another reason, but food policy makers also need to be aware of how an economy stands in relation to its agricultural products consumption and utilisation vis-à-vis agricultural production.

The rationale and results of intended changes in GAFS can be delineated. The management of GAFS is the management of its processes. For those processes to operate at full capacity it is imperative that any departure from an envisaged standard is instantly detected and preventive actions undertaken to rectify it. Another purpose of measuring the phenomenon of GFC is to know the extent of its current level for the purpose of controlling and managing it. An assessor needs to have good knowledge of the measure, nature of the phenomenon and should be non-judgemental in nature. The measure of GFC and the assessor need to convey as much information (copy of questionnaire, individual score of each question, score of each dimension of a phenomenon and overall index/score) as possible to the policy makers concerned so that it is clearly understood which part needs to be taken care of.

How can someone come up with the idea of measuring GFC? Just look at the complexity of GFC. As a system, there is a need to know more about everything in the system. Deming (1994) stated, 'There is no substitution for knowledge and a system cannot understand itself'. We have to gain the knowledge about the system from outside the system, for example GAFS through measuring GFC. It is complex and difficult to measure GFC in an intricate dynamic environment. However, it is crucial to do so. A famous saying is that: 'What you don't measure, you don't know. What you don't know, you can't manage. When you can't manage, you are at the mercy of chance'. Therefore, we must measure the phenomenon of GFC in order to make right decisions regarding food policy options and agricultural investments. Many researchers believe that the true magnitude of food crisis in its totality is not measurable. This is not true. We are able to measure the food crisis at world level, not by hard measures, but by soft measurement.

Fundamental Prerequisites for Measuring Global Food Crisis

As adumbrated earlier, GFC lies at the heart of GAFS. It is, therefore, futile to discuss how to measure GFC in a global economy unless we comprehend what the nature of global economy is. In other words, we are about to measure a system, or more precisely, the behaviour of the system. A basic principle of measuring and managing GFC is to view the global economy as an evolving complex system of interdependent and interconnected sub-systems and the forces connecting them. Then, understanding GFC from complexity perspective and finally, a multivariate model is built and empirically applied by collecting the required information and analysed to infer conclusions and offer food policy prescriptions.

Viewing Global Economy as an Evolving Complex System

In this section we face and need to understand three different questions. Firstly, "What is the nature of global economy?", secondly, "What is a system?", thirdly, "How is the global economy an evolving complex system[xiii]?". Over time, the meaning of the word 'economy' has changed from "household management" to "the management of economic affairs" and further to "the economic system of a country or an area".[xiv] However,

Introduction

the 'global economy' is viewed as the sum total of all commercial activities such as producing, consuming, buying, selling, distributing, giving, taking and such other activities across the world. It is highly integrated with the regular worldwide movements of goods, services, and manpower. It is an economic system wherein the labour, capital and land resources, and the economic agents economically participate in the production, exchange, distribution, and consumption of goods and services in all markets across the world. Through the forward and backward linkages of globalisation, the functioning, behaviour, forces and activities of global economy affect many countries negatively or positively. Thus, over centuries as economies have evolved from local to regional to national to transnational to global, the global economy has grown both in size and complexity. Each sector[xv] of global economy has its own dynamics and this classification is not watertight. A given economy is the end result of a process that involves its technological evolution, history and social organization, as well as its geography, natural resource endowment, and ecology, as main factors. These factors give context, content, and set the conditions and parameters in which an economy functions. Kenneth Boulding (1985) visualised the global economy as an evolutionary total system. Economic patterns are complex and ever-changing in nature and an economy is process-dependent, it behaves like organisms and it is always evolving. Mills (1995) brings to our attention three aspects, namely, complexity, unknown interactions and unseen interactions. An economy consists of human beings and products interacting, often under different cultures and conditions. Therefore, it does not operate in static environment, the parameters affecting the global economy change and must be identified and measured. It is however important to acknowledge here that many important things that must be managed could not be measured due to unknown or unknowable important figures.

Turning to the second question, a system can be defined as an assemblage of interdependent, interacting or interrelated elements or processes that are organised to accomplish the goals as a whole. It is a set of objects together with relationships between the objects and their attributes related to each other and to their environment so as to form a whole (Shoderbek et al., 1990). Deming (1994) argues that *"A system is a network of interdependent components that work together to try to accomplish the aim of a system.*

On Measuring Global Food Crisis

A system maximisation must have an aim. Without an aim, there is no system". For instance, the human body, any organisation, society or global economy is a system of interconnected and interrelated parts wherein everything is connected to everything else. As the phenomenon of GFC is related with global economy, a holistic view of GFC is an important consequence of adopting a systems perspective which needs to be addressed. In understanding the GAFS as a complex and heterogeneous system over space and time, systems approach is helpful in understanding the critical food crisis factors that lead to particular outcomes or the interactions that govern a specific behaviour of interest. There is a difference between an analytical and systems approach. Analytical thinking deals with increasing complexity by trying to *reduce* it into manageable sizes and address them in isolation, whereas systems thinking deals with the interactions among components to understand how the system as a whole functions[xvi]. A move from analytical to systems (synthesis) approach to GFC can be characterized as an evolutionary paradigm *shift* since our world is getting more difficult to manage and detailed information is needed to manage the emerging global issues.

It calls for attention to the importance of studying the phenomenon of GFC on global basis and to the need of establishing coordination mechanisms. Thus, the concept of a system helps in addressing complex problems with multi-causality resulting from interactions among interdependent components. The understanding of global food system elaborated in chapter four lends itself to a "systems" approach as it is a "problem-determined system" rather than a "system-determined problem" (Ison et al., 1997). In propounding the idea of GAFS as complex, heterogeneous over space and time and replete with non-linear feedback, one has to be fully inter-disciplinary with an aim at marriage of different sciences. Thus, systems theory or thinking serves as a bridge for interdisciplinary dialogue between autonomous areas of study as well as within the area of systems science itself. Norgaard (1984) first described agricultural systems as co-evolved social and ecological systems. Berkes and Folke (1998), Folke et al. (2003) and Holling (2001) described coupled social–ecological systems as co-evolved, with mutually dependent and interacting social and ecological components and highly uncertain and unpredictable outcomes. This conceptualization of human–environment interactions is useful for food systems, although the

Introduction

links between the social and environmental components may be indirect in many cases (Ericksen, 2007).

Now viewing the global economy as a constantly evolving complex system it unfolds over time with multiple elements adapting or reacting to the pattern these elements create and they tend to vary from one context to another (Arthur et al., 1997). It contains many sub-systems (national or regional economies) that are also constantly in a dynamic process. Through the working of various forces of globalisation in global economy, national economies (elements) adapt to the aggregate (global economy), i.e. as the national economies react, the global economy changes, and as the global economy changes, national economies (elements) react anew. Thus, the global economic system is hypersensitive to small changes in the dynamics of global markets, international and national political conditions, social interactions, geographical issues, environmental changes, security issues and the like. For example, in global economy economic agents such as international investors, multinational firms, global buyers and sellers, financial institutions, customers, international organisations or stakeholders adjust their market moves together including investing decisions, buying or selling decisions, lending decisions or pricing decisions to the situation. Economic elements (human beings) react with strategy and foresight by considering outcomes that might result as a consequence of behaviour they might undertake which adds a layer of complication to economics not experienced in the natural sciences (Anderson et al., 1988). K. E. Boulding used evolutionary systems approach to economics in his work *Economic Development as an Evolutionary System* (1970). He believed that human economic and other behaviour was embedded in a larger interconnected system. To understand the results of our behaviour, economic or otherwise, we must first research and develop a scientific understanding of the eco-dynamics of the general system, the global society in which we live, in all its dimensions spiritual and material.

For the sake of simplifying its questions, traditional economics deals with the basic question: What are behavioural agents such as actions, strategies or expectations consistent with the aggregate patterns these behavioural elements create together? It studies consistent patterns (patterns in behavioural equilibrium) that would induce no further change or reaction and thus ignores the unfolding patterns its agents create. For example, general equilibrium theory[xvii], game theory[xviii] or rational expectations economics[xix] have been studying consistency of behavioural agents' patterns with the outcomes these agents create together (See Arthur et al., 1997; Arthur, 1999). However, modern economists have been broadening this traditional equilibrium approach by asking the following question: How do behavioural agents react in general to—might endogenously change with— the aggregate patterns they create? They examine problems in economics as complex dynamic processes with random events and natural positive feedbacks, studying the general emergence of structures and unfolding of patterns in the global economy. This perspective of studying economy as an evolving complex system of dynamic processes in economics is being noticed in political economy (Axelrod, 1986; Kollman et al., 1997), in the theory of money and finance (Marimon et al., 1990; Shubik, 1997; Brock et al., 1995; Maddala et al., 1995), in game theory (Lindgren, 1991; Young, 1993; Blume, 1993; Huberman et al., 1997), in learning in the economy (Sargent, 1993; Lane and Maxfield, 1997; Darley and Kauffman, 1997), in economic history (North, 1997), in the evolution of trading networks (Ioannides, 1997; Kirman, 1997; Tesfatsion, 1997) and in the stability of the economy (Bak et al., 1997; Leijonhufvud, 1997). To sum up, viewing global economy as an evolving complex system helps us to deal with the complex phenomena of GFC effectively which is discussed in the next section.

Understanding Global Food Crisis from Complexity Perspective

The term 'complexity' refers to the degree of difficulty in understanding, describing, analysing, managing and predicting the outcomes of a phenomenon like GFC. It points to a condition or characteristic of something with many parts in a system in intricate arrangement and numerous forms of relationships among the elements. However, the complexity of the phenomenon of GFC is relative and changes with time. What is the complexity perspective of the phenomenon of GFC? This is not an easy question to answer as there are multiple blending complications. This complexity multiplies since we have global economy as an evolving complex system with its own forces working in it on one hand and on the other hand, there are key environmental and natural, socio-economic, political-institutional, and technological forces contributing to complexity.

Introduction

Then, we have GFC as a complex multidimensional phenomenon with its own uncertain and diverse forces. The next layer of complication arises from the dynamic nature of GAFS in which the phenomenon of GFC lies. Thus, in the complex global economy, there is a dynamic complex GFAS with the layers of complications created by the behaviour, actions and interactions, and geo-ecological forces that are driving change in GAFS and influence agricultural activities that produce various outcomes such as effects on social welfare, food security and human contestability. Even small disturbances in the GAFS may cause significant adverse socio-economic consequences especially for those dependent upon agricultural sector for their livelihood (Chambers, 1991). The static equilibrium-centred views of conventional agricultural science and development programmes provide inadequate insight into the dynamic character of GAFSs, particularly in an era of global economic and environmental change where factors such as climate change, rapid land use shifts and uncertain political economic conditions in agricultural economies all impinge on the day-today realities of poorer producers and consumers in the developing world (Thompson et al., 2007). Therefore, the complexity perspective of GFC studies the unfolding of these patterns of complicated layers in the system its behaviour or factors create. As a result, it is imperative to study and analyse this phenomenon from complexity perspective. It involves a profound understanding and management of GFC in an ever-increasing complexity of socio-economic reality of our global system. Globalisation as well as political, social and cultural interdependence among various nations of the world has sprung up as a major challenge of our times. Complexity arises from the difficulty of finding description of the overall behaviour of the overall socio-economic system/model, its components and their interactions (relationships), its attributes (properties) of parts and relationships and systems' environment.

The phenomenon of GFC within the GAFS contains multiple elements reacting to the patterns these elements espouse. As mentioned before that the GAFS is very complex, unpredictable and full of shocks and surprise since the political, economic, ecological and social elements play interactively with each other by forming numerous relationships and together in the process these elements adjust to and influence the overall system (Folke 2006; Adger et al., 2005; Walker et al., 2004; Gunderson et al., 1995). In this process, time plays its crucial role through adjustment and change (Arthur,

1999). Traditional agricultural science and policy options do not seem to explain fully the complexity, diversity, uncertainty and non-equilibrium states (Chambers, 1991). Various forces or elements affect each other and produce the aggregate changes and these aggregate changes in turn react and produce fresh changes in elements. Thus, there is a very high degree of interdependence among the elements themselves as well as among the elements and overall system (aggregate). The GAFS is an intricate system in its processes, activities and subsystems and constantly develops, evolves and unfolds over time. For example, complexity creates vulnerability that not only damages people's welfare, but also reduces growth by destroying assets or diverting assets away from more productive activities to those that reduce risk and uncertainty (Ericksen, 2006). Therefore, when modelling and measuring GFC the unfolding of the layers of complications in GAFS is involved which warrant the application of systems' theories. As we know system thinking does not mean ignoring complexity rather organising it in a coherent way that helps in seeing through complexity the underlying structures generating changes and pinpoints the causes of problem and how they can be remedied in enduring ways. The fundamental principle of system thinking is to gain knowledge about the whole relevant system, understand the numerous interrelationships between parts of the system. This is contrary to how most of the GFC measuring agencies and organisations think and act today.

The problems of the GAFS are the typical classic 'systems' problems where aspects of systems behaviour are both multifarious and capricious and where causes, while at times apparently simple, when finally understood are always multiple. These problems are often non-linear in nature, cross-scale in time and space and dynamic in character (Thompson et al., 2007). A critical minority of policy-makers and citizens – both producers and consumers – are demanding integrated solutions that address these issues of uncertainty, diversity and complexity. Where do you turn for an answer to the above complex problems? Agricultural science often provides only limited assistance, largely because it includes not only conflicting voices – witness the debate on genetically modified (GM) crops or arguments over food production vs. population growth–but also conflicting modes of inquiry and criteria for establishing the trustworthiness of different lines of argument.

Multivariate Modelling of Global Food Crisis

Multivariate modelling uses multivariate analysis that deals with data containing observations on two or more variables where there is some inherent interdependence between the variables and each variable measured on a set of objects (Mardia, Kent and Bibby, 1979). It is based on the statistical principle of multivariate statistics which involves observation and analysis at a time. As the phenomenon of GFC encompasses a whole range of economic, political, social and institutional factors, they need to be analysed simultaneously, facilitating or preventing the achievement of food security and social welfare in the prevailing GAFS. It is pertinent to note that the terms 'system' and 'model' are not the same, but sometimes they are wrongly used interchangeably. As adumbrated earlier, a system is a whole with interdependent components that further have subsets and each component can affect the behaviour of whole and vice versa. In order to reduce the complexity of a system, there is a need to construct a model which is a simplification or a simple small scale representation of reality. Any theoretical construction or a deliberate simplified analytical framework which attempts to analyse and explain a phenomenon is called model (Chopra, 1989). It is a small scale replica of reality. A model can be described by a list of endogenous variables, a list of exogenous variables and a list of specifications as to which variables are present in each equation. An economic model is a logical (usually mathematical) representation of whatever a priori or a theoretical knowledge economic analysis suggests is most relevant for treating a particular problem. Usually a model takes the form of a system of equations embodying certain assumed interdependencies among more or less operationally defined variables (Christ, 1966). A model is not a complete simplified representation of reality, but it is an abstraction from the real world. Through the process of abstraction, only relevant and most essential factors are taken into account.

To sum up, a multivariate GFC model is constructed and validated in this study by using a process of abstraction to lead to an analysis of manageable dimensions as both global economy as well as the GAFS are extremely complicated. The degree of abstraction depends upon the number of identified critical food crisis factors and constructs of GFC. Under the set of simplified assumptions, a GFC model by using simultaneous equations modelling approach illustrates the functioning of a GAFS in a most simplified manner. The measurement system is constructed in such a way that it provides the maximum amount of information to understand the reality of the phenomenon of GFC clearly. Since the global economy is constantly changing and the GAFS has to adapt to a continuously changing environment, the multivariate GFC model developed in this study includes the most important elements inside and outside the GAFS that have an effect on the system. Thus, the multivariate model suggests the pathways for managing the phenomenon of GFC in ever-changing environments where the future is unpredictable and surprises are likely to occur and, to be able to explain, let alone respond to, complexity, diversity, uncertainty with inherent seasonal instability.

Using the Multivariate Model for Understanding Global Food Crisis

Once we have constructed a multivariate model within the measurement system for measuring GFC, it is time to start making a practical use of the measurement system to learn more about the behaviour of GAFS and, its outputs and outcomes. It will depend upon the quality and reliability of the identified driving forces, factors and activities in a manner that keeps the policy makers and other stakeholders towards their goals. These factors and activities are not detached, but exhibit symmetrical relationships. The policy makers can improve the performance of any factors resulting in a simultaneous improvement of other related factors specified in the relationships in the model. The advantage of using the multivariate model is that an analyst can determine the strength of factor relationships, collective contribution of critical food crisis factors towards global food crisis, and ways by which the factors can be controlled. Thus, it is only through the understanding of the whole system that we are able to take correct decisions and actions at all times. Global agricultural and food system, food demand-side forces, food-supply-side restrictions, global market distortions and government and co-operative actions failures are the examples of important elements to measure GFC. This way we apply the measurement system to the models and models provide systematic knowledge regarding the phenomenon of GFC.

Objectives of the Study

The fundamental aim of the present study is to propose a reliable measurement tool to measure and analyse the phenomenon of GFC. However, the present study has six objectives: *first*, to conceptualise the phenomenon of the GFC from holistic perspective; *second*, to identify and analyse the diverse critical food crisis factors and system dimensional structure of GFC; *third*, to propose and outline a theoretical framework for studying multiple interactions, the underlying dynamics, processes and critical driving forces that shape the emerging patterns and their implications of GAFS and evaluating the major societal outcomes affected by these interactions: food security, social welfare, development and opportunity, and environmental sustainability and ecological security; *fourth*, to introduce, develop and validate a new GFC measurement system called *Kanji-Chopra Global Food Crisis Measurement System,* based on multivariate modelling research methodology comprising structural equations modelling, systems approach, critical food crisis factors approach and stakeholders approach; *fifth*, to analyse and measure the extent and severity of GFC in terms of dimensional decomposition, strengths of causal connections and overall GFC index that is both generic as well as specific in nature; and *sixth*, to pinpoint and prescribe the food policy options and courses of actions in order to identify what exactly is required from the governments, food policy makers and international organizations to manage food crisis effectively. The basic purpose is to introduce a new measurement system to measure GFC by applying academic insights from vast literature on food problems: food security, hunger, famine, malnutrition, obesity and so on. An attempt has been made to make a contribution to the existing literature on economics and meta-economics of food, in general, and agricultural economics, in particular. The present work is, therefore, purported to be an explicit exercise in the study of measurement, analysis and management of GFC.

Research Questions

In the process of measurement and analysis of GFC, the following twelve research questions have been dealt with:

1. To what extent do the underlying driving forces of global agricultural and food system interact within the system and explain the

phenomenon of global food crisis?

2. How effective are the critical food crisis factors under study in explaining the phenomenon of global food crisis?

3. What is the numerical strength of the relationship between global agricultural and food system and construct of food demand-side forces?

4. To what extent is the global agricultural and food system related to food supply-side dimension?

5. What is the extent of relationship between global agricultural and food system and global agricultural markets failures?

6. To what extent is the GAFS related with public sector interventions and collective actions failures?

7. To what extent do the food demand-side forces contribute to the global food crisis?

8. To what extent do the food supply-side restrictions contribute to the global food crisis?

9. To what extent does the construct of global agricultural market failures contribute to the global food crisis?

10. To what extent do the dimension of public sector interventions and collective actions failures contribute to the global food crisis?

11. What are the significant constituents of the conceptualisation of global food crisis?

12. What is the extent of overall severity of global food crisis?

Structure of the Book

The present research study is based on a structure for measuring and managing the GFC. It has been developed by utilizing three approaches: exploratory, descriptive, and empirical (See Figure 1.1). These categories differ significantly in terms of purpose, research questions, and the data collection methods that are used. The basic purpose of the exploratory work is to seek insights into the general nature of the problem and relevant variables that required consideration. Here, a comprehensive review of literature on GFC is performed to formulate the research problem and to obtain an inventory of critical food crisis factors. The exploratory work is followed by descriptive work which involves linking the identified critical food crisis factors to the

GFC that serve as a premise for developing conceptual model and structural model of GFC. The questionnaire is designed, pre-tested, refined and finalised for required data collection and analysis. The empirical work is strictly based on constructing latent variable structural model based on critical food crisis factors and data collected from respondents on a measurement instrument that was developed to measure the phenomenon of the GFC. Based on data collected, generalisations are made on the relationships among critical food crisis factors and the GFC. The GFC index and indices of the critical food crisis factors are determined using a mathematical equation that takes into consideration the mean scores of measurement items and their ability in providing the empirical content of the GFC dimensions. The strengths of those relationships are applied in an advanced method for improving the situation of GFC and critical food crisis factors.

Significance of the Study

The issue of food security is significant not only to the least developed countries, but also to the developed countries including USA, UK, European countries, and Australia. The responsibility of global governance of world food security is to create a *new* world food system and an environment that provide every human positive freedom from chronic hunger, poverty, food vulnerability, starvation, obesity and malnutrition. This is indispensible for physical and mental growth that can be done by ways of introducing improvements in inputs, mechanisms, processes, outputs and outcomes of GAFS. In order to achieve these improvements, there is a need to measure the intensity and severity of prevailing GFC and the structural causal pathways leading to it.

Previous studies have shown that the GFC is a result of price hike due to various factors such as bio-fuel initiatives, natural disasters, food demand from emerging economies, etc. independent from one another. But these studies only provide a narrow and partial picture of food crisis since they fail to take into consideration all the factors simultaneously and also an order of significance of these factors. However, one should identify all possible critical food crisis factors contributing to GFC in order to be successful in managing the food crisis effectively. Once these factors have been identified, they could be measured, managed and improved.

Figure 1.1:   ***Structure of the Book***

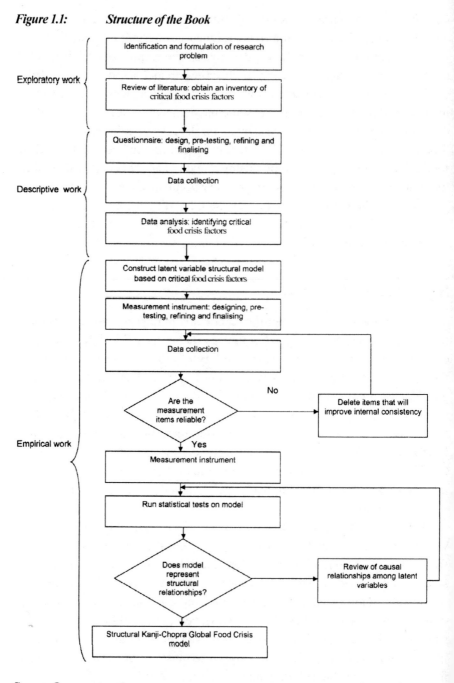

Source: Own construction

Introduction

There is no previous study that measures the phenomenon of GFC holistically. To the best knowledge of the present researcher, the present study is the only study that measures GFC by using systems modelling approach and structural equation multivariate modelling. If an alternative could be found that identifies the weaknesses of GAFS and discovers the causal pathways to GFC, then the world economy will benefit from it in terms of being able to provide good measures of food security, overcome problems in key areas, and provide accurate information to international organisations, governments, policy makers and all other food stakeholders.

Assumptions of the Study

The study is based on the following assumptions:
1. The questionnaire survey method is sufficient to obtain data concerning critical food crisis factors and global food crisis.
2. Respondents are assumed to provide truthful and honest response.
3. Response rate of less than 100 per cent is acceptable as long as it is large enough to do the required analysis of the GFC measurement system.
4. The agricultural analysts, economists and researchers represent the experts on the subject who can provide the required information as specified in the questionnaire.
5. The research results are as accurate as the statistics used to show reliability and validity of the measurement instrument used and the model.

Limitations of the Study

The *first* limitation of the study is the conceptual validity of GFC. There is a tendency in the literature to have various definitions based on different aspects of GFC and hence there is a lack of consensus. The present study takes a holistic view of the phenomenon of GFC. The *second* limitation is always a problem of faking about artificial view of peoples' perceptions. We are dealing with human behaviour that is changeable and unpredictable, so self-reporting and self-awareness can be faked by the respondents. The *third* limitation is that if the measurement model is using more than one scale, scales are treated in isolation and not interconnected to each other to give overall picture. There will be a problem if we include variables that do not form the part of the system into the model like happiness or we take into consideration mixed or combined manifest variables like creativity or intelligence. Cultural biases pose another limitation of measurement. Because of the geographical distance of the respondents, data can only be obtained via mail and electronic mail questionnaire. Consequently, other useful information could not possibly be obtained unless direct observations and direct contact were made. The theoretical development via modelling approach that is employed in this research certainly does not have the luxury of a scientific research where all variables are under the control of the researcher.

Chapter Scheme

This book develops, constructs and validates a new measurement kit. It measures GFC in eight chapters based on multivariate modelling approach and profound statistical thinking. The "Introduction" (Chapter One) is followed by a historical perspective of the food problems. "The Food Problems: A Historical Perspective" (Chapter Two) provides an intellectual historical review of scientific research in food problems and also succinctly reviews the current literature on food issues including GFC. It discusses the six fundamental challenges related to economics and meta-economics of food: a growing problem of world hunger; vicious cycle of intensified poverty and hunger dietary malnutrition; food, diet and health interactions leading to a growing epidemic of obesity; vulnerabilities of agricultural and food systems, and food quality and safety standards. A comparative picture of similarities and differences in the causes and timelines among the food crisis during the 1970s and 1990s and the current GFC have been discussed in this chapter. It traces the historical evolution and development of *global governance* for world food security since the beginning of the last century. It highlights the succession of policy choices and calls for the need of a *new global food governance system* with coherence and transparency of international governance and strategic thinking on world food security, rural poverty alleviation and rural development.

"Research Methodological Structuration" (Chapter Three) outlines the research methodology developed and applied in this study. The statistical understanding of the phenomenon of GFC has been outlined. The research methodology of *Kanji-Chopra Global Food Crisis Measurement System* (KCGFCMS) is based on a foundation of structural equation modelling and three basic pillars or axioms, such as, systems approach, critical food crisis factors approach and stakeholders approach. "A Theoretical Model of Global Agricultural and Food System" (Chapter Four) presents a theoretical framework for global agricultural and food system that initiate and sustain food crisis. The chapter analyses the behaviour of GAFS by studying the multivariate interactions of driving forces within systemically conceptualised GAFS with human resources and technological forces, environmental, geo-ecological and natural forces, political-institutional forces and socio-economic and cultural forces. It identifies key processes and activities, and evaluates major outputs, outcomes contributing to food security and overall societal impact of these interactions in terms of social welfare, development and opportunity, and environmental sustainability and ecological security. The theoretical model of GAFS also allows an analysis of feedbacks from the activities, outputs, outcomes and impact of food system to the driving forces of environmental, human, technological, political-institutional, socio-economic, and cultural change. It enables tradeoffs among the GAFS outputs, outcomes and impact between different scales or levels of decision-making or management in order to have context-specific solutions to manage them. The model can be used to build the typologies of food system interactions.

"System Dimensional Structure of Global Food Crisis" (Chapter Five) develops and analyses the dimensional structure of GFC. It represents a theoretical framework that subsumes the whole range of key factors contributing to GFC. These factors can be grouped into six latent variables or dimensions, namely, GAFS, food demand-side forces, food supply-side restrictions, global agricultural markets failures, public sector interventions and collective actions failures and GFC itself. Each dimension further incorporates critical parameters that play crucial role in the genesis of GFC. The dimensional structure of KCGFCM identifies 48 critical GFC factors that are key areas of risk for the well-being of population. If managed properly, they can improve the overall conditions and performance of different sub-systems and overall global agricultural and food system.

On Measuring Global Food Crisis

The choice of critical food crisis factors depends upon the researcher's judgement, justifications, extensive literature review and emerging empirical evidence. The identification of factors and forces is based on the principle of interactions and holism. As individual food security and welfare is contained in collective food security and welfare, there is a linkage and interdependence between individualism and collectivism at various levels. Moreover, the factors contributing to the GFC are complex, e.g., denial of food access, food availability and exorbitant food prices jointly and singly contribute to chronic hunger, malnutrition, and starvation.

"Developing Global Food Crisis Measurement System" (Chapter Six) develops and constructs the complete measurement system called KCGFCMS to measure GFC. Consistent with the theme of the present work is the development and construction GFC index and decomposition of GFC index. It tackles four distinct problems faced in the measurement of a phenomenon: first, the choice of a criterion of GFC to identify the whole range of critical GFC factors; second, the study of causal structure of GFC by using causal reasoning or casual pathways; third, the dimensional decomposition of GFC index into food demand-side forces index, food supply-side restrictions index, global agricultural market failures index and public sector interventions and collective actions failures index; and fourth, the aggregation of dimensions to account for multidimensionality by constructing an overall index of severity. A conceptual model has been used specifically to highlight the interdependence of various dimensions of GFC. Thereafter, a structural model has been constructed for determining the GFC index where six latent variables are interlinked. The dimensional structure of GFC has been introduced to establish the causal pathways. Its format is the result of the specific questions and problems addressed and requirements specified for GFC index. It is based on well-established theories and approaches specified for GFC criteria and draws on a number of currently used crisis dimensions. A set of manifest (measurable) variables is associated with each of the latent variables and the structure is called the GFC analytical model. A GFC measurement model is also constructed, developed and validated for the construction of causal path diagrams, measurement of elements and indices, to perform reliability analysis, to verify content, construct and criterion-related validity of the model, to conduct sensitivity analysis on research questions and to interpret the results.

Introduction

"Measuring Global Food Crisis" (Chapter Seven) delineates a step-by-step procedure of an application of KCGFCMS. It outlines multivariate model process of validation, testing and estimation. The chapter discusses an empirical application of KCGFCMS along with the measurement instrument, survey methodology, statistical reliability analysis, validity analysis and path analysis. The findings of the study have been analysed and interpreted. "Resume, Conclusions and Policy Options" (Chapter Eight) provides a summary of the study along with its main conclusions, findings on research questions and recommendations. It analyses the contributions of critical food crisis factors towards GFC. It attempts to pinpoint and prescribe the food policy options leading to greater food security, social welfare and environmental sustainability and ecological security. It shows that KCGFCMS is a robust measurement tool and a significant contribution to the understanding of the global food problems.

Notes

i.   The Food and Agricultural Organisation in the United Nations (FAO) Food Price Index is a measure of the monthly change in international prices of a basket of food commodities. It consists of the average of five commodity group price indices (representing 55 quotations), weighted with the average export shares of each of the groups for 2002-2004.

ii.   Food security may be defined as an access by all people at all times to enough food for an active, balanced and healthy life.

iii. World Bank (2011), Food Price Hike Drives 44 Million People into Poverty, http://web.worldbank.org/WBSITE/EXTERNAL/NEWS/0,contentMDK:22833439~pagePK:64257043~piPK:437376~theSitePK:4607,00.html, 15 February.

iv.   Lagi et al. (2012) summarize a sample of the literature on the causes of the food price crisis of 2007-2008. Abbott et al. (2008) provide an earlier summary of causes. The several potential factors the various authors examine are: the change of diet in developing countries, bio-fuels conversion, financial speculation in the commodity futures market, the price of crude oil, and variation in currency exchange rates.

v.   Thompson, W. and Tallard, G. (2010), Potential market effects of selected policy options in emerging economies to address future commodity price surges, OECD Food, Agriculture and Fisheries Working Papers, No. 35, OECD Publishing, OECD, Paris.

vi.   FAO, IFAD, IMF, OECD, UNCTAD, WFP, the World Bank, the WTO, IFPRI and the UN HLTF, Price Volatility in Food and Agricultural Markets: Policy Responses, Joint Policy Report, June 2011.

vii. Sharma, Ramesh, Food Export Restrictions: Review of the 2007-2010 Experience and Considerations for Disciplining Restrictive Measures, FAO Commodity and Trade Policy Research Working Paper, No. 32, May 2011; Mitra, Siddhartha and Tim Josling, Agricultural Export Restrictions: Welfare Implications and Trade Disciplines, IPC Position Paper, Agriculture and Rural Development Policy Series, International Food and Agricultural Trade Policy Council, January 2009; Bipul Chatterjee and Chenai Mukumba (2011), "Food Export Restrictions: Balance importers' and exporters' rights", CUTS CITEE Working Paper No. 1/2011.

viii.   The years 2007–2008 saw dramatic increases in world food prices and as of 2009, food prices have fallen significantly from their earlier highs.

ix.   Agricultural production grew faster than the human population during the past 50 years.

x.   Food insecurity is a situation that exists when all people, at all times, do not have physical, social and economic access to sufficient, safe and nutritious food that meets their dietary needs and food preferences for an active and healthy life.

xi.   At individual and household levels, the ownership and command over adequate amount of food can be established either by growing the food personally (as in the case of farmers or small agricultural co-operatives) or by buying the food in the market place (Sen, 1999). Individuals are affected by food crisis when they fail to establish the ownership and command over the adequate amount of food either due to inability to buy food due to personal human contestability failure (unemployment, lack of income, low wages, lack of assets, illiteracy etc.) or country's social, economic, political and institutional circumstances and arrangements (economic slowdown, absence of social security system, unequal distribution of food, lack of political will or natural disasters such as famines and so on).

xii.   Free system means that the agents/elements in the system are not fixed and adapt to the changes within the system.

xiii.   The term complex means composed of many interconnected parts. Complex systems can be managed systems and adaptive systems (See, Pyzdek, 1999).

xiv.   Ancient Greek defined an economy by using the Greek words οἰκονόμος «one who manages a household» (derived from οἶκος «house», and νέμω «distribute» (especially, manage), οἰκονομία «household management», and οἰκονομικός «of a household or family". However, its meaning changed to "the management of economic affairs" in the case of a monastery during the thirteen century. Thereafter, the meaning of the word 'economy' is recorded in more general senses including "thrift" and "administration". Nevertheless, its currently most frequently used meaning is "the economic system of a country or an area".

xv.   Within the global economy, the different national economies are classified on the basis of four different sectors such as an economy dominating in primary sector (mining, fishing, farming, drilling for oil), governing the secondary sector (all types of manufacturing and building), leading the tertiary sector which includes all types of services to the people such as doctors, bankers and postmen, and controlling the quaternary sector such as think tanks, those who do research and development work, work in policy and development. Another way of classifying different national economies is in terms of distinct sectors such as shipping, mining, tourism, banking, industrial production, retail, exports, textiles, information technology, education, research and development.

Introduction

xvi.   Analysis and synthesis are two approaches used to understand increasing complexity. Analysis, based on mathematical thinking of analytic geometry, means analyzing a complex situation, issue or phenomenon by trying to break it down into component pieces and consider each in isolation from the others. The underlying assumption is that all of the parts are essentially independent of one another. On the other hand, systems' thinking represents synthesis that is based on integrated perspective. In systems approach, first the system is taken apart into different components, understand in isolation and then each link and interaction among different components are established to understand how the system as a whole functions.

xvii. General equilibrium theory asks: what prices and quantities of goods produced and consumed are consistent with-would pose no incentives for change to—the overall pattern of prices and quantities in the economy's markets.

xviii. Game theory asks: what strategies, moves, or allocations are consistent with— would induce no further reactions to—the potential outcomes these strategies, moves, allocations might imply.

xix.   Rational expectations economics asks: what forecasts (or expectations) are consistent with—are on average validated by—the outcomes these forecasts and expectations together create.

Chapter 2   The Food Problems: A Historical Perspective

"Lack of access to food is a social problem and it is not just a question of raising food production vis-a-vis population. Starvation and malnutrition relate ultimately to ownership and exchange in addition to production possibilities. There is, indeed, no such thing as an apolitical food problem"
Amartya K. Sen[i] (1982). Distinguished Indian Economist, Winner of the Nobel Prize in Economics (1998) and Bharat Ratna (1999).

Introduction

We are living in interesting times - an age of perilous socio-political uncertainty, puzzles, extremes and changing landscapes marked by triple interwoven crises namely, global financial and economic crisis, global environmental and depleted natural resources crisis, and global food crisis at assorted scales. Albeit all these crises have numerous multifarious negative consequences for individuals and communities but the food crisis has immediate, direct and more rigorous impact on human well-being and quality of life. The net impact of food problems[ii] has been constantly spreading over society, politics, health, agriculture, economy, psychology and beyond. Food problems are not simply a matter of astronomical basic food prices or food demand-supply mismatch, but fundamentally are linked to the basic challenges of unequal distribution of food, growing obesity, food vulnerability, food utilisation problems, food quality and safety issues, intensifying global poverty, hunger, starvation, and malnutrition and seriously damaged environment. History reveals that severe food problems often occurred amidst copious food supplies (Brinkman and Hendrix, 2011). Various previous studies have coined the legacy of plethora of dimensions of food crisis but various food issues at individual level can be subsumed into the two most important ones: the entitlement dimension and the utilisation dimension. The *entitlement dimension* of food crisis asserts that food problems occur when people cannot establish their command, exchange or ownership over adequate amount of food either due to shocks to people's endowments (loss of employment, income, assets, etc.) or disturbances in food supply or prices or both (Sen, 1981 and 1999)[iii]. This dimension explains people's sufferings from hunger, undernourishment and starvation perspective. Whereas the *utilisation dimension* of food crisis goes beyond the issues of food affordability and shortages. It focuses on the dynamics of food intakes, diets and health interactions linked with food consumption and absorption. This dimension also affects human *body capital* and contributes to food crisis through its linkages with obesity, food wastages, food quality and safety and other issues.

The literature on food problems and its dimensions is spread over different studies and the present chapter takes its concise review. The present chapter is structured in five different sections. The first section reviews an intellectual history of scientific research in food problems including the critical delineation of the contemporary literature on global food crisis. The second section unfolds a paradoxical situation of growing hunger and obesity in the world. This section is further divided into five subgroups namely, growing world hunger; vicious cycle of intensified poverty and hunger; food for healthy living: diet and health interactions (dietary undernutrition and overnutrition or an obese world); vulnerabilities of agricultural and food systems and food safety and standards. The third part is devoted to a succinct comparison between current food crisis and the food crises during the 1970s and 1990s. The fourth segment outlines a historical evolution of the idea of global governance for world food security and the fifth part concludes the chapter.

Scientific Research in Food Problems: An Intellectual Historical Review

Search for food has been a basic challenge for earliest humans to survive. Food problems are as old as human civilisation. They are also endemic in the contemporary world. Throughout human history, there have always been food problems due to different causes ranging from natural disasters, to overpopulation, to government howlers, to wars, human displacements and conflicts (Himmelgreen and Kedia, 2010). Susan George's (1977) observed that famines represent the final stage in an extended process of deepening vulnerability and fracturing of social reproduction mechanisms, this food "crisis" represents the magnification of a long-term crisis of social reproduction stemming from colonialism, and was triggered by neo-liberal capitalist development (McMichael, 2009). In socio-economic context, food problems are studied in agricultural economics by applying the tools, methods and principles of general economics to *economic relations* among persons arising out of land usage, production, storage, exchange, distribution, consumption, and utilization of crops and livestock[iv]. It focuses on maximizing the crop yield with minimizing costs and negative externalities, and maintaining a good soil ecosystem. However, any scientific research in agriculture or food problems gives *fact basis* for clear thinking and right action (Henry, 1928). Be that as it may, tracing the evolution of scientific research in food problems requires a profound insight into intellectual torrents of general economics.

The review of literature on food problems can be divided into four categories for simplicity's sake. The *first category* includes the earliest works from ancient thoughts to the works of T.R. Malthus and its critique and other classical economists' works. The *second category* reviews the major studies from the beginning of the 19th century to the end of the Second World War. The *third category* includes the studies on food problems after 2nd World War. The *fourth category* reviews the research studies particularly on GFC up to the end of year 2011, which is further sub-divided into three categories. The *first sub-category* reviews the research studies linking the food problems with socio-economic issues such as poverty, inequality, rural developments, agricultural development and distribution of food and other resources. The *second sub-category* reviews the studies undertaken by international organisations on the eve of contemporary GFC (during 2007-09). Finally, the *third sub-category* reports on internet blogs, research papers and articles, and a plethora of references and edited books published by individual researchers when the impact and severity of contemporary GFC was felt, noticed and discussed at international level during 2007-2012.

In the *first category*, the ancient thought on food problems, albeit not based on any systematic paradigm, can be imbibed from Hebrew economic thought[v] (2500 B.C.–150 B.C.), based on metaphysical and

The Food Problems: A Historical Perspective

ethical considerations, where agriculture even though traditional was given the most important place in society (Roll, 1933). The economic ideas of ancient Greeks are contained in the teachings of Greek philosophers–Platon (427-347 B.C.) and Aristotles (384-322 B.C.); and in the writings of the contemporary historian-Xylophone (440-355 B.C.) and Epicurus (341 B.C.– 270 B.C.). They laid the true principles of agricultural economy, preferred agriculture as a source of wealth, considered agricultural exports leading to the impoverishment of the peasantry and the interests of merchants and landowners were considered to be clashed. Roman economic thinkers such as Marcus Tullius Cicero (106-43 B.C.), Lucius Annaeus Seneca (4 B.C-65 A.D.), Pliny the Elder (23-79 A.D.), Marcus Porcius Cato (234-149 B.C), Marcus Terentius Varro (116-27 B.C.), and Lucius Junius Moderatus Columella (A.D. 4–ca. A.D. 70) praised agriculture with interests in the improvements of agricultural techniques.

Ancient Indian agricultural thoughts were the first contained in Kautilya's treatise, *Arthasastra* (3rd-4th century B.C.) which regarded agriculture as a continuous process (Nene, 2002)[vi]. Another ancient Indian scholar Valluvar[vii] published his economic ideas in his book *Thirukkural* (during the first or the second century A.D.) and regarded a prosperous nation as one with plentiful harvest, industrial productivity with agricultural inputs, and consequent abundance of production and wealth. However, medieval agricultural ideas covers a vast span of about one thousand years which is divided into two parts: (1) from 476 to the 11th century known as the dark ages in which static or stagnant agricultural economy prevailed and (2) from the 12th to the 15th century–the period with commercial and economic progress. The social structure of the medieval period was raised on the foundations of *feudalism* which appeared in the Western Europe, but the most important feature of feudal economy was the predominance of agriculture. St. Thomas Aquinas's (1225–1274 A.D.)[viii] views were a mixture of the teachings of the Bible and the philosophy of Aristotle. His doctrine of '*justum pretium*' (just price) was based upon the concept of value considered absolute as an objective quality and usefulness inherent in every commodity. Its measure was dependent upon a process of estimation of the cost of production which covered labour. Thereafter, *Mercantilists* (1500-1750) such as Sir Thomas Mun, J.B. Colbert, A. Serra, S.J. Child, and Sir James Steuart, recognized two factors of production namely, land and labour. Petty's famous dictum is repeated here: "Labour is the father, and active principle of wealth, as land is the mother". Land and trade went together. They laid emphasis on the cultivation of agricultural waste land to increase food production and make country self-sufficient in foodstuffs. Food imports were to be restricted, and should be grown in the domestic country.

However, after the post-industrial revolution in Britain and other countries, agricultural research was derived from two different intellectual streams: theoretical and empirical (Federico, 2008; Bohstedt, 2010). The theoretical intellectual stream may be traced back to the 18th century and includes neoclassical political economy, the theory of the firm and other techniques applied to farm production. However, the empirical intellectual stream subsumes strategies and policies for organized marketing of agricultural commodities through collective bargaining and cooperatives. The French *Physiocrates* Francois Quesnay in his *"Tableau economique"* (1758) with the help of input-output analysis and general equilibrium theory provided logical explanation of land as a factor of production, conversion of land inputs into agricultural outputs and profit, and emphasis on surplus production. Arthur Young[ix], a leading agricultural writer of the time, conducted a variety of agricultural experiments and published his first major agricultural work, *The Farmer's Letters*, in 1767. In 1784 he founded the periodical *Annals of Agriculture*, and edited forty-six volumes published as well as contributed a large proportion of their contents. His sample survey investigative procedure undoubtedly represented a pioneering scientific approach to agricultural research (Allen and Ó Gráda, 1988). Adam Smith[x] in his *The Wealth of Nations* (1776) promoted profit-seeking, private property, and free market exchange consistent with strict economic perspective. Smith accentuated on the central role of agriculture as a store of national wealth and agriculture is much more durable and cannot be destroyed by violent convulsions of war and political instability (Runge, 2006). His writings are consistent with many aspects of sustainable agriculture. Smith believed in balancing economic with environmental and social considerations (James, 2006). David Ricardo[xi] coined the *Law of Diminishing Returns*[xii] to land in his *An Essay on the Influence of a Low Price of Corn on the Profits of Stock* (1815)[xiii].

Reverend Thomas Robert Malthus[xiv] in six editions of his celebrated book, *An Essay on the Principle of Population*, published from 1798 to

1826 asserted that "food is necessary to the existence of man" and "the passion between the sexes is necessary and will remain nearly in its present state". Based on these two postulates, Malthus concluded that "the power of population is indefinitely greater than the power in the earth to produce subsistence for man". The basis for this conclusion was his assumption that, "Population, when unchecked, increases in a geometrical ratio. Subsistence increases only in an arithmetical ratio[xv]". Malthus argued that population was held within resource limits by two types of checks: *positive checks* such as hunger, disease and war, which raised the death rate, and *preventative checks* such as abortion, birth control, prostitution, postponement of marriage, and celibacy, which lowered the birth rate.[xvi] "If positive checks were unsuccessful, then inevitably (he said), famine would be the resulting way of keeping the population down. Before starvation set in, Malthus advised that steps be taken to help the positive checks to do their work. In Malthus' opinion, the masses were incapable of exercising moral restraint, which was the only real remedy for the population problem. They were therefore doomed to live always at bare subsistence level." Contrary to the time when Malthus first published his work, the global population has grown more than seven times (less than one billion at his time) and the general standard of living as well as food production and consumption have seen unprecedented increase.

Figure 2.1:   *Malthusian Theory of Population and Resources Growth*

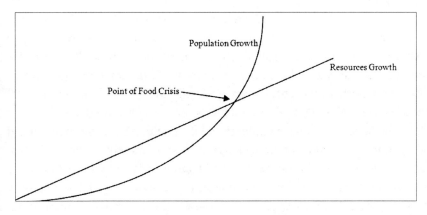

Over the past several decades, some neo-Malthusians or 'catastrophists' have expressed concern about the ability of agricultural production to keep pace with global food demands (Brown and Kane, 1994; Meadows et al., 1992; Ehrlich and Ehrlich, 1990), whereas other 'cornucopians' have forecast that technological advances or expansions of cultivated area would boost production sufficiently to meet rising demands (Conway and Toenniessen, 2003; Evans, 1998; Simon, 1998; Boserup, 1965; Smil, 2002). Thus far, dire predictions of a global food security catastrophe have proved unfounded in the sense that aggregate food supply has kept pace with population growth, although hundreds of millions remain hungry and malnourished. Nevertheless, despite the fact that food production per capita has been increasing globally, major distributional inequalities remain linked primarily to poverty (Thompson, 2003; Drèze and Sen, 1989). As mentioned earlier, Amartya Sen (1999) analysed and discussed the contemporary challenge of hunger and the question of entitlements at a greater length. Hunger is the prevailing subject for Moore Lappé, Collins and Rosset (1998); Boucher and Douglas (1999); Burby (2006); Hall (2006); Standford (2007), Vernon (2007); von Braun, Ruel and Gulati (2008); von Grebmer, Fritschel, Nestorova, Olofinbiyi, Pandya-Lorch and Yohannes (2008); Cribb (2010); Patel, Holt-Giménez and Shattuck(2009), Thurow and Kilman (2009); Bassett and Winter-Nelson (2010); Fraser and Rimas (2010). Global food production has increased by well over 130 percent since the 1960s, yet the fact that almost 78 per cent of countries that report child malnutrition are food-exporting countries dramatically illustrates a 'paradox of plenty' (Mittal, 2006).

In the *second category* of research studies, J.H. Von Thünen (1828)[xvii] was the first agricultural economist among classical economists who developed a scientific and mathematical based model of agricultural land use. He provided an analysis of the extensive margin and the relationship between distance to market and rent. However, during the late 19th and earlier 20th centuries the major scientific foundations for agricultural economics were laid by the neoclassical developments and it came into being as an organised and systematised body of knowledge. Alfred Marshall's very important work, *Principles of Economics* (1920) blatantly established the link from diminishing marginal utility in exchange to decreasing marginal productivity on the supply side (Runge, 2006). To Marshall, the amount of agricultural produce raised and the position of margin of cultivation were both governed by the general conditions of demand and supply. He popularised the notions of price elasticity of demand, price shifts and curve shifts[xviii]. His other main contributions widely used in agricultural economics were quasi-rents, marginalist revolution (marginal costs in relation to agricultural values), marginal utility equals price, economic welfare divided into producer and consumer surplus (known as Marshallian surplus), among others. He made use of the term 'land' in a much broader sense[xix].

The farm depression of the 1870's -1890's gave rise to many new agricultural issues such as marketing, organization, labour interests, farm management, physical, technical and scientific aspects of production and so on. Thorstein Bunde Veblen[xx] (1893) observed that agriculture was assuming the character of an industry in the modern sense. The depression in agricultural farming and food production was not due to bad weather, but due to fall in food prices and high money rents. He elaborated Marshall's theory of the firm. He made an attempt to statistically measure and validate the relationship between input costs, output prices, and farm profits. He distinguished agricultural economics and linked it strongly to the neoclassical syntheses of J.R. Hicks (1939) and Paul Samuelson (1947). Henry C. Taylor was the greatest contributor to agricultural economics with his major work *An Introduction to the Study of Agricultural Economics* (1905). He applied Marshallian principles to farm production, and developed production functions showing increasing, steady and diminishing returns. Étienne Jouzier (1911) was one of the earliest economists to define agricultural economics[xxi]. John D. Black's book *Introduction to Production Economics* (1926) became the standard and he had been described as "the most influential economist in the United States dealing with the problems of agriculture" (Galbraith, 1959). Holbrook Working's (1922 and 1925) econometric explorations were among the first to derive an empirical demand curve. Hotelling (1931) analysed the natural resources as problems of materials shortages and treated as a form of capital.

L.C. Gray (1922, 1933) published his works on agricultural economics, history of agriculture in Southern USA and on plight of rural classes. Frederick V. Waugh (1928) contributed his first quantitative study of quality characteristics as determinants of prices by applying hedonic regression pricing models and appearing as "Quality Factors Influencing Vegetable Prices" in which he noted that if "a premium for certain qualities and types of products is more than large enough to pay the increased cost of growing a superior product, the individual can and will adapt his production and marketing policies to market demand". Warren Cleland Waite (1929) continued his research into different areas including price analysis of agricultural economics. In 1930, Mordecai Ezekiel pursued the empirical work of Warren Waugh with his book, *Methods of Correlation Analysis*, which became an international standard textbook on correlation theory and regression side of correlation with particular stress on nonlinear regression functions. Ezekiel (1938) provided a state-of-the-art description of cobweb and recursive models illustrated by the corn-hog cycle. According to W.W. Leontief (1971), the works of Ezekiel and other early agricultural economists were "an exceptional example of a healthy balance between theoretical and empirical analysis..." and "the first among economists to make use of the advanced methods of mathematical statistics."

The *third category* includes many important research works by Hendrickson (1943), Black (1943), Boserup (1965), Marx (1975), Marei (1977) and Morgan (1980). Hibbard (1948) undertook many studies on agricultural marketing, cooperatives, and farmer movements. Earl O. Heady (1951, 1957, and 1958) broke new grounds with the application of linear programming methods for analyzing how inputs could most efficiently be employed in producing agricultural outputs. He also pioneered the application of computing power to problem-solving in applied economics. This included work on human and animal diet rations and consumption (Heady and Dillon, 1961). Zvi Griliches (1957) contributed new technology and diffusion models. Farrell (1957) measured multifactor productivity and efficiency by involving an empirical application of state level agricultural data. Nicholas Georgescu-Roegen (1960), a demand theorist and econometrician, expressed path-breaking insights into the physical process underlying economic activity, and contributed a deep critique of agrarianism and Marxian misunderstandings of agricultural production. Hildreth (1957), Hildreth and Houck (1968) and Hazell (1971) produced optimization applications in farm management by applying stochastic programming methods and random coefficients regression. Burt and Allison (1963) applied Bellman's dynamic programming principle to optimal wheat rotations. Boussard and Petit (1967), both French economists, applied George Shackle's (1949) "focus loss constraint" concept of uncertainty to agriculture. Dillon (1971) and Anderson, Dillon and Hardaker (1977) surveyed the application of subjective probability concepts to agriculture.

The German agricultural economists Heidhues (1966) and De Haen (De Haen and Heidhues, 1973) contributed by following their analysis on the outgrowth of optimization theory as an analysis of the growth and decline of farms in modern economies. Henderson (1959) studied behavioral adjustment or supply response in agriculture by using recursive programming models, and were generalized by Day (1963), following the path set by Nerlove (1958). Optimal storage rules were analyzed by Gustafson (1958). Spatial issues in agriculture analyzed best-location decisions (Egbert and Heady 1961), and interregional supply-demand equilibrium issues (e.g., Fox, 1953). Two new issues of natural resources and agricultural development in developing countries were brought into agricultural research investigation during 1960s and 1970s. Following the early analytical leads of Hotelling (1931) and Ciriacy-Wantrup (1952), Scott (1955) and Crutchfield and Zellner (1962) studied fisheries; and Burt (1966) and Burt and Cummings (1970) in a series of articles considered groundwater allocation over time as a dynamic program with stochastic state variables. Cummings and Winkelmann (1970) extended these dynamic models to interregional investments in water studies. By the 1970s environmental pollution emerged as a major subject of applied economics that encouraged many agricultural economists to acknowledge the agriculture's negative external effects and market failures.

Various multilateral and bilateral aid agencies such as the World Bank, FAO, and so on, supported and encouraged project evaluations in many areas of agricultural development in developing countries. W. Arthur Lewis (1954), Leibenstein (1957), J.W. Mellor (1966), Chenery and Syrquin (1975), Lipton (1977), Timmer (2002) and others saw the development problem of the LDCs as an imbalance or bias between agriculture (rural) and industrial (urban) sectors and analysed agriculture's sectoral role. The primary data limitations in these countries restricted the full application of optimization models at the microeconomic level. However, T.W. Schultz's was instrumental in establishing econometrics as a tool for analyzing agricultural economics empirically and noted that agricultural supply analysis was rooted in "shifting sand" implying that it was and is simply not being done correctly[xxii]. His classic work *Transforming Traditional Agriculture* (1964) relied mainly on stylized representations of "rational but poor" farmers and descriptive analysis from anthropologists. He was among the first economists such as Johnston and Mellor (1961), Thorbecke (1970) to examine development economics as a problem related to agriculture in 1968[xxiii].

Many agricultural economists (Rosenstein-Rodan, 1957; Oshima, 1958; Mazumdar, 1959; Wonnacott, 1962; Meller, 1963; Kao et al., 1964; Viner, 1964; Sen, 1966; Ghosh, 1977) saw the "farm problem" as one of surplus labour and disguised unemployment. In relation to demand-supply imbalance in agriculture, supplying farm commodities in excess of domestic demand has detrimental impact on agricultural prices. Analyzing low agricultural prices as a matter of chronic oversupply, aggravated by rapid technological improvements and productivity gains in the face of inelastic demand, Cochrane (1958) proposed his treadmill hypothesis: rapid and early adopters of productivity-improving technology would reap the lion's share of rents to innovation, as laggards were forced off the farm, while Brewster (1959) considered the social and policy implications of these trends. This opened the way to consideration of agriculture in an open economy, and a new policy emphasis on the macroeconomics of the food sector (Schuh, 1974, 1976; Cochrane and Runge, 1992; Ardeni and Freebairn, 2002; Abbott and McCalla, 2002). In the 1980's, this open economy analysis was supported by the development of large-scale computable general equilibrium models linking agriculture to trade (e.g., Hertel, 1997) as well as more traditional macroeconomic sectoral forecasting models (e.g., Myers et al., 1987). Together, the large-scale models allowed alternative trade and agricultural policy approaches to be simulated and compared to the *status quo* (e.g., Cochrane and Runge, 1992).

Over the last more than five decades (1960-2012) there have been ten broad areas of contributions made in agriculture and food economics: (a) agricultural productivity, technical progress and economic development (Canning, 1988); (b) manpower and agricultural issues (human capital investment, surplus labour, disguised unemployment in agriculture, wages) (c) institutional factors and government interventions in agriculture; (d) environmental, ecological and natural resources issues; (e) command over food (food security, food vulnerability, hunger, starvation, poverty, right to food, freedom for food, and so on); (f) agricultural risk and uncertainty; (g) world agricultural trade, market structure and agri-businesses organisation; (h) food consumption and food supply chains; (i) price determination and income stabilization; (j) global food crisis and global governance for food security. However, the following section specifically reviews the literature on GFC.

The *fourth category* reviews the research studies particularly on GFC up to the mid of 2012. Its *first sub-category* includes studies on the food problems linking with socio-economic problems. The impact of food crisis on poverty has been studied by various studies such as Ravallion (1990); Ivanic and Martin (2008); Vu and Glewwe (2009); Wodon and Zaman (2010); Skoufias, Tiwari, Zaman. (2011). The issue of right of food in globalisation and food crisis has been discussed by De Schutter and Cordes (2011). The impact of food export restrictions on GFC has been analysed by many studies by Sharma (2011), Mitra, Siddhartha and Josling (2009), Kavi and Parikh (2001), Fischer et al. (2002); Martin and Anderson (2011) and Chatterjee and Mukumba (2011). The *second sub-category* includes some of the important studies that have looked at hunger, food insecurity and malnutrition in the backdrop of the current food crisis, e.g., *The State of Food Insecurity in the World (2008)* by the Food and Agricultural Organization (FAO), *Food Security Assessment (2007)* by the United States Department of Agriculture (USDA) and *Global Hunger Index: The Challenge of Hunger (2008)* jointly published by the International Food Policy research Institute (IFPRI), Welthungerhilfe and Concern Worldwide. These studies provide insightful pictures on the global situation with regard to the food crisis. The FAO and USDA reports mentioned earlier also discuss the reasons for the food crisis and preferred policy options. In addition to these reports, other studies and documents like the World Bank Policy Research Working Paper *Implications of Higher Global Food Prices for Low-income Countries* (hereafter referred as Ivanic and Martin, 2008), World Bank report *Rising Food and Fuel Prices: Addressing the Risks to Future Generations* prepared by their Human Development Network (HDN) and Poverty Reduction and Economic Management (PREM) network (henceforth HDN-PREM study) and the IMF study *Food and Fuel Prices–Recent Developments, Macroeconomic Impact and Policy Responses* (henceforth IMF Report, 2008) have addressed the above mentioned issues.

The HDN-PREM study supported by the World Bank stressed that recent food inflation resulted in an increase in the poverty count and depth of the poverty. The study quoted latest estimates of increase in poverty depth which reveal that 88 per cent of the increase is due to poor households sliding further down into poverty and only 12 per cent is accounted by non-poor households falling under the poverty line. The study detailed the implications of high food prices for health and education. In addition, Ivanic and Martin (2008) analysed household level data for nine low-income countries (Zambia, Vietnam, Peru, Pakistan, Nicaragua, Malawi, Madagascar, Cambodia, and Bolivia) to assess the net effect of food inflation on poverty. They examined whether the positive impact of high food prices on net food sellers in poor nations was outweighed by the negative impact of the same on net food buyers. While noting that the food producers in developing economies stood to benefit from high food prices[xxiv], the authors cautioned that the extent of actual benefit was determined by the net sales of food by the food surplus farmers. Typically, large portions of the food production were used for own consumption in the global south, which partially offset the positive effects of high food prices on food cultivators.

The IMF Report (2008) and USDA (2008) identified the growing economies as one of the central causes behind the food inflation. Over the last two decades, per capita income and economic growth has increased in China and India. As a result, all type households underwent dietary diversification and fast approaching the western dietary patterns that caused an increase in demand for food grains in these countries based on the premise that diversified diets containing higher proportion of animal products led to a larger indirect consumption of grains. In the event of such a development, the total *direct* and *indirect* demand for food grains would undergo significant increases. In the wake of the contemporary food crisis, the UN Secretary-General had appointed a 'High Level Task Force on the Global Food Security Crisis' to recommend policy suggestions to address the current concerns on the global food situation. The Task Force has published the *Comprehensive Framework for Action* in July 2008, which would also be an interesting document for study. These studies not only help us to comprehend the different dimensions of the GFC, but also reveal some of the lacunae that still remain within the global perspective on the food crisis. A deeper and correct understanding of the latter will be crucial for mankind to successfully tide over the current predicament.

The *third sub-category* includes a plethora of internet blogs, research articles (published in journals and newspapers), books (references and edited) which can be grouped in accordance with the issue they address. For instance, food riots are widely debated by Walton and Seddon (1995), Pilcher (2006), Patel (2010), Bohstedt (2010). Ivanic and Martin (2002), Sachs (2005), Holt-Giménez, Patel and Shattuck (2009), Hoekman and Ataman (2010), Innman, (2011), Macan-Markar (2011) enlarge upon the relationship between food prices and poverty. Food insecurity is the major source of debate for Skoet and Stamoulis (2006), United Nations World Food Programme (2006), Wunderlich (2006), Amare (2008), Leyna (2009) and Nord (2009). Other authors have presented food crisis in a global context such as Shaw (2007)[xxv]; Dawe (2008); McCullough et al. (2008); Roberts (2008); Shaw (2008)[xxvi]; Shattuck (2008, 2009); Astyk and Newton (2009); Bello (2009); Cohen and Clapp (2009); Marsden et al. (2009); Nellemann (2009); Patnaik, (2009); Headey and Fan (2008, 2010); Himmelgreen and Kedia (2010); Magdoff and Tokar (2010); Rosin et al. (2011). Hike in food prices have been presented in several books written by Abbott et al. (2009); Cudjoe et al. (2010); and Mitchell (2008).

The above studies dealt with the magnitude, causes, impact, consequences or policy options of GFC by using microeconomic and macroeconomic data. Most of these studies are collections of articles by different experts or highlights of the contemporary controversies on the issues or a comprehensive story-type narration of facts related to GFC. However, none of the works mentioned above addresses the issue of management with measurement of GFC in robust and scientific way directly. The complexity perspective of the phenomenon is missing. Despite its severity as a global phenomenon, no major study is undertaken to conceptualise the phenomenon of GFC as a holistic syndrome and to measure its magnitude, intensity, analyse its causes and sources, comprehend its consequences, and offer policy options to manage it effectively and timely. The present book is primarily designed to measure incidence, depth and severity of the phenomenon of GFC. Thus, the present study points out the knowledge gaps we still have. However, it looks at the phenomenon of GFC from a comprehensive, holistic and systems point of view and does provide a systematic study of the measurement of the food crisis for its effective management.

Starving or Obese Nations: A Paradox of Growing Hunger and Obesity

The ongoing and new emerging forces are driving significant changes in global agricultural and food system. There is an emerging paradox of growing hunger and increasing obesity (also called dead weight) in the world. The number of undernourished as well as obese children and adults is increasing. Their combined effect stands to be a major challenge to food security. A policy of achieving food security in every country ought to involve the maintaining and securing of a stable supply of good-quality affordable food accessible to everyone by increasing domestic agricultural production with imports and stockpile, and an appropriate combination with large investment in rural development resulting in significant reduction in poverty, inequality and maldistribution of food. According to the 'Rome Declaration on World Food Security', governments have to comply with 'the right of everyone to have access to safe and nutritious food, consistent with the right to adequate food and the fundamental right of everyone to be free from hunger' (FAO, 1996). Food security implies a number of conditions which can be summarised in five 'As': availability, accessibility, adequacy, acceptability and agency (Centre for Studies in Food Security, 2011). Focusing on this issue, Rocha (2006) opines that food insecurity can be considered as a *market failure* due to the presence in the global food systems of externalities and public goods. The former follow from negative externalities in shape of pollution generated by agricultural productions; the latter are inherent in the very concept of food security, since it can be enjoyed by many individuals (in a non-rival and non-exclusive way), enhancing public health, another public good (Praussello, 2011). Hermann (2006) is of the opinion that imports of subsidised agriculture goods and provision of food aids in developing countries can help overcome food crises in the short run, but in the longer term can have disruptive effects by giving origin to food shortages. The main contemporary food related challenges are: first, the world hunger is increasing in the South. The main food problem is not a technical one of producing more food, but a political one of ensuring that food is available to hungry poor rural food producers who need it most in the South. Second, the world is becoming more and more obese due to indiscriminate food intake mainly in the North as well as in the South. People consume too much food almost any time and not the right type. Third, global poverty and inequality have intensified the vicious cycle of intensified poverty and hunger. Fourth, malnutrition in poor quality diets is more widespread. Fifth, there is an emerging issue of food safety across the world.

World Hunger: A Growing Problem

In the early 1990s, the number of hungry[xxvii] people started to bottom out, following a two-decade trend of declines. Since then, high food prices made it worse and hunger has been increasing. Recently FAO had estimated that during 2012 there were 1 billion people around the globe facing extreme hunger every day, one sixth of world population making thus the *Millennium Development Goal* target of 420 millions almost impossible. By 2012, food emergencies remained in 37 countries. Vulnerability with regard to meeting the minimum nutritional norms, the fundamental requirement for a healthy life, can lead a household or individuals to trade-off specific secondary yet important expenditures like that on education or health services. This in turn leads to high opportunity costs in the long run. Moreover, excessive pressure of consumption expenditures on the household budget due to rising food prices can trigger the selling of durable assets in a bid for survival. This phenomenon is likely to be more prevalent among the relatively poor households which have a higher share of food in their total expenditure.

Figure 2.2 shows the contribution of various components to 1990, 1996, 2011 and 2012 Global Hunger Index. GHI is highest in South Asia and lowest in Europe. The above adumbrated analysis entails a comprehensive picture of the sudden surge in the number of hungry people in the world in recent times reflecting food crisis. With the upsurge in food prices, progress in reducing the proportion of food insecure people has been reversed in all the regions. Food insecurity, poverty, chronic hunger and nourishment, deprivation are the major problems in urban as well as rural areas around the world today. Not only various types of conflicts, terrorism, corruption, under-development, population growth, environmental degradation and natural and man-made catastrophes are being considered as contributing factors, but the contemporary GFC has also made the situation worse directly and indirectly. Exacerbating these conditions is the extraordinary rise in food prices since 2007-08. Therefore, providing food security is an urgent problem.

Figure 2.2: Contribution of Components to 1990 GHI, 1996 GHI and 2011 GHI

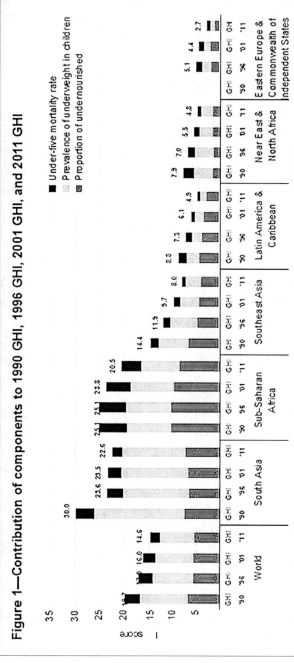

Figure 1—Contribution of components to 1990 GHI, 1996 GHI, 2001 GHI, and 2011 GHI

Notes: For the 1990 GHI, data on the proportion of undernourished are for 1990–92; data on child underweight are for the year closest to 1990 in the period 1988–92 for which data are available, and data on child mortality are for 1990. For the 1996 GHI, data on the proportion of undernourished are for 1995–97; data on child underweight are for the year closest to 1996 in the period 1994–98 for which data are available; and data on child mortality are for 1996. For the 2001 GHI, data on the proportion of undernourished are for 2000–02; data on child underweight are for the year closest to 2001 in the period 1999–2003 for which data are available; and data on child mortality are for 2001. For the 2011 GHI, data on the proportion of undernourished are for 2005–07, data on child underweight are for the latest year in the period 2004–09 for which data are available, and data on child mortality are for 2009.

Source: von Grebmer et al. (2011)

47

The Food Problems: A Historical Perspective

The concentration of hunger is further illustrated when one studies the countrywise figures. Nearly 64 per cent of the world's hungry are located in just seven countries, namely, India, China, the Democratic Republic of the Congo, Bangladesh, Indonesia, Pakistan and Ethiopia. Out of this, just India and China are home to 354 million hungry people, nearly 36 per cent of the world figure. A similar picture of high regional concentration emerges for the increase in the hunger incidence following the high food prices in 2006 and 2007. Table 2.1 shows that there was no increase in the number of undernourished people in the developed world. This can be largely attributed to the negligible price increases in recent times in the prices of meat and beef products which form a sizeable share of consumption in the advanced countries. However, within the developing world, the major share of the increase in hunger incidence occurred in the Asian and Sub-Saharan African regions; of the 75 million new hungry, 65 million were in these two regions alone (FAO, 2008)[xxviii].

There is a sudden increase in food-deprivation for the poor across the world, particularly in the Global South, as a result of the food inflation followed by the global financial and economic crisis. The problem is more intense for the developing and less-developed world in the South essentially due to the fact that there was already a wide hiatus in consumption levels and incidence of hunger between the Northern countries and those in the South even prior to the onset of the recent high food prices or the global economic crisis. The latter now threatens to severely exacerbate food insecurity in the developing countries and throw them well off-track from their Millennium Development Goals (MDG) on hunger reduction (Banerjee, 2011). Table 2.1 presents the *global hunger index*[xxix] jointly published by the International Food Policy research Institute (IFPRI), Welthungerhilfe and Concern Worldwide. It provides us a comparative situation of hunger across the developing world. Out of 120 countries, the study finds 26 countries in the 'alarming' hunger situation and another 7 in the 'extremely alarming' category. The bracket of serious hunger incidence contained 32 countries. More than half of the countries covered in the study exhibited serious or worse situation of hunger incidence. Among the regions, Sub-Saharan Africa and South Asia fared the worst with hunger indices at an 'alarming' level (23.3 and 23.0 respectively). The majority of the individual nations that had a more vulnerable hunger index were also from these two regions. In contrast, South-East Asia recorded a score of less than 10 while the Near-East and North Africa and Latin America both had the index at just over 5. In fact, these are underestimations of chronic hunger since this covered data only till 2006 implying that food deprivation further exacerbated by the recent phenomenal food and fuel price inflation is not captured in the analysis. A large number of nations may have actually entered the category of an alarming situation of hunger incidence after 2006.

Table 2.1: *Categories of Hunger Situation and Number of Countries in each category: 2008-2012*

Range of Hunger Index Score	Situation of Hunger	Number of Countries		
		2008	2011	2012
< 4.9	Low	32	41	41
5.0-9.9	Moderate	23	22	22
10-19.9	Serious	32	33	37
20.0-29.9	Alarming	26	22	17
>30.0	Extremely Alarming	7	4	3

Source: Global Hunger Index: The Challenge of Hunger 2008; IFPRI 2008; Banerjee, 2011, p. 22; IFPRI, 2011 and IFPRI, 2012

Therefore, it is not that people cannot find food, but rather, as the World Food Program (WFP) director Josette Sheeran puts it, "there is food on the shelves, but people are priced out of the market". Then she adds 'high food prices are creating the biggest challenge that WFP has faced in its 45-year history, a silent tsunami threatening to plunge more than 100 million people on every continent into hunger.' (Gimenez and Peabody, 2008).

Vicious Cycle of Intensified Poverty and Hunger

Poverty is the principle cause of hunger and hunger is the also a cause of poverty, and thus of hunger. The main causes of hunger are harmful economic systems, conflicts and large-scale repatriation movements[xxx], climate change[xxxi], and lack of sufficient land to grow, or income to purchase, enough food. By causing poor health, low levels of energy, and even mental impairment, hunger can lead to even greater poverty by reducing people's ability to work and learn, thus leading to even greater hunger (World Hunger Notes, 2012).

Hunger is obviously tied to poverty and countries with high levels of hunger are overwhelmingly low or low to middle-income countries. There is a vicious cycle of poverty and hunger that forces a large numbers of people to live in intransigent poverty and hunger in an increasingly wealthy global economy. This is the major ethical, economic, social and public health challenge of our time. There is a trap of extreme poverty in developing countries wherein poverty begets poverty and hunger begets hunger. "Most of the world's poor people earn their living from agriculture, so if we knew the economics of agriculture, we would know much of the economics of being poor." Theodore W. Schultz, Nobel Prize Laureate in Economics, lecture to the memory of Alfred Nobel, 1979. More than three-quarters of poor people in developing countries – defined as those living on less than USD 1 per day – live in rural areas, and most of them depend directly or indirectly on agriculture for their livelihoods. 162 million people, deemed ultra poor, live on less than \$0.5 a day. They are overwhelmingly concentrated in Sub-Saharan Africa, where their numbers are growing. The ultra poor often live in remote rural areas; are more likely to be ethnic minorities; and have less education, fewer assets, and less access to markets than better-off people. Their extreme poverty makes it next to impossible for them to climb out of poverty: they find themselves unable to invest in assets and in educating their children; they have little access to credit; and hunger and malnutrition reduce their productivity (Chatterjee, 2009). 1.2 billion people do not have enough to eat which is more than the people of USA, Canada and EU. 907 million in developing countries alone were hungry in 2008. Asia and Pacific region is home to over half the world's population and nearly two thirds of world's hungry people (FAO, 2009). More than 60% of the chronically hungry were women. Despite higher economic performance, the greatest social problem of hunger and poverty still remains a great challenge.

The recent rise in food prices has increased poverty considerably. Based on rough estimates by the World Bank, a doubling of food prices in the last three years alone already threatened to push 100 million people back into poverty (Ivanic and Martin, 2008; World Bank 2008a). To quote Skoufias, Tiwari and Zaman (2011), food inflation caused food-deprivation across the world, particularly in the developing and less-developed world. Food insecurity has also been regarded as an outcome of income poverty and inequalities in the demand, production and distribution of food. Various factors have resulted in demand-supply mismatch as well as other socio-economic inequalities in the global market leading to manifold increase in food prices. On one hand, demand for food throughout the world is increasing due to bio-fuel consumption, population growth urbanization, industrialization, and changes in lifestyle and consumption menus due to rising income standards in developing countries like India and China. The demand for meat and dairy products will continue to increase. On the other hand, the supply of internal food production is limited by land endowment, water and energy resources. An increase in world population by millions in the next decades will lead to further rural to urban migration, city and industry growth, and changes in consumption patterns that accompany rising incomes. There will be additional pressure on land, water and other resources. This requires substantially more water in production than grains. At the same time, more land will be needed for transportation infrastructure, housing and energy generation to support the increasingly urban population. Besides this, there are food market and government failures as well as financial speculations involved in the system.

Food for Healthy Living: Diet and Health Interactions

The interactions among food consumption, quality and quantity of dietary contents and health outcomes have broadened the domain of global food crisis. These three separate sectors of food, diet and health are crossing boundaries among each other. Healthy living is also affected by the adequate food consumption and dietary intakes (Amine et al., 2012). Diet and human health interact with each other. Diet profoundly affects health and health conditions of individuals influence dietary intakes. Broadly malnutrition[xxxii] refers to both undernutrition (subnutrition) and overnutrition. People suffer from undernutrition if their diet does not provide them with adequate calories and protein for their body maintenance and growth, or they cannot fully utilize the food they eat due to illnesses or medical conditions. Individuals suffer from overnutrition if they consume too many calories. According to the WHO, malnutrition is the gravest single threat to global public health. Let us take a concise account of dietary undernutrition and growing epidemic of obesity.

Dietary Undernutrition

In both developed and developing nations, the problem of dietary subnutrition is quite widespread. It takes place due to either inadequate consumption of food or poor diet with wrong balance of basic food[xxxiii]. The undernourishment associated with missing macronutrients or micronutrients in poor quality diets is more prevalent than the undernourishment reflected by underweight alone. Among other essential substances, poor or substandard diet may lead to a vitamin or mineral deficiency. Sometimes it may result in scurvy – a condition where an individual has a vitamin C (ascorbic acid) deficiency. Dietary undernutrition can cause complicated diseases to occur. Globally the groups of people at highest risk of malnutrition (subnutrition) are: elderly people in long-term care, individuals in poverty (low income), people with chronic eating disorder, individuals and children vulnerable to lack of food, food prices and distribution problems, individuals convalescing after a serious illness or condition, alcoholics and the like. An estimated 2 billion people suffer from one or more vitamin and mineral deficiencies resulting in shorter life-spans, frequent illnesses, or reduced physical and mental abilities. In developing countries deficiency in vitamin A affects 40-60% of children under the age of five causing blindness and death by compromising immune systems. An estimated 250,000 to 500,000 vitamin A-deficient children become blind every year and half of the children die within a year of becoming blind. Iron deficiency, the most widespread health problem in the world, impairing normal mental development in 40-60% of infants causing more than 130,000 deaths (women and children) each year. In pregnancy iodine deficiency is the most common cause of preventable mental retardation and brain damage on the planet – in 60 countries it is associated with a 10-15% lowering of average intellectual capacity. Malnutrition during childhood usually results in worse health and lower educational achievements during adulthood. Folate deficiency is responsible for around 300,000 severe birth defects every year. Zinc deficiency causes retarded growth, mental disturbances and recurrent infections. Countries may lose 2 to 3% of their GDP as a result of iron, iodine and zinc deficiencies. In China, vitamin and mineral deficiencies represent an annual GDP loss of up to USD 5 billion according to the World Bank.

Table 2.2: *Undernourished Population Distribution across Regions: 2003-05, 2007, 2010-2012 (Millions)*

Regions	2003-05	2007	2010-2012
Asia and the Pacific	542	583	563
Sub-Saharan Africa	212	236	234
Latin America and Caribbean	45	51	49
North Africa and Oceania	5	6	6
Developed World	16	16	16

Source: FAO (2012).

Table 2.2 reveals the spread of the undernourished population across different regions of the world. It is apparent that hunger is not only concentrated within the developing world, but also in other regions. Not surprisingly, the average number of undernourished people in the developed world stood at just 16 million in 2010-2012 less than 2 per cent of the world total. This is quite expected as the developed North Atlantic countries through their economic transition have historically achieved income and consumption levels that are way ahead of that prevalent in the Third World. The more interesting insight revealed is that even within the developing world, the incidence of hunger is mainly concentrated in two regions. The Asia and the Pacific regions had the highest number of undernourished persons at 542 million in 2003-05, nearly 65 per cent of the hungry population in the world and much more than the 212 million in Sub-Saharan Africa. In contrast, the latter region had the highest proportion of undernourished in the population. By 2003-05, more than 30 per cent of the population in Sub-Saharan Africa was below the threshold energy levels. The same figure for the Asian region was around 16 per cent in 2003-05. The number of undernourished people increased by 75 million in 2007 and 40 million in 2008, largely due to higher food prices (FAO news release 9 Dec 2009). One third of South Asian and one fourth of African people are predicted to be undernourished by 2020.

Growing Epidemic of Obesity

The world is facing another food paradox. It is the co-existence of hunger and growing epidemic of obesity. Today we live in an obese and excess weight world. Obesity is a growing global health problem. The incidences of chronic food-related diseases[xxxiv] such as diabetes are growing. The world obesity epidemic affects individuals, families, communities and nations across the globe with calamitous consequences for health, well-being, life expectancy, economic productivity and quality of life. According to WHO (2012) there are more than 1.6 billion overweight, compared to 100 million fifty years ago and 400 million obese people in the world and the number is expected to rise to 2.3 billion overweight and 700 million obese in 2015. There are 25 million children under five overweight (childhood obesity) in 2011 with a higher chance of premature death and disability in adulthood. Statistics from the most recent large-scale survey in the UK shockingly reveal that 25 percent of boys and 33 percent of girls aged between two and 19 years are overweight or obese – and there's little sign the incidence is slowing[xxxv]. New figures of NHS on childhood obesity revealed that almost one in five year-six pupils in England (19.0%) is now obese. Obesity can also affect child's emotional (low confidence or self-esteem) and mental health (bulimia and depression). Diet is one of the leading risk factors for chronic illness. When overweight children become adults they are most likely to develop diet-related diseases such as obesity, heart disease, musculoskeletal disorders, especially osteoarthritis, high blood pressure, liver disease, asthma, development problems in feet, sleep apnoea, stroke and diabetes. Cardio-vascular disease is a leading cause of death in both industrialised and developing countries, killing 17 million people each year, according to the World Health Organization (WHO, 2010). The European Union warns that over-eating and inactive modern lifestyles have raised obesity to the number one public health challenge of the 21st century with rapidly increasing childhood obesity of particular concern. Moreover, United States tops in overweight people in the world followed by Mexico, Canada, UK, Germany and Finland. There are more female overweight than male in these countries except Canada, Finland and Germany. The obesity epidemic is not restricted to these developed countries but has spread in Eastern Europe, Australia, Asia, the Middle East, the Pacific Islands, North America and China.

A dramatic transition has altered the diet and health of hundreds of millions of people across the developing world. Undernourishment and overconsumption coexist in a wide range of countries and may be found within the same community and even within the same household. This double burden is caused by inadequate pre-natal, infant and young child nutrition, followed by exposure to high-fat, energy-dense, micronutrient-poor foods and lack of physical activity. Unbalanced diets are often related to low intake of fruits and vegetables and high intake of fats, meat, sugar and salt. Many traditional foods, however, are rich in micronutrients, and expanding their role in production systems and diet could have health benefits (Popkin, 2003).

Vulnerabilities of Agricultural and Food Systems

The concept of 'vulnerability' is both relative and dynamic. It is defined as the propensity, likelihood or susceptibility of diminished capacity[xxxvi] of individuals, households, groups and communities to an adverse natural or man-made event. Although most often associated with poverty, but it can also arise when people are isolated, insecure and defenseless in the face of risk, shock or stress. The hypothesis[xxxvii] that vulnerability is inversely related to resource endowments is empirically applicable in most of the cases (Antle et al., 2004). In context with agriculture and food system, farmers or farm households differ in their exposure to risk as a result of their economic vulnerability, crop vulnerability to biophysical stresses, agricultural production vulnerability to ecosystem services, financial vulnerability of poor farmers, and so on. For example, a crop may be vulnerable to total failure (i.e., a zero grain yield) because of climate change stresses such as drought, floods, heat stress, or frost. Likewise, a farm household (farmer) may be vulnerable to bankruptcy if its financial resources fall below a critical threshold (Antle, 2009). However, a holistic perspective instead of a threshold approach to 'vulnerability' of agricultural and food system is important to its comprehensive understanding for appropriate and suitable food policy formation and execution.

First of all, the growth and productivity of most crops are vulnerable to adequate water availability, temperatures such as minimum, maximum and cumulative heat stress (degree days), competition for groundwater and surface resources and other such critical thresholds. These stresses interact in complex ways with site-specific soil and other environmental conditions (aspect, slope, and elevation), atmospheric CO_2 concentrations, and management (Parry et al., 2007; Hatfield et al., 2008). There is a need for agronomic studies to effectively quantify these vulnerabilities of crops to failures at aggregate level. For example, the U.S. assessment indicates that the South and the West are the regions most vulnerable to the adverse impacts of climate change as a result of increased heat stress, drought, and competition for surface and groundwater resources (Reilly et al., 2003; McCarl, 2008; Antle, 2009). Secondly, the farm households are economically vulnerable to agriculture and food systems including climate change for their income and livelihood. The main resilience for small farmers is diverse mix of crops and livestock, non-farm income, government subsidy, community support, and government income support. However, larger farms tend to be more vulnerable to climate changes, but are financially stronger, specialised to risk management, sell in national and international markets and receive larger income from government subsidies. Most of the research on climate change impacts has not addressed the vulnerability of agriculture in the sense of assessing the likelihood of production or incomes falling below critical thresholds (for details See, Antle et al., 2004; Antle, 2009). Thirdly, the financial vulnerability of farm business is affected by climate change and adaptation. A structural model is required to quantify the financial vulnerability by taking into consideration production income, debt structure, nonfarm income, and the use of financial risk management tools such as futures markets, crop insurance, and agricultural subsidies. Undoubtedly small farm households in developing countries still face periodic financial crises during adverse economic or climatic conditions due to high debt-to-asset ratios and imperfect capital markets such as high interest rate, non-availability of microfinance, unorganised banking and non-banking sectors and so on. Another feature of farm household businesses that may increase their financial vulnerability is that a much larger share of their total wealth is invested in their business than is typical of nonfarm businesses (Antle, 2009). Another much neglected area of research is the vulnerabilities of ecosystem services. Agricultural lands produce ecosystem services that are valued by individuals and society (Backland et al., 2008). For example, extreme weather events such as droughts, may lead to overgrazing, making arid pasture lands vulnerable to erosion and the loss of soil organic matter. Both biophysical and economic thresholds may exist, making soil degradation and other losses of natural capital irreversible (Antle et al., 2009). Intensive agricultural chemical use can magnify water quality problems.

Food Quality and Safety Standards

Food quality and safety standards are affected through several mechanisms (Food and Agriculture Organization of the United Nations, 2008). Right from the water supply and pesticides to veterinary drug residues (e.g. antibiotics, hormones) or transgenic plants and to various contaminants like heavy metals or mycotoxins, food safety is a major issue that can affect human organs, slow poisoning to death and can damage brain as in mercury poisoning through eating contaminated fish and seafood by pathogens and toxins, including through the increased pesticide contamination that is likely to be associated with climate change. Increased disease incidence in livestock is likely to increase the use of veterinary drugs and thus increase the risk of food contamination, antibiotic resistance, and related health issues. Addressing these increased risks will require the adaptation of existing public information, disease surveillance, and intervention practices (Antle, 2009).

Contaminated water supply through industrial waste and pollution can result in outbreak of fatal diseases. The residues of pesticides can build up in human body causing damage to organs. The heavy metal toxics in food can also have the same effect on human body. The lack of pasteurisation of milk and other food products may seriously damage human health. The lack of proper freezing and preservation of meat can give birth of food bacteria such as Salmonella, Botulism, and the like. There can be incidences of lead poisoning through faulty and unsafe food packaging adversely affecting human health. All above food-health concerns, the avian influenza pandemic and more recently outbreaks of porcine influenza and other diseases transferred from food, e.g., mad cow disease have sharpened the demand for food safety standards. There has been a highlight of the importance of animal-human link in the food value chain. Mad cow disease in the UK, salmonella in US eggs, and dioxin-affected Belgian chickens are just some of the recent examples of the food risks engendered by insufficiently and inappropriately regulated industrial food production and processing in the North. Moreover, increased CO_2 may increase plant growth but may result in lower protein content of grains may be impacted due to this increase. In addition, food quality and safety of vegetable and fruits are highly vulnerable to temperature and water stresses (Hatfield et al., 2008). All in all, health issues are likely to gain importance in the food landscape and to increasingly shape the global agricultural and food system.

Looking Back: Comparing the Current Food Crisis to the Food Crises during the 1970s and 1990s

The contemporary GFC is not new as we experienced similar food crises during 1972-1974. However, the following section will thrash out the similarities and differences in the causes and ramifications of these two food crises:

Global Food Crisis: Past and Present

As discussed earlier in the prolegomena of this book, the world experienced a remarkably similar food crisis in the early to mid-1970s which was similar to the current food crisis both in scale and scope. In constant dollar terms, price levels of the four staples (rice, wheat, maize, and soybean) during 2008 to 2010 were as high as they were during 1970-74 in real terms. For example, in the case of wheat, increasing 180 percent during 1970–74 versus 110 percent from 2005 to May 2008, but the maize price increase has been slightly higher (80 percent in 1972–74 versus 90 percent during the current crisis). The increase in rice prices has been roughly the same (a little more than 225 percent in both cases). Changes in fertilizer prices have been about the same, although percentage changes in oil prices were much higher in the 1970s. Finally, the sudden decline in international food prices from June 2008 to March 2009—contrary to the predictions of leading organizations and prominent experts—also closely follows the decline in food prices after mid-1974 (Gulati and Dutta, 2009). By our calculations, real prices of staple grains dropped by a little more than 40 percent from 1974 to 1978, and from June 2008 to March 2009 staples dropped by 35 percent on average. Hence the inter-temporal and inter-commodity profiles of price changes across the two crises are remarkably similar (Headey and Fan, 2010). In their recent paper, Peters et al. (2009) discussed the similarities between the patterns of the recent food price hikes compared with those in the 1970s and 1990s. An examination of a variety of internal and external factors[xxxviii] determining the present as well as future food-related crises reveal various causal pathways leading to GFC. Chapter 5 of this book provides a detailed discussion on the six different transmission mechanisms that through trade allows international food price movements to affect the domestic prices in both food importing and food-exporting countries. This suggests that large segments of the developing world's population remain vulnerable to food price shocks. A quick look at Figure 2.3 reveals that prior to the price rise, the real prices of staple foods were in steady decline for almost 30 years (as was the case during the 1974 food crisis). In May 2008, the price increases have been very sharp and can be compared to the 1974 food crisis when the price rose by 200% (255% in the current crisis).

The current food crisis may seem to have started exerting its real force on the poor since 2006 onwards, but the foundations behind the crisis started their origins around the beginning of the 21st century. The year 2002 saw a steady and seminal depreciation of the US dollar that continued for eight years. During 2003, the oil prices rose in international markets inflating oil costs at local levels, and rising transportation and fertilizers costs. With global demand for bio-fuels on the increase due to the oil price increases taking place since 2003 and the desire to reduce oil dependency as well as reduce GHG emissions from transportation, there is also fear of the potential destruction of natural habitats by being converted into farmland (Bounds, 2007). Russia and Ukraine were struck hard with severe strikes of drought and Australia had its worst multi-year dry spell in a century during 2005. The year 2006 observed a diversification of investors and hedge funds into agricultural commodities as cereal production fell by 2.1 per cent and prices of cereals increased by 21%. Floods hit northern Europe and droughts dried southern Europe, Turkey, northwest Africa and Argentina during 2007 and cereals prices rose by 31% in comparison to the previous year, thus further contributing to GFC. During 2007-2008 some countries imposed export restrictions to protect their food stocks that increased food prices by 49% during the first quarter of 2008 on the IMF's market prices indices, 2005-2008. 'Between April 2007 and April 2008 alone prices increased by 85%.

The Food Problems: A Historical Perspective

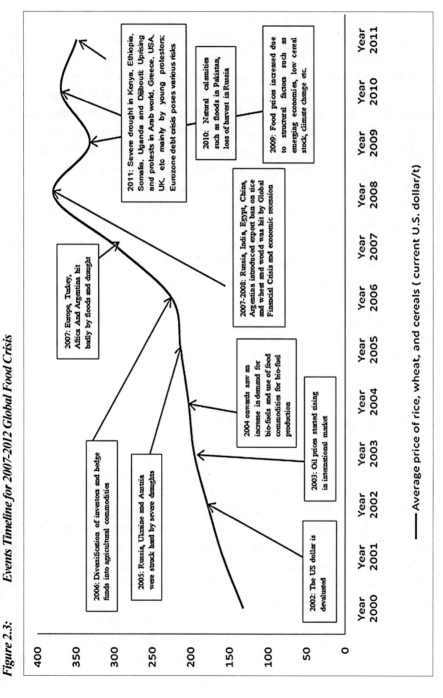

Figure 2.3: *Events Timeline for 2007-2012 Global Food Crisis*

— Average price of rice, wheat, and cereals (current U.S. dollar/t)

This price rise has been broad-based, led by wheat, then maize, followed by rice whose price has tripled since September 2007 and soared by 160% between January and April 2008 alone' (UNCTAD, 2008). The GFC is also closely related to global economic recession in 2008. The late 2000s global financial crisis, worst financial crisis since the Great Depression of the 1930s, resulted in the collapse of large financial institutions and housing market, the bailout of banks by national governments, failure of key businesses, prolonged unemployment for millions, decline in economic activity, increased debt burden, and downturns in stock markets around the world, leading to a severe global economic recession in 2008. Thus, the end of 2008 saw almost 1 billion people without adequate nutrition. During 2009 the food prices stayed high and even increased due to structural factors such as increased prosperity in emerging economies, low cereal stock, bio-fuel production and climate change[xxxix]. The year of 2010 was a landmark year for food inflation (food prices rose by 32%) as local food prices returned to their inflation peak levels across the globe. Wheat prices have doubled between July and August 2010 due to natural calamities such as drought, floods in Pakistan, loss of harvest in Russia and so on. During 2011, the severe drought across Kenya, Ethiopia, Somalia, Uganda and Djibouti has left an estimated 11.5 million people on the brink of starvation.

Food Crisis during the 1970s: Causes and Events Timeline

The main causes of 1972-74 food crisis were: rising oil prices, pressure on food demand side, shocks on food supply, longer term pressures on international food commodity markets and many others. Figure 2.5 reveals the causes and timeline of events leading to food crisis during 1972-74. In June 1971 Nixon liberalised grain exports to China and Eastern Europe. In July 1972 the USSR procured a large amount of grain from the international markets (Schuh, 1983). This prompted similar central command economies to follow this trend. As a result, there was a global demand for commodities. Between 1971-72 world wheat exports increased nearly 29%. In addition to this, countries flush with petrodollars also entered the market and as a result the global commodity market received a further fillip. During 1971-74 the US dollar depreciated as the US government sought to delink the dollar from the gold standard and adopt a floating exchange rate. Consequently, exports and prices rose. This increase in demand coupled with poor harvests worldwide, starting in 1972 till 1974, sparked off an international commodity price rise. The situation was further aggravated by the decision of countries like the US and Australia to cut government stocks and idle cropland. Due to the existence of large grain reserves during the 1950s and 1960s, the USA, Australian and Canadian governments drastically reduced the production, stocks and reserves of grains during 1970-74 (Johnson, 1975). In a reactionary move countries began to adopt protectionist policies which prevented the flight of domestically produced food-grains, but contributed to the increase in international grain prices.

Just like the current food crisis, many of the causes of the 1972–74 food crisis were related to the US production and trade conditions, especially with respect to wheat and other coarse grains (See, Headey and Fan, 2010). The earliest contributing factor to the crisis was probably the US policies regarding wheat production (Johnson, 1975; Destler, 1978). During 1973-74, OPEC countries quadrupled price of petroleum. In November 1974 World Food Conference was held in Rome. Rich nations committed to 19 new food security measures and increased foreign aid. During 1974 Green revolution farmers suffered heavy losses due to high fertilizer prices and rich nations implicitly restricted fertilizer exports during 1974-75. During October 1976 the USSR and the US signed new bilateral agreement on grain exports. During the period 1974-78 aid commitments to agricultural development increased substantially including food aid. New institutions were built for agricultural R&D and increased monitoring of food security. During the same period, world food production increased but highly unevenly (Dawe, 2008). Asia's Green Revolution was successful in increasing food security, but Africa was heavily hit by drought and famine. Africa became increasing dependent on cereal imports and food aid. Rapid population growth was a bigger problem in both Sub-Saharan Africa and North Africa (Egypt, Algeria, and Morocco) where cereal imports were becoming an increasing portion of total food demand. Other factors contributing to rising cereal prices were not shocks, but rather long-term factors that fostered tighter international food markets (Timmer, 2009). "The direct effects on agricultural production were severe, because the major food production systems in the world were by that time already highly energy intensive. Rising oil prices were therefore directly transmitted to rising food prices in the United States and other major producers, and these elevated prices were then transmitted to other markets because of North America's vital role in the grains trade" (Heady and Fan, 2010).

Similarities between the 1972–74 and 2007-12 Food Crises

There are many similarities between the two crises which suggest that there is scope for contemporary policymakers to learn from the successes and failures of the 1972–74 crisis. The most important factors in both crises were: rising oil prices, decline of the US dollar, large demand shocks, export bans, long-run supply constraints, hoarding and weather shocks. In 1972–74 the demand shock came from the USSR which following its own crop failure that year, purchased more than one-quarter of US wheat production in 1972. In 2005–08 the primary demand shock came from the US bio-fuels industry which also absorbed one-quarter of US production in 2007, this time in maize. Consistent with this story is that the 1972–74 crisis was characterized by large price increases in wheat rather than in maize whereas the reverse was true of the 2008 crisis. Like the food crisis of the 1970s, the crisis which began in the mid-90s was also characterized by a depreciating dollar. The East-Asian financial crisis occurred during this period, and as growth suddenly dipped, so did global demand for commodities. As in the 1960s, net exporting (producer) countries, once again decided to cut reserves and reduce the area under cultivation. It is clear that relatively speaking the price hike in the mid-90s was lesser than the 1970s price hike. Peters et al. maintained that this was due to the low levels of foreign currency held by net importing countries which prevented them from adopting protectionist policies, which would have led to hoarding and further price rises.

Food Crisis during the 1990s

By now it is apparent that certain similarities exist between the current food crisis and the crises of the 1970s and 1990s. Demand from emerging economies accounted for 67% of US exports in 2007. Additionally, the value of global agricultural trade has increased by 50% from 2000 to 2006. As observed recently, the dollar has once again undergone depreciation. Countries around the globe became repeat-offenders when they continued

Figure 2.4:   *Events Timeline for 1972-74 Food Crisis*

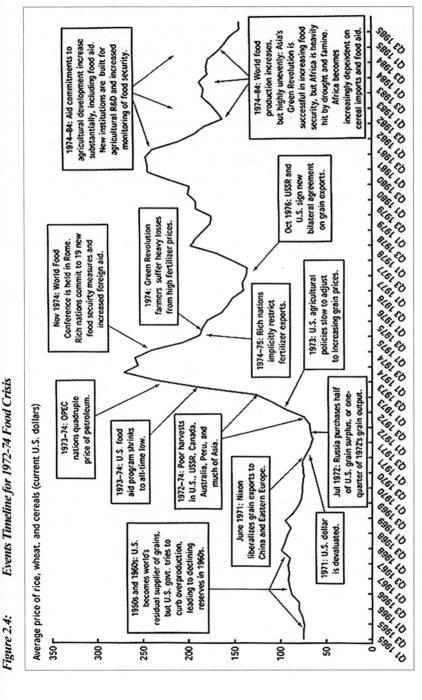

Average price of rice, wheat, and cereals (current U.S. dollars)

1950s and 1960s: U.S. becomes world's residual supplier of grains, but U.S. govt. tries to curb overproduction, leading to declining reserves in 1960s.

1973-74: OPEC nations quadruple price of petroleum.

1973-74: U.S. food aid program shrinks to all-time low.

1972-74: Poor harvests in U.S., USSR, Canada, Australia, Peru, and much of Asia.

June 1971: Nixon liberalizes grain exports to China and Eastern Europe.

1971: U.S. dollar is devaluated.

Jul 1972: Russia purchases half of U.S. grain surplus, or one-quarter of 1972's grain output.

Nov 1974: World Food Conference is held in Rome. Rich nations commit to 19 new food security measures and increased foreign aid.

1974: Green Revolution farmers suffer heavy losses from high fertilizer prices.

1974-75: Rich nations implicitly restrict fertilizer exports.

1973: U.S. agricultural policies slow to adjust to increasing grain prices.

Oct 1976: USSR and U.S. sign new bilateral agreement on grain exports.

1974-84: Aid commitments to agricultural development increase substantially, including food aid. New institutions are built for agricultural R&D and increased monitoring of food security.

1974-84: World food production increases, but highly unevenly: Asia's Green Revolution is successful in increasing food security, but Africa is heavily hit by drought and famine. Africa becomes increasingly dependent on cereal imports and food aid.

Source: Heady and Fan, 2010, p. 83.

to implement internationally harmful policies such as farmer subsidies and export restrictions. A new entrant in this crisis is the role played by bio-fuels, which has diverted crops away from consumption into the energy sector, further reducing supply and inflating prices. It remains to be seen what steps the market will take in order to adjust itself against increasing prices. The 1997 East-Asian Financial Crisis resulted in Asian countries rolling back their demand and reducing consumption, leading thus to a global dip in demand and a reduction from the 1994-96 price hike. The dollar has begun to appreciate again since late 2008 and increased planting has been undertaken in the face of high crop prices. One can only watch and wait, and see what the outcome will be.

Global Governance for Total World Food Security: A Historical Overview[xl]

The evolution of collective food security governance can be traced back to the commencement of human society and the any deviation from it resulted in hunger, social unrest, lack of human well-being, malnutrition and starvation throughout the human history. Historically, it was thought that the issue of food insecurity could be tackled within the boundaries of a nation. However, the capability and capacity of a single household, community or a nation to ensure adequate nutritious food supply for its members/citizens depend upon the factors and forces ranging from domestic to global level. Therefore, global governance[xli] for food security has increasingly become an intricate maze of overlapping and contradictory policies, regulations and actions of multiple international institutions in a *new* globalised economy. Considering the internationalised nature of food insecurity phenomenon, constant greater changes happening both in the dynamics of GAFS and in understanding of changing international relations of countries, international agencies and non-government actors, and impacts of globalization on agriculture and food industry (Nair, 2010), it can be safely concluded that global governance for world food security is already here that has been taking shape throughout the human history.

The historical evolution of global governance for world food security can be traced back to the formation of an idea of an international organization for food and agriculture in the late 19th and early 20th century. After a series of

The Food Problems: A Historical Perspective

international meetings held at Rome, Italy from the 29th May to the 6th June, 1905, a Convention was passed on the 7th of June 1905 in Rome, Italy, which led to the creation of an official and permanent International Agricultural Institute (IAI). The *League of Nations* was formed after World War I in 1919 to improve nutrition, food security and farming as well as it provided a debate venue about the co-existence of widespread malnutrition and global over-availability of food (McKeon, 2009). The Second World War effectively ended the IAI which was officially dissolved by resolution of its Permanent Committee on the 27th of February 1948. However, in 1943 the United States President Franklin D. Roosevelt called a United Nations Conference on Food and Agriculture with representatives from 44 governments gathered at the Homestead Hotel, Hot Springs, Virginia, from the 18th May to the 3th June. The commitment of these governments was fulfilled on the 16th October 1945 with the creation of *Food and Agriculture Organization of the United Nations* (FAO) in Quebec City, Canada. The First Session of the FAO Conference was held in the Chateau Frontenac at Quebec, Canada, from the 16th October to the 1th November 1945. The original vision of its founders to combat hunger is still valid today: "Progress toward freedom from want is essential to lasting peace; for it is a condition of freedom from the tensions, arising out of economic maladjustment, profound discontent, and a sense of injustice, which are so dangerous in the close community of modern nations"[xlii]. The FAO's first Director-General Lord John Boyd Orr asserted that food was more than a commodity and the world required a food policy based on human needs. He proposed World Food Board as a means to accomplish some of the governance functions that are recognised as crucial today: stabilising world agricultural prices, managing an international cereal reserve, and co-operating with the organisations responsible for agricultural development loans and international trade policy to ensure that the measures they took were coherent with food security (McKeon, 2011). The food policy emphasis to fight post World War II hunger was to grow more food by using latest science, technology and innovations (Lang et al., 2009). The General Agreement on Tariffs and Trade (GATT) was established in 1947. The signing of the Uruguay Round Agreement of the General Agreement on Trade and Tariffs (GATT) mandates member countries to open up their economies to the world market forces.

The independence of formal colonies during the period between 1940s and 1970s shifted balance of power in the UN that led to the establishment of G77 in 1964, group of developing countries, and a more equitable *New International Economic Order* (NIEO) with two new important institutions namely *United Nations Conference on Trade and Development* (UNCTAD) and the *UN Center on Transnational Corporations* (established in 1974 and shut down in 1992). The famines of 1970s, rise in the cost of oil, the peak of Green Revolution paradigm, neo-liberal thesis, market liberation, and intellectual property rights on seed varieties and related input packages[xliii] dominated world's food system. The establishment in 1971 of the Consultative Group on International Agricultural Research (CGIAR) with headquarter at the World Bank had already excised science from the UN system. The UN *World Food Conference* (1974) proposed the creation of a top-heavy policy body, the *World Food Council* that was doomed to failure but nonetheless eroded the FAO's normative power. As for the financing of agriculture, it was hived off from the FAO and entrusted to the newly established *International Fund for Agricultural Development* (IFAD). Finally, World Food Programme (WFP) was separated from the FAO and established as an independent UN agency in order to react to food emergencies[xliv]. Nevertheless, the national governments continued to be the main players in food governance and the states still played a considerable role in regulating and supporting agriculture through mechanisms such as food stocks, supply management, and subsidies[xlv].

The period between 1980s and 2008 was dominated by success of globalization, dominance of free-market, the emergence of alternatives, and growth of food corporations. Early 1980s was dominated by the international financial institutions such as World Bank and the IMF which drastically curtailed the policy decision-making space of national governments, opened up the markets of developing countries, and cut back severely on state support to regulate agriculture. The creation of the WTO[xlvi] in 1995, promulgation of global trade regulations, emergence of G7/G8 as a powerful alternative forum, institutionalization of structural adjustment, free trade, dominance of productionist paradigm and global market integration constituted a recipe for addressing world food problems. The goal of 'eradication of hunger' was declared in World Food Summits of 1996 and 2002 convened by FAO and its efforts led to the inclusion of the goal into the MDGs. However, researchers questioned the sustainability of industrial agriculture and the negative consequences of structural adjustments on poverty, malnutrition, rural livelihoods and hunger were noticed[xlvii]. Moreover, right to food, food sovereignty[xlviii], and agro-ecology entered the dome of global governance for the first time. In 2002 the *International Planning Committee for Food Sovereignty* (IPC)[xlix] was established on four principles: the right to food and food sovereignty, mainstreaming agro-ecological family farming, defending people's access to and control of natural resources, and trade and food sovereignty.

Three major agricultural institutions, namely IFAD, FAO, and CGIAR, were externally evaluated since 2005 that uncovered severe institutional failures. The WTO Doha Round was brought to a standstill on agricultural issues in 2005. Moreover, the World Bank for the first time in 25 years dedicated its *World Development Report* of 2008 to agriculture and development by admitting that it had made a considerable blunder in neglecting agriculture as a source of growth. However, the eruption of the food crisis in late 2007-2008 unveiled a void in global governance. In the absence of an authoritative and inclusive global body governing food issues, decision making in this vital field was being carried out by international institutions like the WTO, the World Bank, the G8/G20, FAO, and the like. Food crisis sparked a range of international institutional initiatives, of which the most significant were the UN *High Level Task Force on the Food Security Crisis* (HLTF), the *Global Partnership for Agriculture and Food Security* (GPAFS), the reform of the *Committee on World Food Security*[l], and a *Comprehensive Framework of Action on Food Security* (CFA). In July 2008 the G8 proposed the creation of a *Global Partnership on Agriculture, Food Security and Nutrition* (GPAFSN) with three objectives: increased investment in agriculture, enhanced expertise brought to bear on food security issues, and a global policy forum whose location was not finalized. However, GPAFSN had no real existence and has had a strong opposition from the FAO, some G77 countries, small food producers and civil society organizations. Interestingly CFS took the unusual step of opening up the reform process to all stakeholders on equal basis including governments, organizations of smallholder food producers (OSFPs), international NGOs, civil society organisations and other global institutions such as FAO and IFAD. Thus, the networks of OSFPs had an impact on government policy by engaging governments and intergovernmental forums at national, regional, and global levels, and building alliances with other sectors of civil society. Locally, alternative food networks and fair trade movements are working at the community level where they promote agro-ecological production and food webs as an alternative to the industrial food chain (Dolan and Humphrey, 2001).

Recently the globalization of economic, political and social movements has facilitated the emergence of alternatives and brought pressure on governments. The *International Assessment of Agricultural Knowledge, Science and Technology for Development*[li] (IAASTD) study published in 2008, sponsored by the World Bank, the FAO, UNEP, and UNDP, has provided momentous scientific support for alternatives, called for a fundamental paradigm shift in agricultural development and advocated strengthening agro-ecological science and practice. *Bill and Melinda Gates Foundation* is a new entrant in the field of health, food and agriculture with its investment from 1994 to September 2011 of more than $2.6 billion in promoting a 'new green revolution' and focusing on improving people's health and giving them the chance to lift themselves out of hunger and extreme poverty in developing countries[lii]. Further, in May 2011 *Global Forum on Food Security and Nutrition* hosted an electronic debate on global food governance and concluded that there is a crisis of confidence in the current conglomeration of global institutions[liii]. It should therefore endowed with the power, authority and resources to act effectively on the really critical issues that affect our ability to ensure that all people can eat adequately, now and in the future. The agricultural sector remains of primary importance for many non-OECD economies. As a result, the 2011 *OECD Global Forum on Agriculture* focused on improving agricultural market information and analysis for better policy decisions and enhanced food security. In addition to covering the newly-launched *Agriculture Market Information System* (AMIS), the Forum looked at the medium-term commodity outlook and scenario analysis, capacity building actions and technical assistance in terms of how improved market information and outlook analysis could lead to better policy actions and improved policy coherence and coordination in response to future price spikes/ food crisis events.

To sum up, the above brief historical review concludes that none of the international institutional initiatives succeeded in ensuring the food security of developing countries[liv]. The contemporary food crisis, climate change and financial turmoil have questioned the dominant paradigms, food insecurity and governance both in global South and in the North. There are nine different types of international organizations[lv] with different primary focuses which are directly or indirectly involved in the issues of food security that are market-oriented, dominated by rich countries and have contradictory inadequate objectives. This reflects the international community's failure to tackle hunger and ensure world food security. There is a widespread recognition that the world agricultural and food market has failed to ensure the food security of poor households of developing countries. Moreover, the prevailing structure of global governance for food security is patchy, illogical, obscure, objectionable and unacceptable. It is dominated by the interests of the private sector and the food policies are inadequate in dealing with the challenge of hunger, obesity, malnutrition and starvation. Hence, there is a need for global governance for food security that is based within UNO as a democratic set up fully represented by all nations and agricultural and food organizations with an aim of protection of small farmers and markets in developing countries, global food reserves and supply management, agroecology as a climate-friendly approach to agricultural production.

Concluding Remarks

Adequate balanced diet is essential for healthy living. Unfortunately, food problems are affecting human health since dawn of humanity. Despite exhaustive research and numberless policy efforts, tackling these food problems is still an increasingly difficult task in a globalised world involving multiple layers of complexity and decision-making. As a distinct event of the 21st century, the prevailing GFC should be looked at involving a mix from agricultural economics, economic history, politics, sociology, political economy and other disciplines. In line with neo-Malthusian predictions that global food output has expanded to keep pace with multi-fold global population increase, it has been increasing evident that the fundamental food problem is not a technical one in nature of producing more food worldwide but a political one of ensuring adequate and nutritious food availability to those who need it. The world faces a paradoxical situation of growing hunger and obesity[lvi]. Globally more people suffer and die from obesity (overweight) related illnesses such as diabetes type 2, heart diseases, and stroke than from hunger. One sixth of global population is hungry with majority of poor rural food producers in the developing world maintaining a vicious cycle of intensified poverty and hunger. At the same time, there are 1.6 billion obese in industralised world and other parts of the world due to overconsumption and unsuitable diets. A comparison of previous global food crises and the present GFC reveals many similarities in the causes and events timeline. Over the last six decades food crisis did not travel alone. The externalities or spillovers of agriculture have also been on the same journey accompanying food crisis. Climate change and the energy crisis have shown that a food system based on the intensive use of petrol products and chemicals is not sustainable. Biodiversity losses, arable land degradation, water pollution, greenhouse gases due to the use of nitrogen fertilisers derived from rarefying petrol have been affecting the entire GAFS. Although the food policies and regulations formulated since 2nd World War are a overlapping or contradictory complex web, there is a call for a *new* global governance for world food security that not only focuses on agricultural production and food processing, but also on food distribution sector down the food chain, multinational chains, consumption, and ultimate utilization of food for better health and quality of life.

Notes

i. Excerpted from Amartya K. Sen (1982), "The Food Problem: Theory and Policy", *Third World Quarterly,* 4(3), 447-459.

ii. The main food problems are food insecurity, hunger, food crisis (food-demand, food-supply, food production, food prices, and so on), starvation, malnutrition, obesity, and so on.

iii. "What we have to concentrate on is not the total food supply in the economy but the 'entitlement' that each person enjoys: the commodities over which she can establish her ownership and command. People suffer from hunger when they cannot establish their entitlement over an adequate amount of food" (Sen, 1999).

iv. Economic relations arise in agricultural and food system when some people have the food to sell and others. But the problem is agreeing the price at which the food products will be transferred. Other economic relations arise from the use of land, purchase of equipments and tools, hiring of labour, buying raw materials such as seeds etc. In all these relations, the economic relations centre at price fixing, i.e., agreeing upon the rental or lease for land, agreeing wages for labour, agreeing

The Food Problems: A Historical Perspective

prices for equipments and raw materials. A farmer has to make choices in these economic relations to get maximum profits and he bases these choices in terms of relative prices and relative costs.

v. The Old Testament is the most important and original source of information regarding the economic thought of the Hebrews. From a description of the contemporary society in the Old Testament it appears that it had some of the characteristic features of a capitalist society.

vi. Chapters 1, 2, 3, 9, 13 and 14 of *Arthasastra* include all the vital aspects of agriculture, as we practice it today. Main points covered were managing agriculture, measurement of rainfall, astrology and astronomy related to agriculture, meteorological aspects of agriculture, kinds of crops, advantage in cultivating certain classes of crops, the growth of crops, treatment of seeds, manuring and harvesting. For instance, paragraph 1 says,"Possessed with knowledge of the science of agriculture, water management, and managing crops and trees, or assisted by those who are trained in such sciences, the superintendent of agriculture shall in time collect the seeds of all kinds of grains, flowers, fruits, vegetables, bulbous roots, roots, fruits of creepers, fiber-producing plants such as hibiscus and cotton."

vii. Tiruvalluvar (Valluvar) was the greatest Tamil (South Indian) poet, sage, seer, and a scholar whose book Thirukkural, a work of underlying classic and ethics par excellence, is one of the most important works of the Sangam era. It deals with the fundamentals of life. He opined that for the prosperity of a country, three factors are indispensable: farmers (Land), merchants (Capital) and virtuous people (Labour).

viii. He was the most renowned scholastic philosopher born in Italy.

ix. Arthur Young (1741-1820) was born in London. Young assembled comprehensive data on production, rents and land tenure in Great Britain. Serving as editor of the *Annals of Agriculture* from 1768-1770, he collected his data and observations into nine volumes of 4,500 pages, which have proven of continued value especially to economic historians (e.g., Allen, 1992). Most famous are his Tours of England, Ireland and France, which mixed travel diaries with facts, figures and critical commentary on farming practices. He was consulted by agriculturists and politicians at home and abroad, including George Washington, and received numerous honours.

x. Like all 18th century political economists, Smith could not ignore agricultural questions, even if he gave them less primacy than the Physiocrats. He, together with Ricardo, Von Thünen and Malthus, provided commentary on the difficulties of agricultural specialization, returns to land as a factor, issues of space and distance to market, and the long-run relation between arithmetic increases in food supply an dgeometric increases in demand due to population growth. Many pages of the *Wealth of Nations* (1776) dealt with agricultural questions, including the differential capacity for specialization and routinization of agriculture versus industry and the arts of husbandry at the microeconomic level (pp. 16; 143).

xi. The main economic ideas of David Ricardo were published in *The Principles of Political Economy and Taxation* (1921). His coined a modified version of the labour theory of value. He was a main contributor in creating classical economics. He fought for free trade and free competition without government interference by enforcing laws or restrictions.

xii. The Law of Diminishing Returns states that as we add more units of the variable input (i.e. labour) to fixed amounts of land and capital the change in total output will first rise then will begin to fall. Diminishing returns to labour occurs when marginal product starts to fall. This means that total output will increase at a decreasing rate when more workers are employed.

xiii. According to Ricardo, rent is that portion of the produce of the earth which is paid to the landlord for the use of the original and indestructible powers of the soil. As rents rise, profits fall. In essence, rent costs gobble up profits as the population increases. He also distinguished between productivity enhancements due to augmentation of the soil and improvements in machinery and the capitalization of various investments or policies (e.g., taxes) into the value of land. He held the view that the *Corn Laws*, in particular, constituted a burden to the agricultural economy. He believed that these trade barriers kept food prices artificially high and encouraged a bloated rent rate.

xiv. T.R. Malthus (14 February 1766 – 29 December 1834) was an English scholar and a writer of great significance. He coined great theories of population, popularized the economic theory of rent, criticized the *Poor Laws* and supported the *Corn Laws*, which introduced a system of taxes on British imports of wheat. His revolutionary ideas became an intellectual stepping-stone to the idea of natural selection by Charles Darwin.

xv. Gilbert, G. Introduction to Malthus, T.R. *An Essay on the Principle of Population.* 1798. Oxford World's Classics reprint. Viii.

xvi. Bloy, M. 'Thomas Malthus' "Essay on Population"'. 2003. Accessible at http://www.victorianweb.org/economics/essay.html .

xvii. J.H. Von Thünen (1783-1850), a prominent 19th century classical economist, was north German landowner, who in the first volume of his treatise, *The Isolated State* (1826), developed the first serious treatment of spatial economics, connecting it with the theory of rent. The importance lies less in the pattern of land use predicted than in its analytical approach. The Von Thunen model is an excellent illustration of the balance between land cost and transportation costs. As one gets closer to a city, the price of land increases. The farmers of the Isolated State balance the cost of transportation, land, and profit and produce the most cost-effective product for market. Of course, in the real world, things don't happen as they would in a model.

xviii. Alfred Marshall'ssupply and demand functions as tools of price determination, were previously discovered independently by Cournot.

xix. According to Alfred Marshall, the term land refers to the whole of the materials and forces which nature gives freely for man's aid in land, water, in air and light and heat. It includes all natural resources that human being get free from air, water and land.

xx. Thorstein Bunde Veblen (1857-1929), American sociologist and social critic, studied economics under the guidance of J.B. Clark and was critical of capitalism as evident by his best known book *The Theory of the Leisure Class* (1899).

xxi. Étienne Jouzier in his book, *Économie Rural* (1911) defined, "agricultural economics is that branch of agriculture science which treats of the manner of regulating the relations of the different elements comprising the resources of the farmer whether it be the relations to each other or with other human beings in order to secure the greatest degree of prosperity to the enterprise".

xxii. See, Schultz, T. W. (1956). Reflections on Agricultural Production, Output and Supply. *Journal of Farm Economics*, 38 (3), 748–762.

xxiii. See, Schultz, T. W. (1968). *Economic Growth and Agriculture*. New York: MacGraw-Hill.

xxiv. Seven food items were considered for the first experiment namely, Beef, Dairy, Maize, Poultry, Rice, Sugar and Wheat. For the second experiment, Beef and Sugar were excluded as the price increases of these items were negligible between 2005 and 2007. The percentage price changes in this period for Dairy, Maize, Poultry, Rice and Wheat were 90, 80, 15, 25 and 70 respectively (Ivanic and Martin 2008).

xxv. This book is not a study of GFC but a study of historical pathology of food security.

xxvi. *Global Food and Agricultural Institutions* is indeed a very general book on food and hunger, and as such, it does not address the measurement and management issues of the global food crisis.

xxvii. The FAO labels —hungryǁ those people being deprived of access to sufficient food on a daily basis - receiving fewer than 1800 calories a day.

xxviii. Although the actual estimates of hungry people in 2007 by the USDA study are higher, the regional concentration of hunger incidence that emerges is similar to the FAO study.

xxix. This study constructed the hunger index for 120 countries using a fairly simple methodology. It uses three variables namely, the proportion of undernourished as a percentage of the population, the prevalence of underweight in children below five years and the mortality rate of children below five years. The index is a simple average of these three somewhat inter-related variables. The GHI classifies the countries into five categories of hunger situation based on their hunger index score (see Table 2.1).

xxx. By the end of 2008, the total number of refugees under UNHCR's mandate exceeded 10 million. The number of conflict-induced internally displaced persons (IDPs) reached some 26 million worldwide at the end of the year. Providing exact figures on the number of stateless people is extremely difficult But, important, (relatively) visible though it is, and anguishing for those involved conflict is less important as poverty (and its causes) as a cause of hunger.

xxxi. Increasing drought, flooding, and changing climatic patterns requiring a shift in crops and farming practices that may not be easily accomplished are three key issues.

xxxii. Malnutrition can also be defined as the insufficient, excessive or imbalanced consumption of nutrients. Several different nutrition disorders may develop, depending on which nutrients are lacking or consumed in excess. http://www.medicalnewstoday.com/articles/179316.php.

xxxiii. The right balance of nutrients from major food groups includes carbohydrates, fruit and vegetables, protein, dairy and fats.

xxxiv. Obese people, who consume more calories than they need, may suffer from the subnutrition aspect of malnutrition if their diet lacks the nutrients their body needs for good health.

xxxv. http://www.weightlossresources.co.uk/children/childhood_obesity.htm.

xxxvi. The capacity can be described as the resources available to individuals, households and communities to cope with a threat or to resist the impact of a hazard. Such resources can be physical or material, but they can also be found in the way a community is organized or in the skills or attributes of individuals and/or organizations in the community.

xxxvii. The results supported the hypothesis that the most adverse changes occur in the areas with the poorest resource endowments and when the mitigating effects of CO_2 fertilization or adaptation are absent. The study also found that the vulnerability of agriculture to climate change depends on how it is measured (in relative versus absolute terms, and with respect to a threshold) and on complex interactions between climate change, CO_2 level, adaptation, and economic conditions.

xxxviii. See, Chapter 3 for detailed discussion on the factors affecting global food crisis.

xxxix. This discussion has been imbibed from http://www.wfp.org/photos/gallery/food-crisis-timeline. See this website for detailed discussion on the timeline and pathways to global food crisis.

xl. This section has imbibed and drawn heavily from McKeon (2011), www.boell.de

xli. The term 'global governance' is made of two terms, 'global' means transnational and 'governance' means systems of rules and regulations at all levels of human activity to direct and control (Rosenau, 1995). Global governance is any purposeful activity intended to control or influence someone else that either occurs in the arena occupied by nations or occurring at other levels, projects influence into that arena. Global governance is governing, without sovereign authority, relationships that transcend national frontiers. Global governance is doing internationally what governments do at home (Finkelstein, 1995). Global governance for food security refers to the international system, in the absence of global government, that contains processes, relationships and mechanisms among nations, organizations, markets, and individuals to control, manage and improve the situation of food security at global, regional, national and local levels by sharing responsibilities and abilities to facilitate and enforce decisions, programs and global food policies.

xlii. United Nations Interim Commission on Food and Agriculture, *The Work of FAO*, Washington D.C. 1945.

xliii. The six largest agrochemical and seed corporations are filling sweeping, multi-genome patents in pursuit of exclusive monopoly over plant gene sequences that could lead of control of most of the world's plant biomass ....under the guise of developing 'climate ready' crops.

xliv. It is important to note that different food crises led to a series of new institutional initiatives to improve global governance on food security, including the World Food Program (WFP), the International Fund for Agricultural Development (IFAD), the reform of the Committee on World Food Security, launched in April 2009, and the short lived World Food Council. The agricultural ministers of G20 have yet again underlined the need for strong global governance to improve food security. Typically, food crises have also led to summits and pledges to cut global hunger. Today, almost every country subscribes to the global target of halving hunger between 1990 and 2015 despite the fact that the number of hungry people is rising in the world.

xlv. However, urban bias – then as now – pushed the governments of developing countries to favour cheap food for the more unruly urban population over the interests of rural producers.

The Food Problems: A Historical Perspective

xlvi.   The birth of WTO gave stimulus to networking among the victims of globalization, liberation and privatisation.

xlvii.   The independent evaluation of the World Bank's assistance to agriculture in Africa published the same year acknowledged the negative impacts of two decades of structural adjustment policies.

xlviii.   The principle of food sovereignty was introduced by La Via Campesina at the 1996 forum. In February 2007, an important global encounter on food sovereignty held in Mali brought together more than 500 delegates from local movements in all regions and deepened the common understanding of what food sovereignty means, what to fight for, and what to oppose. See, www.nyèleni.org

xlix.   The IPC is an autonomous, self-managed global network of some 45 people's movements and NGOs involved with at least 800 organizations throughout the world. Its membership includes constituency focal points (organizations representing small farmers, fisher folk, pastoralists, indigenous peoples, agricultural workers), regional focal points, and thematic focal points (NGO networks with particular expertise on priority issues). It is not a centralized structure and does not claim to represent its members. It is rather a space for self-selected civil society organisations that support the food sovereignty agenda adopted at the 2002 forum.

l.   Established in 1974 as an intergovernmental body, the Committee on World Food Security served as a forum for review and follow-up policies concerning world food security. Besides preparing and following up on the two World Food Summits of 1996 and 2002, this body had a task to negotiate the Voluntary Guidelines on the Application of the Right to Food at national level. It had failed to function as an effective policy forum. However, the only international initiative with global significance was the effort to transform the FAO Committee on World Food Security from an ineffectual talk shop into an authoritative policy forum.

li.   The IAASTD was a four year process involving 400 experts from all regions.

lii.   In comparision, the FAO's budget for the year 2010-2011 was $1 billion approved and monitored by 192 member governments. See, http://www.gatesfoundation.org/about/Pages/foundation-fact-sheet.aspx.

liii.   Global institutions through their technical assistance, financing, rules and regulations, and reliance on markets, promoted directions on agricultural development and trade that respond too much to global corporate interests and western values rather than to the people on whose lives they impact through their actions. Nations are increasingly becoming dependent on each other for their food supplies that make them vulnerable to global crises such as financial, economic, water, food or climate. See, http://km.fao.org/fsn/discussions/global-governance/en/.

liv.   Particularly those whose governments succumbed to World Bank advice to sell their commodities on the world market and purchase "cheap" food in exchange – as well as of the need, instead, to promote smallholder food production for domestic consumption.

lv.   The first category of international institutions includes the WTO, Bretton Woods institutions, IMF and the World Bank for whom food security is hardly core business. The second includes G8/G20, groups of the most powerful economies. The third category includes multinational corporations who have disproportionate impact on global food policies. The fourth category includes financial speculators who influence food prices considerably. The fifth category includes WHO, UNICEF etc. which deal with the nutrition and food-health issues. Sixth category includes ILO that deals with labour laws and human rights. The Seventh category includes FAO, IFAD and the like that concentrates on the issue of right to food. Eighth category includes small food producers organisations and civil society organisations. The ninth category includes international institutional and forums such as WIPO, WTO-TRIPS, CBD, ITGRFA and the like.

lvi. Although the League of Nations was already the venue of acrimonious pre-World War II debate about the co-existence of widespread malnutrition and global over-availability of food (McKeon, 2009).

Chapter 3   Research Methodological Structuration

"Probably at no point in the history of man has there been so much discussion about the rights and wrongs of the policy makers... (Citizens have) begun to suspect that the people who make the major decisions that affect our lives don't know what they are doing... They don't know what they are doing simply because they have no adequate basis to judge the effects of their decisions. To many it must seem that we live in an age of moronic decision making".
Charles West Churchman (1913-2004), a Systems scientist, *The Systems Approach* (1968).

Introduction

Albeit a delicate and fine dissimilarity exists between the terms 'method' and 'methodology', but these terms have been used interchangeably in the present chapter. This chapter outlines the methodological structuration of Kanji-Chopra Global Food Crisis Measurement System (KCGFCMS) by considering its various methodological dimensions. It is a powerful statistical approach in that it combines the multivariate measurement model and the structural equation model into a simultaneous statistical analysis. It involves a mix of economic theory, economic history, agricultural economics and a holistic and system modelling approach that constructs a series of models to measure GFC within certain boundaries of the whole agricultural and food system. The KCGFCMS estimates simultaneously a series of interrelated interdependent relationships for uncovering causality by providing parameters' estimates of the direct and indirect association between observed variables and tests how well a model explains covariance in the data. There are many analytical planes to the methodological boundaries of KCGFCMS. However, the suitability and applicability of a measurement system depends upon its philosophy, principles and tools. If sciences are the trees, philosophy is the soil that makes forest possible. The philosophy of KCGFCMS is a comprehensive system of ideas pertaining to the nature of measurement and the reality we live in. It is a guide for measuring the phenomenon of GFC by addressing its basic and fundamental issues and factors involved. The principles of KCGFCMS are the elementary propositions, maxims, axioms or postulates that guide the entire measurement process. A tool is a utility that helps to complete a task or a set of tasks. The tools of KCGFCMS are instruments to aid at evaluating the variables involved in GFC wherein the philosophical tenets and implementation prescriptions become interwoven and this relationship between theory and practice, significant for developing a measurement system, becomes important in managing the phenomenon of GFC and putting evidence into practice.

The research methodological structuration developed in this study incorporates four principal interconnected methods namely systems thinking or approach incorporating holism[i] and interactions[ii], structural equations modelling, stakeholders' approach and critical food crisis factors approach. This structuration includes both structure and agents as described by Ghosh (2002) (See, for details, Hodgson, 2002), and basically studies the interactions of various factors and forces (See, chapter 5 for details), organisations, institutions and individuals in a global economy. Indeed in this methodological structuration the ultimate focus is on poor individuals in the functioning of the entire world food system who face food insecurity or vulnerability. All individuals are the true entities and their welfare is linked with the overall welfare of the global economy. Moreover, the present research methodological structuration conceptualises GFC as a holistic phenomenon determined by a large number of interconnected determinants, so it warrants a multivariate modelling approach in its measurement. A path or structural equation modelling, a multivariate technique, with latent variables combines econometric prediction with psychometric modelling of variables indirectly observed by multiple manifest variables (Fornell and Cha, 1994).

The present chapter is organised in the following manner. The section following details the statistical understanding of the phenomenon of global food crisis and the next section examines the methods of analysis at some length. It discusses the structural equation modelling (SEM) wherein the assumptions, arrangement of model, structural models with latent variables, partial least squares method, factor analysis approach, path analysis and step by step application of SEM. The next part thrashes out the systems approach along with the system dimensions of GFC, system components and measurement consequences and systems environment. A section is devoted to stakeholders approach incorporating identification and relationships management of stakeholders in GAFS. The next section discusses the critical food crisis factors approach that subsumes the identification process of CFCFs, application of CFCFs and measuring CFCFs. The last segment of the chapter presents the concluding remarks of the chapter.

Statistical Understanding of Global Food Crisis

The logic of statistical reasoning and understanding of GFC originates from the fact that a complex set of interacting factors rather than any single factor is involved. As a global phenomenon and a distinct event, GFC is not merely complicated, it is *complex*. That means the relationship between cause and effect is uncertain. It lies in the GAFS pertaining to an ever-changing complex world where everything is connected to everything else. Thus this system is a very complex, profound, dynamic and ever-changing process. Any small change in any interdependent component or subset of the system affects the behaviour or properties of the components as well as the behaviour of the whole system. The question is: Why do systems fail and lead to a crisis such as GFC? The answer to this question lies in the reflective statistical understanding of the phenomenon of GFC. Factors that seem mysterious or counter-intuitive suddenly make sense and enable researchers to see a bigger picture that makes more statistical sense of their world. It provides a sound theoretical basis for their new ideas. The role of statistical concepts and analysis in the development of agricultural economics is nothing new. However, a rudimentary statistical analysis and tools such as production or consumption trends, ratios, averages, statistical approach by graphical methods and so on in assessing, measuring and managing the contemporary GFC have quite limited application in this context.

The fundamental aspect of statistical understanding is the variation that exists in every process of a system and the decisions are made on that basis. If the variation is not known in a process, then the required output of that process will be difficult to manage. It is also very important to comprehend that every process has an inherent capability and the process will be doing well if it operates within that capability. However, sometimes one can observe that the resources are wasted in solving a problem, simply not realising that the process is working at its maximum capacity. For a multidimensional phenomenon such as GFC, it is important to uncover causality among different factors. In order to understand the variability, the control of variation, uncovering causality and establishing causal pathways leading to GFC, it is necessary to be aware of the basic statistical concepts. These concepts are simple to understand, learn and provide tools to the policy makers for higher productivity, food self-sufficiency at affordable prices. In this complex interconnected world, international organisations and policy makers normally operate in an uncertain environment and therefore the major emphasis is on the immediate or short-term problems. In their everyday life they deal with problems where the application of statistics occurs in pursuit of their organisational objectives. However, as we know, this complex world is ever-changing and the policy makers along with other players such as economists, politicians, administrators, etc are adopting this change and also learning how to manage it. For many people, the best way of adopting this change is to focus on statistical understanding of the phenomenon of GFC because it permeates all aspects of GFC. We know that 'all work is a process' and therefore identification and reduction of a variation of processes provides opportunity for improvement. Here, the improvement process, which recognises that variation is everywhere, takes help from the statistical world for this 'management with measurement' journey. In general, policy makers can take many actions in order to reduce variation to improve hunger and food insufficiency.

Kanji-Chopra Global Food Crisis Measurement System

Scientific measurement of a phenomenon such as global food crisis is an integral part of any research process. A measurement system is a set of interconnected scientific tools and techniques that can convert raw data into valuable, relevant and actionable information based on statistical reasoning. The present study takes into the whole range of key factors affecting GFC so that it can be understood in its totality. A multivariate modelling approach has been used to construct conceptual model, operational model, latent variable structural model and measurement model in order to drive the global food crisis measure within certain boundaries of the GAFS.

Methods of Analysis

The usual methods of frequency tables and bar charts are used to report the results. The tools such as step by step procedure of obtaining GFC index, reliability of measurement scale, Partial Least Squares method, construction of the causal path diagrams, measurement instruments, measurement software, content, construct and criterion-related validity of the model and sensitivity analysis have been used in analysing the data (See, chapter 7). Apart from this, for the analysis of GFC, the KCGFCMS uses the techniques of structural equation modelling, systems approach, critical food crisis factors approach (CFCFs) and stakeholders approach. It is evident from the Figure 3.1 that the architecture of KCGFCMS is based on three pillars and uses a powerful statistical tool of structural equations modelling as a foundation that combines factor analysis, regression analysis and causal pathways approach. The first pillar is systems thinking or approach that looks at the phenomenon of GFC as a whole and asserts that it is the behaviour, components and structure of the system that matters. The second pillar of KCGFCMS is the identification of CFCFs that have significant impact on the accessibility, adequacy and availability of food. The third pillar is the stakeholders' approach that takes into consideration all the stakeholders involved from the production to the utilisation of food. These three pillars are supported and held together by structural equation modelling that give a solid measurement foundation cementing these pillars' activities to create a robust measurement system to measure GFC. It also provides a solid single measurement structure.

1. Structural Equation Modelling

KCGFCMS uses structural equation modelling (SEM)[iii], also called simultaneous equation modelling, as a foundation to test and estimate the postulated causal (cause-effect) relationships that form the measurement models that has its origins in econometric analysis. Structural equations models are multivariate (i.e., multi-equations) regression models. SEM is a very general predominantly linear and cross-sectional statistical modelling technique and it is a largely confirmatory[iv], rather than exploratory, technique (Kline, 2005). SEM is also a multivariate technique combining aspects of multiple regression and factor analysis to estimate simultaneously a series of interrelated dependence relationships (Bollen, 1989). Factor analysis, path analysis and regression all represent special cases of SEM (Loehlin, 1998). Such models include one or more linear regression equations that describe how the endogenous constructs depend upon the exogenous constructs; their coefficients are called path coefficients[v] or sometimes regression weights. It provides parameters estimates of the direct and indirect association between observed variables and tests how well a model explains covariance in the data. SEM is a powerful statistical approach or technique in that it combines the measurement model and the structural equation model[vi] into a simultaneous statistical analysis (Aaker and Bagozzi, 1979). Thus, SEM is also a multivariate technique combining aspects of *multiple regression, path analysis*[vii] and *factor analysis*[viii] to estimate a series of interrelated dependence relationships simultaneously. However, whereas the factors in factor analysis are calculated after running the procedure, in SEM the latent variables are defined before with the model defining the weights of the variables that feed into each latent variable.

To sum up, SEM is a factor analysis technique used for confirmatory factor analysis, since the structure and number of factors is constrained or defined *a priori* and SEM measures how the observed variables are loaded on particular constructs (Anderson and Gerbing, 1998). Unlike the more traditional multivariate linear model, however, the response variable in one regression equation in an SEM may appear as a predictor in another equation; indeed, variables in an SEM may influence one-another reciprocally, either directly or through other variables as intermediaries (Fox, 1984). These structural equations are meant to represent causal relationships among the variables in the model. Accordingly, SEM is not a method for discovering causative relationships, but rather a means by which theoretical relationships can be tested. By accounting for random measurement error, SEM produces more reliable coefficient estimates. An SEM implies a structure of the covariance matrix of the measures (hence an alternative name is "analysis of covariance structures"). Once the model's parameters have been estimated, the resulting model-implied covariance matrix can then be compared to an empirical or data-based covariance matrix. If the two matrices are consistent with one another, then the structural equation model can be considered a plausible explanation for relations between the measures.

Figure 3.1:   ***Foundation and Three Pillars of KCGFCMS***

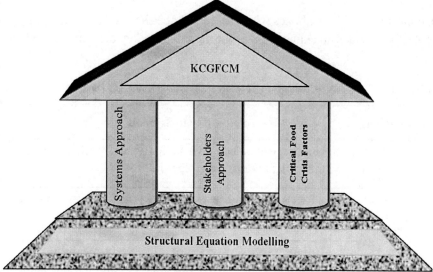

Source: Adopted from Kanji and Chopra (2010).

Assumptions of Structural Equation Modelling

In SEM, the qualitative causal assumptions are represented by the missing variables in each equation as well as vanishing co-variances among some error terms. These assumptions are testable in experimental studies and must be confirmed judgmentally in observational studies. SEM traditionally has some assumptions (Reisinger and Turner, 1999) namely: (1) Independence of variables; (2) Random sampling of respondents; (3) Linearity of all relationships; (4) Multivariate normality of distribution; (5) No kurtosis and no skewness; (6) Appropriate data measurement on interval or ratio scale; and (7) Sample size between 100 and 400. However, the relative importance of meeting these conditions depends also on the estimation methods used. Some estimation methods can adjust for the violation of some of these assumptions. As mentioned earlier, the PLS method is used in the simultaneously estimation of the weights of the constructs of the system pertaining to the phenomenon of GFC.

The Symbolic Representation of an SEM

In creating an SEM the boxes with different shapes have different meanings. Table 3.1 provides an explanation of the meanings or key to symbols in SEM diagram:

Table 3.1:   *Key to Symbols in Structural Equation Modelling Diagram*

Symbols	Key to Symbols
$\boxed{\eta_1}$	Unobserved or latent variable (typically representing a theoretical construct or factor.
Y_1	Observed or manifest variable (typically represented as an item (question) on a questionnaire)
ε_1	Unique observed or latent variable (typically used to represent either: 1. Disturbance in equation, measurement, or both, and/or 2. Unobserved variables unique to the manifest variable it is affecting).

Source: Own construction

Model Arrangement

SEM incorporates several different approaches or frameworks to representing different models. An SEM must be arranged in a particular way if it is to be recognised as being such by both humans and computers. Figure 3.2 shows an example of a basic SEM with one latent variable.

The observed variables (Y_1 to Y_3) all fed by the unobserved endogenous latent variable, η_1. ε_1 to ε_3 are disturbance terms or measurement errors usually each associated to observed variable. The disturbance is treated as a latent variable. Directly observable variables or manifest variables are enclosed in rectangular boxes, and unobservable variables are enclosed in circles. In case of only one latent variable, the data in the observed variables could be analysed by simply calculating the means, variances, etc for each of the variables. However, the strength of the SEM comes from the fact that instead of the calculations been solely based on the data within one particular variable, the SEM also takes into account the responses made to the other variables before a weight for each observed variable is calculated. In simple terms, the SEM model takes into account a respondent's responses to all questions rather than isolating a particular question. Most SEMs will have more than one latent variable (See Figure 3.2). Therefore, arrows from one latent variable to another latent variable build up the model. The arrows indicate an influence or cause from one latent variable to another.

Figure 3.2: **Basic Structural Model (A Single Factor Model)**

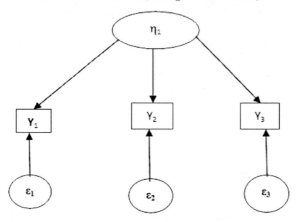

Source: Own construction

In the Figure 3.3 the circles identified with a 'ξ' (Greek character, 'ksi') indicate exogenous (not caused) latent variables while the circles identified with a 'η' (Greek character, 'eta') indicate endogenous[ix] (i.e., caused) latent variables or constructs. The boxes containing a 'X' are the observed (manifest) variables which feed the exogenous latent variables and the boxes containing 'Y' are the observed (manifest) variables which feed the endogenous latent variables. The subscript numbers indicate a particular variable's location within the matrices which are used for calculation purposes. The two types of constructs included in a structural equation model, i.e., exogenous and endogenous, are distinguished on the basis of whether or not they are dependent variables in any equation in the system of equations represented by the model. Exogenous constructs are independent variables in all equations in which they appear while endogenous constructs are dependent variables

Figure 3.3:   *An Example of a Simple Structural Equation Model*

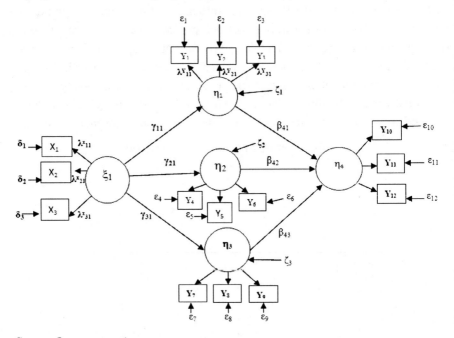

Source: Own construction

in at least one equation although they may be independent variables in other equations in the system. In graphical terms (Figure 3.3), each endogenous construct is the target of at least *one* one-headed arrow while exogenous constructs are only targeted by *two* one-headed arrows. The Figure 3.3 shows a hypothetical simple SEM with three X variables of one exogenous latent variable (ξ_i). There are four latent endogenous variables (η_i), each with three Y indicators. Finally, there are three kinds of errors. One kind of error is a stray cause of the latent endogenous variables called zeta (ζ), also called measurement errors (unreliability) or structural disturbances or errors in equations. There are also errors of the observed or manifest variables. For the observed exogenous variables, these errors are called delta (δ) and for the observed endogenous variables, the errors are called epsilon (e). Each of these is labelled in the figure. The character representing λ^x_{11} is structural parameter or regression coefficient linking latent exogenous construct to its measures (manifest variables) and the character representing λ^Y_{11} is structural parameter or regression coefficient linking the latent endogenous variable to its measures (manifest variables). Parameters representing regression relations between latent constructs are typically labelled with the Greek character, γ_{11}, γ_{21} (gamma) for the regression of an endogenous construct on an exogenous construct, or with the Greek character β_{41}, β_{41} (beta) for the regression of one endogenous construct on another endogenous construct.

Hair et al. (1998) define endogenous construct as construct or variable that is the dependent or outcome variable in at least one causal relationship. In terms of a path diagram, there are one or more arrows leading into endogenous construct or variable. An exogenous construct is a construct or variable that acts only as a predictor or 'cause' for other constructs or variables in the model. In path diagram, exogenous constructs have only causal arrows leading out of them and are not predicted by any other constructs in the model. An illustration is given in the Figure 3.4 below.

Figure 3.4:   *An Illustration of Endogenous and Exogenous Variables*

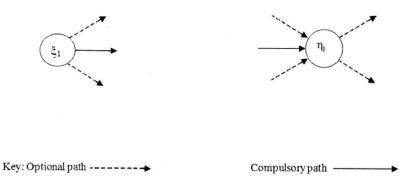

Key: Optional path ┈┈┈▶   Compulsory path ──────▶

What is a Latent Variable?

From the point of view of the present research, latent variable, also known as hidden variable or hypothetical variable is an unobserved variable that is not directly observed but is rather inferred through a model from other variables that are directly observed or measured (Borsboom et al., 2003). Global food crisis is a latent variable which means it is not measured directly, but it is dependent on other variables which are also of a latent construct. Therefore, the dimensions of global agricultural and food system, food demand-side forces, food supply side factors, global agricultural market failures, public sector intervention and collective actions failure, and global food crisis are all latent variables of the latent variable structural models that have been experimented with throughout the course of this research. Latent variables cannot be observed directly, but their values can be implied by their relationships to observed variables. Two or more measured variables are necessary to determine a value for a latent variable.

What is a Manifest Variable?

As opposed to latent variables, manifest variables are observable variables and can be observed and measured directly. Manifest variables are the indicators of latent variables. Each manifest variable is represented by a question in the measurement instrument. Researchers use manifest variables (actual measures and scores) to ground their latent construct with the real data. In SEM, there are two types of manifest variables, i.e., exogenous manifest variables and endogenous manifest variables. The manifest variables associated with exogenous constructs are labelled X while those associated with endogenous constructs are labelled Y. There is no fundamental distinction between these measures, and a measure labelled X in one model may be labelled Y in another.

Thus, the components that are analyzed as part of the regression are known as latent vectors or latent variables. Latent variables were chosen to provide maximum correlation with the dependent variables (DVs). In the case of the KCGFC model, critical food crisis factors were the underlying latent variables that accounted for variations in the responses of the manifest variables. The KCGFC model measures the relationships between latent variables corresponding to the KCGFC concepts. The latent variables are an operationalization of the theoretical constructs of GFC. The variable of GAFS and the core concepts mentioned (FDSFs, FSSRs, GAMFs, and PSICAFs) are latent variables because they cannot be directly measured, but are represented by the manifest variables instead. The manifest variables in the model are represented by the directly observable values indicated by the answers to the questions. These observations are made by a person who establishes a value according to his or her perception. Multiple manifest variables link to one latent variable. By combining several manifest variables into one latent variable, the overall representation is strengthened through correlation weights (Singleton and Straits, 2005). PLS regression analysis was used in the BERS to calculate the scores of the various parameters. These scores were analyzed for each construct and linked to the manifest variables in the model. Together, these scores showed which measurements needed to be increased. A reliability analysis was based on mathematical tests using Cronbach's alpha and chi-square test results.

Different Techniques of Structural Equation Modelling

Structural equation modelling incorporates several different approaches or frameworks to representing these models. The two mostly used techniques are maximum likelihood (ML) and fixed-point estimation(FP). An understanding of these two methodologies is required before progressing any further. Each of these methodologies has a corresponding computer programme which aids in the calculations. Maximum likelihood uses AMOS (LISREL) while fixed point uses the Partial Least Squares (PLS) methodology.

(a) Structural Models with Latent Variables

There are several indicators to measure a latent variable. These produce the following measurement model. In SEM, the structural model includes the relationships among the latent constructs (Bollen, 1989). The equation for manifest variable for exogenous construct becomes:

$$X_1 = \lambda^x_{11} \xi_1 + \delta_1 e_{11}$$

Here, X_1 is the manifest variable indicator for exogenous variable, λ^x_{11} is structural parameter or regression coefficient linking latent exogenous construct to its measures (manifest variables), ξ_1 is the latent exogenous variable, δ_1 is the measurement error term or disturbance variable, and e_{11} is a structural parameter (regression coefficient or weight) relating measurement error to manifest exogenous variable i.e., it is used to indicate the effect of a disturbance variable on an exogenous manifest variable. Similarly, we obtain the equation for manifest variable for endogenous constructs as follows:

$$Y_1 = \lambda^Y_{11}\eta_1 + \varepsilon_1\alpha_{11}$$

The structure among the exogenous and endogenous latents then becomes:

$$\eta_1 = \gamma_{11}\xi_1 + \zeta_1\alpha_{\zeta 11}$$

Here, η_1 is an endogenous latent variable, γ_{11} is structural parameters (weights or regression coefficients) relating exogenous variables to endogenous (inner coefficients), ξ_1 is the exogenous latent variable, ζ_1 is the measurement error of the latent variable in equation, and $\alpha_{\zeta 11}$ is the inner coefficient or structural parameter relating the measurement error (ζ_1) to latent endogenous variable (η_1). However R^2 measures how well h can be predicted by ξ_1. The R^2 value indicates how much of an effect the model before the latent variable is having on that particular latent variable. For example, if the R^2 value if 0.5, this indicates that the model before this latent variable explains 50% of the variation in the latent variable. These formulae can then be developed for the particular methodology that is required for calculation purposes. However, the general structural equation model can be represented by three matrix equations:

$$\eta_{(m+1)} = B_{(m \times m)} * \eta_{(m \times 1)} + \Gamma_{(m \times n)} * \xi + \zeta_{(m \times 1)}$$

$$Y_{(p \times 1)} = \Lambda Y_{(p \times m)} * \eta_{(m \times 1)} + \varepsilon_{(p \times 1)}$$

$$X_{(q \times 1)} = \Lambda X_{(q \times n)} * \xi_{(n \times 1)} + \delta_{(q \times 1)}$$

(b) The Maximum Likelihood Method (LISREL)

Karl Gustav Jöreskog provided an operative algorithm for maximum likelihood estimation of factor models in 1967, and the maximum likelihood algorithm LISREL (Linear structural relations) was developed in 1970 (Jöreskog, 1970). Retherford and Choe (1993) illustrate the maximum likelihood method as it can be seen below. Consider the simple model:

$$\text{Logit } P = a + bX$$

which can be written as

$$P = \frac{1}{1 + e^{-(a + bX)}}$$

Assuming the mathematical forms of these equations are correct, we do not know the values of a and b, which are treated as unknowns. The first step is to formulate a likelihood function, L. L is the probability of observing particular sample data under the assumption that the model is true. That is, we assume that the mathematical form of the model, as given above, is correct, but we don't yet know the values of a and b. We choose a and b so that L is maximised. In other words, we choose values of the unknown parameters that maximise the likelihood of the observed data and call these parameters best fitting parameters. The method can be thought of as considering all possible combinations of a and b, calculating L for each combination, and picking the combination that yields the largest value of L (Retherford and Choe, 1993).

Certain assumptions are made when using maximum likelihood. It assumes that the data is normally distributed and that the variables are made up of continuous data.

- The multivariate normality is determined by the covariance matrix Σ.
- Calculate the observed covariance matrix Σ_0 for all the manifests.
- Use the structural model to obtain a theoretically derived covariance matrix Σ_T
- This includes the coefficients: $\lambda, \gamma, \delta^2$
- Insert starting values $\hat{\lambda}, \hat{\gamma}, \hat{\delta}$ to obtain $\hat{\Sigma}$
- Compare the differences $\Sigma_0 - \hat{\Sigma}$
- If it is close enough stop, otherwise obtain new values for $\hat{\lambda}, \hat{\gamma}, \hat{\delta}$ and continue.

The difference between the observed and estimated covariance matrices is minimised and the likelihood based on the multivariate normal is maximised (ECSI Seminar, 1999).

(c) Fixed Point Estimation (Partial Least Squares Method)

Partial Least Squares (PLS) method is a second-generation multivariate analysis technique used to estimate the parameters of causal models. It embraces abstract and empirical variables simultaneously and recognises the interplay of these two dimensions of theory development. It was originally introduced as an alternative to maximum likelihood LISREL as a way to avoid problems of improper solutions and factor indeterminacy as well as the violations of distributional assumptions (Fornell and Larcker, 1981; Fornell and Bookstein, 1982; Fornell and Cha, 1994). The PLS approach was initially developed by Herman Wold (1981), who questioned the general fitness of covariance structure models as implemented by LISREL (Fornell and Cha, 1994). In many studies, this one included, the data generated is not normally distributed, a requirement of the LISREL maximum likelihood approach. Weight relations for each of the observed variables are calculated under the PLS methodology.

By using weight relations, PLS estimates case values of the latent variables, and therefore, the problem of factor indeterminacy is eliminated (Fornell and Cha, 1994). In addition, the least squares estimation method used by PLS eliminates' the problem of improper solutions (Fornell and Cha, 1994). PLS has been used on several marketing studies including the customer satisfaction index approach in both the United States and Sweden (Fornell, 1992). A theoretical explanation for PLS can be seen below.

Because the estimate process for PLS is different to maximum likelihood, the measurement models are reversed in comparison to AMOS (the arrows from the manifest variables to the latent variables point in the opposite direction for PLS when comparing the same model with the AMOS), see Figure 3.5.

The hypothetical PLS model in the Figure 3.5 shows seven X (exogenous manifest variables) as indicators of three latent exogenous variables (ξ_1 to ξ_3). Note that X_3 is an indicator for both ξ_1 and ξ_2. There are two latent

Figure 3.5:   *An Example of a Hypothetical PLS Model*

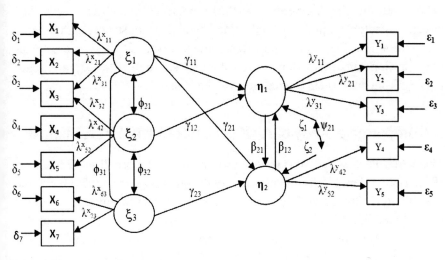

Source: Own construction.

endogenous variables (η_1 and η_2), η_1 with three endogenous manifest variables (Y_1 to Y_3) and η_2 with two endogenous manifest variables (Y_4 and Y_5). Few researchers expect to perfectly predict their dependent constructs, so the model typically includes a measurement error or structural error term or disturbance variable. The model involves errors or disturbance variables in equations ζ s (the Greek character 'Zeta'). Researchers attempt to model the measurement imperfection and measurement error terms with X measures (exogenous manifest variables) are labelled with the Greek character δ (Delta) while terms associated with Y measures (endogenous manifest variable) are labelled with the Greek character ε (Epsilon). In this figure, one-headed arrows represent regression relations while two-headed arrows represent correlational relations, i.e., shared variation that is not explained within the model. The structural parameters (weights) relating exogenous variables to endogenous (inner coefficients) are typically labelled with the Greek character γ (Gamma) for the regression of an endogenous construct on an exogenous construct. The structural parameters or coefficients relating endogenous variables to endogenous variables (inner coefficients) are typically labelled with the Greek character β (Betta) for the regression of one endogenous construct on another endogenous construct. Typically in

SEM, exogenous constructs are allowed to co-vary freely. Parameters labelled with the Greek character ϕ (Phi) represent these co-variances. The Greek character 'Lambda' is used to label the latent constructs to their measures through a factor analytic measurement model, λ^x_{11} to λ^x_{73} are 'loadings' linking constructs to measures on the X side and λ^y_{11} to λ^y_{52} are 'loadings' linking constructs to measures on the Y side.

A Comparative Study of AMOS (LISREL) and PLS Methods

There are wide discussions (Fornell and Larcker, 1981; Fornell and Bookstein, 1982; Lohmöller, 1989; Green et al., 1995; Igbaria et al., 1995; Hackl and Westblund, 2000; Gorst, 2000) on the advantages and disadvantages on the use of Fixed Point Estimation type of PLS versus the Maximum Likelihood Estimation type of LISREL and AMOS (Arbuckle, 1994). One of the chief difference between PLS and AMOS (LISREL) is the theory behind how they make their calculations. PLS is based on the fixed point methodology (FPM) while AMOS is based around, maximum likelihood methodology (MLM). FPM differs from MLM in its principles and assumptions. In ML estimation, the probability of the observed data given the hypothesised model is maximised. However, PLS estimation minimises residual variances under a FP constraint (Fornell and Bookstein, 1982). The major advantage of the AMOS package is its ability to show the SEM in a graphical format that allows us to see what is happening within the model and make necessary changes quickly. Moreover, if a variable is unidentified[x], it will tell the user how many additional constraints are required. In comparison, if the SAS. PLS methodology cannot execute, the error message is far more complicated and points to a line in the programme where it failed to execute. However, it is important to note that the PLS methodology does not require additional constraints on the influences between different latent variables. Since it is a maximum likelihood procedure, the asymptotical properties are known, that is to say standard errors and goodness of fit statistics can be computed. ML approach aims at selecting the best fitting model.

The main disadvantage of AMOS is that the chi-square can sometimes be misleading, i.e., it may indicate a good fit between the model and the data even though the measures and theory are inadequate (Fornell and Larcker, 1981). Secondly, if the sample size is small, it may not be chi-squared distributed, which does not provide an accurate representation of what is happening. Thirdly, AMOS methodology requires data to be normally distributed and is sensitive to data that is skewed. Fourthly, it requires continuous data and a large number of observations (500). Moreover, ML methodology inverts the matrices and it cannot be done if data is ill-conditioned. However, PLS enables the analysis of very small samples (Lohmöller, 1989 and Lgbaria, et. al., 1995), these can be as small as ten times the number of indicators on the most formative construct (Green et al., 1995). The PLS results are interpreted in two stages, firstly, the assessment of the reliability, and, validity of the measurement model. Second is the assessment of the structural model (Green et al., 1995). Due to the robustness of the PLS methodology, the technique is particularly applicable in research areas where theory is not as well developed as that demanded by LISREL (Igbaria et al., 1995). For our purpose, PLS is employed and used extensively throughout.

Factor Analysis Approach

Factor analysis is a method used to describe the variability among observed and correlated variables in terms of a potentially lower number of unobserved, uncorrelated variables called factors. It purports at describing the covariance relationships among many variables in terms of a few underlying, but unobservable, random quantities called factors (Johnson and Wichern, 1992). Karl Pearson and Charles Spearman among others were some of the first researchers to develop factor analysis to define and measure 'intelligence' or psychometric measurement. The purpose of factor analysis is to discover simple patterns in the pattern of relationships among the variables. However, the advent of powerful computing helped in its development as a statistical method. Factor analysis is helpful in identifying the underlying, not directly observable, constructs through a process involving the observed correlations of the variables. For example, variables such as poverty ratings of communities in a survey can be expressed as a function of factors such as income, consumption and human capital. Throughout the research a factor analysis has been carried out on each of different sets. The initial purpose of using factor analysis was as a way of explaining structural equation modelling. In addition, the factor analysis carried out also go some way towards supporting the allocation of the manifest variables to the relevant latent variables.

There are two types of factor analysis: exploratory factor analysis (EFA) and confirmatory factor analysis (CFA). EFA is used to uncover the underlying structure of a relatively large set of variables. The researcher's *a priori* assumption is that any indicator may be associated with any factor. This is the most common form of factor analysis. There is no prior theory and one uses factor loadings to intuit the factor structure of the data. CFA seeks to determine if the number of factors and the loadings of measured (indicator) variables on them conform to what is expected on the basis of pre-established theory. Indicator variables are selected on the basis of prior theory and factor analysis is used to see if they load as predicted on the expected number of factors.

Causal Path Analysis

Path analysis[xi], also called causal pathways or causal modelling, is a straightforward extension of multiple regression. It is used to describe the directed dependencies and estimate the magnitudes and significance of hypothesised causal connections among sets of variables. It can be viewed as a special case of structural equation modelling (SEM) – one in which only single indicators are employed for each of the variables in the causal model. That is, path analysis is SEM with a structural model, but no measurement model. Path analysis was developed around 1918 by geneticist Sewall Wright. It has since been applied to a vast array of complex modelling areas, including sociology and econometrics. Path Analysis is a variation SEM which is essentially a type of multivariate procedure that allows an examination of independent variables and dependent variables. Variables can be continuous or discrete. SEM works with measured variables and latent variables. Path Analysis uses measured values only. Measured variables can be observed and are measurable.

Path analysis can be best explained with the help of a path diagram (Figure 3.6). Causal modelling generally involves the construction and use of diagrammatic representations of the causal assumptions expressed as directed acyclic graphs (DAGs). Such graphs have cognitive benefits, for example by facilitating user inferences involving the underlying causal models (Griffiths and Tenenbaum, 2005; Larkin and Simon, 1987).

Diagrams and language are two ways of externalizing thought to reduce memory load and facilitate inferences (Scaife and Rogers, 1996). A path diagram improves their accuracy in finding all direct and indirect effects of one variable on another, a task that is equivalent to specifying all the causal paths between those variables. A path diagram is constructed by writing the names of the variables and drawing an arrow from each variable to any other variable we believe that it affects. There are two types of path diagrams: an *input path diagram* that is drawn beforehand to help plan the analysis and represents the causal connections that are predicted by our hypothesis and an *output path diagram* that denotes the results of a statistical analysis and shows what was actually found.

Causal models provide researchers with several key benefits (Hulland, 1999):

a. they make the assumptions, constructs, and hypothesised relationships in a theory explicit;
b. they permit a more complete representation of complex theories;
c. they add a degree of precision to a theory since they require clear definitions of constructs, operational, and functional relationships;
d. they provide a framework for constructing and testing both theories and measures.

Figure 3.6: **A Hypothetical Path Diagram of Causal Pathways**

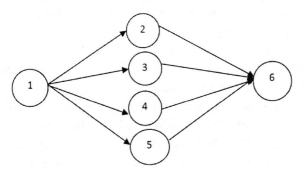

Source:Own construction

One of the strengths of SEM is to construct the latent variables[xii], variables which are not measured directly, but are estimated in the model from several manifest or measured variables. The principles and concepts embedded in

Kanji-Chopra measurement system cannot be directly measured. Rather they need to be translated into a set of manifest variables[xiii] (indicators). These indicators not only have to adequately cover the domain of the latent constructs, but also need to meet requirements of measurement validity and reliability. The manifest variables are measured using measurement items and serve as indicators of the latent variable. A measurement instrument (questionnaire) is then developed and used to obtain scores from respondents on a variety of quality attributes that provide an empirical content to the model's constructs. In our case, the *latent variable structural model* (LVSM) is used to represent the causal relationships among latent variables (critical global food crisis factors and GFC). A LVSM is expressed into a system of simultaneous equations known as structural equations. The components of a structural equation are the latent variables, structural parameters and a disturbance term. Then an *index* is obtained using structural equation models that simultaneously measures the impact of all the variables on a phenomenon.

SEM is also used to examine scale validation and possibly modify scales for better psychometric properties (Chau, 1997). It is also concluded that a simultaneous system approach rather than a partial model approach is required for this analysis in order to estimate the entire set of relationships at once. Hence, both the measurement systems derive from a structural model based on a probabilistic approach using simultaneous equation estimation techniques for the measurement of a phenomenon. The estimates for the structural parameter component can be determined by using computer programs such as LISREL, SAS, PLS and AMOS. The structural equations generate a hypothetical variance/covariance matrix of manifest variables. The degree to which a structural equation model reflects reality is given by the degree to which the hypothetical variance/covariance matrix is similar to, or has a good fit with, the empirical variance/covariance matrix for the same manifest variables. However, KCGFCMS uses specially designed measurement software based on Partial Least Square path modelling approach[xiv] in the simultaneous estimation of the weights of the constructs or dimensions of the system of a phenomenon. It calculates these weights in a way that maximizes the goodness of fit of the models and, thus, the ability to explain performance excellence as the ultimate endogenous variable.

Steps Involved in the Application of Structural Equation Modelling

The steps involved in the application of SEM are pictured in the Figure 3.7.

Figure 3.7: **Structural Equation Modelling Stages**

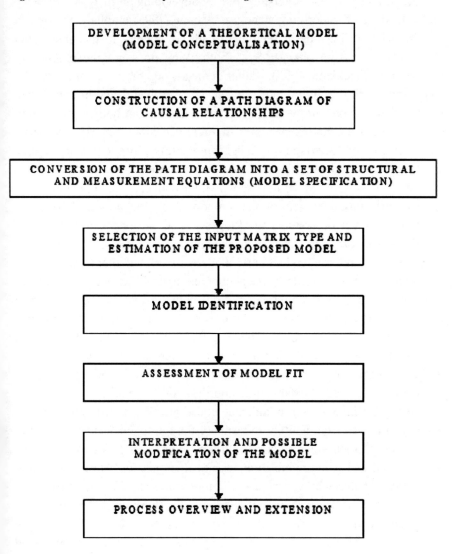

Source: Own construction

2. Systems Approach

The term 'systems approach', also known as 'system dynamics', 'system theory' or 'system thinking', has various definitions. According to Barry Richmond (1993), "Systems approach is the art and science of making reliable inferences about the behaviour by developing an increasingly deep understanding of underlying structure". Senge (1993) emphasises "the art of systems thinking lies in seeing through complexity to the underlying structures generating change. System thinking does not mean ignoring complexity (Checkland, 1997). Rather, it means organizing complexity into a coherent story that illuminates the causes of problems and how they can be remedied in enduring ways". Whether it is a human body, organisation or society, it is a complex system of interconnected and interrelated parts. Everything is connected to every other thing in this universe like organisms, and this relation involves the emergence of a relational quality. In systems approach all systems are composed of inter-connected components. The connections cause behaviour of one component to affect another. Therefore, systems approach or systems thinking serve as the prime foundation of KCGFCMS in order to measure a phenomenon holistically. Systems are made of highly interdependent parts that must work together to achieve the system's overall aim. Similarly, the phenomenon of GFC conceives the global economy as a system that interacts with its demand-side forces, supply-side restrictions, agricultural markets failures and public sector interventions. Thus, the holistic view of the phenomenon of global food crisis is an important consequence of adopting a systems perspective. It calls attention to the importance of implementing a phenomenon of GFC on a global level basis and to the need of establishing coordination mechanisms.

Let us begin with a fundamental question, "What differentiates one country or region from another in terms of food problems?" Discussions in economics, political science, agricultural economics, sociology and history have offered us a wide menu in answer to this question. However, I shall argue that all these have serious limitations and shall try to present an alternative answer from complexity and systems thinking perspectives that need a good deal of attention in the literature on food problems. I shall argue to propose an answer to this question by looking into the current global agricultural and food system. In fact, it is the *behaviour* of the world food system[xv] that makes all the difference. Furthermore, systems have different levels of complexity[xvi].

The accepted 'analysis approach' deals with increasing complexity by *reducing* it into manageable "bites" and address them in isolation. We analyze a complex situation or issue by trying to break it down into component pieces and consider each in isolation from the others. This kind of thinking has its roots in analytic geometry where one basic axiom is that *the whole is equal to the sum of its parts*. Think about that for a moment. The underlying assumption behind this conclusion is that all of the parts are essentially independent of one another. However, this approach fails and is counter-productive when applied to dynamic, homeostatic, or cybernetic systems. A holistic or whole system approach is considerably better suited to study complexity we usually encounter today. It represents *synthesis*-thinking with an integrated perspective about the whole phenomenon. Prior to synthesizing, we must first analyze, i.e., we first take the system apart usually conceptually to understand the functions of each link or component. Once the components are fully understood in isolation, we study the interactions among components to understand how the system as a whole functions. Understanding these interactions requires *integrating* the components into something larger and more capable than the components represent alone. Thus, there is a paradigm[xvii] shift here, from analytical thinking to systems thinking.

Therefore, systems thinking or approach is used here as the prime foundation in order to drill through the layers of complexity of international system. Why systems thinking? Firstly, a global country is viewed as a system and behaves as organisms made of highly interdependent components such as economic, political, financial and social components organised in a particular way with their complex relationships. Secondly, all these components must work together like different parts of body to achieve the global economy's overall aim. Thirdly, a systems thinking is as *an art and science of making reliable inferences about systems behaviour by developing and increasing deep understanding of underlying structure.* Fourthly, it does not ignore complexity rather facilitates in seeing through complexity to the underlying structures generating changes. Fifthly, within a system the behaviour of one component affects the behaviour of the other as well as of the entire system. To understand a systems' total behaviour, we must understand its structure. Structure is the pattern of component connections which is how the system is organized. Thus, the structure of a system determines its behaviour.

Sixthly, the components, their degree of interconnectivity, structure of a system and its complexity are constantly changing. For example, the system of global economy is always changing due to a number of reasons such as globalisation, increasing interdependencies among nations, organisations and people, advancement of technology and communication, space race, emergence of giant multinational, increasing social, economic and political problems and tensions, growing threats from global terrorism, environment problems, growing ethical concerns and so on. All these factors jointly interplay in varying degrees in different situations making the world a place full of surprises and sudden shocks such as global financial crisis, climate change, recent global banking crisis, global food crisis, economic recession, and the like.

As adumbrated earlier, the phenomenon of global food crisis lies within global agricultural and food system that interacts with its environment (surrounding). The global economy operates in a complex and dynamic environment and has to adapt to the continuously changing economic, political, financial or social arrangements. This environment up to certain extent is outside the control of a policy maker. Moreover, there are two types of factors that affect the situation of global food crisis, internal factors and external factors. Figure 3.8 shows the internal and external factors that jointly lead to the measurement of global food crisis within an international system's boundary. For example, if a neighbouring country has flood or famine, it may increase the food insecurity of a country and may adversely affect its food crisis assessment. Similarly, location of a country is also an external factor affecting global food crisis assessment.

System Dimensional Approach

The core concepts associated with the global agricultural and food system are as follows:
  a. Synergy – in that the totality of the system is greater than the sum of its components elements;
  b. System boundary – which delineates the system and which may be

open, partially open or closed in relation to exchanges between the system and its environment;

c. Subsystems – comprising interrelations between particular elements within the total system and which themselves have the characteristics of a system;

d. Flow – a system has several streams of processes throughout;

e. Feedback – serves to keep the system in a state of dynamic equilibrium with respect to its environment.

Figure 3.8: *Global Agricultural and Food System in Interaction with Its Environment*

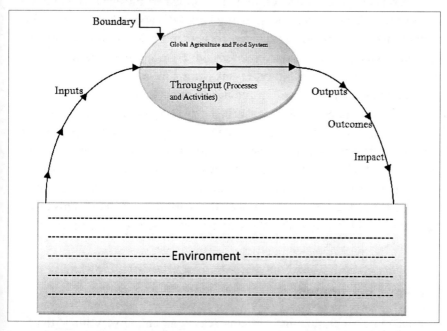

Source: Own construction

System Components and Measurement Consequences

If we regard global economy as system, i.e. "network(s) of interdependent components that work together to try to accomplish the aim of a system" (Deming, 1986), the main components of GFC measurement are necessarily inputs, processes (throughput), outputs and outcomes. There are, however, problems associated with the measurement of each of these aspects, especially in what concerns to outcomes (Sanderson, 1994). Accordingly, global systems are made up of elements – people, materials, and processes – that interact with each other to pursue an overall and collective purpose. To some extent, this necessarily implies the transformation of inputs into outputs and outcomes and finally into impact. Accountancy and financial measures usually work quite well for the inputs part, even if they do not consider many intangible assets such as agricultural workers' competencies or food corporation know-how.

In terms of outputs, headcounts and workload are the most common type of measures (Gaster, 1995), but they say very little about the quality of food products achieved and how the customers perceive it. Moreover, the pressure for high headcounts can lead to counterproductive consequences in terms of quality. Assessing outcomes requires measuring the impact of a food service or agricultural activity upon its recipients, including its consequences or effects. Furthermore, when measuring global food crisis the attributes of the system are in focus. Those attributes are, for example, production, productivity, responsiveness, customer satisfaction and responsibility. It is clear as Ackoff (1994) stresses that "the way that the behaviour or properties of each part of a system affects its behaviour or properties depends on the behaviour or properties of at least one other part of the system". This means that interdependence between the various dimensions cannot be discarded when measuring GFC.

Systems Environment

A final note goes to the systems environment. Everything that is external to the global agricultural and food system and not included in the system can be viewed as the system environment. Thus, the system boundary demarcates the environment from the system. Typically, global environment is dynamic and forces continuous change and adaptation. The environment's characteristics determine important aspects of global food crisis measurement. It is true that food problems have an impact on society. It is also a fact that some general environmental features strongly influence food security and social welfare. Clearly, when measuring global food crisis the focus is on the controllable environmental parameters. Since the GFC lies within GAFC, a system modelling approach must be adapted to it in which world food system is described in terms of components, subsystems, transformation processes, inputs, outputs, outcomes and impacts. From there analytical models involving the potential key drivers of food crisis are developed, tested and validated. Using a system modelling approach, one can understand the world food system's performance looking at the entire system including all main elements and their interactions within the system and towards their environmental patterns at the same time.

3. Stakeholders Approach

Stakeholders in GAFS can be defined as any constituencies (persons, communities, groups, or organizations) that have direct or indirect stake in the world agricultural and food system and are affected by the system's decisions, activities and actions. All stakeholders are not equal and different stakeholders are entitled to different considerations. For example, farmers are entitled for fair trading practices as food producers but they are not entitled for same consideration as food consumers. Stakeholders are the interest groups with a direct or indirect stake or interest in the GAFS.

Stakeholders Identification in Global Agricultural and Food System

Stakeholders may be identified either *a priori* based on knowledge of the country and reform context, or through informal consultations with government or study partners or in the research process as a result of social analysis. Such a process is appropriate where ethnic diversity is minimal or stakeholders are "obvious." In some cases the appropriate stakeholders may be identified through consultations and research. However, stakeholder identification may not always be followed by an analysis of their interests or "stakes". Broadly, there are two categories of stakeholders: primary and secondary. The primary stakeholders can be identified at grass-root level by the research team members themselves. The secondary stakeholders groups sometimes identified in focus-group discussions with local counterparts.

Figure 3.9:   *Stakeholders of Global Agricultural and Food System*

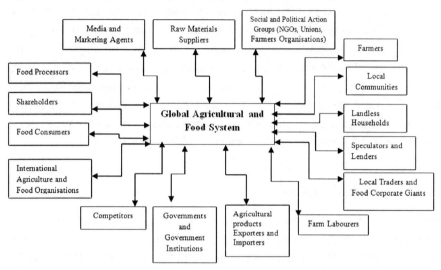

Source: Own Construction

Figure 3.9 shows that the main stakeholders of GAFS are farmers, landless households, farm labourers, local communities, speculators and lenders, local traders and food corporate giants, agricultural products exporters and importers, governments and government institutions, competitors, international agriculture and food organisations, food consumers, shareholders, food processors, media and marketing agents, raw materials suppliers, and social and political action groups (NGOs, unions, farmers organisations)

Managing Stakeholders Relationships in Global Agricultural and Food System

The relationship between the GAFS and its stakeholders is twofold. If it is true that stakeholders have power to influence the GAFS's activities and actions. It is equally true that the GAFS has a major impact over its stakeholder's behaviour and decisions. Managing these relationships has become essential for smooth functioning of the world food system. By knowing how its stakeholders think and act, it will be easy to control the GAFS and its environment, understanding how it is changing and developing appropriate responses to those changes. In order to achieve positive outcomes and impact of GAFS, there is a need to understand stakeholders' needs and how the quality of the food products and services provided by GAFS is perceived. Different stakeholders are expected to have different (and sometimes even conflicting) views on these matters. Therefore, the system used to measure GFC must be able to capture the views of the key stakeholders of the GAFS. Thus, the stakeholders' approach is an integral part of our measurement system since it suggests and encourages the policy makers and international agricultural organisations to start by considering the needs and requirements of stakeholders. A large number of interactions and trade-offs must be managed in order to satisfy the interests of different stakeholders. Measuring how outputs, outcomes and impact are perceived by the stakeholders of GAFS allows the identification of the relative importance of various dimensions to different groups.

Measuring GFC according to the key stakeholders' perceptions not only contributes to a more accurate and realistic picture of GAFS performance, but also gives important indications of the key areas where improvement is vital. By combining the assessment of key stakeholders, the new system is expected to provide an integrated view of GAFS performance. Different stakeholders require different performance indicators. That inevitably places important pressures on the new performance system, calling for synthesis and integration. For KCGFCMS, such integration essentially comes from the use of a critical global food crisis factors approach, as explained next.

4. Critical Food Crisis Factors Approach

The term 'critical food crisis factors' has been specially coined and developed in this research to be used in the world of agricultural and food economic analysis. Critical food crisis factors (CFCFs) approach is essential to determine the central forces and their behaviour in the context of global agricultural and food system (GAFS). CFCFs are the factors, activities or things that are generating crisis in any economy. Thus, CFCFs are the elements that are vital for an understanding of world food crisis. These factors can be referred to as 'cold sweat factors', i.e. things that are of main concern and therefore must be achieved in order to succeed in managing food crisis.

CFCFs can also be described as those variables that stakeholders can influence through their decisions that can affect significantly the overall food security position of the global economy. The CFCFs are those few areas of agricultural and food activity in which favourable results are necessary in order to achieve the desired goals. Such system is based on the critical food crisis factors (CFCFs) which are the limited number of areas in which results, if satisfactory, will ensure successful management of the world food crisis. The CFCFs concept has not yet been applied in previous studies in agricultural and food economics, which first of all, involves identifying those *vital few* dimensions that are supposed to have a major impact on world food system's performance and, then, including them in the measurement of world food crisis.

Identification Process of Critical Food Crisis Factors

In amalgamating food problems into the strategy of global governance for world food security, any mission that has already been developed is changed into critical food crisis factors to coerce and move it forward. The identification of critical global food crisis factors is a very important step for applying them in process. It provides a means by which a researcher or policy makers can assess threats and opportunities in world food system's environment. CFCFs also provide a set of criteria for assessing the strengths and weaknesses of global agricultural and food system. In integrating the global food crisis into the dynamics of global agricultural and food system, it is essential to determine the central driving forces that are changed into critical global food crisis factors that are vital for a strategy of food security to be successful. The CFCFs concept ought to be applied to the food security mission which first of all involves identifying these vital few dimensions or factors that are supposed to have the major impact on the food crisis situation and, then, grouping them into different dimensions that indicate their degree of importance and including them in the measurement of global food crisis. In this case, the measurement of GFC will involve determining weightings and causal connections strengths of CFCFs.

The research is responsible for listing CFCFs in order to gain understanding the key areas producing crisis and if measured and managed properly, that will improve the food security situation. Hofer and Schendel

(1978), and Leidecker and Bruno (1984) observed that CFCFs can easily be identified through a combination of sensitivity and elasticity analyses. However, the major problem is assessing relative importance. A global level of analysis goes beyond country's boundaries for the source of CFCFs. One needs to perpetually scan the system's environment (economic, social, political, and ecological) to provide sources that will be the determinants of global food crisis. There may be eight techniques to indentify CFCFs: (a) a thorough review of literature, (b) environmental analysis, (c) analysis of global economy's structure, (d) individual agricultural economists' opinions, (e) analysis of agricultural and food market competition and structure, (f) analysis of global agriculture and food system, (g) a thorough literature review, (h) opinions of experts with leading world institutions such as WTO, World Bank, IMF, United Nations, International Food Policy Research Institute, Bretton Woods Institutions, etc., (i) temporal and intuitive factors, (j) information system, and (k) characteristics of the agricultural and food industry. The present study utilised the techniques of an exhaustive literature review, analysis of global agriculture and food system and repeated discussions with experts, and identified 48 agricultural-industry specific CFCFs and grouped them into six categories essential for laying foundation to the analysis and measurement of GFC. The identification of CFCFs has particular significance for governments and policy makers at national and international levels. Identification of CFCFs can be done by evaluating the agricultural strategy, environment, resources, operations, markets, coping with food inflation, ensuring the adequacy and accessibility of food to all, and strategic development. However, the present study is the first study to apply critical food crisis factors approach to the analysis of the food problems.

Application of Critical Food Crisis Factors Method

There has been no previous study that has applied the critical food crisis factors approach in relation to the analysis of GFC. A selection of CFCFs is based on the assumption that the outcomes and impact of global agricultural and food system output depends on the quality of inputs (seeds, fertilizers, soil, labour, etc.) and the quality of the process and activities (See, chapter 5 for further details.). Each CFCF is assessed against a string of criteria for world food crisis. Each criterion is weighted and its score determined. The product of the weight and score gives the weighted score for that criterion. The overall crisis indicator, which is the sum of the weighted scores for all criteria, reflects the quality for a given critical food crisis factor. The KCGFCMS is a versatile approach that can be scaled up to include larger parts of the entire global economy. Conversely, it may be scaled down to focus on more detailed processes or smaller units.

Measuring Critical Food Crisis Factors

Once CFCFs (core forces) have been identified and synthesised, world food crisis measures for CFCFs can be developed. These factors are used as the basis for identifying the food crisis indicators. The indicators can be used in measuring short-term progress towards long-term objectives of social welfare and environmental security. The indicators must satisfy the specifications of being reliable, simple, timely, operational, and indicative. In order to achieve the reliable measurement, initial selection of measurement items for each critical food crisis factor, pre-testing the instrument, and finalisation of the measurement items have been used to develop the measurement instrument for measuring GFC. The data collected on CFCFs were factor analysed and resulted in six critical food crisis factors of food insecurity.

Concluding Remarks

The quantification of the phenomenon of GFC is *de rigueur* for its effective and successful management. It requires following a scientific research methodology structure in order to arrive at meaningful conclusions for apposite policy options. The present study proposes a theory of treating a GAFS as a living system using inputs, functions and activities and knowledge to measure and manage the global food crisis. GAFS is the prime in the entire measurement system. However, the KCGFCMS is very powerful and robust as it is based on six very powerful but easy to use measurement tools and they are: systems approach, stakeholders' approach, critical success factors approach, structural equation modelling, survey methodology and specially designed measurement software depending upon the nature and type of dimensions of the phenomenon under investigation. The previous studies do not provide evidence of taking into consideration the whole range of determinants responsible for the food crisis. KCGFCMS treats this phenomenon in a multivariate context wherein causal connections among different dimensions are tested. The concepts or ideas applied in the KCGFCMS are specific and give sufficient information to policy makers to take appropriate policy actions to control and manage this food crisis. The four models, discussed in the next chapter, of the KCGFCMS have been proposed and developed. They have been tested for their reliability, construct, content and criterion-related validity.

Notes

i.   Holism as a methodological process not only takes into account the mutuality of the relations, but also considers the totality of the influence on a phenomenon.

ii.   Interactions are reciprocal two-way relations. Interactions, interdependence and integration exist through the global agricultural and food system. These interactions can be found to exist at many analytical levels of GFC.

iii.   The geneticist Sewall Wright (1921), the economist Trygve Haavelmo (1943) and the cognitive scientist Herbert Simon (1953), articulated the definitions of SEM and Judea Pearl (2000) formally defined it by using a calculus of counterfactuals. SEM allows both confirmatory and exploratory modelling, meaning they are suited to both theory testing and theory development. Confirmatory modelling usually starts out with a hypothesis that gets represented in a causal model. The concepts used in the model must then be operationalized to allow testing of the relationships between the concepts in the model. The model is tested against the obtained measurement data to determine how well the model fits the data. The causal assumptions embedded in the model often have falsifiable implications which can be tested against the data.

iv.   Confirmatory factor analysis, in statistics, is a special form of factor analysis. It is used to test whether measures of a construct are consistent with a researcher's understanding of the nature of that construct (or factor). In contrast to exploratory factor analysis, where all loadings are free to vary, it allows for the explicit constraint of certain loadings to be zero. It has built upon and replaced older methods of analyzing construct validity such as the MTMM Matrix as described in Campbell and Fiske (1959).

v.   Path coefficients are the standardised regression weights used to examine the possible casual linkages among statistical variables in SEM. The standardization involves multiplying the ordinary regression coefficient by the standard deviations of the corresponding explanatory variable: these can then be compared to assess the relative effects of the variables within the fitted regression model.

vi.   Most SEM applications deal with research problems related to the study of causal relationships among latent variables. For the requirements of performance evaluation it is necessary for the system to deliver meaningful results in terms of causal (cause-effect-oriented) relationship and a structural approach (meaning that the analysis shall be model-based). SEM provides a means by which theoretical relationships can be tested.

vii. Path analysis, in statistics, is used to describe the directed dependencies among a set of variables, as such, models equivalent to any form of multiple regression analysis, factor analysis, canonical correlation analysis, discriminant analysis, as well as more general families of models in the multivariate analysis of variance and covariance analyses (MANOVA, ANOVA, ANCOVA).

viii. A statistical method, first developed by Karl Pearson and Charles Spearman to measure intelligence, used to describe variability among observed variables in terms of a potentially lower number of unobserved variables called factors.

ix. Variables that are not influenced by other variables in a model are called exogenous variables. Thus, an exogenous variable is not caused by another variable in the model and usually it causes one or more variables in the model.

x. A model is said to be identified, if there is one optimal value for each unknown parameter. If the model is identified, the iterative procedure usually converges to an optimal solution with parameter estimates that best fit the data.

xi. Other terms used to refer to path analysis include causal modelling, analysis of covariance structures, and latent variable models.

xii. Latent variables (as opposed to observable variables), are variables that are not directly observed but are rather inferred (through a mathematical model) from other variables that are observed (directly measured may be called manifest variables). Variables such as value, satisfaction, intelligence, loyalty, and quality are latent variables.

xiii. Manifest variables also called observable variables, are the variables that can be observed and directly measured.

xiv. Partial Least Squares (PLS) copes well with some departures from the usual assumptions (and normality in particular), whereas other popular tools, such as LISREL, are particularly sensitive to distributional characteristics of the data. This technique is also considered as better suited to data exploration.

xv. A system is network of a set of inter-connected and interdependent components that work together and establish interactions and relationships between the components and their attributes related to each other and to their environment so as to form a whole.

xvi. Bounding classifies different systems into nine levels of complexity. The first three levels are physical and mechanical systems and the next three levels deal with biological systems. The last three levels of humans, social organizations and transcendental systems (See, Schoderbek et al., 1990).

xvii. Thomas Kuhn, in 1962, coined the word 'paradigm' to depict a pattern of knowledge, assumptions, rules or thinking. The difference between an analytical approach to food problems and a synthesis approach can simply be described as a paradigm *shift*, or a significant change in the "rules of the game." Paradigm shifts can be either evolutionary (i.e., a slow pace of change) or revolutionary-dramatic, short-term, and immediate high impact.

Chapter 4   A Theoretical Model of
Global Agricultural
and Food System

"...Facts can be applied in any field. Our curse is ignorance. Facts are our scariest raw material. This is shown by the economy by which we use them. One has to dig deep for them because they are as difficult to get as they are precious to have. I shall be happy if we can substitute the calm findings of the investigator for the blatant explosions of the politicians"
Owen D. Young (1874-1962), An American Industrialist Businessman, Lawyer and Diplomat.

Introduction

Agricultural and food systems have globalised in both developed and developing countries(Kennedy et al., 2004). The global agriculture and food system has not been adequately theorized in existing literature. As a consequence, the dynamics of the driving forces and their interactions, processes, activities, outputs, outcomes and impacts of global agricultural and food system (GAFS) are misunderstood or not properly interconnected. The key to theorizing global agriculture and food system is the recognition that its behaviour is extremely intricate given that individuals, groups and organisations have their own purposes. The objects of GAFS and their attributes are related to each other and to their environment. This chapter attempts to apply systems approach and complexity perspective as the prime foundation of the *new approach* to GAFS that come from the tendency to regard it as organisms being made of highly interdependent parts that must work together to achieve the aim of hunger and obesity free world. It attempts to develop a theoretical model of GAFS which will incorporate (1) a clear conceptualisation of GAFS, (2) a lucid delineation of salient features of GAFS, (3) an identification of mechanism and processes involved as inputs, throughput, outputs, outcomes and impacts of GAFS, (4) an unambiguous understanding of driving forces and dynamics involved connecting to food security, social welfare, ecological security and environmental sustainability, (5) the detection of sources of pressure of GAFS towards global food crisis (Giménez and Peabody, 2008).

Food related facts linked with hunger, obesity, vulnerability and hardships bring to light the predicament of adults and children who continue to slip through the nutrition safety net and are likely to be hungry, undernourished, and in poor health with high rates of obesity, heart disease, diabetes, and other nutrition-fueled health problems. The phenomenon of food insecurity is undeniably complex due to intertwining political, social, agricultural, environmental, economic, cultural, and geographical forces. Right from the life threat of Roman Emperor Claudius in AD 51 from hungry crowds, and bread riots that helped spark off the French Revolution[i] in 1789 to the present food crisis riots during 2007-2012[ii], food and bread riots led to the fall of governments and political systems in many countries including Tsarist Russia, USA (Southern Bread Riots), France, British Rule in India in 1947 hastened by bread and salt riots, and Egyptian bread riots in 1977 (Bush, 2010; Berazneva and Lee, 2011; Fortson, 2012). Therefore, a structured and smooth functioning of GAFS or food regimes[iii] is an indispensable foundation for peace and prosperity of a stable global economy and a wider society that is capable of reproducing itself. The importance of GAFS lies in its linkages with food production, food demand, processing, distribution, and consumption networks at local, regional and global levels (Smith, 1998; Ericksen, 2006).

We live in a global village where the most basic need of nutritionally adequate and safe food is satisfied on the basis of a system with global reach and global price and production interconnections. Our planet's seven plus billion people need a daily diet of grains, oils, and protein, and the most important of these foods are produced within the context of a global trading system. In relation to world food problems, a system is made up of a conversion process, some resource inputs into that process, the outputs resulting from the conversion of the inputs, short to medium term outcomes in terms of food security, long term impact in terms of social welfare, development and opportunity, ecological security and environmental sustainability, and information feedback about the activities in the system. This perspective illustrates a general agricultural and food system that has given rise to the whole food production-consumption cycle. The GAFS presents a theoretical framework that subsumes the driving forces that originate, sustain and lead to food crisis. These forces provide profound insights across a wide range of real issues related to the deficiencies, gaps and inequalities in different constructs of global food system facilitating or preventing the achievement of food security and social welfare. By increasing awareness and understanding regarding the underlying forces of food crisis, one can also realise the fact that the stability and effectiveness of the world food system can no longer be taken for granted. This endeavours to resolve the puzzles of food crisis by identifying the whole range of causes and their relative importance. Furthermore, a fresh look into the prevailing world agricultural and food system will broaden our theoretical and analytical understanding of the economic, political, social and institutional factors contributing to food crisis. In this sense, world food system brings a structural perspective to the understanding of agriculture and food system's role in the crisis generation across time and space.

Human resources in terms of labour, education, technical know-how, skill generation and agricultural research and development are required to sustain the world food system. The political economy of GFC causation and prevention involves institutions and organisations, but it depends, in addition, on perceptions and understandings that accompany the exercise of power and authority. Food's central role is in social reproduction, and therefore in reproducing changing forms and relations of power. Global agriculture and food have played a strategic role in creating the construction of the world capitalist economy. Contradictory relations within food regimes produce crisis, transformation, and transition to successor regimes. Food regime analysis underlines agriculture's foundational role in political economy and ecology. Food regime analysis brings a structured perspective to the understanding of agriculture and food's role in capital accumulation across time and space. The identification of factors and forces is based on the principle of interactions and holism. Since individual food security and welfare is contained in collective food security and welfare, there is a linkage and interdependence between individualism and collectivism at various levels. Moreover, the factors contributing to the global food crisis are complex, e.g., denial of food access, food availability and exorbitant food prices jointly and singly contribute to chronic hunger, malnutrition, and starvation (Chopra, 2011). Thus, these factors constitute various causal pathways leading to global food crisis.

Conceptualising Global Agricultural and Food System

On complexity level ordering basis of a system, the conceptualisation of global agricultural and food system (GAFS) is both easy and complex. In simple terms, food system is used with reference to agriculture, food, health, nutrition, and community's socio-economic development. At a lower level of complexity, a food system simply includes a range of basic activities, processes and infrastructure involved in feeding population at household and local levels. However, the structure of contemporary agriculture and food system is being reshaped over a period of time with a range of newly emerging features and forces. It simultaneously operates at various levels ranging from local to global and in a complex, dynamic and open environment with multiple political, socio-economic, financial, geographical, ecological, institutional, cultural and environmental determinants. Therefore, at a higher complexity level, the world food system is much more comprehensive as it operates within multi-disciplinary contexts and involves interactions among different driving forces, activities, processes, outputs, outcomes and impacts at various levels that are unquestionably complex. It includes much wider range of activities such as growing, harvesting, processing, packaging, transporting, marketing, consuming, and utilising food and food-related items in various sizes, shapes and variety. The nature and intensity of these forces, interactions, activities and processes have been undergoing rapid changes due to growth in bio-fuels, food miles enhancing the costs of food, the juxtaposition of relationships of 'overconsumption' and 'under-consumption' of food, food regime of capital, biotechnology as the central technology for capitalist agriculture, accelerating urbanization resulting in much more complex food handling and distribution systems, globalization of the food system through international trade, new technologies which are coming on stream and dispersing rapidly across production areas, agricultural trade reforms, transformation from manufacturer-dominated supply chain to supermarkets own brands, the marked intensification of food production, the tremendous growth of processing and packaging of food products, corporate concentration in retailing and distribution, and the rising influence of large numbers of urban consumers.

Keeping this in view, in simple terms, GAFS refers to a set or chain of activities ranging from agricultural production to food consumption (from farm to plate). A broader definition of GAFS must include driving forces, their interactions, activities and processes along with their resulting outputs, outcomes and impact. It operates within and is influenced by social, political, economic and environmental contexts. The GAFS can be holistically conceptualized as a set of components forming an integrated whole incorporating *forces* bringing changes, *interactions* among critical food factors, *activities* related to sectors of food production, processing, distribution and consumption, *processes* producing control over market and integration and *outcomes* and *impact* of activities for food security, social welfare and sustainable development at individual, households, communities, national, regional and global levels. Thus, a GAFS is an integrated, complex, diverse and unpredictable network of interdependent and interwoven components or elements that work together to feed the growing world population. It constitutes the global food production, markets, food policies, food foreign aid and public sector regulations with regards to various aspects of food security and social welfare. In GAFS the functioning and behaviour of the components is important rather than the elements in themselves. Concisely stated, it includes the all inputs needed (including infrastructure) and outputs generated at each stage of food production, processing, distribution, consumption and utilisation.

Objectives of Global Agricultural and Food System

The central aim of GAFS is largely to satisfy the aim of producing sufficient good quality nutritious food to feed the world's growing population. However, the main objectives of GAFS include: (a) to produce sufficient food to feed the global population, i.e., greater enhanced food security; (b) to attain equitable distribution of food at various levels; (c) to achieve economic growth through agricultural and food system, i.e., act as an engine of development; (d) to attain greater eco-efficiency; (e) to attain food quality and safety standards; (f) to arrive at sustainable agriculture; (g) to increase in the efficiency and productivity of food systems in reducing the prevalence of hunger and improving malnutrition; and (h) to contribute in managing diet related diseases such as obesity caused by the consumption and utilisation of excessive food energy intake from energy-dense foods such as those high in fat and sugars.

Prerequisites of a Sustainable Global Agricultural and Food System

The main prerequisites of sustainable GAFS to ensure that every human being has access to adequate food are: (a) increase in investment agriculture sector in developing countries through a combination of higher public investment and better incentives for farmers and the private sector to invest their own resources; (b) meet growing and diverse food needs of the world; (c) greater priority to agricultural research and development; (d) preserve and regenerate soil, water and biological resources upon which production depends, and avoid adverse impacts on the environment; (e) give a rational rate of return to small and medium farmers to sustain families, infrastructure, and communities in rural sector; (f) guarantee a realistic rate of return to public and private providers of farm inputs, information, services and technologies; (g) increase efficiency, productivity and yields to meet the growth in diverse food demand; (h) stick on to social norms and opportunities in terms of transparency, correct labeling, fairness and equity, regulations, fair trading, food safety, and ethical treatment of workers, animals and other creatures sharing agricultural landscapes; and (i) effective functioning of global markets.

Typology of Global Agricultural and Food Systems

On the basis of farm-to-plate food model, there are either *conventional* or *alternative* GAFSs. The conventional GAFSs were the oldest food systems based on economic models such as vertical integration, economic specialization, and global trade, operated on the economies of scale with an aim to maximise efficiency in order to reduce consumer costs and increase overall production. The development of conventional GAFS can be traced back to the origins of agriculture and production of surplus food that contributed to the development of ancient civilisations in settled areas. GAFS further enlarged with the growth in the system of international trade of foodstuff such as salt, spices, fish, grains, etc. in East Asia, North America, South America, and Sub-Saharan Africa. With the developments of significant events in the history timeline, new foods were introduced in the world and food system began to intermingle on a global scale. After

A Theoretical Model of Global Agricultural and Food System

World War II, the advent of industrialised agriculture, Green Revolution and development of more robust global trade mechanisms, new models of food production, presentation, delivery, consumption and disposal emerged[iv].

The alternative food systems include *local food systems, organic food systems, cooperative food systems* and *fair trade in global food system. Local food systems* (LFS) are direct networks of food production and consumption that are geographically and economically accessible. In contrast with industrial food systems, LFS operate as face-to-face relationships between the farmers and consumers with stronger sense of trust and social connectedness, reduced transportation, environmental beneficial and more direct marketing. However, this system can lead to narrow inward-looking attitudes and elitist food culture. Examples of local food systems are farmers markets, farm to school programs, community-supported agriculture and garden sharing that have been associated with the 100 mile diet, low carbon diet, food sovereignty movement and slow food movement. *Organic food systems* (OFS) are based on organic produce without the chemical pesticides and fertilizers of industrial food systems and livestock is reared without the use of antibiotics or growth hormones. So, there is a reduced dependence on chemical inputs and an increased transparency and information for consumers to identify organic food. Organic agriculture is promoted for the ecological benefits of reduced chemical application, the health benefits of lower chemical consumption, the economic benefits that accrue to farmers through a price premium, and the social benefits of increased transparency in the food system.

Cooperatives in food systems exist both at the consumer end of food consumption and the farmer end of food production. Consumer cooperatives are socially owned where members buy a share in the food stores like cooperative grocery stores. They do not work for profit. Farming cooperatives refer to arrangements where farmers pool resources either to cultivate their crops or get their crops to market. Recently many new cooperatives like community-supported agriculture and garden sharing have emerged. The benefits of cooperatives are largely in the sharing of risk and responsibilities among all the members. However, in this food system a reduced competition can reduce efficiency. *Fair trade in global food system* has emerged to achieve a greater balance between the price and cost of food. It is a direct trading system whereby producers have greater control over the conditions of trade and a fair and just return for their work, decent working environment and living conditions.

Salient Features of Global Agricultural and Food System

The emerging GAFS is an open system that interacts with its environment. Economic and technological changes occurring in agriculture sector are contributing to the contemporary global food system faster and more profound than many realize. This emerging global system offers great promise to enhance food security, stimulate economic development, increase the reliability, efficiency and environmental soundness of global agriculture, and meet new demands for food quality—if it develops in an open, market-based manner. The resulting increase in demand and in rising expectations cannot be met by domestic production alone in most countries, especially with mounting constraints on available land and water resources and intensifying demands for environmental protection. The old, commodity-based thinking about farming has gradually been replaced by the emerging GAFS wherein the focus has shifted to the affordable food supply, human well-being, food security, food quality and safety and environmental efficiency. This emerging new paradigm for the food and agricultural system has been built on expanded two-way trade flows anchored in comparative advantage. This GAFS has its own contributions, perils and pitfalls. The prevailing food system is global in scope, horizontally and vertically integrated, multi-food product system, and open commerce. Globalisation, trade liberalisation, socio-ecological issues, environmental concerns, demands for global food security, global distribution and branding strategies, emerging global fast-food chains and supermarkets and technological changes occurring in agriculture are creating a new corporate global food system faster.

Table 4.1 makes a comparative analysis of different food systems. It highlights twenty two different features of the fast emerging new paradigm of GAFS such as neo-liberal deregulation and market liberation, eco-efficiency and environmental consciousness; food quality and safety revolution; greater integration of agricultural with manufacturing and service industries; mass consumerism; rapid growth of corporate ownership resulting in concentration and integration in the food system; systemic risks to cope with customer satisfaction, food safety and standards and quality; diverse

A Theoretical Model of Global Agricultural and Food System

global food demand requirements; increased consolidation and vertical coordination along the supply chain between producers and processors highly complex global food supply chain management; consumers demand for information on food quality and nutrition based on a scientific foundation of safety standards; co-existence of public sector intervention and collective action, emerging global food market failures and promise to enhance food security along with alleviating rural poverty, hunger and malnutrition. Agriculture has a number of features that distinguish it from other productive sectors. Among other things, it is mainly a private activity implemented locally mostly by households, but it has also many dimensions of collective action, it is deeply affected by global forces and depends greatly on public interventions for its structure, its support and its development (Thompson et al., 2007). This broader conceptualisation of agriculture suggests that the GAFS is a dynamic system of interactions in complex, diverse, risk-prone environments and explores how agriculture-food pathways can become more resilient and robust in a turbulent age. However, a vulnerable global agriculture and food system has inherent problems that are multiple, often non-linear in nature, cross-scale in time and space and dynamic in character (Ericksen, 2006). Therefore, even small disturbances in such a system can lead to, through various pathways, dire consequences for the poor and most vulnerable people of the world.

This paradigm would replace commodity-specific, nation-based, mercantilist trade concepts with a highly integrated, global food system built on expanded two-way trade flows anchored in comparative advantage e.g. the rise of 'non-traditional exports' of fruits and vegetables from the global South, and shaping subsequent research on various commodities such as shrimp, poultry, canned seafood, canned pineapple and fresh fruit from Thailand (Goss and Burch, 2001), green beans, baby carrots and corn, and snow-peas from Kenya (Dolan and Humphrey, 2000), corporate tomatoes from Mexico (Barndt, 2008), and Pritchard and Burch's (2003) global analysis of different sources and forms of tomato production. In other words, the emergence of a global food system opens up new ways of looking at agriculture's old issues. The old, commodity-based thinking about farming ought to be replaced by a focus on what is involved in meeting human nutritional requirements. The national boundaries of agricultural systems can dissolve into a food system without borders. And the old, mercantilist idea that exports are good and imports are bad should be replaced by a systemic approach to production and distribution that emphasizes the gains from two-way food trade flows. A new regime seems to be emerging not from attempts to restore elements of the past, but from a range of cross-cutting alliances and issues linking food and agriculture to new issues. These include quality, safety, biological and cultural diversity, intellectual property, animal welfare, environmental pollution, energy use, and gender and racial inequalities. The most important of these fall under the broad category of environment.

Table 4.1:   *A Comparative Analysis of Global Agricultural and Food Systems*

Global Agricultural and Food System Features	1st Global Agricultural and Food System	2nd Global Agricultural and Food System	Present Global Agricultural and Food System
Approximate commencement period	1870-1940s	1950s-1970s	From 1980s to present
Main driver or decision maker	Nation (especially settler) states, and farmers	Processing company	Retailers
Mode of regulation	State control	Managed Keynesianism	Neo-liberal deregulation and market liberation
Output	Basic foodstuffs for home preparation (food for self-sufficiency)	Basic and processed foodstuffs for home preparation and 'out of-home' dining	Basic, processed and manufactured foodstuffs for home preparation; convenience and 'flexi-eating' (Mass consumerism)
Food consumption	Basic staples (un-branded and/or undifferentiated products)	Branded unprocessed products	Processed food with a brand name, supermarket own brands, generic labels; more animal products
Food production system	Seasonal farming, diverse, small farms and varied productivity	Continuous diverse, small farms production with emphasis on high productivity via Green Revolution	Coexistence of flexible batch production (marketed on price, novelty, retail loyalty, convenience) and few crops predominate; intensive, high inputs and bio-fuels initiatives

Continue...

A Theoretical Model of Global Agricultural and Food System

Consumers	Have minimal influence on quality and presentation of marketed products	Accept durable foods as desirable	Are increasingly discerning about food quality, food safety and food price volatility
Environmental concern	Soil degradation, land clearing, and pests	Environmental degradation, droughts, floods and effects of extensive farming	Environmental spillovers, nutrient loading, chemical runoff, water demand, greenhouse gas emissions
Role of the State	Encouragement for family farming	Support for productivist agriculture and food manufacturing	Encourage global free trade and private regulation by agriculture-food firms
Underlying dynamics	Availability of products, application of technologies	Availability and price of products, technological dominance	'Greening' of consumers, risk society
Market power concentration	Not much concentration of market power	Controlled by local middle-men (food grain traders)	Global food chains have control over market power (Rapid growth of corporate ownership resulting in concentration and integration in the food system)
Food quality and safety standards	No emphasis on food quality and safety standards	Some emphasis on food quality and safety standards	Greater emphasis on food total quality management
The role of speculation	No role played by speculation	Little role played by speculation	Greater role of speculation in food markets
Principal employment in food sector	In traditional agriculture	In food production	In food processing, packaging, transporting and retailing
Supply chain	Short and local	Medium and regional	Long and global 'food miles and nodes' (triumph of globalisation, global market integration and free market)
Typical farms	Traditional large family based large farms	Nuclear family based small to medium farms	Large industrial farms for global production

Continue...

Governments/states involvements in food governance	The governments played role in food policy of human survival	States emphasis on food production (Green Revolution), food technology and innovation	States continue to play a considerable role in regulating and support-ing agriculture through mechanisms such as food stocks, supply manage-ment, and subsidies in global, national, and local food systems
Commercial inter-ests and agribusiness	Very low commercial interests in farming and agribusiness	Low to medium level commercial interests in agribusiness	Powerful commercial interests on global scene, profit-based agriculture and protection of intel-lectual property rights on seeds and other inputs
International financial institutions (IFIs) such as World Bank, IMF, etc.	No involvement of IFIs in global gover-nance on food	Some involvement of IFIs in global food governance	Dominance of IFIs in the global governance of food
Global governance for world food security	Emergence of a new multilateral architec-ture the establishment of the Food and Agri-culture Organization (FAO) in 1944	Food governance crumbles in the face of a global food crisis during 1970s	Proliferation of global institutions (CGIAR, WTO, IPCFS etc.), domi-nance of G8/G20, failure of WFC and institutional failures of IFAD, FAO, CGIAR etc. led to call for a new global food governance
Emergence of new alternatives and principles	No emergence of alternatives	Emergence and growth in neolib-eral and productionist paradigm (NPP)	Emergence of alterna-tives to NPP (rural social movements, civil society forums, regional peas-ants organisations, etc.) and principles of right to food, food sovereignty and agro-ecology
Health concerns	Chronic undernutrition	Undernutrition	Co-existence of obesity and undernutrition
Main food shocks sources	Droughts, floods and food production shocks	Food prices, dis-tribution and trade problems	Prices, high costs and household income shocks lead to food poverty and hardships

Sources: http://www.ijsaf.org/archive/13/1/burch_lawrence.pdf; Maxwell and Slater (2003); Heffernan and Hendrickson (2006); Ericksen (2007); McKeon (2011).

Mechanism of Global Agricultural and Food System

The working of the GAFS involves a whole range of questions such as (a) Inputs – How expensive, extensive and widespread are the forms of agricultural inputs innovations including technology that are changing the GAFS? Is there a 2nd Green Revolution underway? (b) Throughputs – What are the various institutions through which food is produced? Is it peasant farming, family farming, large scale corporate farming and food processing? (c) Outputs – what are the trends in productivity (output per hectare, output per unit of inputs, output per labour day and so on) in agriculture? Does growth in food supply match growth in human population (macro-stability)? (d) Outcomes – What are medium terms outcomes of GAFS? Are we achieving food security? (e) Impact – How do rural conditions and quality of life change as a result of emerging changes in the GAFS (socio-economic impacts)? How is GAFS affecting the ecological security and environmental sustainability and vice-versa? How is GAFS affecting macroeconomic development and opportunity? (f) Institutions and agreements – What are the affects of international trade institutions and free-trade agreements (WTO, NAFTA) on grain production, food prices, incomes to stakeholders, and future of corporations and food commodities markets?

By exploring and synthesising the widespread and incongruent empirical literature on world food system, food security, hunger and malnutrition and sustainable agriculture development, the present section brings out the multiple interactions of various forces within and outside GAFS, identifies key processes and determinants and evaluates the major societal outcomes affected by these interactions: food security, poverty, hunger and malnutrition, social welfare (quality of life) and sustainable agriculture in a given place or time (Asian Development Bank, 2008). The fundamental research question is how a change in driving forces will interact with the GAFS, and what impact it will have on outcomes. By adopting a holistic approach to understanding the mechanism of global agriculture and food system interactions, the present work proposes a broad framework for world food systems, which includes feedbacks and interactions among driving forces and considers ultimate multiple outcomes (See Figure 4.1). The framework in the Figure 4.1 subsumes driving forces and their interactions, activities, actors and critical processes involved in the GAFS and the output influencing the normative and may be conflicting goals of food security, social welfare and sustainable development outcomes at a point or space of time. It is built on the idea that within open complex systems like GAFS, one can identify the key forces, processes and determinants that influence the outcomes. It uses the idea behind adaptive management approach[v] that an appropriate conceptual framework will lead to better decisions in the face of uncertainty and unpredictable outcomes. The framework is based on the assumption that the GAFSs are managed for the welfare and benefits of individuals. How well the GAFS will fulfill the objective of food security is open to debate and contestable. This objective may not be achieved due to existence of multiple objectives, agricultural markets failures, government failures and other institutional failures, etc.

Figure 4.1 reveals the mechanism of GAFS wherein land, human, materials and financial resources and activities enter as inputs into the system and thereafter raw food is processed and transformed into outputs in terms of products and services as an immediate short term effect. The differences between the outputs, outcomes, impact of GAFS are significant and important. Therefore, it is important to understand these differences since they can help the policy makers to come up with other ways to achieve the same results and have more flexibility in solving the global food problems. The output is what the global food system actually delivers immediately. Outcomes are what the individuals gain from the output in short to medium term. Impact is the results that are the medium-term to long-term consequences of delivering outputs. The short to medium term achievements are the outcomes of the system in terms of food security (food availability, accessibility, acceptability, adequacy and agency). The long term overall impact of the interactions of forces, activities and outcomes are on social welfare in terms of quality of life, stability and equality, sustainable development in terms of economic development, human development, and social development and ecological/environmental security in terms of ecosystem services, access and availability of natural resources and ecosystem stocks and flows (Anderson, 1995). However, a brief description of the forces, activities, outputs and outcomes of framework follows:

Figure 4.2 reveals the above discussed dynamics of the GAFS with multiple influencing factors. The framework exhibits the multiple

A Theoretical Model of Global Agricultural and Food System

Figure 4.1: **The Mechanism of Global Agricultural and Food System**

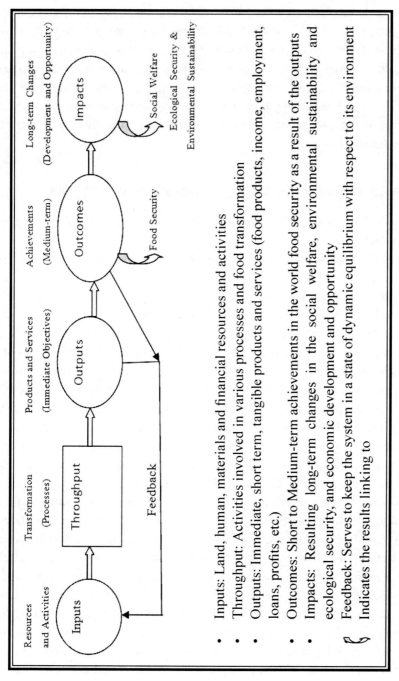

- Inputs: Land, human, materials and financial resources and activities
- Throughput: Activities involved in various processes and food transformation
- Outputs: Immediate, short term, tangible products and services (food products, income, employment, loans, profits, etc.)
- Outcomes: Short to Medium-term achievements in the world food security as a result of the outputs
- Impacts: Resulting long-term changes in the social welfare, environmental sustainability and ecological security, and economic development and opportunity
- Feedback: Serves to keep the system in a state of dynamic equilibrium with respect to its environment
- Indicates the results linking to

Source: Own Construction

cross-scale interactions among driving forces and actors in different arenas and at different levels namely local, regional, national and global. It shows the broadly defined GAFS and evaluates the resultant activities, immediate outputs of system in terms of products, services, employment and financial results (income, profits, etc.), major food related outcomes in terms of food security and finally long-term major societal impacts in terms of social welfare, development and sustainability and ecological security affected by these interactions.

Driving Forces of Global Agricultural and Food System

The typology of GAFS key driving forces that bring changes in GAFS are discussed as follows:

(a) Environmental, Geo-Ecological and Natural Forces: These are the forces of nature. There is a two-way interaction between the forces of nature and GAFS. Environmental forces such as water availability and quality, increasing land degradation and pollution, tropical storms and hurricans such as Katrina and Sandy, nutrient availability and cycling, the loss of biodiversity, sea currents and salinity and sea level affect agriculture unfavourably (Defries et al., 2005). On the other hand, there are environmental impacts of agriculture in terms of the theory of externalities or environmental spillovers in terms of variety of externalities such as greenhouse gas (GHG) emissions leading to continued excessive atmospheric warming and climate destabilization, pest externalities, air and atmosphere externalities, spatial externalities, trade and regulation externalities and so on (Meade, 1952; Coase, 1960). Broadly the externalities are spillovers—effects outside of commercially measurable parts of economic activities. Externalities are defined as situations where actions of agricultural business affect the state of the environment, the societal and spatial structures of a region or country, and the welfare of people who are external to those decisions. This includes all agents in the business of cultivating the soil, producing crops and raising livestock. Externalities identify either positive (recreational areas, pleasant landscape, sustainable societal and spatial structures), negative (soil eroded, water polluted, etc.) or conflicting aspects (multiple-use of water, space, biodiversity, etc.). Externalities of agriculture are numerous[vi] as reported in international literature but the purpose of the study we shall focus on negative

A Theoretical Model of Global Agricultural and Food System

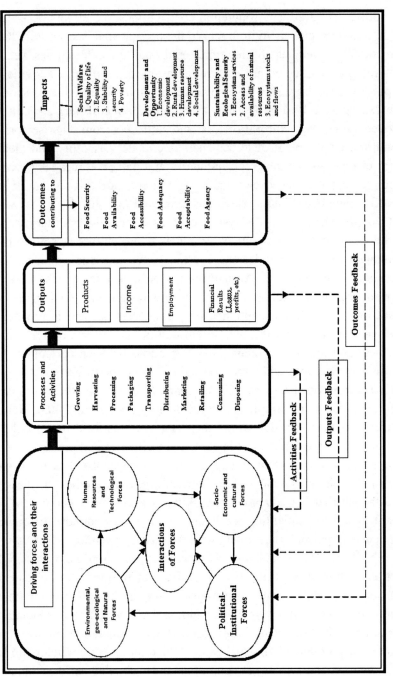

Figure 4.2: **Dynamics of Global Agriculture and Food System**   **External Influences Factors**

Source: Own Construction

externalities as purely environmental contributions, the effects of agriculture activities on global environment in the present analysis. Tisdell (2005) has mentioned examples of three types of agricultural externalities, i.e., agricultural externalities on agriculture (a variety of productive activities in one part of agriculture can have negative externalities on other parts, e.g., chemicals sprayed by a farmer may affect other framers land); agricultural spillovers on non-agricultural sectors; and spillovers from other sectors on agriculture. Geo-ecological forces such as climate variability and means, habitat change, extinctions, and humanity and natural forces such as tornadoes, volcanoes, solar cycles, tsunami, drought, earthquakes, hurricanes etc., affect the GAFS (Blum, 2005; de Gorter and Just, 2010).

Thus, the changes in this system such as increasing land degradation and the loss of biodiversity and externalities of agriculture as spillovers of greenhouse gas (GHG) emissions and air, water and land pollution have tremendous affect on GFC. Agriculture not only includes goods (food and fibre) and services ("agri-tourism") that are bought and sold in market transactions (with few exceptions), but its conceptual size is broadened by considering the natural inputs to agriculture and effects of agriculture on society and the environment. The interactions between agriculture and environment are captured by the externalities of agriculture.

(b) Human Resources and Technological Forces: Another set of driving forces are human resources and technology (Fan et al., 2003). Human resources are narrowly defined as the manpower involved in agriculture. What matters is the capability of people to be effective and productive economic agents, in short, human capital (literacy, agricultural skills, health, nutrition). In the particular case of agriculture, most studies on the subject establish that the education and skills of agricultural people are significant factors in explaining the inter-farm and inter-country differences in agricultural performance, along with the more conventional factors such as availabilities of land and water resources, inputs, credit, etc. Basic education can improve significantly the efficacy of training and agricultural extension work which in turn affect agricultural production through: (a) enhancing the productivity of inputs, including that of labour; (b) reducing the costs of acquiring and using information about production technology that can increase productive efficiency; and (c) facilitating entrepreneurship and responses to changing market conditions and technological developments

A Theoretical Model of Global Agricultural and Food System

(Schultz, 1988). The relationship between education and agricultural development cuts both ways and the two are mutually reinforcing, with demand for schooling rising as rural incomes increase. Thus, the amount and quality of trained technical and professional manpower in agriculture are critical factors, both in agricultural development and more general human resource development.

However, a broader view on human resources considers trends in demographic profile (population, age, gender or social class), diversity (variations within the population) and skills and qualifications. Technological forces are the influences that developments in technology have on agriculture sector, farmers, consumers and society in general. Agricultural science, technology and innovations (ST&I) also bring changes in the GAFS. Phil Kerstin Cuhls (2006) in her short report to the SCAR Expert Working Group/EU Commission on Science, Technology and Innovation Drivers has grouped the agricultural technologies as „major driving forces" and 'minor and single driving forces' for agriculture. The 'major driving forces' play large in agriculture and include information and communication technologies, low cost infrastructures a mix of competing infrastructures, technologies and operators source (imaging, wireless transmission, software and hardware for precision farming), radio frequency identification[vii], simulations for weather forecasts[viii], nanotechnology[ix] to design food by shaping molecules and atoms, nanoscale biotech and nanobio-info will have big impacts on the food and food-processing industries (Amato and Dagostino, 2011), biosensors in agriculture for smell, taste but also for bio-chemical detection or to detect single molecules have been developed, new fertilizers, herbicides and pesticide, biotechnology[x], genetics[xi], functional food[xii] technology, 2nd, 3rd generation transgene plants including molecular farming[xiii] and green gene technology, drugs[xiv] for safety, energy, bio-fuels, photovoltaics (energy generation), application of brain research systems in agriculture, education, better system to memorise, human motivation, ecological systems research, artificial meat (The Economist, 2012) and internet of things[xv].

The 'minor and single driving force' include materials such as biolubricants, new wood products, functional packaging, "green" fibres, oils from plants, biomaterials, etc; production such as biocatalysts, robust production microorganisms and bioreactors; drugs, medicines, etc. such as metabolomics, metabonomics, antibodies from plants, toxicogenomics, hormone therapy, xenotransplantation, and stem cell transplantation; crops such as toxicoproteomics, biomass for energy and biological crop protection; animals technology such as biological clock research and communication technology between human beings and livestock; climate, water, environment technology such as algae's mechanisms of CO_2 absorption and concentration, assessing the impacts of global climate and environmental change, water saving in agriculture, efficient revegetation in deserts and water treatment technologies; soft sciences such as economics, business administration, management, humanities, philosophy, cultural studies, etc. have been playing their role in shaping the future of agriculture.

(c) Socio-economic and Cultural Forces: Socio-economic and cultural forces are influences in the society with the capability to cause change. The influence of social, cultural, and economic forces such as societal change, women's workload, control over economic resources, change in institutions, resource accessibility, demand and supply of agricultural goods, economic conditions, social class, poverty, socio-cultural beliefs, social-economic values, and attitudes, customs, interest rates, level of inflation and employment level per capita and long-term prospects for the economy Gross Domestic Product (GDP) per capita, and so on, affect GAFS and can also have a significant influence on family nutritional well-being in terms of food choice and food-sharing behaviour within the family. In many societies some foods are highly priced than others and no meal is considered complete without them. Cultural food beliefs and taboos are often related to foods of animal origin and frequently apply to women and young children. Culture can be a strong behavioural determinant and can dictate preference or avoidance of certain foods, especially during illness and pregnancy. While some cultural beliefs and habits are nutritionally harmful, others which are beneficial should be promoted through positive messages to raise household members' and especially women's knowledge and awareness of the benefits of a nutritious diet using locally available foods.

(d) Political and Institutional Forces: The frame of GAFS is also shaped by the government interventions and institutional and policy factors. Some of the factors play their role within the system and others are external constraints within which the players of the global markets follow their strategies as to production, retailing, price setting and consumption choices (Praussello, 2011). Political forces include the political parties, personalities,

pressure groups that strongly influence the economic and political stability of a country through their actions and pronouncements. Institutional forces are crises or changes in national institutions or systems such as national economic, fiscal, or political crises. Political arena has a huge influence on agriculture and food system and spending power of consumers and farmers. How stable is the political environment? Will government policy influence laws that regulate or tax your business? What is the government's position on marketing ethics? What is the government's policy on the economy? Is the government involved in trading agreements such as EU, NAFTA, ASEAN, or others?

Processes and Activities of Global Agricultural and Food System

The main steps or activities in the GAFS are: growing, harvesting, storing, transporting, changing (processing), packaging, marketing, retailing, preparing, consuming and disposing. The activities involved in the agricultural and food system are grouped into following five categories:

(a) Growing and Harvesting: The cultivation of animals, plants, fungi and other life forms for foods, fibers, bio-fuels and raw materials used to sustain life involves all those human activities that are concerned with growing and harvesting these products. Foods include cereals, vegetables, fruits, milk, and meat. Fibers include cotton, wool, hemp, silk and flax. Raw materials include lumber, bamboo, and other useful materials produced by plants, such as resins. Bio-fuels include methane from biomass, ethanol, and biodiesel. Cut flowers, nursery plants, tropical fish and birds for the pet trade are some of the ornamental products. Thus, this category includes the whole range of activities from the process of obtaining inputs such as land, labour and capital, breeding animals (intensive poultry and pig farming, sheep husbandry), planting crops or obtaining young animal stock, (aquaculture, dairy farming, grazing, hydroponics, livestock, orchards), caring for the growing food material and then harvesting or slaughtering it. These activities are determined by a variety of factors ranging from available resources and constraints, geography and different climates, cultures, technologies to government policy intended to protect or promote production, economic, social and political pressure, land tenure, input prices, agricultural technology

and the philosophy and culture of the farmer.

(b) Transporting and Distributing: Transporting food includes all activities involved in moving the food from one location to another. It involves infrastructure, vehicles, and operations. The modes of transport include road, water, rail, cable, pipeline or air. The initial transportation may be human-powered (the farmer or his labourer), carrying the produce themselves or using animal-drawn carts. Alternatively, traders may send agents around to farmers to collect produce for assembly in one central area. Transport costs will vary according to the distance between farmer and market, but they will also depend on the quality of the roads. The transportation of finished and processed food to the cities involves a complex spatial interaction purported at overcoming space which is shaped by both human and physical constraints such as distance, political boundaries, time and topographies. The food distribution system involves activities and elements such as wholesale, intra-urban linkages, (e.g., packaging, transport, market information and credit), formal-informal and traditional-modern retailing (markets, shops and supermarkets), street food, restaurants and household food delivery. The distribution of food is heavily influenced by transportation infrastructure, trade regulations, government transfer programs, and storage requirements. The dynamism of food transport and distribution system involves activities that adapt to changing conditions and is important to food security problems stemming from changes in internal as well as external factors.

(c) Processing and Packaging: Food processing means changing the food's form, substance and presentation that may be once or several times. It is a set of methods and techniques used to transform the raw material materials (cereals, vegetables, fruits, animals) into food for consumption by humans or animals (e.g., processed dog or cat food). Given the market for processed foods, suitable technology, infrastructure facilities, food processing activities, substantially different than food production, include raw materials, ingredients and safe water procurement, refining, distillation, and centrifugation; granulating, cooking and drying; blending, mixing, and homogenisation; pasteurisation and sterilisation; pumping and heating; cooling and refrigeration; bulk storage, packaging, bottling or canning; and finished products. For example, wheat undergoes extensive processing and packaging before it becomes bread. Right from crude processing of prehistoric

ages[xvi] to the 21st century, food processing has progressed significantly due to many developments such as spray drying, juice concentrates, freeze drying, artificial sweeteners, colouring agents and preservations such as sodium benzoate. Many products such as dried instant soups, reconstituted fruits and juices, and self cooking meals such as meal ready to eat (MRE) food ration were developed.

Apart from its many disadvantages such as loss of nutritional density (loss of vitamin C in processing), health risks of food additives, and risk of food contamination, food processing has many advantages such as cheap mass production than individual home cooked food, time saving in cooking, toxin removal, preservation, easing marketing and distribution tasks, alleviating food shortages, improving the overall nutrition of populations and increasing food consistency. In also increases seasonal availability of diverse foods, enables transportation of delicate perishable foods across long distances and makes many kinds of foods safe to eat by de-activating spoilage and pathogenic micro-organisms. Food packaging and labeling include all range of activities to protect, to preserve, to easily transport and to make food look attractive. A range of materials (plastics, modified-atmosphere packaging, Paper, card, metal and glass) can be used for packaging, some of which are environmentally friendly. The EU Food Labeling Regulations of 1996 requires certain information by law on all pre-packed foods for the consumers. Both food processing and packaging activities add economic value to raw food by altering its appearance, storage life, nutritional value, and contents.

(d) Marketing and Retailing: Food marketing and retailing involve a range of human activities directed at understanding and identifying customer's food requirements and needs in order to satisfy them and keep the customers. Retailing is the direct sale of food to ultimate consumer, i.e., the transfer of food from the producer or seller to the consumer or buyer and is influenced by activities such as advertising, location, market organisation, shipping to customers, storing and selling. Food marketing involves marketing audit (market analysis, market segmentation and marketing strategy), market research (quantitative analysis, qualitative analysis and consumer tests), and marketing mix (4Ps, i.e., product, price, place and promotion). The food transfer mechanism takes place in many ways such as counter service, delivery (ordering by phone, on internet, newspaper, etc), door-to-door,

and self-service. Marketing and retailing of food is determined by various factors such as government restrictions, unfavourable taxation structure, absence of developed market chain, high competition, and lack of management and educated and trained staff.

(e) Consuming and Disposing: Consuming and disposing food is connected with the utilization of food. For humans and animals, consuming and disposing food is an activity of daily living. It involves a range of activities right from deciding what to select, preparing daily food menu, cooking, eating and digesting food for nutritional needs, particularly for energy and growth. After consuming the food, all packaging need to be disposed of or recycled. Thus, we all participate in the food system each day by eating. Consuming food is determined by factors such as prices, income levels, physiological need, cultural traditions or preferences, social values, education and health status. In the global food system different people in most of the countries are having diverse choice in food to eat via advertisement, globalised food supply chain, and the availability of variety of food. Individuals across different cultures have been more concerned with the issue of healthy eating and diets. Various techniques such as dieting, fasting, special low fat diets, vegetarianism have been encouraged in many societies either as a part of culture or for the pursuit for better health. Hunger triggers the need for eating. However, there are numerous physical, cultural and psychological conditions (emotional eating, depression, food allergies, bulimia, anorexia nervosa, pituitary gland malfunction, other health problems, and eating disorders) that can affect appetite and disturb eating patterns. A serious lack of nutritious food can cause various illnesses eventually leading to starvation or even famine.

Outputs of Global Agricultural and Food System

The outputs of the processes and activities of GAFS are products, services, employment and financial results in terms of income, loans and profits, involved in feeding billions of people across the globe. Outputs are produced at each step or activity of GAFS. Products (food and raw materials) are the most important contributions of world food system. The *products* of GAFS provide the provision of wage goods and of industrial raw materials to secondary sector and agro-based industries such as textiles, sugar, grain milling, hide processing, etc. People working in agricultural sector and other occupations require food for their sustenance. The dependence of people on GAFS for wage goods will be as strong as ever unless, of course, new scientific innovations also result in the production of perfect synthetic substitutes for food grains. Agriculture constitutes the main source of *employment* of the majority of the world's poor. Through assured access to remunerative markets for agricultural produce through linkages with agro-industries dramatically raises rural incomes, generate millions of on-farm and non-farm employment opportunities, eradication poverty and usher in a prosperity movement throughout rural sector. The GAFS provides livelihood to millions of people and many financial benefits in terms of income to farmers, wages to workers and profits to stakeholders at every step of the process. On negative side, it may leave many small scale framers in debts and loans if the costs go up or harvest is destroyed due to bad weather conditions.

The vulnerability of GAFS results in instability of agriculture in terms of fluctuations in prices, income and output in agriculture sector. The fluctuations in agricultural prices will ultimately result in fluctuations in the income of farmers, standard of living, demand for non-agricultural products and thus adding to the overall instability of the economy. This results in inefficient crop planning by farmers and other problems. The reasons for greater price fluctuations in agriculture lie in the nature of their demand and supply. Both demand and supply for most of agricultural products is relatively less elastic. People's demand for food is inelastic as it is biologically determined.

Outcomes of Global Agricultural and Food System

The outcomes of agricultural and food system are analysed in terms of its contributions to food security. As discussed earlier that food security refers to a situation when food deficit individuals, households, communities, countries, regions, or global economy should be able to have physical and economic access to sufficient, safe and nutritious food to meet their dietary needs and food preferences for an active and healthy life on a year to year basis. It involves: (a) *Food availability*: It has to do with the supply of food. There should be the production of sufficient quantity of quality and variety food for all people at all times. It includes food production, distribution and exchange. (b) *Food accessibility*: It encompasses ensuring all levels physical and economic access to food for all at affordable and relatively stable prices at all times. It addresses the demand for the food. It is influenced by economic factors, physical infrastructure and consumer preferences. Hence food availability, though elemental in ensuring food security, does not guarantee it. Thus, it includes affordability, allocation and preferences. (c) *Food adequacy*: It is about the access to food for households and individuals within them that is nutritious and safe, and produced in environmentally sustainable ways. It is concerned with the notion of *food utilisation*, i.e., nutritional value, social value and food safety. It should ensure an adequate consistent and dependable supply of energy and nutrients through sources that are affordable and socio-culturally acceptable to them at all times. Ultimately food security should translate to an active healthy life for every individual. For this to take place the nutritionally adequate diet should be biologically utilized so that adequate performance is maintained in growth, resistance or recovery from disease, pregnancy, lactation and/or physical work. Hence adequate health and care must be provided in addition to adequate food. (d) *Food acceptability*: It is the access to culturally acceptable food which is produced and obtained in ways that do not compromise people's dignity, self-respect or human rights. There is a role of consumer perception and attitudes. It is regarding the understanding of the factors affecting food choice, acceptance and consumption since these influence all aspects of its activities. (e) *Food agency*: It refers to the policies and processes that enable the achievement of food security. Thus, a nation, region, household is considered as food secure when its occupants do not live in the fear of hunger or starvation. They have availability and access to food supply at affordable prices. A GAFS is said to have deficiencies and failures if it has not managed to solve the challenge of food insecurity (hunger, starvation, obesity and other diet-related health problems).

The methodological and analytical literature on food security has evolved since late 1970s. It first focused on aggregate food production, stocks and supply. During 1980s, the research emphasis shifted on two fronts: first from *availability of food* to *access to food* and second from aggregate/national level to household/individual level (Sen, 1981; Dreze and Sen, 1989). Due to tremendous growth in urban population, more and more people do not grow their own food. This insight elucidates inequality in food distribution and allocation, a crucial determinant of food security, based upon income, political and social power (Ericksen, 2007). During the 21st century a further shift took place from access to food to consumption patterns, preferences and utilisation (absorption) of food that has further broadened the food security research framework. It has been increasing recognized in public health research that the human body food absorption and different nutrients, calories and protein needs are influenced by various factors such as age, health, disease, food quality, diet (fat, sugar, added chemicals and salt contents), poor hygiene, food preferences, physiological condition, and so on. Thus, the phenomenon of food security has taken global perspective with applicability in every country, region and local area where both rich and poor nations, households and consumers are affected the health outcomes of food.

Impact of Global Agricultural and Food System

The long term impact of GAFS can be captured in terms of impact on development of different sectors (the primary sector, the secondary sector, and tertiary sector) and overall global economy, impact on social welfare and impact on ecological security.

(1) Impact on Social Welfare: It refers to the welfare of the entire society. It includes the factors like quality of life, equality, stability and safety, and poverty. The quality of life is used to evaluate the general well-being of individuals and societies. It is not same as standard of living but is more concerned with the quality of life that includes factors such as the quality of the environment (air, soil, and water), level of crime, extent of drug abuse, availability of essential services as well as religious and spiritual aspects of life. The GAFS has an impact on lowering poverty and helping people afford a better quality of life. It also affects the equality of individuals in the society. The economic and social equality can move in any direction, i.e., it can increase or reduce the equality. If the rich farmers, food traders and supermarkets get more income and resources out of the food system, there is an adverse impact of equality and vice versa. The long term impact of GAFS can also impact stability, safety and poverty levels in a society.

(2) Impact on Development and Opportunity: The long term impact of GAFS can be grouped into economic development, rural development,

social development and human resource development. According to Simon Kuznets, agriculture and food system makes three types of contributions to the overall growth of an economy: (a) the factor contribution, (b) the product contribution, and (c) the market contribution. The GAFS provides valuable resources (transfer of capital and labour) to non-agricultural sectors that are productive in nature and large contributor to the economic growth and hence it is called 'factor contribution of agriculture'. The product contribution of GAFS is in terms of wage goods, raw materials provision to industries, processed food and fast food for people. The GAFS also provides a market to other sectors for its inputs. While helping the development of the other sectors, it also finds the income for its people increasing. This increased income, in turn, leads to an additional demand for the products of other sectors not only for consumption purposes, but also for production. The GAFS also contributes to the development of international trade. The GAFS helps to increase human development when agriculture and food processing and retailing use improved capital intensive technology and thus by employing well educated and well trained people. Among other factors, rural development is achieved by the economic actions and activities of processing of food stuff and raw materials in the GAFS via actions and initiatives taken to improve the standard of living in non-urban neighbourhoods, countryside, and remote villages. Another long term impact of the GAFS is the social development or change in the rural and non-rural societies in nature, social institutions, social behaviours or social relations. It involves the change in the socio-economic structure, for instance a shift away from feudalism and towards capitalism.

(3) Ecological Security and Environmental Sustainability: There is a long-term impact of the GAFS on the sustainability (carrying capacity of natural systems) and ecological security or environmental security that refers to the relationship environmental events (such as environmental asset scarcity, environmental risks or adverse changes, or environment-related tensions or conflicts) and security of individuals, nations, global community and nature. The GAFS also contributes to global environmental change and future trends e.g. increased demand for food with increases in incomes and populations will have consequences for global environmental change processes that encompass changes in the bio-geophysical environment which may be due to natural processes and/or human activities.

Sources of Pressures of GAFS on Global Food Crisis

The GAFS constitutes various factors and forces. GFC is determined by how the GAFS works and behaves. The phenomenon of GFC can be managed by increasing our awareness and perception regarding the theoretical, analytical and empirical understanding of the underlying forces of GAFS. These forces are the sources of various pressures of GAFS towards expansion of production and distribution. These pressures may be the particular reasons for the forms of environmental degradation which these cause and the ecological consequences of this degradation for the continuance of farming itself. Agriculture and food works involve various processes dependent on the biosphere. Considering this, the KCGFC model identifies and takes into consideration the following eight manifest variables:

1. *Environmental, Geo-ecological and Natural Forces*: As mentioned earlier, the GAFS is affected and affects the environmental, natural and ecological system.

2. *Human Capital and Technical Manpower Forces*: Human resources and technological forces bring changes in the GAFS that in turn affects the food security and food crisis.

3. *Socio-economic and Cultural Forces*: A close relationship exists between social systems and agroecosystems. The socio-economic and cultural factors influence the decision making process in rural farming/cropping systems.

4. *Political-Institutional Forces*: The political and institutional forces have their tremendous affect on the GAFS and hence, on food security and world food crisis.

5. *Corporate Global Food System*: Farming is no longer the dominant economic activity in the overall GAFS. The processing and packaging of raw materials into food products and distribution and retail, globalisation of food trade and role and number of supermarkets have increased corporate concentration up and down the food supply chain (vertical integration).

6. *Greater Sectoral Integration*: There has been an outgrowth of large industrial farms for global demand requirements and greater integration of agricultural with manufacturing, international trade and service industries.

7. *Technological Dominance*: The emerging GAFS has witnessed a technological dominance and a transition from techno-corporate food in the global agricultural-food system sectors of agricultural production, food processing and retailing to alternative agriculture-food movements such as organic agriculture, fair-trade and food localization movements.

8. *Systemic Risks*: There are many systemic risks in the GAFS to cope with shocks and stresses of food safety, quality standards, animal welfare and hygiene.

Concluding Remarks

This chapter endeavours to theorize the global agriculture and food as a system by applying systems thinking and complexity perspective. It illustrates GAFS in an integrated mode and a systems approach is used to explore, synthesise and describe not only the component parts, but also the mechanism to unfold the theoretical patterns of interactions among food systems, their components, various driving forces, inputs, activities, outputs, outcomes and impacts. It can be concluded that the origin and perpetuation of food problems lie within the GAFS. It is the behaviour of the GAFS that brings significant changes in food problems and hence, in food crisis at the global scale as well as widespread locally. The above suggested theoretical model of GAFS is an essential framework for unfolding empirically interactions among different food systems such as slow or fast mechanisms, food systems, local, national or global food systems; organic, cooperative, fair trade food systems and so on. Like previous food regimes, the contemporary GAFS is also a specific constellation of governments, global institutions, corporations, collective grassroots organisations, civil society, farmers and individuals that benefit some key actors while marginalising others and likely to strengthen and intensify inequalities between rich and poor eaters. The phenomenon of global food security is indeed a dynamic and complex condition. Over the years it has engorged in depth and scope with the help of a variety of insights from different disciplines and areas of research such as poverty, vulnerability, inequality, agricultural economics, health economics, welfare economics, human development, political economy, and so on.

A Theoretical Model of Global Agricultural and Food System

Notes

---

i. The main causes of French Revolution were economic difficulties, fiscal crisis (debt), and extremely unpopular high taxes compounded by the food scarcity caused by famine during the 1780s. Bread prices rose by 80 per cent in 1788-89 that led to 'bread riots', starvation and hence revolution. Marie Antoinette, the Queen of France during the French Revolution, who said "let them eat cake" when told the peasants were starving because they had no bread. The monarchy was overthrown and her husband Louis XVI was executed by guillotine on the 21st of January and she was beheaded on the 16th October 1793.

ii. Food and bread riots are caused by harvest failures, hoarding, food prices, attacks by pests, inappropriate distribution system, and the like. There is a logical connection among rising prices, hunger and violent civil unrest and if food prices were allowed to rise too high, the situations sometimes end up in wars. In January 2011, food prices were identified as one trigger for Tunisia's unrest as well as for riots across much of northern Africa, including Egypt, a country that depends heavily on Russian grain (See, Fraser and Rimas, 2011).

iii. The first formulation of the concept of 'food regime' was given by Harriet Friedmann (1987).

iv. The impact of conventional food system is to lower food costs and to achieve greater food variety. Agronomic efficiency is driven by the necessity to constantly lower production expenses, and those savings can then be passed on to the consumer. Also, the advent of industrial agriculture and the infrastructure built around conventional food systems has enabled the world population to expand beyond the "Malthusian catastrophe" limitations. However, lowering the production costs can lead to compromising of local, regional, or even global ecosystems through fertilizer runoff, nonpoint source pollution, and greenhouse gas emission. The globalization of food production can result in the loss of traditional food systems in less developed countries, and have negative impacts on the population health, ecosystems, and cultures in those countries.

v. It is a structured, iterative process of optimal decision making in the face of uncertainty, with an aim to reducing uncertainty over time via system monitoring. In this way, decision making simultaneously maximizes one or more resource objectives and, either passively or actively, accrues information needed to improve future management. Adaptive management is a tool which should be used not only to change a system, but also to learn about the system.

vi. Meade (1973) defined externalities as situations where actions of agents affect the production possibilities of the economy and the welfare of people, who are not fully consenting parties in reaching production decisions, as they are in sales and purchases. No compensation is made for welfare losses and gains. In addition, true externalities (which remain uncompensated and are called technological externalities) are distinguished from pecuniary externalities (which are income-related effects that can be captured within the market economy). Other types of externalities are societal and spatial effects as well as purely environmental contributions.

vii. Radio Frequency Identification (RFID) for are active or passive tags on all kinds of products including agriculture that replace common barcodes system and have a huge impact on agriculture and marketing of products.

viii. Simulations for weather forecasts for strong rain, landslides, for earthquakes, volcano eruptions etc. have a growing importance in risk assessment and But simulations can also be used in agriculture directly, e.g. to simulate when crops are ripe and harvests are due. The "virtual plant" as a computer model is another endeavour. This will have a huge impact on the design of plants and the management of farming.

ix. Nanotechnology is an emerging science and, if used to develop novel foods and processes, approval would be required under the 'Novel Foods Regulation' (Regulation (EC) No 258/97) to ensure products are safe. Nanotechnology is the manufacture and use of materials and structures at the nanometre scale (a nanometre is one millionth of a millimetre). Nanotechnology can be defined as the design, characterisation, production and application of structures, devices and systems by controlling shape and size at the nanometre scale. It covers a very wide range of activities, so it is probably more correct to refer to 'nanotechnologies'. Nanotechnology is a topic in nearly every foresight with different assumptions, different aims, applications and time horizons. For agriculture, mainly new materials, packaging, new food ingredients (e.g. for taste or better health), sensors and actuators, and NEMS seem to be of relevance in the time frame until 2020. Also new fertilizers, herbicides and pesticides are discussed if these are not produced in the "classical" chemical way but by manipulating different atoms and molecules, or by a more efficient and safe administration, means pesticides, herbicides and fertilizers are controlled precisely when and where they are released (Kuzma/ VerHage 2006).

x. Biotechnology is and will be the major driver for agriculture, be it in plant breeding, farming or food processing. The general aim of biotechnology is to make use of a biological system (e.g. cells, tissues...) to produce something or degenerate products. It is more than genetic engineering or DNA technology. Biotechnology also plays a role in the health debate. In biotechnology, there is a lot of old culture available (joghurt, beer, cheese, wine...) which is directly linked to agriculture and improved successively.

xi. Genetics will lead to the design of new plants and modified plants (for better harvests, resistance against enemies, drought resistence, salt resistence and so on) in a much faster way than the evolutionary biotechnologies or breeding techniques were able to. This is one of the major drivers for agriculture but will still take time.

xii. Functional food is food or ingredients of food with special functions and an additional value for the consumer, mainly for a higher quality of life and health or a reduced risk of nutrition-based illnesses. The impacts of functional food are caused by (a higher amount of) certain ingredients in food. Also food with reduced potentially harmful parts (e.g. allergens) are called functional food.

xiii. The definition of the 2nd and 3rd generation of transgene plants is not very clear until now. In general, the second generation are those in the "pipeline", means in the industrial development and shortly before the approval. The third generation are those in research and early development. A list of them and their applicability is found in Sauter/Hüsing 2006. These new plants will have an impact on different areas of agriculture, e.g. direct food production, whereas the plant-made pharmaceuticals will have a low impact because they will be the subject of industry more than of agriculture. Plant-made industrials, e.g. oil design, production of enzymes, bio polymers, which all involve the large scale use of plants may be interesting for agriculture and have a certain impact.

xiv.   Drugs will continue to play a large role in agriculture, for plants and for animals. If pharmaceuticals against certain illnesses like BSE, SARs, Avian 'Flu, Foot and Mouth Disease etc. are available that will have no impact on the animal products directly but a huge impact on the safety in agriculture and on food safety, and therefore the whole sector.

xv.   The model of the internet of things means that physical transport is possible like data transfer in the internet. Logistics and management are facilitated when technology for quick and "intelligent" transport, even in different ways are developed.

xvi.   Prehistoric crude processing incorporated slaughtering, fermenting, sun drying, preserving with salt, and various types of cooking (such as roasting, smoking, steaming, and oven baking). Salt-preservation was especially common for foods that constituted warrior and sailors' diets, up until the introduction of canning methods. Evidence for the existence of these methods can be found in the writings of the ancient Greek , Chaldean, Egyptian and Roman civilizations as well as archaeological evidence from Europe, North and South America and Asia.#

Chapter 5   System Dimensional Structure of Global Food Crisis

"How can you frighten a man whose hunger is not only in his own cramped stomach but in the wretched bellies of his children? You can't scare him -- he has known a fear beyond every other".
John Steinbeck in *"The Grape of Wrath"* (1939).

Introduction

The previous chapter developed and analysed a theoretical framework to understand the behaviour and mechanism of GAFS holistically and to discover the sources of pressures on GFC. The GAFS serves as a foundation of system dimensional structure which also involves other various dimensions of the phenomenon of GFC. The present chapter, however, takes a complete view of the theoretical-analytical schema of GFC. It develops and presents the system dimensional structure of GFC. A system dimensional structure is a systematic means to organise the critical food crisis factors into various dimensions. It is designed to provide both the support and mechanism for effective conduct of agricultural and food related activities in the system. It is the study of sets of interacting entities of GFC. It lays bare the various factors and forces subsumed in various dimensions that created circumstances necessary for world food crisis (Abbott, 2009). One of the central controversies of economics is whether prices are controlled by actual demand and supply, or they are affected by other factors that can cause artificial panics and bubbles. The food prices changes also come across this controversy. Considering supply and demand of food products only is committing a fallacy of not being consistent and ignoring other factors in the actual dynamics and incidences of worldwide food crises. Wild swings in food prices and insecurity cannot be explained by normal demand and supply dynamics alone. The weaknesses of demand-supply method stem from the fact that such method addresses different types of food crisis factors independent from each other and limited to food demand and food supply only. Many conceptual characterizations, quantitative analyses and qualitative discussions of the causes of GFC suggest that multiple factors are simultaneously important and involved. In fact, in certain situations one critical food crisis factor may interact with other food crisis factors in a multiplicative way, whilst in others it may interact with other food crisis factors producing reciprocal compensatory and attenuating effects. The present study considers six different dimensions or transmission mechanisms: global agricultural and food system (discussed in the previous chapter), food demand-side forces, food supply-side restrictions, global agricultural market failures, government or public sector interventions and collective actions, and the construct of GFC.

Constructs of Global Food Crisis

The above adumbrated six constructs of the contemporary GFC highlight various influences and causes of GFC. These forces affect both food-surplus and food-deficit countries and contribute to world food crisis in varying magnitudes. After having thrashed out the construct of GFAS in the previous chapter and the five constructs of GFC can be discussed as follows[i]:

Food Demand-Side Forces

Food demand is a crucial dimension of the GAFS. The demand for food crops is biologically determined with low price elasticity of demand whereas demand for fibre crops is more elastic than that of food crops. However, factors such as income, price (own), price (substitutes and complementary food), population, habits, customs, preferences, dietary diversity etc. are responsible for fluctuations in food demand causing instability in agriculture leading to GFC (Geo, 2012). Engel's law states that as income increases, people spend a smaller proportion of their total income on food. Bennett's law states that the richer one becomes, the less he or she spends on starchy staples. Traditionally economists calculate the rate of growth in aggregate demand for food (D) by considering change in rate of population growth (P), income elasticity of demand (n) and rate of growth of per capita income (g), i.e., $D = P + ng$. However, there are many other factors that have affected the recent GFC via affecting the food demand. Apart from population growth, age structure, fertility rates, number of pregnant women, height of population and dependency ratio determine the calorie needs at different ages and demand for food. Global demand for food has been affected by a number of factors such as an increase in crop consumption under bio-fuel initiatives; production or 'bio-fuel rush' (corn-based ethanol or soybeans for biodiesel); large dietary diversification (dietary changes from grain to more diversified diet like meat and dairy products) due to changes in lifestyle and consumption patterns; increasing demand for feed (1 kg of meat requires 8 kgs of feed); a food demand increase due to more larger, prosperous and urban population; an increase in food demand due to global population growth; sustained food demand from emerging markets, agribusiness in new markets; panic buying for the purpose of hoarding buffer stock and an increase in demand in industrial sector for agricultural raw material and wage goods (Watts, 2007). However, the present work has identified the following eight determinants or forces of food demand:

1. Bio-fuels Initiatives: Apart from fossil fuels (oil, natural gas, and coal), nuclear fuels, renewable resources such as hydroelectricity, and non-commercial biomass e.g. wood, hay and fodder, bio-fuels, are considered as a viable renewable energy source and many countries favour and facilitate the growth of bio-fuel production and consumption. The use of bio-fuels as engine oil was first tried in 1895 by Dr. Rudolf Diesel (1858-1913). Biodiesel refers to a non-petroleum based diesel fuel made by transesterification of vegetable oil which can be used alone or blended with conventional diesel in unmodified diesel-engine vehicles. A shift of farming to produce wheat, sugar crop, maize, corn, etc. for the production of bio-fuels has tremendous negative effects on food security, food prices, rural poverty, hunger, environmental destruction and water scarcity[ii]. However, this food-fuel conflict is controversial. One group of experts argue that bio-fuels are not the main factors and should not be blamed for high food prices (Armah et al., 2009; Harrison, 2009; Tyner, 2010; Block, 2012). Farmers[iii] also love the ethanol programme because it guarantees a market and a good price. There is another group of various recent studies that blame biofuels for food problems. These studies include International Energy Agency (2006)[iv], Greenfield (2007)[v], Ragan and Kenkel(2007)[vi], World Bank(2008)[vii], Sachs(2008)[viii], Goodall(2008), IFPRI(2008), Elliott(2009), FAO(2009)[ix], Fischer et al.

149

System Dimensional Structure of Global Food Crisis

(2009)[x], Holt-Giménez and Leahy(2008), Collins(2008), Rajcaniova, and Pokrivca(2010), Rajagopal et al.(2011), Walsh(2011), Chen and Khanna (2012). These studies have also concluded that the bio-fuels initiatives have increased the demand for food grains tremendously. Taking nearly 40 per cent of a depleted crop to put into cars rather than feeding people just does not make sense. In 2007 there were only 20 oil producing nations meeting the needs of over 200 nations. By the year 2020, more than 200 nations will become biodiesel producing nations and suppliers. This demand for oil-bearing crops is not only reducing the land available to produce food crops in Europe, it is also driving the clearing of rainforests in Indonesia and Malaysia for palm oil plantations. The ultimate beneficiaries of this bio-fuels resolution will be grain merchant and big players. It is also feared that the waste lands currently being accessed by the poor people (used as grazing lands or some general purpose) will be taken away for bio-fuel plantations and subsequent denial of access to them. Some studies have examined the impacts and responses of biofuels (Arndt et al., 2009).

2. Increase in Dietary Diversity: Dietary diversity or dietary variety is defined as the number of different foods or food groups consumed over a given reference period (Ruel, 2003). It is universally recognized as a key component of healthy diets. A growing wealthier middle class population demand more diversified diet (including meat, dairy products, eggs, cereals) more variety in preparation, dietary quality and nutrient adequacy at afford-able prices. The (over)consumption of meat and other animal-sourced foods (ASF) is happening in emerging economies due to changes in demographic pattern and profile, lifestyle and consumption patterns. Researchers also list growing demand-driven meat consumption as a reason for the upward trend in global food crisis as it stimulates demand for animal-feed (Brown, 1995; Benson, 2008; Gale and Henneberry, 2009). For instance, the average meat consumption in China was 20 kg in 1980 which in 2012 rose to 52 kg and isn't likely to stop until it reaches the 70 kg that the Taiwanese consume (Fortson, 2012). The growth rate in the demand for cereals is expected to rise again to 1.4% per year up until 2015, slowing to 1.2% per year thereafter. In develop-ing countries, overall cereal production is not expected to keep pace with demand. The net cereal deficits of these countries, which amounted to 103 million tonnes or 9% of consumption in 1997-1999, could rise to 265 mil-lion tonnes by 2030 when there will be 14% of consumption. There are now some 3 billion people moving up the food chain, eating greater quantities of grain-intensive livestock and poultry products. The rise in meat, milk, and egg consumption in fast-growing developing countries has no precedent. Total meat consumption in China today is already nearly doubled that in the United States (Li, 2011).

3. *Livestock Revolution and Increased Demand for Animals Feed:* Another factor that is determining the food demand and ultimately intensifying the GFC situation is a combined impact of livestock revolution[xi] and an increase in demand for animals feed. 1 kg of meat requires 8 kgs of feed. The increased cereal requirements to feed the pig and poultry population to meet the increased demand would require over the next two decades an additional area of about 65 million hectares more than the size of France. China will need another 80m-100m tonnes of grain to satisfy meat demand. This will require 20m hectares of land, pretty much the entire land mass of Britain. And that is just to satisfy the additional meat demand from a single country, China. The livestock revolution is a dynamic structural phenomenon in global agriculture and it is here to stay (Delgado et al., 1999; Delgado, 2003). It has profound implications for our health, livelihoods, environment, and the intensified world trade of meat products and rising food prices. Livestock food sectors across the globe are undergoing many changes[xii] and contributing to GFC in many different ways. First, livestock (animals) consume much more than they produce in terms of meat or milk. Eating 1,000 calories of meat could easily use 5,000 calories in feed. Second, poor countries like Ethiopia, Kenya and other countries, practice food export to wealthy countries to be used to feed animals and produce meat while their own large populations remain hungry and food-insecure resulting in starvation and deaths. Third, the global meat consumption will double between 2000 and 2050 according to the United Nations. Within the first ten years, this prediction is on track increasing 20% from 50 billion land animals dying for food production to 60 billion. Fourth, the excessive nitrogen, phosphate, and heavy metal levels in the effluent of intensive livestock farms cause environmental pollution and loss of biodiversity[xiii] (World Bank, 2005a).

In recent years there has been an increase in the demand for grain-intensive livestock and poultry due to rise in demand for meat and poultry products the lower and middle-income countries even though their per capita consumption is still far less than the US, Europe and other industrialized and high-consuming countries. Besides population growth, the impact of the increasing consumption of resource-intensive animal source foods (ASF) greatly compounds the problem. Left unchecked, it will continue to rise. According to the International Food Policy Research Institute report on Livestock in 2020: "The demand-driven livestock revolution is one of the largest structural shifts to ever affect food markets in developing countries and how it is handled is crucial for future growth prospects in developing country agriculture, for food security and the livelihoods of the rural poor, and for environmental sustainability".

4. Urbanisation and Declining Ratio of Food Producers to Food Consumers: Another factor influencing demand for food is urbanisation and declining ratio of food producers to food consumers[xiv] (Stage, 2010). Urbanisation influences domestic food production and consumption, promotes rural-urban competition for resources, and stimulates social and economic change (von Braun et al., 1993). The rural–urban migration of population driven by rapid economic growth and job possibilities in urban areas has changed the type of foods that consumers demand and where they allocate their food expenditures. These trends have significant implications for food exporting countries (Smit et al., 1996). The low to middle income countries have more than three-quarters of urban population. Satterthwaite et al. (2010) concluded that world's level of urbanisation is likely to continue increasing and it is putting an immense pressure on GAFS due to loss of agricultural land to urban expansion and water restrictions. Any discussion of the ways in which urbanization may affect food demand and supply needs to take into account the complexity of the linkages between rural and urban people and enterprises, and to recognize the capacity of food producers to adapt to changes in urban demand. This brings major challenges for food security in urban areas. Urban food security depends on households being able to afford food within other needs that have to be purchased (Cohen and Garrett, 2009). Rae(1998) found that in six East Asian countries urbanisation has been a significant contribution in the consumption function of total animal-driven food products. The process of urbanisation has a positive impact on the overall demand for food products since the individuals living in cities do not produce their own food and have to rely on supermarkets.

5. Global Population Growth: The phenomenon of world population and food output growth imbalance has been widely discussed in literature (Malthus, 1799; Ehrlich et al., 1993; Evans, 1998; Sen, 1999). Malthus asserted during the late 18th century that "the period when the number of men surpassed their means of subsistence has long since arrived". However, quite contrary to this assertion, not only there is no real decline in world food production per head, but also the largest per capita increases have come in the more densely populated areas of the world (Sen, 1999). World population has been increasing for centuries. It took the world millions of years to reach first billion around 1800, then 125 years (1925) to get to the second billion followed by 35 years (1960) to the third billion, 14 years to the fourth billion, just 13 years (between 1974 and 1987) to the fifth billion, 13 years to 6 billion in the year 2000 and 10 and half years to reach 7 billion in October 2011 and expected to increase to 9 billion in 2050. We are living in an overcrowded world and still adding 80 million people each year. Tonight there will be 219,000 additional mouths to feed at the dinner table and many of them will be greeted with empty plates. Another 219,000 will join us tomorrow night. At some point, this relentless growth will begin to tax both the skills of farmers and the limits of the earth's land and water resources. The worst part is most of the world's population growth occurs in developing parts of the world that are unable to produce enough food stock to feed themselves (Clemmitt, 2008). Rapid population growth means there will be more people to feed that will damage earth's resources including food and water and will diminish human well-being and quality of life (Boserup, 1965). Some social scientists argue that there is enough food to support the world population while others dispute this belief.

6. Emerging Markets: The five largest emerging markets (EMs) are China, India, Indonesia, Brazil and Russia. There is a sustained food demand and agribusiness from emerging new markets new. The emerging countries' large population and their fast growing economies have provided a significant market for food and agricultural commodities because of land and other resource limitations. Gale and Henneberry(2009) described how domestic production and imports have accommodated dramatic improvements in living standards and dietary change during the last three decades. Barichello and Patunru(2009) identified the key issues in Indonesia's agricultural sector, including slow productivity growth, producer–consumer conflicts over high farm prices, politics and public support for bio-fuels, poverty, and environmental challenges. Gulati, Landes and Ganguly(2009) described India's agricultural challenges to most effectively make the transition from ensuring adequate wheat and rice supplies to improving food grain management, enhancing the safety net for the poor, and managing rapid agricultural diversification. Liefert, Liefert and Serova(2009) concluded that Russia has become the second largest agricultural importer in the world among emerging markets after China and a major exporter of grain. Meat imports in particular are substantial. Recent socioeconomic shifts in Brazil have led to structural changes in food demand. Valdes, Lopes and Lopes (2009) discussed Brazil's bio-fuels industry and its effect on the availability of grains and oilseeds for domestic food and feed uses and exports are discussed.

7. Panic Buying: Another significant factor determining the food demand is the panic buying for the purpose of hoarding buffer stock in the anticipation of a large price increase, perceived disaster, food shortages or simply lack of preparation. The giant build up of grain is inconsistent with normal supply and demand dynamics. Countries dependent more on agricultural imports might exacerbate food inflation by going on a buying spree and by stockpiling. The year 2000 saw the panic buying of food and water. The global rice shortage of 2008 due to export restrictions by many governments gave birth to panic buying and rationing sales of rice by retailers led to the rise in rice prices worldwide. Blas(2011) concluded that first the crop failures; second the export restrictions; and third the initial food riots on the back of rising prices. Now food importing nations including Morocco, Jordan, Iraq and South Korea are responding with a steep increase in purchase and hoarding, driving agricultural commodities prices even higher (Robinson, 2012).

8. Increase in Demand for Agricultural Raw Materials and Wage Goods: Traditionally agriculture played a major role in overall economic development and industrialisation. However, the recent years have seen a tremendous increase in the supply of agricultural raw materials to industrial sector. The overall global food demand is also influenced by the changes in the demand for agricultural raw materials and wage goods (mainly food) in agro-based and other industries. The production and demand linkages from agriculture to industry have pushed up the demand for agricultural products.

Food Supply-Side Restrictions

Food supply-side restrictions on global food crisis, a significant dimension of GAFS, subsume many factors determining the production and supply of agricultural products. Producing an adequate supply of healthy and nutritious foodstuffs is essential for global economic security and political stability, and further reducing barriers to trade being crucial to achieving that goal. The relationship between supply of agricultural products and wellbeing of individuals is controversial. Samuelson described this as a phenomenon of 'poverty amids plenty', if one farmer worked hard and produced more, he would get richer (in money terms). But if all farmers worked hard and produced more, everyone would become poorer (in money terms) when compared with the original situation due to oversupply and fall in grain prices. In many backward countries there is an existence of backward-sloping supply curve where people mainly produce for their own subsistence and sell some portion of produce in the market. If price of food grains rise, the supply falls due to the fact that the farmers will sell less amount of food grains to take home same amount of money in cash. This phenomenon may not be fully applicable now. However, the supply of agricultural products has low or inelastic price elasticity due to peculiar nature of costs, biological nature of the production process, existing market structure, inflexibility in the total area under cultivation, immobility of labour and, and so on. T.W. Schultz (1953) argues that agriculture reacts to change in market conditions by taking the major part of the impact on prices while maintaining production almost intact. Industry, on the other hand, reacts to the changed market conditions by adjusting its production and the prices remain rather stable. Food supply available to people across the world depends upon various factors such as environmental, technical, geographical, socio-political and economic. Uncertainty and instability in production due to vagaries of nature and weather shocks such as floods, rain, drought, earthquakes, etc.; shortage of food supply due to scarcity of resources (water, credit and the like), changing farm structure, serious degradation and loss of arable and fertile soil (urban-rural land use conflicts); shocks (low crop outputs) resulting from pests, animal disease (mad cow disease) etc. in key grain regions affecting and afflicting agricultural production; decline in research expenditure (R&D) affecting new agricultural biotechnology, innovations and higher return farming; growing costs of factors of production (inputs) including fertilisers, water, labour, energy, oil, seeds and credit; Increasing storage and transportation costs (food miles); food supply conditioned by the rules of the global food market, global geopolitics, global food trade and lack of decoupling agricultural support (government policy to discourage food production) and ecological constraints on the exploitation of new lands or ocean exploration for sea food.

Thus, the factors responsible for fluctuations in food supply are many and varied. Many of these operate simultaneously and may even be working in different directions. The dimension of food supply-side restrictions subsumes the following manifest variables:

1. Scarcity of Resources: Food supply-side dimension of GFC is immensely determined by the availability of resources/inputs such as seeds, fertilizers, irrigation, credit, proper know how, energy, etc. In the absence of their adequate availability, the production of crops may not increase at all or sufficiently when their prices increase. Moreover, the supply responses for wheat, rice, etc. may be different from different regions due to differences in irrigation, improved seeds, or other inputs scarcity.

2. Land Constraints: The food supply is determined by land constraints in terms of inflexibility in the total area under cultivation, urban-rural land use conflicts, changing farm structure, serious degradation and loss of arable and fertile soil even as longstanding ones such as soil erosion intensified. Approximately one third of the global cropland is losing topsoil faster than new soil is forming through natural processes and thus, it is losing its inherent productivity. After the US dust bowl of the 1930s two recent dust bowls are forming, one across northwest China, western Mongolia, and central Asia and the other in central Africa. Satellite images show a steady flow of dust storms leaving these regions, each one typically carrying millions of tons of precious topsoil. In North China some 24,000 rural villages have been abandoned or partly depopulated as grasslands have been destroyed by overgrazing and as croplands have been inundated by migrating sand dunes.

In countries such as Mongolia, Haiti, North Korea and Lesotho have been experiencing severe soil erosion that lowers yields and shrinking grain harvests and eventually leads to cropland abandonment. The result is widespread hunger and chronic dependence on imports or food aid. The recent phenomenon of aquifer depletion is sharply shrinking the amount of irrigated area in the Arab Middle East mainly in Saudi Arabia, Yemen, Syria,

Iraq, India, China and the United States (states such as California and Texas) due to large-scale use of mechanical pumps to exploit underground water. At present, about half the world's people live in countries where water tables are falling as over-pumping depletes aquifers. Sooner or later falling water tables translate into rising food prices.

3. Climate and Ecological Constraints: The food crisis or more exactly the shortage in production of grains particularly in some of the major food-grain exporting countries has been attributed to environmental factors such as global warming and climate change. For instance, the demand-supply mismatch in the global market leading to manifold increase in wheat prices was triggered by the drought-led Australian Wheat disaster, the fall in wheat production in Ukraine in 2006-07 or the decline in production in Argentina. As well as this, without a doubt the ecological constraints on the exploitation of new lands or ocean exploration for seafood and threat of 'environmental dumping' (exports at prices below the full cost of production including the social costs of pollution) have played a major part in the actual food crisis. Nevertheless, uncertainty and instability in production due to vagaries of nature and weather shocks such as floods, rain, drought, earthquakes etc. are the main climate and ecological constraints which have fuelled the food crisis all over the world. The rising temperature is also making it more difficult to expand the world grain harvest fast enough to keep up with the record pace of demand. Crop ecologists have their own rule of thumb e.g. for each 1 degree Celsius rise in temperature above the optimum during the growing season we can expect a 10 per cent decline in grain yields. This temperature effect on yields was all too visible in western Russia during the summer of 2010 as the harvest was decimated when temperatures soared far above the norm. Another emerging trend that threatens food security is the melting of mountain glaciers.

4. Pests and Animal Diseases Shocks: Food grains supply is considerable influenced by the amount of pests and animal diseases shocks such as DDT, foot and mouth disease. Moreover, studies have shown that the chemicals used to control pests and other plant diseases can cause many human health issues, contaminate water and harm species. Thus, shocks (low crop outputs) resulting from pests, animal disease (mad cow disease) etc. in key grain regions are affecting and afflicting agricultural production.

5. Agricultural Research and Development Expenditure: Agricultural products supply is also considerably affected the agricultural research and development expenditure. A decline in research expenditure in agriculture will influence the new agricultural biotechnology, innovations and higher return farming. The last decade has witnessed the emergence of yet another constraint on growth in global agricultural productivity: the shrinking backlog of untapped technologies. Rice and wheat yields are not rising at all due to lack of new technologies.

6. Peculiar Nature of Costs: The variable costs of agricultural products are quite small in comparison to fixed costs in both developed and developing countries. Production of crop and other food products is spread over a span of time. Therefore, as time passes variable costs turn into fixed costs resulting in variable costs to be even smaller. For instance, the cost of seed is variable costs and as soon as the crop is sown, cost of seed will become a fixed cost and will not, therefore, influence the decision to continue with the crop if the price falls after it has been sown. It is the same case with other costs like fertilizers, irrigation, etc. So long as the price will be considered to cover the variable cost, the production of crop will not fall. However, the rising costs of storage and distribution will increase the food prices and termed as food miles.

7. Biological Nature of the Production Process: The biological nature of the production process or crop explains why its production cannot be increased when its price rises, especially during a season. The distinction between fixed costs and the variable costs explains why no attempt is made to reduce the supply of crop after it has been sown when its price falls. Similarly, once the crop has been sown and prices start rising, it may not be possible to bring more area under cultivation during that season simply because the climate suitable for the sowing of that crop is no longer there.

8. Access to Finance: Another factor determining the supply of agricultural products is the farmers' access to finance (Buera et al., 2011). New farm technology requires larger amount of finance. The marginal and small farmers have deficit budgets due to low per capita income derived from the small, scattered, uneconomic and non-viable holdings, inadequate availability of basic inputs, lack of savings, wasteful expenditure on litigation, etc. These farmers and food processors have a very limited access to finance that may be through money-lenders, relatives, commission agents, landlords, friends, co-operative banks for both investment and consumption.

Global Agricultural Markets Failures

Market failures represent imperfections in the economic system based on economic welfare theory that includes farmers on supply side and consumers on demand side. It is widely acknowledged that *per se* agriculture and food markets displays a good number of market failures and are often characterised by the lack of competition in its different forms, above all in the fields of commodity trade and food processing and distribution (Harmon et al., 2010). Market failures occur when freely-functioning markets fail to deliver efficient allocation of resources and lead to the loss of economic and social welfare for a society as a whole. Market failures are thought to be the result from structural rigidities that is lack of responsiveness in price signals. Agriculture markets as an institution fails to deliver optimal outcomes from the allocative and social points of views. With the globalization of the market, however, comes a globalization of market failures due to the fact that prices do not to capture 'external' costs and benefits to third parties (Boyce, 1999). In the current GFC the international agricultural and food markets failed because export restrictions played a dominant role in turning a critical situation into a full-blown crisis, especially in the case of rice (Nedergaard, 2006). Adam Smith in his *The Wealth of Nations* (1776) argues against public sector regulation and unnecessary government interventions in agriculture markets and favours the 'invisible hand' whereby the social goals can be achieved by individuals following their own self-interests. However, there are circumstances when markets fail to allocate resources efficiently and exchanges between the buyers and sellers are impeded and efficiency is compromised. Agricultural markets failures occur if a market fails to provide a competitive outcome and an efficient price. It is a situation when individual decisions guided by self-interest are at odds with an efficient allocation of resources from society's perspective. There are many reasons/ types for agricultural markets failures: negative and positive externalities such as water or air pollution, public goods, lack of price transparency, informational gaps, demerit goods, inequality, factor market imperfections e.g. factor immobility and market power. Along with a sufficient number of buyers and sellers not being able to affect voluntary prices, enough flexibility of demand and supply schedules are lacking. For example, when supply falls short of demand it can rise only with a time lag and this often produces an overshooting which gives rise to a 'cobweb' process where an alternation of dampened supply and demand excesses can take years to reach an equilibrium point (Praussello, 2011). However, the following manifest variables have been included in the dimension of GAMFs:

1. Trade Distortions and Emergence of Oligopolistic and Oligopsonistic Structures: Trade distortions in terms of barriers to entry, monopoly power, consolidation, lack of market transparency, integration and coherence, exchange rates fluctuations. International trade can play a role in improving food security and in addressing the issue of food price volatility (Buetre et al., 2004). Open and well-functioning markets are essential to allow more investment in agriculture. This is critical to ensure an increase in agricultural production and productivity to meet growing demand in the coming years. A stable, predictable, distortion free and transparent system for trade allows the unrestricted flow of food and agricultural commodities contributing to food security. Global food production is much more substantial than trade, but trade remains important. Even though total food grain trade is only 15% of world grain production (FAO 2007), and rice trade is less than 5% of global rice production (FAO, 2009b), trade has a powerful impact on domestic prices. Of course, the price impact varies as amongst countries and social classes. Grain exporters welcome higher prices, poor consumers are devastated by them. There is no 'win-win' here. The market power concentration in global agricultural industry as a source of market failures can be hardly exaggerated. Market dominance by monopolies can lead to underproduction and higher prices than would exist under conditions of competition. The large companies involved in food global markets exhibit their monopolistic or better oligopolistic and oligopsonistic behaviour (i.e., factors moving them away from competitive conditions) as a source of market imperfections and disequilibria and have become a significant factor responsible for crisis in the global food system (Reardon et al., 2003). Among recent drivers that have enhanced market imperfections one can quote the examples of commercial seed production on the one hand and of spreading of supermarkets and fast food chains (multinational agri-business and food giants such as Wal-Mart, the largest global food retailer) in retailing sectors all over the world on the other (Murphy, 2006). Moreover, it is widely recognised in literature that state trading enterprises in agriculture based in developed countries possess monopoly power large enough to affect international markets and world food prices(FAO, 2008).

Companies acting in Life Science area where seeds are going together with other crucial inputs such as pesticides and agriculture chemicals are discovering and patenting genetically modified hybrids that often bring into being sterile seeds, acquiring a monopolistic power over industrial agricultural producers, who are obliged to buy the commercial seeds from them (Saruchera and Matsungo, 2003). As a result commercial seed markets are highly concentrated and companies such as Monsanto are in command of important market shares: in this instance about 40 per cent of world market of commercial maize seeds and 25 per cent of soybean seeds. At a global level, the first 10 multinational seed companies have a market share that exceeds 50 per cent (Praussello, 2011).

A high company concentration is being monopolized by a series of transnational agribusiness interests that place their own economic interests above the good of the public and the community (Smith et al., 2010). Today, the food system no longer responds to the nutritional needs of people, nor to sustainable production based on respect for the environment, but is based on a model rooted in a capitalist logic of seeking the maximum profit, optimization of costs and exploitation of the labour force in each of its productive sectors. Common goods such as water, seeds, land, which for centuries have belonged to communities, have been privatized, robbed from the people and converted into exchange currency at the mercy of the highest bidder.

2. Displacement of Natural Fibres by Synthetic Substitutes: Another manifestation of global agricultural market failures is the displacement of natural fibres by synthetic substitutes for example jute by synthetics resulting from competition in which the higher pollution costs associated with the latter are not internalized in world prices. The renewable natural raw materials including cotton, jute, wool, sisal, and rubber have lost international markets to synthetic substitutes. The environmental costs associated with the production and consumption of synthetics typically are considerably larger. Hence, the competition between natural raw materials and synthetics pits relatively clean producers in the South against relatively dirty producers in the North - the opposite of what is commonly assumed in discussions of the environmental impacts of North-South trade. The competition between jute and polypropylene is a case in point (Boyce, 1999). Polypropylene wins the competition due to price advantage, but its major environmental impacts are air pollution and energy consumption.

3. *Factor Market Imperfections:* Factor immobility causes unemployment hence productive inefficiency. There are many factors that are the sources of factor market imperfections in the global agricultural and food system. Rural factor markets are characterised by many imperfections such as unequal land ownership distribution, imperfect competition in land tenancy market, unequal access to finance, farm and off-farm employment gaps, rural credit market imperfections and so on.

4. *Markets Failures in Terms of Erosion of Crop Genetic Diversity:* The relationship between crop genetic diversity, food security and farm household well-being has received extensive study from economists (Cavatassi et. al., 2005). Bruinsma(2003) estimated that agricultural intensification will be the primary source of crop production growth globally over the next 25 years. However, the main concern is that the erosion of crop genetic diversity through the widespread replacement of traditional, landrace varieties with improved modern varieties has arisen during the last four decades. The fact is that agricultural markets have failed to reward the farmers for the provision of the erosion of crop genetic diversity. This is a trade-driven market failure.

5. *Negative Externalities Related to Agricultural Production and Consumption Activities:* Negative externalities such as water pollution arise when buyers or sellers are neither charged nor compensated (high transaction costs and free riders) for the economic impacts of their choices on others. It is a type of market failure where welfare of some economic agents depends upon an activity under the control of somebody else and its effect is not taken into account by normal market behaviour. As long as farmers can discharge agricultural chemicals into waterways without being charged for the costs their actions impose on other water users, the prices of the food they produce (and the chemicals they use) will not reflect full societal costs. Also, if prices are not accurate indicators of costs, markets cannot allocate resources efficiently. Market prices encourage farmers to produce more crops and more water pollution than if pollution's costs were reflected in those prices. This source of market failure is known as a negative externality. The true marginal costs and/or marginal benefits associated with the goods and services traded in the market are not reflected in a market when an externality exists. It does not lead to the attainment of a Pareto optimum in a competitive economy because individuals acting in their own self-interest will not have the correct incentives to maximize total surplus, i.e., the invisible hand of Adam Smith will not be pushing people in the right direction. Externalities may be related to production activities, consumption activities, or both. Production externalities occur when the production activities of one individual imposes costs or benefits on other individuals that are not transmitted accurately through a market, for example, air pollution from burning coal, ground water pollution from fertilizer use, or food contamination and farm worker exposure to toxic chemicals from pesticide use. Consumption externalities occur when the consumption of an individual imposes costs or benefits on other individuals that are not accurately transmitted through a market, e.g., cigarette smoking, illicit drugs (Zilberman, 1999).

6. Cobweb Process: Cobweb model or theorem or process, first analysed by Nicholas Kaldor in 1934, is based on time lag between (lag between planting and harvesting rubber and corn for example) and cyclical fluctuations in demand and supply decisions in agricultural markets. Prices of agricultural products are assumed by producers to be based on observations of previous prices. For example, due to unexpected bad weather farmers go to market with an unusually small crop of cucumbers that will result in high prices. If farmers expect these price conditions to continue, then in the following year, they will raise their production of cucumbers relative to other crops. As a result, they will go to market with high supply which will result in low prices. If they expect low prices to continue, they will decrease their production of cucumbers for the next year, resulting in high prices again (Ezekiel, 1938).

7. Rising Expectations and Financial Speculations: Rising expectations and financial speculations in the agricultural commodity markets have been regarded to have played their crucial role in compounding the problem of world food crisis (Epstein, 2008; FAO, 2009b). The transfer of capital from the stressed US Real Estate market to the commodities markets which have pushed up prices. The falling US dollar value played a crucial role in determining the food security of countries linked to the USD, as one saw in the recent case of the rice price hikes where the Philippines paid $1,100/ton of rice imported during April 2008. The New York Times of April 22, 2008, reported that "This price boom has attracted a torrent of new investment from Wall Street, estimated to be as much as $130 billion." According to the same article, the Commodity Futures Trading Commission noted that "Wall Street funds control a fifth to a half of the futures contracts for commodities like corn, wheat and live cattle on Chicago, Kansas City and New York exchanges."[xv] Lagi et al.(2011) developed an analytical model and estimated that at least half the food price increase from January 2004 to March 2011 was due to explosion of financial speculation such as commodity traders and investment banks.

8. *Information Asymmetries:* Information plays a very critical role in agricultural markets and information asymmetries exist between various stakeholders such as farmers, traders, speculators, corporations, inputs manufacturers, logistics, packagers, government, policy makers and consumers due to location, socio-economic situations, distance, financialisation, and rising globalisation of economic policies. Imperfect information means nutritious and good quality foods are underproduced while fatty fast foods are overproduced or overconsumed. Due to these asymmetries there is an overreaction situation in global agricultural markets since all stakeholders are aware of these asymmetries and quickly react to any new information. For example, the 2007 announcement that the wheat production would be 50% lower than estimated (production gap in global production fell by 2% only) and Australia instigated a panic movement on international markets.

Public Sector Interventions and Collective Actions Failures

The concept of government failures or political failures was coined by James M. Buchanan (1979), which represents imperfections in the political system, explained by rational choice theory, including politicians, bureaucrats, and policy makers on the supply side and farmers and consumers on the demand side. Rational choice (or public choice) theory has been established as an independent theory regarding the political decision making. When global agricultural markets fail, governments often take policy actions in terms of public sector interventions in an attempt to regulate the markets and private groups also undertake collective actions in an anticipation to achieve better results. The role of public sector (government) in agriculture is twofold: providing 'social overhead capital' (infrastructure) and to undertake activities that would compensate for market failures. However, both governments' policies and collective actions, like markets, fail to and are imperfect. By products of these government failures large-scale and visible corruption often emerges. Further, government policies and programmes often benefit the rich although objective is to help the poor (Krueger, 1990).

Government failure can be defined as the sum total of all actions and failures to act which resulted in a less-than-Pareto optimal situation. There have been colossal government failures, both omission and commission, in agricultural and food industry that significantly overweight the market failures. Failures of commission include exceptionally high costs of public sector enterprises, engaged in variety of manufacturing and other economic activities such as state marketing boards, providing subsidised inputs to farmers, state ownership of shops for the distribution of food and other essential products, state operation of mines and manufacturing activities, state enterprises accorded monopoly rights for importing varieties of commodities, nationalised agricultural banks and insurances, inefficient and wasteful government investment programmes, government public sector deficits, negative consequences of urban-bias investment strategy, and saving behaviour. Complementary to these failures are failures of omission such as deterioration of transport and communication facilities in rural sector, failure to maintain existing infrastructure facilities, buttressed by exchange controls and import licensing, insistence upon nominal interest rates well below the rate of inflation with credit rationing so that government could supervise credit allocation among competing claimants.

There is no substitute to allowing the individuals–food producers, traders, processors, and consumers – determine what is good for them. More government intervention in agricultural production and distribution is creating more problems than solutions. The rules governing non-tariff issues like food safety, quality standards, regulation of new technologies and products, animal welfare and competition policy are not always as transparent, uniform or scientifically grounded as they need to be food quality and safety. This dimension of GFC is concerned with the effectiveness of public policy and collective action of farmers' organisations. Agricultural is usually supposed to be a very specific industry requiring a vast involvement of government through dedicated public policies. The market manipulation and manifold market failures that characterise the sector have also been blamed for the current food price spikes around the world. Low income elasticities of consumption (a well-known phenomenon of Engel curves) remain a structural element of global food markets. Hence public sector interventions in the form of government regulations, taxation, subsidies in agriculture production and distribution are required to take care of its intrinsic slower dynamics, compared with manufacturing and services sectors, to offset market failures and to achieve a number of national economic objectives dealing with agricultural production, trade, distribution, development, international trade and price and income guarantees. Therefore, government interventions in the domestic agriculture markets are persistent.

A collective action literally requires collectivity and an action. By a narrow sense, collectivity implies group work in which all the members are requested to participate and an action implies physical movement. Collection actions[xvi] may have good effect on the quality of natural resources or on the economic activities based on the natural resources or may be many inefficient, non-functioning collective actions (Olson, 1965; Sakurai, 2002). Although a collective action is defined at community level, we can have two kinds of variable for the collective action. One is community level variable for the existence or the emergence of the collective action in community. And the other is individual/household level variable for the participation in the collective action at individual/household level. Collective action counteracts a number of conditions that retard agricultural development: market failures, deterioration of customary institutions, and lack of empowerment of vulnerable groups. It is relevant for a broad range of developmental activities, including technology innovation, enterprise development, policy change, improvement of community outcomes, and alleviation of poverty. But it has special relevance in the case of natural resource management. Collective action can be a means of overcoming the absence of markets in specific sectors, as in the case of environmental externalities. The very nature of many natural resources (non-divisibility, high variability and uncertainties) require collective action in order to provide effective management. Where communications among users are important, collective action can reduce costs of information and knowledge flows. The ways institutions form opportunities and incentives for collective action are critical to outcomes. Collective action is influenced by the institutional structure in which the community is embedded (including government policies, cultural and religious values, social capital, ethnicity, property rights structure, etc.).

And as societies are complex, defining appropriate scales and institutions for collective action is complex. Communities and institutions are nested within other communities and institutions, and boundaries are not always clear. There will be sub-groups with their own interests and claims. One area in which World Bank staff deal with collective action is the common property arena. World Bank project managers are increasingly aware that there are opportunities for management of natural resources through the collective action of communities, and that is critical to get right the organizational arrangements for collective action, as well as securing rights in the resource. Countries are within their sovereign right to secure their food-stocks; however, with better foresight and some collective action, there are possibly better and more effective ways to address the challenge related to food security so that all countries benefit. This is a typical challenge of supra-national collective action.

However, the management of GFC requires an international coordination of policies as a result the national governments fail to cope with global food challenges. The misguided public policies do not result in more food for more consumers at more or differentiated price levels.

1. Fiscal Policy Interventions Failures: Government's fiscal policy interventions (indirect tax, subsidies, tax relief, tariffs) in the price mechanism of agricultural products to change the allocation of resources to improve economic and social welfare. However, these interventions fail when desired goals are not achieved. High taxes on oils and agricultural products make food very expensive for consumers. Financial support given by the government to one set of producers rather than another will always create "winners and losers". Taxing one product more than another will similarly have different effects on different groups of consumers.

2. Public Sector Agricultural and Food Enterprises Failures: Government intervention in agricultural production may encourage farmers to produce less food when they are capable of producing more prevents local food prices from falling, which should have benefited consumers. This perverse use of tax payers money then making the same taxpayers pay more for food that could have been made available at a lower price is insensitive public policy. Encouraging farmers to continue producing particular commodities even if their prices have gone down (due to big local harvest due to improved productivity, due to big harvests abroad and imported cheaply, etc.) to non-profitable levels is not good. Taxpayers should be spared from shelling out more money for price differential subsidy. With current high prices of many food products, farming is becoming more profitable. But when governments maintain, if not increase, various farm insurance and price subsidy, this means those governments have no intention of allowing cheaper farm production in the future. There is a serious problem of corruption and bribes in public sector agricultural enterprises. Clientelism and elite capture culture lead to exposure to corrupt officials and mismanagement of public budgets.

3. State Monopoly on Food Imports and Exports: Another controversial factor of goverment interventions in food system is the export-import restrictions as a response to food crisis (Abbott, 2010 and 2012; Buetre et al.. 2004; Dollive, 2008). Another failure of public sector interventions is the state monopoly on food exports and imports. The policy of food protectionism penalizes consumers, including many farmers themselves who experience crop damage or small harvest (due to strong typhoons, pest or insect attack, prolonged drought, civil conflict, etc.). A better option is to cut, if not abolish, those tariffs on food products, have full free trade in food and other commodities and services. Producers of food-surplus countries will benefit through higher income, while consumers of food-deficient countries will benefit through lower price. Export-import policy imposing restrictions on grain exports, implementation of import tariffs, regressive direct export bans by some governments have worsened the difficulty of net rice importing countries through even higher rice prices. Global supply is disrupted and some farmers in rice-surplus countries are discouraged from higher production since the opportunity to earn higher at exporting rice was killed. Allow freer trade, have few or zero restrictions, in mobility and trading of commodities that experience high price increases so that producers will have more incentives to produce more. Whilst many countries instinctively close their borders upon threat of a food shortage, these actions have proven to have detrimental effects both domestically and globally due to market distortions. Export restrictions on grains were one of the key drivers of the food crisis and price spikes during the 2007-11 period. The food crisis of 2006-08 saw significant exporters begin to limit international sales. The issue of export restrictions was again brought to the fore of the agricultural negotiations by Japan and Switzerland when they expressed, once more, the need to address the issue of export bans and taxes. In an informal paper submitted in April 2008, the two countries proposed checking WTO Members ability to restrict food exports and requiring them to consider how such policies affected countries that depended on food imports. In the current crisis international markets failed because WTO statutes did not prevent countries from imposing export restrictions that induced so much unnecessary volatility. It has also been recognized that reforms proposed in the July 2008 Framework Agreement did not include provisions to discipline export taxes or bans, nor would special safeguard mechanisms in the agreement have approximated a free-trade arrangement (Abbott et al. 2008).

4. Deterioration of Existing Infrastructure Facilities in Rural Sector: Another manifestation of government failure in agricultural sector is the deterioration of existing transport, communication and infrastructure facilities in rural sector (Brandt and Otzen, 2007). Investment in transport, communication and infrastructure in rural areas is a part of capital accumulation required for agricultural development and have an impact on socioeconomic measures of welfare. Thus, investing in infrastructure is a means of stimulating the economy especially during recession. There are severe constraints on the supply side of the provision of infrastructure in Asia. The infrastructure financing gap between what is invested in Asia-Pacific (around US$48 billion) and what is needed (US$228 billion) is around US$180 billion every year (Kingombe, 2011).

5. Inefficient Government Rural Development Programmes: Within policy, research, and development agendas, there has been a re-emergence of interest in agriculture and pro-poor growth[xvii] in rural areas (Gulati *et al.* 2007). The problem of rural development and poverty are rampant, massive and widespread in rural areas of developing countries of the world. The World Summit on Sustainable Development in Johannesburg in September 2002 concluded that the progress in five areas such as water, energy, health, agriculture and biodiversity is essential for having severe poverty by 2015. This has not happened due to inefficient and wasteful government rural development programmes, which is another manifestation of government failures. For instance, Integrated Rural Development Programme (IRDP), a single major instrument of rural poverty alleviation in India since 1978, could not make any significant impact on rural poverty eradication due to various loopholes, perils and pitfalls (Chopra, 2003).

6. Collective Actions Institutions Failures: The benefits of collective actions institutions (such as rules and norms, farmers organizations and agricultural cooperatives) are clearer in making markets work for poor particularly in high value products (e.g. fruits, vegetables, poultry and fish) and accessing credit, seed, and fertilizer (Miehlbradt and McVay 2005). They are often seen as key factors in enhancing farmers' access to markets and a means to promote governance decentralization and business development in the rural areas. However, these institutions are also not free from failures and ineffectiveness in achieving desired results. Many research studies have concluded that these failures are reflected in producer organizations' limited business skills, failures of institutions in securing market access for smallholders (Markelova and Meinzen-Dick, 2006), non-replicable organizational models for linking producers to markets, relatively low transaction costs associated with market access, limited impact of farmers organization on prices due to a large number of buyers and sellers, and need for substantial public and private investment to establish and maintain these organizations (Salifu, *et. al.*, 2010).

7. Food Health and Safety Regulations Failures: Those strict health, sanitation, environmental, animal welfare, and labour standards were imposed by farm lobbies and bureaucracies of rich governments, not so much by consumers. If some rich consumers want these strict regulations, they can do so by demanding labelling and purchasing only those products (local or imported). Poorer consumers, who may not be too strict with those standards and just want cheaper and safe food, need not be forced to pay more. If food products are indeed unfit for human consumption, they should be banned, not over-taxed to make it very expensive for consumers.

8. Urban-bias Investment Strategy: There is acontinuing debate on the thesis of urban bias (Lipton, 1977, 2005; Byers, 1979; Bates, 1988; Ghosh, 1990; Chopra, 2012; Varshney, 1993; Jones and Corbridge, 2010). Urban bias is a strategy of development which discriminates against rural and agricultural sectors in favour of the urban and industrial sectors in terms of inadequate public investments and access to resources to rural sector. Urban based policy makers, allocate more and more investment to the urban areas although these areas do not deserve it on the grounds of economic efficiency and equity. Allocative bias and transfer of resources from rural to urban sector[xviii] are the manifestations of urban bias. Another manifestation of urban bias is reflected in the higher incomes, standard of living and welfare of urban people as compared to those of the rural farmers and poor people. Over the years various forms of urban bias have persisted (e.g., the international trade regime) and even intensified (e.g., government expenditure and foreign aid) (Bezemer and Headey, 2008). Urban biased investment strategy in labour-surplus developing economies leads to intensification of rural poverty, increase in sectoral inequalities, a decline in employment generation in rural sector, out-migration of farmers from villages leading to labour shortages in agriculture and fall in agricultural output. Thus, inefficient allocation of resources leads to government failure in reducing rural poverty.

Global Food Crisis as a Construct

The complexity of GAFS and dynamic nature of GFC dimensions constantly determine the severity of GFC. All latent and manifest variables contribute to GFC in varying degrees. The ultimate outcomes and impacts of the severity of GFC results in rising food prices, unequal access to food, food insecurity, utilization of food, over-eating and under-eating of food, social welfare, poverty, freedom and right to food and food vulnerability. The phenomenon of GFC complements a range of accounts of global political economy that focus, conventionally, on industrial, corporate and technological power relations as vehicles of supremacy. It is also complemented by commodity chain analyses, dependency analyses, and fair trade studies that focus on particular food relationships in international trade. And, finally, there are studies of agriculture and food that focus on case studies, questions of hunger, technology, cultural economy, social movements, and agribusiness that inform dimensions of food regime analysis, once positioned historically within geo-political relations. The difference made by food regime analysis is that it prioritises the ways in which forms of capital accumulation in agriculture constitute global power arrangements, as expressed through patterns of circulation of food.

1. Rising Food Prices: The first most significant ramification of GFC is the sharp and continue rise in food prices. Poor households are more than three times more vulnerable than the rich to the "plague" of rising food prices. As a bigger proportion of their income goes on food, the purchasing power of poor households is more significantly eroded when prices rise.

The percentage of income needed to purchase a healthy basket of food for a single person on social assistance rose by 10 percentage points between 2005 and 2009 alone, highlighting the mounting pressure faced by social assistance recipients to afford a nutritious diet.

2. Utilisation of Food: Utilization is commonly understood as the way the body makes the most of various nutrients in the food. Sufficient energy and nutrient intake by individuals is the result of good care and feeding practices, food preparation, diversity of the diet, and intra-household distribution of food. Combined with good biological utilization of food consumed, this determines the *nutritional status* of individuals. Deficiencies in utilization of food worsen the phenomenon of food crisis. The cereal intake as well as food energy intake levels of the poor are tremendously adversely affected during food crisis despite the fact that the overall economic growth in the economy is stable and this can be attributed to changes in consumer preferences. The distortions in the utilization of food gives rise to the phenomenon of overeating and is termed as 'luxus consumption' leading to storage of body fat, obesity, health problems, and excess resource utilization (Blair and Sobal, 2006). The concept of 'luxus consumption' has been beneficial in estimating the effects of excess food utilisation on human health. This phenomenon contributes to overweight and obese and is a significant contributor to GFC.

3. Environmental Sustainability and Ecological Security: The changes in the driving forces of the GAFS and other dimensions of GFC bring changes in ecosystem services, access and availability of natural resources, and ecosystems stocks and flows that contribute directly to quality of human well-being. Unrestricted growth in population, industralisation, food production, pollution, and food consumption will lead to widespread famine, resource shortages and environmental crisis. These stresses are intensifying and will increasing determine the quality of human life on our planet. Once these stresses become severe then they deny many millions of people basic food, shelter, health, jobs or any hope for betterment.

4. Least Traded Food Commodities: Commodities that often experience huge price spikes are those that are least-traded. Rice that is traded internationally is only about six per cent of global food production. So when certain countries experience supply shortfall for whatever reasons, the leeway for emergency supply from imports is small, resulting in huge price spikes and hence, economic difficulty for poorer consumers of those countries. Public policy intervention for achieving food self-sufficiency invites agricultural protectionism in order to shield local farmers from foreign competition, which may turn them off from continued farming, which can result to "food insufficiency" someday. Some countries produce particular agricultural commodities more efficiently than others by virtue of their geography (wide flat lands, few mountains, lots of lakes and rivers, away from usual typhoon path, and so on), soil condition, conservation practices and entrepreneurial spirit of farmers, etc. Hence, it will give justice to both local consumers to avail of such natural and social advantages in other country that allow them to produce cheaper food than what local producers can provide.

5. *Food Paradox and Food Wastage:* The phenomenon of food paradox exists due to the food, diet and health interactions. It is related to the co-existence of hunger (dietary malnutrition) and obesity on one hand and food wastage on the other hand. It denotes a paradoxical existence of food under-consumption, overconsumption and food wastage culture in the economy (Buzby and Hyman, 2012). It is a less known issue that about half of the food grown is either lost, converted or wasted "from field to fork". There are varied forms of food waste such as uneaten food in households, buffet parties, restaurants, wedding parties, and supermarkets; unpalatable and unhealthy food that ends up in a bin, overeating, eating significantly beyond our caloric needs really is a form of food waste, out of date food waste in supermarkets, lack of leftovers tolerance culture, vending machines firms overproduce food than expected to sell, food wasted at homes, restaurants, parties, production, storage and distribution stages, and so on. According to a recent report by FAO (2012), food waste is a growing concern next to food losses. Global food losses and waste are estimated at 1.3 million tonnes yearly all along food supply chains, i.e., primary production, post-harvest, processing, distribution and consumption. However, overeating is food waste to a severe extreme (Wansink, 2007). Almost all Western countries including Japan introduced laws requiring food products to display "consume by" dates on all food products. While aimed at protecting consumers, the law exacerbated waste to the point that the amount of food being discarded annually by convenience stores and supermarkets, an estimated 6 million tons in Japan alone, was equivalent to roughly 80 per cent of the food assistance being supplied to needy countries (Schreiber, 2011).

6. *Distortions in Food Distribution System:* Increased food production will not automatically transfer to the poor unless it is coupled with adequate distribution mechanism. Food distribution system can be private supply chain management and public distribution system. Among all the safety net operations that exist, public distribution system is wider in terms of subsidy expenditure and coverage. However, distortions in food distribution system will not provide access to food for the poor. The benefits of public distribution system for the poor are also questionable. Another distortion in food distribution system is the inter-regional variations in supply. For example, the regions with high incidence of poverty and hunger may receive lower share of food supply and vice versa. The efficiency of the food distribution system determines the situation of food security to a greater extent.

7. *Conflicting Food Policies of International Institutions and National Governments:* International institutions like the World Bank, WTO, IMF, FAO as well as the Alliance for the Green Revolution in Africa, the government of the United States and the European Union support directly and indirectly a set of big multinationals that control each of the links of the agricultural-food chain that prioritise the profits of these companies over the nutritional needs of people and respect for the environment. A few corporations rake in big profits thanks to a liberalized and deregulated agricultural-business model.

8. *Food Vulnerability:* Another ramification of the interactions of the forces of GAFS and the dynamic nature of the dimensions of GFC is an increase in food vulnerability[xix] at national, household and individual levels. The situation of food crisis worsens both at micro and macro levels, when more and more people feel vulnerable to experiencing food insecurity, hunger in future and shelter to emergency food centers, such as food banks, food pantries and soup kitchens (Scaramozzino, 2006). The countries are more vulnerable to GFC if they have (a) high food dependency as measured by the share of cereal imports in total cereal consumption, (b) high food import burdens as measured by the share of cereal imports in total imports, (c) increased demand for food aid, and (d) low income as measured by a gross national income (GNI) per capita that results in weaker policy, fiscal, and administrative capacities to respond to food crisis. The vulnerable countries have weak capacity to provide social safety nets. Food vulnerability has negative consequences for vulnerable poor people in terms of health problems, emotional well-being, acquiring and/or maintaining employment, stress and anxiety, fear of long-term indebtedness, and so on.

Concluding Remarks

The world and its countries, communities, regions, and people face serious food crisis, which is even worse than its predecessors and is expected to get much worse before it gets better. Global agricultural and food markets are not efficient from the point of view of social justice and economic equity (fairness). Agricultural markets generate an unacceptable distribution of income and consequent social exclusion. The process of GAFS generates a market failure in terms of social injustice or unfairness in divisions of rewards and burdens and other forms of inequalities. The occurrence of GFC is rarely down to one factor. Food problems occur due to poverty-inequality, demand-supply mismatch, ecologically fragile regions, social and political conflicts, uninterested corrupt governments, market failures, collective actions failures, constraints to food imports, channelling aid and distribution, poor infrastructures and so on. The overall functioning of GAFS is hindered by certain barriers such as discrimination, oppression, racism, casteism, classism, ableism, ageism, sexism, prejudice, and stereotyping. The above systematic discussion reveals that GFC has complex causal theories and correlations with multiple pathways. Its system dimensional structure incorporates six latent variables with multiple indicators, i.e., forty eight critical food crisis factors (CFCFs) synthesised into six different dimensions. These CFCFs are the keys areas of activities with direct and indirect effects on GFC. In other words, these are the critical areas in which if things do not go right then the global agricultural and food system does not function smoothly. All these CFCFs directly or indirectly in varying degrees contribute to GFC. The dimensions of GFC affect the social welfare of human beings. The situation of worsening food insecurity results in more hunger[xx], malnutrition[xxi], poverty[xxii], inequality, marginalisation of small farmers by agribusiness, the 'planet of slums', poor quality of life, and lack of stability and insecurity. Social welfare has been hit hardest by the food crisis in the countries of the South where they have experienced the aggravating structural poverty for decades.

Notes

i. The latent variables and manifest variables of the Kanji-Chopra Global Food Crisis Model have been first discussed in, Chopra, Parvesh K. (2011), " Global Food Crisis: A Systems Modelling Approach to Measurement", In: B.N. Ghosh (Ed.), *Global Food Crisis: Contemporary Issues and Policy Options.* Leeds: Wisdom House Publications, pp. 47-90.

ii. A food-fuel conflict may be imminent as bio-fuel crops are also known to consume plenty of water. The problems of water for agriculture probably will be much more important, in this context. World agriculture will have to use its water supply much more efficiently in the coming decades. With the rising competition from bio-fuel crops, the supply of water for food production may be at stake.

iii. Even cattle farmers whose profits could be wiped out by the increased cost of feed, are pushing for bio-fuel programs.

iv. The study indicated a strong relationship between agricultural prices and the share of first generation bio fuels in transport fuels. For example, the cereal price in India increases by 20% with bio fuel share of 4% and by 40 % with 7% bio fuel target. The market effect of increased biodiesel production and use in the United States would likely drive up the price of soya bean oil while driving down the price for soyabean meal used in livestock feed. The overall net impact on farm incomes is estimated to be an increase of about 0.3%.

v. Palm oil 'now used widely in food products ranging from instant noodles to biscuits and ice cream, has become so integrated into energy markets that its price moves in tandem with crude oil price'.

vi. Kenkel and Regen (2007), in their study indicates that Oklahoma producers would shift land to biodiesel feed stocks which may result in a reduced winter wheat output. Further, the signals are that the major source of cellulosic feedstock production as from conversion of existing crop lands rather than from marginal lands.

vii. According to World Bank report, two thirds of global increase in maize production between 2003 and 2007 went to production of bio fuels.

viii. 'This wrong-headed policy, pushed by an aggressive farm lobby, gives a 51-cent tax credit for each gallon of ethanol blended into gasoline.' Sachs further adds "Consequently, up to a third of the U.S. mid-Western maize crop this year will be converted to ethanol, causing a cascade of price increases across the food chain" (Sachs, 2008).

ix. The bio diesel sector in EU is estimated to have absorbed about 60% of the member states rapeseed output in 2007 (FAO 2009). IFPRI (2008) and FAO (2009) estimates that 30% of recent increase in cereal prices as of due to bio diesel production.

x. If the bio-fuel consumption is twice compared to that in 2008 the impact on crop prices in 2020 is very substantial, of the order of 30 % compared with the reference run without bio fuels. It may vary between 15-30 % depending upon the level of bio fuel adoption. The largest price increase is projected for coarse grains at 50 % and that for protein feeds at 30-40%. An additional 200 million people may be at risk of hunger, under varying scenarios of the bio fuel adoption, most of which concentrate in South Asian and African countries (Fischer *et al.*, 2009).

xi.   Delgado et al. (1999 and 2003) introduced the term "Livestock Revolution" for the phenomenal growth in supply and demand of milk and animal products (meat such as beef, pork, poultry and so on). The main characteristics of this revolution they identified are: (1) rapid worldwide increases in consumption and production of live stock products; (2) a major increase in the share of developing countries in total livestock production and consumption; (3) ongoing change in the status of live stock production from a multipurpose activity with mostly non tradable output to food and feed production in the con text of globally integrated markets; (4) increased substitution of meat and milk for grain in the human diet; (5) rapid rise in the use of cereal- based feeds; (6) greater stress put on grazing resources along with more land- intensive production closer to cities; and (7) the emergence of rapid technological change in live stock production and processing in industrial systems.

xii.   These changes include trade liberalization; investment in trade infrastructure (roads, ports, refrigeration facilities); privatization of production and marketing; deregulation of internal markets; and reduced government spending on research, extension, and inspection.

xiii.   More than 130,000 square kilo meters of arable land in China and 30,000 square kilo meters in Thailand, (together an area about four times the size of the Netherlands), have an estimated annual livestock nutrient waste production of phosphate of at least 20 kilograms per hectare per year in excess of the adsorptive capacity of the surrounding ecosystem. The extent of nitrate nutrient loading is probably even more severe (World Bank, 2005).

xiv.   One important way in which urbanization in poor countries may affect food prices is that it increases the number of households that depend on commercial food supplies, rather than on own production, as their main source, and hence are likely to hoard food if they fear future price increases.

xv.   Quoted in Jacques Berthelot, "Sorting the truth out from the lies about the explosion of world agricultural prices," *Solidarité*, May 18, 2008.

xvi.   The examples of collective actions include forest management activities in community forest, such as weeding, pruning, and thinning; maintenance of common irrigation facilities, such as canal cleaning and bund repairing; patrolling of community forest; construction of irrigation systems and community wells; community forest management, water users, association for tank irrigation management, and collective land ownership in lowland. A member of collective action organisation can pay cash or in-kind or hires a labourer instead of participating by him/herself.

xvii.   Pro-poor growth is growth that is good for the poor (DFID 2004). One definition of pro-poor growth considers only the incomes of the poor and the extent to which growth is 'pro-poor' depends on how fast the incomes of the poor are rising. Pro-poor growth can be seen as the average growth rate of incomes of poor people.

xviii. The instruments through which the transfer of resources takes place are: taxation, unfavourable terms of trade for agriculture and skill and cash drain from rural areas. The rural areas do not receive the quid pro quo for the resources that are transferred (Ghosh, 1990).

xix.   Vulnerability is defined in terms of three critical dimensions: (a) vulnerability to an *outcome*; (b) from a variety of *risk factors*; and (c) because of an *inability to manage those risks.* Indeed, a person can be vulnerable to hunger even if he or she is not actually hungry at a given point in time.

xx. Hunger is usually understood as an uncomfortable or *painful* sensation caused by insufficient food energy consumption. Scientifically, hunger is referred to as food deprivation. Simply put, all hungry people are food insecure, but not all food insecure people are hungry, as there are other causes of food insecurity, including those due to poor intake of micro-nutrients.

xxi. Malnutrition results from deficiencies, excesses or imbalances in the consumption of macro- and/or micronutrients. Malnutrition may be an outcome of food insecurity, or it may relate to *non-food factors*, such as: inadequate care practices for children, insufficient health services; and an unhealthy environment.

xxii. While poverty is undoubtedly a cause of hunger, lack of adequate and proper nutrition itself is an underlying cause of poverty.

Chapter 6   Developing Global Food Crisis Measurement System

"Now, what I want is, Facts. Teach these boys and girls nothing but Facts. Facts alone are wanted in life. Plant nothing else. And root out everything else. You can only form the minds of reasoning animals upon Facts: nothing else will ever be of any service to them. This is the principle on which I bring up my own children, and this is the principle on which I bring up these children. Stick to Facts, sir!"
Charles Dickens, *"Hard Times"*(1854)

Introduction

After having built up the dimensional structure of GFC, the present chapter develops its measurement system. In the measurement of GFC, four distinct problems must be faced, viz., first, identifying the whole range of critical food crisis factors that are likely to affect the smooth functioning of the GAFS and impinge on availability, accessibility, adequacy and utilization of food at different levels. This problem has been addressed in the previous two chapters wherein interconnected forty-eight critical food crisis factors have been identified and synthesised. Second, by using causal reasoning, discovering and testing the complex causal theories and mechanisms (web of relations) underlying the complex phenomenon of GFC, developing thus an understanding of casual connections or multiple pathways among different constructs of GFC where all causes are interconnected. Third is to decompose the global food crisis index into food demand-side forces index, food supply-side restrictions index, global agricultural market failures index, government or public sector interventions and collective actions index. Fourth is to construct an index of global food crisis using the available information on the critical global food crisis factors of a global economy. The first problem involves the choice of a *criterion of global food crisis* (food insecurity, food prices, distribution of food, food demand or food supply). The second problem is concerned with the study of *causal structure of global food crisis*, whereby the interconnections among different food crisis factors are analysed. The multiple causal pathways among different dimensions of global food crisis are interpreted by path analysis in causal context (causal modelling). The third problem in the measurement of global food crisis involves *dimensional decomposition of global food crisis index* wherein the severity of different dimensions of worldwide food crisis can be compared across the countries. It employs two forms of criteria: one within each dimension to determine whether a country or global economy is experiencing food crisis in that dimension and second across different dimensions that identifies the country or global economy by counting the dimensions in which a country, region or global economy is in food crisis. The fourth problem involves the aggregation of dimensions to account for multidimensionality by *constructing an overall index of food severity* (a single number between one and 100) in such a way so as to allow a direct comparison of food crisis across each food crisis factor while at the same time being able to compare the food crisis in different countries, global economy as a whole as well as measured over time.

Significant contributions have been made in tackling the first and/or second problems during the 20th century as evident from the enormous scattered literature on food problems such as food insecurity, food vulnerability, hunger, malnutrition, rural poverty and so on. Undoubtedly, these contributions exhibit the gradual improvements in terms of conceptualisation, measurement techniques and analytical competence; however, none of them is adequate in terms of its subject matter, scope and coverage. Our world is increasingly becoming more complex, inter-connected, inter-dependent and ever-changing that makes it essential to look at new variables and measurement techniques that may be significant for analysis and interpretation of global food crisis. Kanji-Chopra Global Food Crisis Measurement System (KCGFCMS) proposed in this work takes care of all four above adumbrated problems simultaneously. Be that as it may, it subsumes conceptual model, operational model, latent variable structural model and measurement model of global food crisis (Chopra, 2011). The discussion of the present chapter is structured in the following sequence. The introduction which forms part one of the discussion is followed by the unfolding of the KCGFCMS in part two that includes four interlinked models namely, conceptual model, operational model, latent variable structural model and measurement model of GFC. It then discusses the GFC multiple causal pathways. The next section outlines a step-by-step procedure for obtaining GFC indices. The final part will lead the discussion to the concluding observations of the chapter.

Global Food Crisis Conceptual Model

The conceptualisation of GFC requires a systematic, multifactor, all-inclusive and integrated approach. It is the preparatory point of measuring a phenomenon such as GFC. The concept of GFC in the index is holistic, multidimensional and multidisciplinary. A quick review of literature on GFC reveals that global food crisis can be defined in different ways such as high food prices, food insecurity, hunger, malnutrition, political and civil turmoil, and the like. However, in real life GFC is a function of a large number of interrelated and interdependent factors such as global agricultural and food system, food demand side forces, food supply-side restrictions, global agricultural markets failures, and public sector interventions and collective actions failures. Therefore, GFC is a complex multidimensional phenomenon. It can be conceptualised as the combination of various internal and external interconnected and interwoven risks and crises attached to food security, food prices, hunger and malnutrition in a country. It is an aggregate of critical global food crisis factors obtained by weighted scores of a number of critical risks and uncertainties that affect the cost, demand, supply, availability and accessibility of food and hence, affects the wellbeing of the poor. Thus, the global food crisis conceptual model consists of an assessment of global agricultural and food system, food demand side developments, food supply side developments, agricultural food market failures and public sector intervention separately or together in a region, country or global economy which may adversely affect the welfare and development of human beings. In turn, each dimension of global food crisis is comprised of multiple factors that are often a combination of subjective evaluations and more objective macroeconomic statistics. The extent to which a country or global economy exhibits a risk to global food prices, availability and accessibility depends upon the system of positive and negative linkages.

181

It is possible to perform a synthesis between GFC and system dimensions for the purpose of developing a comprehensive GFC model. There is a means of doing it is by way of a conceptual model that integrates various concepts as shown in Figure 6.1.

Figure 6.1:   ***Global Food Crisis Conceptual Model***

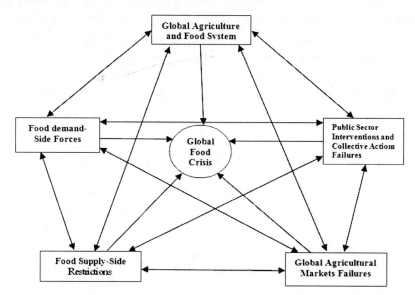

Source: Own construction

A complete GFC conceptual model in Figure 6.1 shows the multiple causal pathways (indicated by the arrows) interlinking global agriculture and food system, global agricultural markets failures, food demand-side forces, food supply-side restrictions, global agricultural market failures and public sector interventions and collective actions failures drivers with global food crisis are entwined with each other (as shown by double pathway arrow ◄────►) and they all are jointly leading to and contribute to global food crisis (as shown by the single pathway arrow ────►). All these factors have multiple causal relationships with each other. The GAFS is designated as a prime that controls the behaviour of every other dimension of GFC. In addition, a system is established for measuring multiple causal pathways that is equipped with a mechanism for providing feedbacks from the outcomes. Global agricultural and food system interacts with food supply-side restrictions, food demand-side forces, global agricultural markets and public sector interventions. Similarly, food demand-side forces of a certain level affect and are affected by others dimensions and produce impact on overall global food crisis. Food supply is also interwoven with other four constructs and contributes to GFC. Similarly, the construct of public sector interventions and collective actions failures also affects the GFC through multiple causal pathways. The GAFS result in economic and political turmoil as it happened in various economies recently. A significantly high level of control over market share can also lead to food crisis. It can be concluded that all these latent variables are significantly interdependent and interwoven with each other and jointly contribute to overall global food crisis.

Critical Food Crisis Factors: The Operational Model

The second stage of measurement system transforms the conceptual model into operational model by unfolding the complexity through looking deeper into the underlying diverse factors within each dimension of the phenomenon of GFC. It is at this stage that one needs to identify various critical indicators (variables) generating food problems within each complex dimension or critical food crisis factor (CFCF) in a region, country or global economy. For example, the construct of food-demand side forces is further influenced by many issues called indicators or manifest variables such as bio-fuel initiatives, increase in dietary diversity, livestock revolution and increased demand for animals feed, urbanisation and declining ratio of food producers to food consumers, global population growth, emerging markets, panic buying, and increase in demand for agricultural raw materials and wage goods. Similarly, other dimensions of GFC are influenced by their own respective determinants. As adumbrated in the previous chapters, the present study has identified that there are in total six CFCFs contributing jointly to GFC. Thus, the KCGFCMS identifies and takes into consideration forty-eight manifest variables that are key areas of food crisis for global economy, if managed properly they can improve the overall conditions and food security related to different dimensions and to overall GFC. The choice and selection of CFCFs and manifest variables will depend upon the researcher's judgement, justifications, extensive literature review, emerging empirical evidence and so on. However, the CFCFs can be arranged on the basis of their degree of importance depending upon the degree of their contributions to GFC. There may be different ways of assigning weights or importance to these factors. However, in the case of KCGFCMS the measurement of GFC index will involve determining weightings of CFCFs. A latent variable structural model of CFCFs is constructed and the strength of causal connections among the latent variables are analysed. The weights of the CFCFs will be automatically determined by the global food crisis measurement software. Depending upon the nature and type of the factors involved, the conceptual model is operationalised by adopting complexity perspective that assigns manifest variables to different latent variables of GFC (See Chopra, 2011). It is imperative to reveal here that the constructs of GFC cannot be directly measured but their empirical content can be obtained by identifying their respective manifest variables and using a measurement instrument that consists of a multi-item scale developed for each construct.

Global Food Crisis Latent Variable Structural Model

The third step in the GFC measurement system is to convert the operational model into latent variable structural model. This is a stage of model specification. Before the measurement system can be applied to measure GFC a latent variable structural model must be developed for measuring CFCFs and exploring their multiple causal connections. In addition, model relationships among the elements of model must be established in order to add value to the GFC. For this reason the operational model of GFC has been transformed into the structural model that defines CFCFs and GFC as model constructs. The mathematical equations are established to express the causal relationships among latent variables in the *structural model*. In a latent variable structural model the *inner model* is the part of the model that describes the relationships between the latent variables that make up the model. In this sense, the *path coefficients* are inner model parameter estimates (inner coefficients)[i]. The inner models are also frequently referred to as the structural models. Latent variables as opposed to observed variables are variables that are not directly observed but are rather inferred (through a mathematical model) from other variables that are observed (directly measured). The latent variables in global food crisis measurement system will be measured by their manifest variables which in turn will be represented by measurement items in a questionnaire. A latent variable structural model is a hypothetical or theoretical construct which means it is an unobserved variable presumed to exist within a structural model but for which direct measurements are not available. A latent variable structural model is a graphical model that specifies the presumed structure of causal connections among latent and manifest variables (Kanji, 2002; Chopra and Kanji, 2010a; Chopra and Kanji; 2010b, Chopra and Kanji; 2011). The latent variable structural model is used to represent the casual relationships among latent variables (Figure 6.2). The purpose of this work is to estimate the strengths of the causal connections among the latent variables and to test the goodness-of-fit of the structural model. To estimate the strength of these causal connections it is necessary to operationalise each of the latent variables in terms of manifest variables (measurement items). The manifest variables are measured using measurement items and serve as indicators of the latent variable. A latent variable structural model is expressed in a system of simultaneous equations known as structural equations for the original model. The structural equations generate hypothetical variance/covariance matrix of manifest variables. The degree to which a structural equation model reflects reality is given by the degree to which the hypothetical variance/covariance matrix is similar to, or has a good fit with, the empirical variance/covariance matrix for the same manifest variables. The chi-square for goodness-of-fit statistic is used to evaluate whether manifest variables are related to their respective latent variables. It is also used to test whether the structure among the latent variables is consistent with the data. This new model will provide a deeper understanding and greater theoretical knowledge about the management with measurement of global food crisis.

Variables Development

Variable development is the specification of variable of interest subsumed in the data e.g. in the KCGFCMS variables developed for constructs (latent variables) and their indicators (manifest variables). Other variables (e.g., path coefficients, GFC indices and correlations) are the results of mathematical transformations and planned analytic or statistical procedures performed on the data sets. The variable list is given in Figure 6.2.

Figure 6.2: A Matrix Equation Explicit Rendering for Simultaneous Equations System for Global Food Crisis

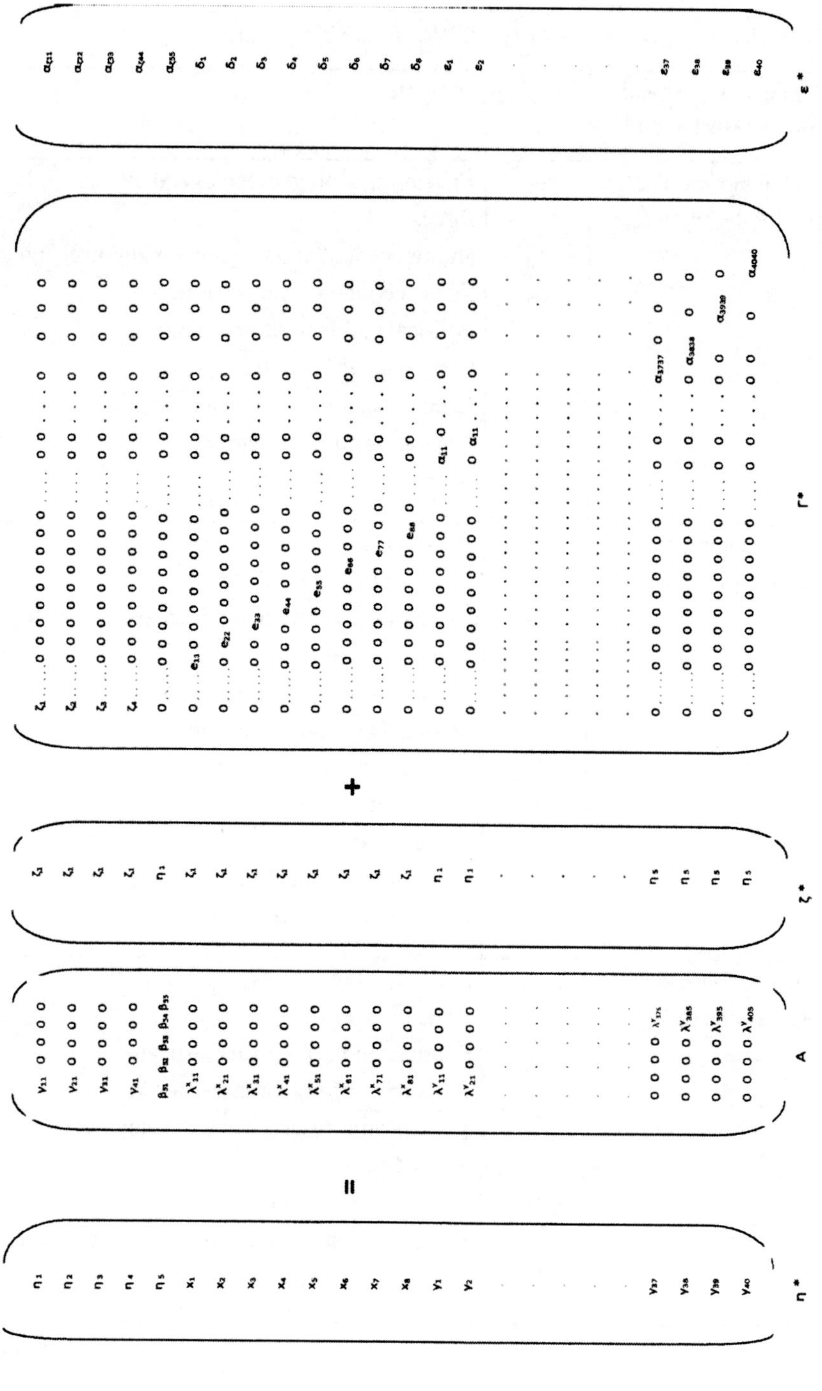

Table 6.1: *Variables List for Global Food Crisis Model*

Dimension: Critical Food Crisis Factor	Label	Variable
Global agriculture and food system (ξ_1)	x_1	Environmental, geo-ecological and natural forces
	x_2	Human capital and technical manpower forces
	x_3	Socio-economic and cultural forces
	x_4	Political and institutional forces
	x_5	Corporate global food system
	x_6	Greater sectoral integration
	x_7	Technological dominance
	x_8	Systemic risks
Food demand-side forces (η_1)	y_1	Bio-fuels initiatives
	y_2	Increase in dietary diversity
	y_3	Livestock revolution and increased demand for animals feed
	y_4	Urbanisation and declining ratio of food producers to food consumers
	y_5	Global population growth
	y_6	Emerging markets
	y_7	Panic buying
	y_8	Increase in demand for agricultural raw materials and wage goods
Food supply-side restrictions (η_2)	y_9	Scarcity of resources
	y_{10}	Land constraints
	y_{11}	Climate and ecological constraints
	y_{12}	Pests and animal diseases shocks
	y_{13}	Agricultural research and development expenditure
	y_{14}	Peculiar nature of costs
	y_{15}	Biological nature of the production process
	y_{16}	Access to finance

Continue...

Global agricultural markets failures (η_3)	y_{17}	Emergence of oligopolistic and oligopsonistic structures
	y_{18}	Social justice and economic equity
	y_{19}	Factor market imperfections
	y_{20}	Agricultural commodities trade distortions
	y_{21}	Externalities related to production and consumption activities
	y_{22}	Cobweb process
	y_{23}	Rising expectations and financial speculations
	y_{24}	Information asymmetries
Public sector interventions and collective actions failures (η_4)	y_{25}	Fiscal policy interventions failures
	y_{26}	Public sector agricultural and food enterprises failures
	y_{27}	State monopoly on food imports and exports
	y_{28}	Deterioration of existing infrastructure facilities in rural sector
	y_{29}	Inefficient government rural development programmes
	y_{30}	Collective actions institutions failures
	y_{31}	Food health and safety regulations failures
	y_{32}	Urban-bias investment strategy
Global food crisis (η_5)	y_{33}	Rising food prices
	y_{34}	Utilisation of food
	y_{35}	Environmental sustainability and ecological security
	y_{36}	Food security and self-sufficiency
	y_{37}	Phenomenon of overeating and food wastage
	y_{38}	Social welfare, social justice and economic equity
	y_{39}	Policies of international institutions and organisations
	y_{40}	Food vulnerability

Structural Equations

The latent variable structural model of the global food crisis is given in Figure 6.2. The model contains a latent exogenous[ii] variable (ξ_1), five latent endogenous[iii] variables (η_1 to η_5), eight observed (manifest) exogenous variables (x_1 to x_8) which feed the exogenous latent variables, and forty observed (manifest) endogenous variables (y_1 to y_{40}) which feed the endogenous latent variables resulting in total forty-eight manifest variables. Thus, ξ_1 is operationalised by eight indicator variables (x_1 to x_8) and is a cause of latent endogenous variables η_1, η_2, η_3, η_4, and η_5 as indicated by arrows from ξ_1 to η_1, η_2, η_3, η_4, and η_5. Eight manifest endogenous variables (y_1 to y_8) serve as indicators of η_1 as indicated by the arrows from η_1 to these variables in squares in Figure 6.2. The subscript numbers indicate a particular variable's location within the matrices which are used for calculation purposes. Each operationalisation of the model's latent variables is made in a similar way. The model recognises that the measures are imperfect and we make an attempt to model this imperfection. Thus, the model includes terms representing measurement errors or structural disturbances or errors in equations. The measurement error terms associated with 'x' measures are labelled with the eight Greek character 'delta' (δ_1 to δ_8) and each 'x' is also associated with structural parameter[iv] (regression coefficient) relating measurement error to manifest exogenous variable (e_{11} to e_{88}, i.e., these are used to indicate the effect of a disturbance variable on an exogenous manifest variable. The measurement errors associated with 'y' (y_1 to y_{40}) are labelled with Greek letter 'epsilon' (ε_1 to ε_{40}) and each 'y' is also associated with structural parameter (weight or coefficient) relating measurement error to manifest endogenous variable (α_{11} to α_{4040}, inner coefficients, i.e., these are used to indicate the effect of a disturbance variable on an endogenous manifest variable). The measurement errors associated with endogenous variables are labelled as ζ_1 to ζ_5 and the structural parameters relating these disturbance variables to latent endogenous variables are labelled as $\alpha\zeta_{11}$, $\alpha\zeta_{22}$, $\alpha\zeta_{33}$, and $\alpha\zeta_{44}$ (inner coefficients). The characters γ_{11}, γ_{21}, γ_{31}, and γ_{41} are the structural parameters relating exogenous variable to endogenous variables (inner coefficients). The Greek characters β_{51}, β_{52}, β_{53}, and β_{54} are structural parameters relating the endogenous variables to another endogenous construct.

Figure 6.3 *Latent Variable Structural Model of Global Food Crisis*

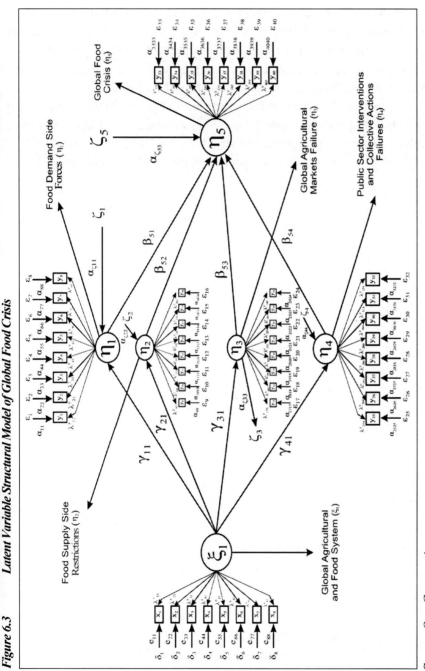

Source: Own Construction

The KCGFC model in Figure 6.2 can be expressed by a system of simultaneous equations. One variable is developed for each latent or manifest variable which means that there are altogether fifty three equations. Each equation includes the latent and/or manifest variables that have a direct effect on the endogenous variable including disturbance variables. Thus, the components of a structural equation are the latent variables, structural parameters and a disturbance term. Other endogenous variable will have similar equations. Latent variables structural model of global food crisis is expressed by a system of simultaneous equations. This system of equations is as follows:

$$\eta_1 = \gamma_{11} \, \xi_1 + \zeta_1 \alpha_{\zeta 11}$$
$$\eta_2 = \gamma_{21} \, \xi_1 + \zeta_1 \alpha_{\zeta 22}$$
$$\eta_3 = \gamma_{31} \, \xi_1 + \zeta_1 \alpha_{\zeta 33}$$
$$\eta_4 = \gamma_{41} \, \xi_1 + \zeta_1 \alpha_{\zeta 44}$$
$$\eta_5 = \beta_{51} \eta_1 + \beta_{52} \eta_2 + \beta_{53} \eta_3 + \beta_{54} \eta_4 + \zeta_5 \alpha_{\zeta 55}$$
$$x_1 = \lambda^x_{11} \xi_1 + e_{11} \, \delta_1$$
$$x_2 = \lambda^x_{21} \xi_1 + e_{22} \, \delta_2$$
$$x_3 = \lambda^x_{31} \xi_1 + e_{33} \delta_3$$
$$x_4 = \lambda^x_{41} \xi_1 + e_{44} \delta_4$$
$$x_5 = \lambda^x_{51} \xi_1 + e_{55} \delta_{58}$$
$$x_6 = \lambda^x_{61} \xi_1 + e_{66} \delta_6$$
$$x_7 = \lambda^x_{71} \xi_1 + e_{77} \delta_7$$
$$x_8 = \lambda^x_{81} \xi_1 + e_{88} \delta_8$$
$$y_1 = \lambda^y_{11} \eta_1 + \alpha_{11} \varepsilon_1$$
$$y_2 = \lambda^y_{21} \eta_1 + \alpha_{22} \varepsilon_2$$

$$\cdots$$

$$y_{37} = \lambda^y 3_{75} \eta_5 + \alpha_{3737} \varepsilon_{37}$$
$$y_{38} = \lambda^y_{385} \eta_5 + \alpha_{3838} \varepsilon_{38}$$
$$y_{39} = \lambda^y_{395} \eta_5 + \alpha_{3939} \varepsilon_{39}$$
$$y_{40} = \lambda^y_{405} \eta_5 + \alpha_{4040} \varepsilon_{40}$$

In the above equations, we have the following definitions:
- ξ_1 = Global agricultural and food system (latent exogenous variable)
- η_1 = Food-demand side factors (latent endogenous variable)

- η_2 = Food-supply side factors (latent endogenous variable)
- η_3 = Global agricultural markets failures (latent endogenous variable)
- η_4 = Public sector interventions and collective actions failure (latent endogenous variable)
- η_5 = Global food crisis (latent endogenous variable)
- λ^x_{11} = Structural parameter or regression coefficient linking exogenous construct to its measures (exogenous manifest variables)
- λ^y_{11} = Structural parameter (regression coefficient) linking endogenous construct to its measures (endogenous manifest variables)
- γ_{11} = Structural parameters (regression coefficients) relating exogenous variables to endogenous (inner coefficients)
- e_{11} to e_{88} = Measurement errors associated with manifest exogenous variables
- ζ_1 to ζ_5 = Measurement errors associated with endogenous variables
- ε_1 to ε_{40} = Measurement errors associated with manifest endogenous variables

Structural Errors

As it is very rare to expect to perfectly predict the dependent constructs, it is important to include error term in the latent variable structural model, labelled as the Greek character 'zeta' (ζ). In order to achieve consistent parameter estimation these error terms are assumed to be uncorrelated with the model's exogenous constructs. The violation of this assumption comes about as a result of the excluded predictor problem. However, the structural error terms have been modelled as being correlated with other structural error terms. This specification indicates that the endogenous constructs associated with those error terms share common variation that is not explained by predictor relations in the model.

Matrix Equations

A matrix of equations representing the fifty three variablemodel is given in Table 6.2. *Dependent variables* are represented in a random vector η^* that may be portioned as $\eta^{*\prime} = [\eta', x', y']$, where η' is a (transposed) random subvector of latent endogenous variables, x′ is a (transported) random subvector of manifest exogenous (independent) variables and y′ is a (transposed) random subvector of manifest endogenous (dependent) variables. The number of latent dependent variables in η′ is indicated by m_1, the number of manifest exogenous variables is indicated by m_2, and the number of manifest dependent variables in y′ is indicated by m_3. The total number of dependent variables is indicated by m, where $m = m_1 + m_2 + m_3$. The order of η′ is thus m x 1.

Independent variables are included in a single random column vector ξ*. Thus, we may write ξ* = [ξ′,$η_1$′] where ξ′ stands for a (transposed) subvector of latent exogenous variables, and $η_y$′ stands for a (transposed) random subvector of manifest endogenous variables. The number of latent exogenous variables included in ξ′ is n_1: the number of manifest endogenous variables in $η_y$′ is equal to m (the number of dependent variables). The number of independent variables in ξ* is thus $n_1 + m = n$, and so the order of ξ* is n x 1.

The *path coefficients* (inner) $γ_{ij}$ that relate independent to dependent latent variables, path coefficients (inner) $β_{ij}$ that relate pairs of dependent variables and path coefficients (outer) λxij and $λ^y_{ij}$ that relate latent variables with their manifest variables are included in matrix A. Each row of A corresponds to one of the dependent variables and contains structural parameters corresponding to the variable's connections with independent variables that cause it. The *path coefficients* (outer path coefficient or structural parameter) $λ^x_{ij}$ relate latent exogenous variable to its manifest variables and the path coefficients (outer) $λ^y_{ij}$ relate latent endogenous variables to their manifest variables. The elements of diagonal of A are thus ordinarily zero, meaning that a dependent variable does not cause itself, i.e., A zero element of ith row and k^{th} column of means that the kth exogenous variable is not the cause of the variable.

The *structural errors* ($ζ_{ij}$) associated with latent endogenous variables, structural errors (e_{ij}) linking measurement errors to manifest exogenous variables and structural errors ($α_{ij}$) linking measurement errors with manifest endogenous variables are contained in the matrix Γ*. The matrix Γ* = [Γ: e: Δ] is partitioned into 'm x 1' matrix; Γ into 'm x n' and 'm x m' for matrix Δ. The rows of Γ correspond to the different dependent variables. The column of Γ corresponds to only one exogenous variable. In the present example Γ is a 5 x 1 submatrix. The submatrix 'e' contains measurement errors relating to manifest exogenous variables, and 'e' is a 8 x 8 submatrix. The submatrix Δ contains structural errors linking measurement errors to manifest endogenous variables. The rows of Δ also correspond to the different manifest variables which correspond to different disturbance variables. In the present example, Δ is a 40x40 matrix.

The *disturbance variables* are included in a single random column vector ε^*. This vector may be partitioned to distinguish between manifest and latent exogenous disturbance variables. Thus, we may write $\varepsilon^* = [\alpha\zeta'$, δ', $\varepsilon']$ where α_ζ' stands for a (transported) sub vector of latent disturbance variables, δ' stands for a (transported) subvector of manifest exogenous disturbance variables, and ε' stands for manifest endogenous disturbance variables. The number of latent disturbance variables in α_ζ' is n_1, the number of manifest exogenous disturbance variables in δ' is m_1, and the number of manifest endogenous disturbance variables in ε' is equal to m_2. The number of disturbance variables in ε^* is thus $n_1+m_1+m_2$.

A more compact for the general matrix formulation of the linear structural equation model with latent manifest variables is given by

$$\begin{bmatrix} \eta \\ x \\ y \end{bmatrix} = A \begin{bmatrix} \xi \\ \eta \end{bmatrix} + [\Gamma : e : \Delta] \begin{bmatrix} \alpha_\zeta \\ \delta \\ \varepsilon \end{bmatrix}$$

or more simply

$$\eta^* = A\xi^* + \Gamma^*\varepsilon^*$$

The goal of structural equation model is to show how relationships among manifest variables (given by either correlation or covariance) can be explained in terms of structural equations relating manifest variables to other (possibly latent) variables of the model. To reach this goal it is required that a certain 'selection' equation draws out manifest variables in the subvectors x and y, from the larger vectors η^* and, of variables. The selection equation is

$$y=[0:I] \begin{bmatrix} \eta \\ x \\ y \end{bmatrix}$$

or

$$y = G_y \eta_1^*$$

$G_y = [0{:}I]$ is a partitioned (m_2 x m) 'selection' matrix with 0, an m_2 x m_1 null matrix and I, an m_2 x m_2 identity matrix. In other words, G_y contains zero elements everywhere except for a single element of unity in each row placed in the appropriate column of G_y to 'select' a corresponding manifest dependent variable for η^*.

The matrix reflecting the variances and covariance among independent variables of the model is

$$\Phi = E(\xi^* \; \xi^{*\prime})$$

The model requires that exogenous variables are independent of disturbance variables. This requirement is expressed mathematically by the requirement

$$E \; \varepsilon[\xi']$$

where E is the expectation operator.

The effect of this requirement appears in the matrix and may be seen in a partitioning of this matrix as

$$\Phi = \begin{bmatrix} \eta & 0_{\varepsilon\varepsilon} \\ y & \Phi_{\varepsilon\varepsilon} \end{bmatrix}$$

where $\Phi_{\varepsilon\varepsilon} = E(\xi\xi')$ and $0_{\varepsilon\varepsilon} = E(\varepsilon\varepsilon')$
The terms $E(\varepsilon\xi')$ and $E(\xi\varepsilon') = 0$ in above equation.

The variance/covariance matrix among manifest variables is given by

$$\Sigma_0 = \Sigma_{yy}$$

where according to the model,

$$\Sigma_{yy} = \Sigma(yy') = G_y B^{-1} \Gamma^* \Phi \Lambda^{*\prime} B^{-1\prime} G_y'$$

The above equation implies that a predicted or hypothetical variance/covariance matrix Σ_0 for the set of observed variables in random vector y may be derived from the parameter values of a hypothetical structural equation model. Therefore, the degree to which the hypothetical structural equation model reflects reality is given by the degree to which the hypothetical matrix Σ_0 is the same as the empirical variance/covariance matrix Σ for the same variables (in y) obtained from measurements of these variables in the world. To make the comparison between the hypothetical matrix Σ_0 and the empirical matrix Σ is the goal of a confirmatory analysis using structural equation models with latent and manifest variables. In practice, Σ_0 and Σ are replaced with sample estimates namely, Σ_0' and S respectively.

Model Identification and Path Coefficients

Before the values of path coefficients can be obtained the structural equation model must be specified in such a way that the 'model' is 'identified'. Identifying a model involves fixing the values of some coefficients (fixed parameters) and using data to estimate values of other coefficients (free parameters) that would result in a unique hypothetical population covariance matrix of manifest variables (James, Mulaik and Brett, 1982). The least squares estimation method is used to minimise the sum of squared differences between the elements of sample covariance matrix (S) and the hypothetical population covariance (Σ_0') matrix for manifest variables.

Analysis of path coefficients begins with the outer path coefficients. For every relationship all measurement items with values of path coefficients that are less than 0.1 are removed from the model. This is to ensure that only manifest variables that adequately reflect the empirical content of latent variables are retained for further analysis. Usually PLS has to be run several times to remove all manifest variables that are poorly linked to latent variables. The outer coefficients of remaining manifest variables are then used to compute critical food crisis factor and global food crisis indices for the study samples by using a mathematical expression that takes into account item mean scores and number of points in the scales. Following the analysis of outer coefficients, the research is then concerned with inner coefficients which represent the amount of change in a dependent variable, expressed as multiples of standard deviation, when the value of its independent variable is changed by one unit.

Standardised inner coefficients cannot be compared across groups of sample, nor can those that are produced by the same population over time. However, standardisation of data simplifies the computation of path coefficients because correlation matrix of manifest variables is used instead of the covariance matrix. In the PLS method, the values of inner coefficients for causal connections that do not involve a single dependent variable can be easily determined by reading their values directly from the correlation matrix. The values of inner coefficients for causal connections that involve a single dependent variable, however, have to be solved from the following equation (Namboodiri et al., 1975):

$$r_{ij} = \sum_k p_{ik} r_{kj}$$

where i = endogenous variable $(I > k, j)$; j = causal variable; and k begins with I-1 and ranges down to 1 (i.e. η_1).

Global Food Crisis Measurement Model

The fourth step in the global food crisis measurement model (GFCMM) is to convert the structural model into a measurement model. The equations that express the relationships between latent variables and their indicators are referred to as the *measurement model*. The *outer model* is the part of the model that describes the relationships between the latent variables and their indicators. The outer models are also frequently referred to as the measurement models. Thus, the outer models containing weights and loadings are also referred to as measurement models. At this stage, the latent constructs, which are not directly measurable, are translated into a set of indicators (manifest variables). Each latent variable is usually associated with multiple measures. The measurement model is the mapping of measures onto theoretical constructs. The latent constructs are most commonly linked to their measures (manifest variables) through a factor analytic measurement model, i.e., each latent variable construct is modelled as a common factor underlying the associated measures. These 'loadings' linking latent constructs to measures are labelled with the Greek character 'lambda' (λ) and there are two separate 'lambda matrices', one on the X side (λ^x_{11}) and one on the Y side (λ^y_{11}) as shown in Figure 6.3. The global food crisis measurement model is the congeneric measurement model, where each measure is associated with only one latent construct, and all covariation between measures is a consequence of the relations between measures and constructs. Most of the models in use are indicative or non-prescriptive models whereas GFCMM is an improvement or prescriptive model. For the measurement of global food crisis, the main objective is to develop a suitable latent variable structural model that shows relationship between variables, other intervening variables and ultimately global food crisis. A measurement scale must be developed so that the model can be used to profile global food crisis practices.

Figure 6.4:   *Global Food Crisis Measurement Model*

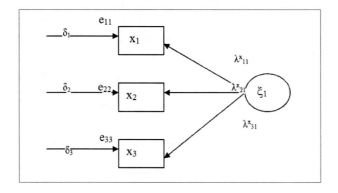

Measurement Error

Almost every measure is acknowledged to include some error since the measures are imperfect and this imperfection is modelled by including terms representing measurement error in the equation. These measurement error terms are uniquenesses or unique factors associated with each measure. Measurement error terms associated with X measures are labelled as the Greek character 'delta' (δ) while terms associated with Y measures are labelled with 'epsilon' (ε).

To estimate the strengths of causal relations, it is necessary to operationalise each of the latent variables in terms of manifest variables that are believed to be caused by a latent variable. In this sense, each latent variable has the role of a common factor, and the manifest variables serve as manifest indicators of the common factor. The empirical content of each manifest variable is reflected directly by assigning observable events to values on the measurement scale of the variables. The measurement model contains the following:

Global Food Crisis Multiple Casual Pathways

Figure 6.5, a graphical representation of the KCGFCMS, matches the paths and interrelationships to the variables. In this step a model was used to establish the set of structural and measurement elements that link the diagram to the constructs of the theory. Structural equations were used to link the constructs. Variables were assigned to the specific constructs showing which variables measure which constructs. A set of matrices was used to indicate the hypothesized constructs from the critical food crisis factors to the constructs or variables. The KCGFCMS was designed to identify the manifest variables to the latent variable constructs.

Figure 6.5:   *Global Food Crisis Multiple Casual Pathways*

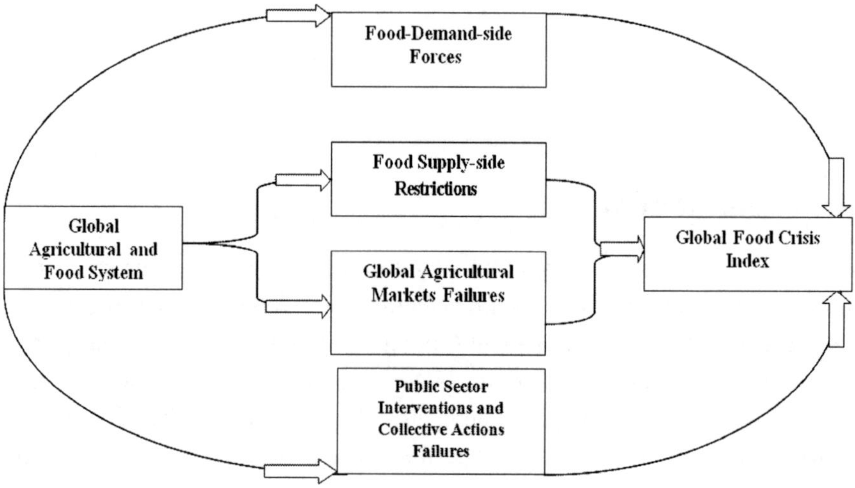

All the variables in the KCCRMS are dependent variables except global agricultural and food system which is independent variable. All dependent variables are directly connected with independent variable except global food crisis. Therefore, dependent variable global food crisis is indirectly linked with independent variable global agri-food system through four causal pathways. In PLS, functional equations are formatted for every causal connection. These equations take into account path coefficients and variable mean scores. It is possible to calculate the contribution of each variable toward global food crisis from the value of path coefficients. KCCRMS has four pathways going through it each starting from global agricultural and food system and ending with global food crisis as shown in Figure 6.6. The arrow ◄────► shows that the pathways is on both sides, it means that a unit change in global agricultural and food system produces change in food demand and subsequently in global food crisis and vice versa.

Figure 6.6:   *The Four Pathways through the Global Food Crisis Model*

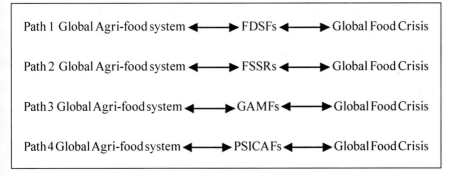

Measurement of the Elements

The measurement of the elements is based on the Analysis of Covariance Structures (Nunnally and Bernstein, 1994). The model used matrix notation in a statistical package to set up the simultaneous equations. All structural parameters assume values that reflect the strengths of causal relationships. Specially, each structural parameter reflects the amount of change in an effect (endogenous variable) that results from a unit of change in a cause (exogenous variable or preceding endogenous variable) with all other causes of that effect held constant. A key objective of representing the KCGFCMS as a latent variable structural model is to do a confirmatory analysis to estimate the values of the structural parameters. The ε_i's associated with each endogenous variable are the 'disturbance terms'. Disturbance terms involve variation in an endogenous variable that is not to be attributed to the causes of that variable included explicitly in a structural model. In the structural model the sources of variation include (a) random shocks and/or unmeasured or omitted causes, (b) random measurement errors in the effect and the causes where the primary concern is error in one or more of the causes, and (c) non-random measurement such as bias in scales of measurement and method variance. The inclusion of the disturbance variation in the KCGF-CMS makes it a probabilistic model.

Functional Relations

The causal relations in the model can be expressed as functional relations, that is a function of an effect on one or more causes. The functional relations are asymmetric because their causal directions are unidirectional. It can be observed from the structural model that there are four types of functional relations: (a) relation between an exothermic latent variable and endothermic latent variable; (b) relation between an exothermic latent variable and manifest indicator variables; (c) relation between an endothermic latent variable to one or more endothermic variable(s); (d) relation between a latent endothermic variable with manifest indicator variables. In structural models functional relations are analysed by using structural equations.

Structural Equations

The above four types of functional relations can be expressed as a system of equations known as functional equations. For the KCGFCMS there is one endogenous variable and forty eight manifest variables which mean that altogether there would be forty eight equations in the system of functional equations.

Empirical Support for Functional Equations

The confirmatory analysis using manifest variables may proceed only if the manifest variables are reasonably accurate representations of the constructs. The objective of such an analysis is to check whether a structural model can be confirmed. Confirmation implies that a structural model and functional equations representing the model are useful for making causal inferences to explain how variables occur (excluding purely exogenous variables). Non-confirmation implies that the structural model (functional relations and equations) are not useful in this respect. The functional relations and equations in a linear structural model may be used to drive a set of predictions regarding the observed correlations (or variance/covariance) among the manifest variables. A structural model is confirmed if the predictions regarding correlations (variance/covariance) among manifest variables are consistent with the observed (i.e. empirically derived) correlations (variance/covariance) among manifest variables. Non-confirmation is implied if predictions and observed correlations (variances/covariances) are inconsistent.

Confirmation of predictions implies support for the structural model represented by the functional relations as equations. Non-confirmation of predictions implies that one or more components of structural model (functional relations and equations) is (are) false, in which case it is concluded that the structural model proposed originally is invalid. Predictions regarding correlations (variances/covariances) among manifest variables and confirmation/non-confirmation of these predictions can be addressed empirically by testing predictions regarding the magnitudes of estimates of structural parameters.

Solutions and Estimates of Structural Parameters

Structural equation modeling (SEM) provides a means by which relationships can be tested. The purpose of the approach is to estimate the strength of the causal connections among the latent variables and to test the goodness of fit of the structural model (KCGFCMS). To estimate the strength of these causal connections it is necessary for each of the latent variables to be operational in terms of manifest variables (measurement items). In reality, the manifest variables are measured by using measurement items such as questionnaires; also, they serve as indicators of the latent variable. A measurement instrument (i.e. questionnaire) is then developed and used to obtain scores from respondents on a variety of attributes that provide an empirical content to the model's constructs.

The importance of meeting these conditions depends on the estimation methods used. Some estimation methods can adjust for the violation of some of these assumptions. In structural models with latent variables we make the assumptions that the distribution of the manifest variables is a function of their variance/covariance matrix. By making this assumption, it is possible to determine the non-fixed parameters of the model. The estimated and fixed structural parameters of a structural equation model determine a hypothetical variance/covariance (correlation) matrix for the manifest variables (Y_o) under the assumption that the model is valid. The structural parameters y and α computed are actually unstandardarised regression coefficients of the structural equations. In the PLS method, the structural parameters of structural equation linking latent variables and manifest variables are called structural weights. As recommended by Anderson and Gerbing (1998), SEM analysis should be performed in two stages with the first stage aiming at the development of a measured model marked with a solid goodness of fit and the second stage targeting at the analysis of the structural model. In the study, the first stage of SEM analysis utilized CFA (confirmatory factory analysis) to examine the model's goodness of fit and to check if sufficient convergent validity and discriminant validity exist in each dimension.

Global Food Crisis Measurement Software

The statistical reasoning behind KCGFCMS is relatively complex, but the user will not need to have any particular mathematical expertise, although some basic skills and statistical knowledge will help. To support the implementation of KCGFCMS, Kanji-Chopra Global Food Crisis index measurement (KCGFCIM) software package calculates the estimates of the parameters of structural equation models, all the associated indices and produces some standard graphics. As mentioned before, KCGFCMS is based on a structural equation modelling technique which combines aspects of multiple regression and factor analysis to estimate simultaneously a series of interrelated dependence relationships. The Kanji-Chopra software, which essentially uses the Partial Least Squares (PLS) method in the simultaneous estimation of the weights of the constructs of the model, calculates these weights in a way that maximises the goodness of fit of the model and thus, has the ability to explain contestability excellence as the ultimate endogenous variable. It is not necessary to have any particular expertise to work with the software package. Anyone who feels comfortable working with Windows usual software programs will soon become familiar with this package. The software generates several types of outputs: outer coefficients (γ, a); inner coefficients (γ, a); Pearson correlation coefficient square (inner r^2); Pearson correlation coefficient (inner r) and Cronbach coefficient (α).

Outer Coefficients (Structural Weights)

The outer coefficients are the unstandardized structural weights of manifest indicator variables. Structural weights must have values significantly different from zero for a confirmation or non-confirmation of a model. Specially, each structural weight reflects the amount of change in an effect (endogenous variable) the results from a unit of change in a cause (exogenous variable or endogenous variable) with all other causes of that effect held constant.

Inner Coefficients (Structural Parameter of Latent Variables)

Structural parameters are the coefficients of functional equations linking latent variables. Structural parameters must have values significantly different from zero for confirmation or non-confirmation of the model. These values reflect the strengths of causal relationships. Specifically, each structural parameter reflects the amount of change in an effect (endogenous variable) that results from a unit of change in a cause (exogenous variable or preceding endogenous variable) with all other causes of that effect held constant.

Variability Analysis

The variability analysis has been undertaken by taking into using Standard Deviation. The standard deviation is the standard error of sample estimate of a structural parameter associated with a causal connection. It provides information on the spread of the parameter estimate from the mean.

Coefficients

The t-coefficient of a structural parameter is the confidence interval around the estimate of the structural parameter. By using the standard error of the parameter, if the confidence intervals constructed around the structural parameter differ significantly from zero, then it can be concluded that there exists a causal connection between the variables in question.

Causality Analysis

The causality analysis is done with the help of: *(a) Correlation Matrix (γ_{ij}):* This is the Pearson correlation, r, matrix among all the exogenous and endogenous variables in the model. Values in the matrix corresponding to latent variables that have cause and effect relationship provide additional indication of strength of their relationship; (b) *Coefficient of Determination (r^2):* The coefficient of determination (r^2) represents the proportion of regression sum of squares corresponding to latent variables. The regression model explains the proportion of the total variation due to the cause-variable and the proportion due to randomness and other variables; (c) *Pearson Correlation Coefficient (r):* Pearson correlation coefficient r is the correlation of latent variables that have causal connections. The closer this value is to ±1, the stronger is the relationship between the variables in both directions.

Model Validity

A valid measurement scale is one that does what it is supposed to do and measures that it is supposed to measure (Nunnally, 1978). There are several types of validity measures. However, the present research is concerned with three: content validity, construct validity and criterion-related validity. Content validity is concerned with the degree to which scale items represent the domain of concepts under study. Construct validity deals with the degree to which the scales represent and act like the concepts being measured. Statistically, there are two types of construct validity: convergent validity and discriminant validity (Campbell and Fiske, 1959). Convergent validity is commonly defined as the degree of association between two maximally different measurements that purport to measure essentially the same concepts. Discriminant validity is defined as the degree to which the measurement scale may be differentiated from other scales purporting to measure maximally different concepts. It is mainly adopted to test the distinction or discrimination between dimensions representing similar concepts. The criterion-related validity sometimes called predictive or external validity is concerned with the extent to which the measurement instrument is related to an independent measure of a relevant criterion (Bohrnstedt, 1970).

Cronbach Alpha (Coefficient α)

Coefficient α value provides an indicator of internal consistency of latent variables (data) that are being empirically reflected by manifest variables. It is calculated using variance of individual questions and covariance between items. The formula is:

$$\alpha = \frac{k}{k-1} \left\{ 1 - \frac{\Sigma \sigma_i^2}{\Sigma \sigma_i^2 + 2\Sigma \ \Sigma \sigma_{ij}^2} \right\}$$

where, k = the number of items in the scale, σ_i^2 = the variance of item i, and σ_{ij} = the covariance of the items i and j. Computing alpha divides total variance into signal and noise components. In other words, the total variance that is equal to the signal is equal to alpha. The second term in brackets represents the noise in the model (DeVellis, 2003). According to Nunnally (1978), the alpha value should exceed 0.7 to suggest an acceptable reliability. Thus, in terms of Composite Reliability (CR) and Average Variance Extracted (AVE) all variables and dimensions should show a CR value exceeding the acceptable level of 0.7 and an AVE value over 0.5, testifying to the fine reliability of the measurement scale and internal consistency of the analysis model (consistency of the questions).

The Global Food Crisis Index Derived

KCGFCMS uses a ten-step scale in order to provide reliable data. All these variables are scored based on the average score on their respective questions. This average is useful when analysing how well a certain area is performed in a country. GFC is not the total average of all the variables, the Global Food Crisis Index (GFCI) is based on how well or badly all other areas are performing. GFCI is dependent on how the variables correlate and thereby produce global food crisis.

Knowing the relationship between CFCFs and GFCI is useful in examining the strength of CFCFs to determine which one needs to be improved by how much, and in what ways in order to improve global food crisis. GFCI is also influenced by the structural weights and the scores of manifest variables that are linked to it as specified by the GFCI mathematical formula as follows:

$$GFCI = \left[\frac{\sum_{i=1}^{n} w_i\, x_i - \sum_{i=1}^{n} w_i}{(N-1)\sum_{i=1}^{n} w_i} \right] \times 100$$

where N = number of points on the scale; x_i = manifest variables for each latent variable; and w_i = outer coefficients. The index value has a range of 0 to 100. 0 indicates no GFC and the values scores closer to zero indicate low-GFC pole of the scale, values between 25 to 50 are medium food crisis countries, the score between 51 to 75 are highly food crisis and score above 76 and closer to 100 indicate extremely-food crisis pole of the scale. The latent variable scores were calculated by using a mathematical expression derived by Fornell (1992) using the weight (w) and the arithmetic mean (x) for each question. Since the weights indicate the strength of relationship between variables, they could be used to determine the amount of improvement needed in different CFCFs in order to improve the situation of food crisis.

Sequence for Obtaining Global Food Crisis Indices in KCGFC Model: A Step-by-Step Procedure

The issues involved in the specially designed KCGFCMS are as follows:

1. Latent variables corresponding to concepts cannot be measured directly. They are operationalisations of constructs in a structural equation model. In KCGFCMS global agricultural and food system, food demand-side forces, food supply-side restrictions, global agricultural market failures, public sector interventions and collective actions failures, and the construct of GFC are all latent variables. Since they cannot be directly observed, they must be represented by manifest variables.

2. Manifest variables are, therefore, observed values for specific items or questions which are used as indicators of latent variables. In KCGFCMS a set of manifest variables were identified to adequately cover the domain of each construct. The manifest variables

correspond to the questionnaire items.

3. Sometimes the set of manifest variables that represent one particular latent variable is referred to as a measurement scale. Measurement scales must obey certain conditions. Apart from adequately representing the domain of the concept (validity), scales are expected to be unidimensional (representing a single construct) statistically reliable (stable and consistent for which, in the KCGFCMS approach, Cronbach's coefficient a is calculated).

4. That is obviously different from the simple notion of scale as the range of values a variable assume. In KCGFCMS questionnaire each item is answered on a one to ten scale.

5. The weights in the structural equation model are usually designed as path coefficients and represent the strength of the relationships among different variables. In a structural equation model, both inner and outer coefficients are estimated.

6. Inner coefficients reflect the strength of causal relationships among variables. They are the coefficients of the equations linking latent variables and each inner coefficient represents the amount of change in an effect variable that results from a unit change in a cause variable. The coefficients in KCGFCMS are expected to be all positive, showing that all dimensions contribute to the phenomenon and reinforce each other.

7. Outer coefficients correspond to the weights of the manifest variables. The higher they are, the more relevant they become in explaining the correspondent manifest variable.

8. Indices are the scores obtained for each manifest variable, based upon the correspondent manifest variables and the path coefficients in the model.

The implementation of this study includes an explanation of the data collection, survey developments, data analysis, sensitivity analysis, and summarisation. This plan is a customisation of the concepts of the GFC. Figure 7.1 is a graphical model of the step-by-step procedure for implementation plan of KCGFCMS to drive GFC indices which reflects the steps of each phase of the development of the study and demonstrates the approach used in this study to build the theoretical constructs, collect data, build the model, make comparisons, and draw conclusions about the

Figure 6.7: **Step by Step Process for Deriving Global Food Crisis Indices in KCGFCMS**

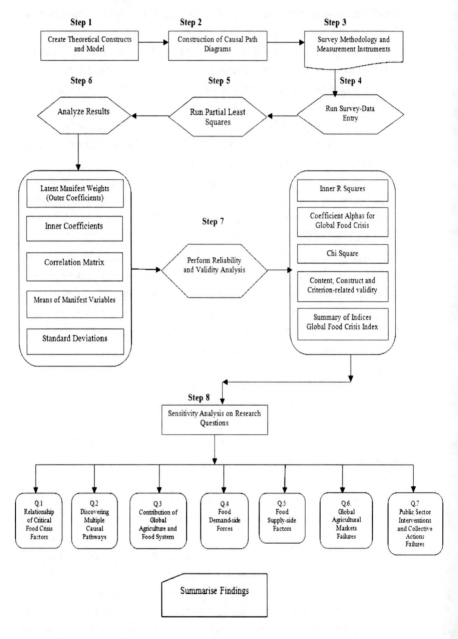

research questions.

Each step in the process of the measurement of various global food crisis indices is discussed as follows:

1. Explanation of Theoretical Model: The first step in KCGFCMS is to identify the critical risk factors in order to develop a theoretical model of Global Food Crisis with strong theoretical foundations. The identified critical food crisis factors are grouped in the relevant constructs or dimensions with logical causal connections proposed and the specification error considered. In KCGFCMS, the structural model was developed to represent the major aspects of food crisis. The dimensions and critical food crisis factors (variables) were carefully identified and are consistent with the thinking of the most prominent researchers in the relevant field. Variables in a structural model are categorized as latent or manifest. Latent variables are both endogenous and exogenous, and they share the common definition that they cannot be explicitly tested. Latent variables are causal to manifest variables which are assumed parametersthat can be tested for accuracy, validity, influence, and reliability, as representing the constructs of the model. The KCGFCMS explained that cause and effect relationships within a structural model are expressed as functional relations in a structural model that can exist between the effects on one or more causes. An example in the KCGFCMS is that global agricultural and food system (an exogenous latent prime variable) affects the CGFCFs (endogenous latent variables). Exogenous indicators and constructs are assumed to be determined by sources outside the model. An exogenous variable is by definition never assumed to be caused by any other construct (Nunnally and Bernstein, 1994). Conversely, endogenous indicators may be influenced by or caused by other constructs within the model (Nunnally and Bernstein, 1994). Endogenous variables or indicators can be influenced by other endogenous or exogenous indicators. Influences between variables may be called cause and effect relations, and the relative strength can be measured between one or more endogenous latent variables and with manifest variables. Each of these functional relations within the structural model is stated using equations (Kanji, 2002). Confirming an analysis requires that the manifest variables reflect the latent variables, a process that utilizes a set of predictions among the manifest variables. Correlations were made between the consistencies of the manifest variable predictions and the observations and the magnitude of their differences using variances and covariance matrices. The strengths of these relationships were denoted as structural weights. Their disturbances are defined in the next step.

2. *Construction of the Causal Path Diagrams:* It involves the following two things:

*(a) **Model Configuration:*** Construct a path diagram which depicts in a diagram a series of causal connections that represent the predictive relationships among constructs. The direction of the inward or outward directions of the latent variables was built into the program. A latent variable is inward if the information is entering into the model structure; it is outward if it is leaving the structure. GFC is only outward variable. This corresponds to the usual way KCGFCMS is pictured in this chapter (Figure 6.7) as a series of interrelated constructs. The diagram gives an indication of the flow of information and assumed relationships. In some cases, these relationships can loosely be considered causal, but in this research, it is not considered a fact of causality. Influences between variables may be called cause and effect relations, and the relative strength can be measured between one or more endogenous latent variables and with manifest variables. Each of these functional relations within the structural model is stated using equations. The model iterates the outer coefficients from estimates of the relationships. Outer coefficients are the unstandardized structural weights of manifest indicator variables. The structural weights are used to reflect the number of changes in an effect variable resulting from a unit of change in a cause variable. The effect variables are endogenous; the cause variables can be endogenous or exogenous. All other causes of that effect are held constant. The disturbance terms between the endogenous variables of the model are measured by ε_{ji}. Disturbance terms indicate the variations of the endogenous variable that are not attributable to other endogenous variables (Kanji, 2002). The parts of the model that are sources of variation are: (a) random shocks and/or unmeasured or omitted causes, (b) random measurement errors in the effect the causes where the primary concern is error in one or more of the causes, and (c) non-random measurement such as bias in scales of measurement and method variance (Kanji, 2002).

Inner coefficients are known as the endogenous latent variables or the independent variables (IVs). These parameters cannot be compared across groups, nor can those that are produced by the same population over time. The amount of change represented on each effect variable is reflected in the causal strength of the relationship to the preceding endogenous or exogenous variable. The standard deviation is the standard error of the sample estimate of the equation. It provides information on the spread of the means.

(b) Measurement of the Elements: The measurement of the elements was based on the Analysis of Covariance Structures (Nunnally and Bernstein, 1994). The model used matrix notation in a statistical package to set up the simultaneous equations. The exogenous variable in the KCGFCMS is global agricultural and food system which is represented in the model as ξ_1. The other latent variables are denoted by η_i, with subscripts where i = 2 to 6. These latent variables cannot be directly observed, but they are defined by the manifest variables, which are labelled y_i. Each manifest variable is an endogenous variable. Structural parameters that associate the strength of each connecting line of directional causation are designated as γ_{ji}, α_{ji}, δ_{ji}. The structural variable connecting the exogenous variable to the endogenous variables is designed by the symbol γ_{ji}, where the j subscript indicates the number of the endogenous variable and the i subscript indicates the number of the exogenous variable connected by the arrow. The structural variable used to indicate the cause and effect relationship is denoted by α_{ji} where the subscript j is the endogenous variable that is the effect while the i is the endogenous variable that is the cause.

Thus, we convert the path diagram into a set of structural and measurement models. At this stage, the model is specified through a series of equations that defines (1) the structural equations linking constructs; (2) the measurement model specifying which variables measure which constructs; and (3) a set of matrices indicating any hypothesized constructs among constructs or variables. Before applying any software or making any calculations in the KCGFCMS, set of indicators (manifest variables) for each latent variable is decided. This means that by then the questionnaire made up of the selected indicators for each construct of KCGFCMS is ready.

3. Survey Methodology and Measurement Instruments: Administer the questionnaires (measurement instruments) to the selected sample and obtain the measurement items from the results of the questionnaires. Sample size decision is also a very important aspect of global food crisis research. This decision is dictated by the structural equation model used, although a large sample size is required to achieve a reliable result with Chi-square test. For this reason, Bentler (1990) has introduced the comparative fit index (CIF) that is capable of indicating model validity for small samples as well. Therefore, in KCGFCMS a sample size from 100 to 400 is the best to achieve reliable results.

4. Run survey and Data Entry: Data were entered manually into an Excel spreadsheet to check for accuracy. Estimate the proposed model, run the equations on computer to get estimates for the path coefficients and the factor indices. SEM uses the variance-covariance of the correlation matrix as its input data. Once the input data type is selected, it is necessary to decide how the model will be estimated. In the KCGFCMS case the correlation matrix is used and the estimates calculated according to Partial Least Squares (PLS) and the PLS regression calculation was embedded in the Kanji-Chopra global food crisis measurement software. The estimates for all coefficients are calculated simultaneously.

5. Run PLS Regression: PLS is a second-generation multivariate analysis technique used to estimate the parameters of causal models which does not impose distributional assumptions on the data, and accommodates both continuous as well as categorical variables (Fornell, 1996). PLS regression is a method for constructing predictive models whereby a relatively large number of descriptor factors (manifest variables) can be transitioned to a smaller number of highly collinear orthogonal factors known as latent variables (Tobias, 1997). The PLS approach was initially developed by the econometrician Herman Wold in 1966 as an alternative to the LISREL (Linear Structural Relations) who questioned the general fitness of covariance structure models as implemented by LISREL (Fornell and Cha, 1994). In many studies the data generated is not normally distributed, a requirement of the maximum likelihood approach.

In general, the method takes I observations described by KDVs and stores them in an $I x K$ matrix denoted as Y. The J predictors values are then stored in $I x J$ matrix X. "The objective of PLS is to predict Y from X and to describe their common structure" (Abdi, p. 1). By performing a simultaneous decomposition of the IVs X and Y, the components explain the covariance between X and Y (Abdi, 2003). The PLS programme is run using the Statistical Analysis Systems (SAS®) under Microsoft Window environment. It is used to calculate the weights (the outer coefficients) that are then used for the calculation of the index scores for KCGFCMS. There are a number of parameters to be initialised before the programme can be executed.

6. Analyze Results for Goodness of Fit: The results for the model estimation must be carefully analysed. Sometimes it is necessary to identify/correct offending estimates. Since KCGFCMS is a theoretical model with sound theoretical justifications, these situations seldom occur. Besides evaluating overall model fit, it is necessary to analyse whether or not the measurement of each construct fits the requirements of unidimensionality and reliability. An analysis was carefully done on the results. The model was then judged on goodness of fit using a chi-square test. The weights of the path coefficients represent the strength of the relationships among the different variables. This structural equation model uses inner and outer co-efficients that were estimated as part of the iterative method.

7. Perform Reliability Analysis: The r^2 was analyzed to assess the power of the explanation of each measurement scale and of the structure of the model as a whole. Coefficient of determination r^2 is an indicator of randomness within the model between variation due to cause variables and variation due to randomness. If the values differ from zero significantly, it may be concluded that causal connections exist. Cronbach's α is used as a reliability measure (Cronbach, 1951). It is a general method that was used to determine the internal consistency of latent variables (items) that belong to the same dimension in the measurement instrument and are being empiri-cally reflected by manifest variables of the items (Kanji, 2002).

8. Validity of Empirical Measurements: Content validity of the test instrument depends on how well the researcher has created the specified domain to cover the content of variables under study. The content validity of the KCGFCMS is based on how adequately the samples tested the breadth of the concepts representing global food crisis. The KCGFCMS contained the various latent variables, and the KCGFCMS contained the various latent variables, a validated model. *Construct validity* can be established by how well the questionnaires capture the meaning of the concepts being mea-sured. Various unique manifest variables represented the domain of the corresponding latent variables. The meaning of each manifest variable was measured by its mean score. *Criterion validity* can be defined as how well the criterion in the test instrument corresponds to what is intended to be measured. To claim that criterion-related validity exists for the model, the critical food crisis factors (CFCFs) had to be collectively highly and posi-tively correlated to global food crisis. The CFCFs used in this instrument were evaluated by the strength of the weights of the relationships between the variables (See Kanji and Chopra, 2010b).

9. Conduct Sensitivity Analysis on Research Questions: After the in-ternal validity constructs and reliability assessments were satisfied, the next step is to conduct sensitivity analysis on research questions. This required a careful review of the results and possible elimination of the offending constructs. To be able to apply the research questions, the strengths and weaknesses between the inner and outer coefficient were significant (>.01). If the strength of the correlations indicated that the questions were not significant, then one or more questions had to be explained for management. The assumption was that the questions not addressed from this particular survey instrument were important for a refinery but not understood by the respondents. An explanation was offered based on the analysis of the data and the construction of the question. Conversely, questions that had strongly correlated data within the model were determined to be significant indicators.

10. Interpretation and Eventually Refine the Model: Conclusions and recommendations to address weaknesses and strengths were based on the research questions.

Concluding Remarks

The present chapter develops a measurement system encompassing four interlinked multivariate models of global food crisis. After specifying the model, it needs to be identified, estimated, tested and manipulated. The relationships among the variables (both measured and latent) are shown in the measurement model. Only the relationships between the latent variables are shown in the structural model. One important benefit of using latent variables is that they are free of random error. The error associated with the latent variables is statistically estimated and removed in the SEM analysis. Only a common variance remains. Each construct of GFC is operational using multiple questionnaire items and the entire system is estimated using PLS method. The structure of conceptual, operational, latent variable and measurement models have been shown to be consistent with the theories of perceptions of many agricultural writers, especially with regards to relationships between variables as specified in the model. Relationships other than those specified in the model have not been explicitly reported in the literature. Clearly, GAFS operates on GFC through its relationships with food demand, food supply, agricultural markets and public sector interventions and collective actions. Each latent variable is a distinct construct. The influence of factors in GAFS's external environment is not explicitly portrayed in the model but it is accounted for by 'measurement' concept.

The PLS path modelling offers a way to build 'proper indices' for unobservable critical food crisis factors and to estimate the relationships between them. The procedure is free from the danger of tendency to overestimate or underestimate outer or inner relationships. Many studies have concluded that the estimates so obtained are robust since when the number of observed variables and sample size increased, the quality of the PLS path modelling estimates increased. This modelling methodology offers a number of advantages over other measures. First, the use of multiple questionnaire items for each construct increases the provision of the estimate of GFC. Second, the individual questionnaire items are measured on a ten-point scale in order to enhance reliability. Third, the GFC measure is constructed by weighting the individual items, that is, GAFS, FDSF, FSSR, etc, such that the resulting index has a maximum correlation with stakeholders' value. Last but not the least, the identification and assessment of various CFCFs provide a feasible means for strategically integrating various concepts and captures, validate and distribute new knowledge fast enough to change strategic direction of food policy makers and resource allocation to prosper in global turbulent environment.

Notes

---

i. In a structural equation modelling analysis, there are two models called as inner model (structural model) and outer model (measurement model). The inner model describes the relationships between the latent variables of model. The path coefficients of inner model are called as inner coefficients. The outer model illustrates the relationships between the latent variables and their indicators (manifest variables). The path coefficients of outer model are called as outer coefficients (weights and loadings).

ii. An exogenous variable is a variable that is not caused by another variable in the model. Usually this variable causes one or more variables in the model.

iii. An endogenous variable is a variable that is caused by one or more variable in the model. Note that an endogenous variable may also cause another endogenous variable in the model.

iv. Structural parameter or coefficient is a measure of the amount of change in the effect variable expected given a one unit change in the causal variable and no change in any other variable. Although like a regression coefficient this coefficient may not be estimable by multiple regression.

Chapter 7   Measuring Global Food Crisis

"Everything has a cause and for everything there is an effect"
Walter J. Turner (1889-1946), An Australian-born Writer and Critic.

Introduction

After having constructed the structure of measurement system in the previous chapter, the present chapter provides the basis for empirical work by way of developing survey methodology including measurement instrument, research questions associated with critical food crisis factors, multivariate model validation, reliability and accuracy, multiple causal pathways leading to GFC, sensitivity analysis on research questions, and GFC indices. The present chapter undertakes an empirical application of the measurement system with three-fold rationale. First, the survey assesses the perceptions on critical food crisis factors of KCGFCMS to determine the extent to which each and every factor contributes to GFC. Secondly, it uncovers the multiple causal connections among these critical food crisis factors. Thirdly, measuring GFC involves estimating the various parameters of model and calculating the indices for each dimension as well as the overall GFC index (GFCI) with the help of measurement software. Given that all food crisis aspects are interrelated and mutually interdependent, the indices for the different latent variables of the model are calculated simultaneously considering the whole data set. Through the results provided, the food policy makers will know how each criterion impacts on the overall GFC index (structural or path coefficients) and where improvement efforts are more likely to have a greater impact. To achieve the purposes of the present study, this chapter has been organised in six different parts. *Part One* presents survey methodology that includes sampling design, developing measurement instrument (questionnaire), data sources, data collection, data analysis, and data presentation. *Part Two* develops an analytical framework in order to establish relationships among particular research questions and specific critical food crisis factors (latent variables) and manifest variables of the KCGFC model for the global economy in the empirical study. *Part Three* presents the results and findings on the reliability, validity and accuracy of the model. *Part Four* uncovers the multiple causal pathways to GFC. *Part Five* conducts sensitivity analysis on research questions by considering results on manifest variables, averages and outer coefficients and carefully reviewing the results with possible elimination of the offending constructs. It uncovers measurement tool on the basis of system dimensional structure of GFC. *Part Six* presents the emerging results on GFC indices and concluding observations on the measurement of GFC. The KCGFC measurement system provides a widespread representation and suitability for pinpointing the complex food problems being faced worldwide.

Survey Methodology

Survey methodology is a scientific field that is concerned with the development and application of survey techniques. It is a plan (arrangement of conditions) that seeks to identify principles about the design, collection, processing, and analysis of survey data in a manner that aims to combine relevance to the research purpose with the economy of procedure. It includes techniques of sampling design (selection of a sample, i.e., sampling method, sample size and representativeness and reliability of sample), questionnaire developing techniques, interview process and analysis of data (data cleaning, screen data, data entry, run PLS regression, analyse results for goodness of fit, perform reliability analysis, validity analysis and conduct sensitivity analysis on research questions, frequency analysis, descriptive analysis, cross-tabulation, correlation). A survey methodologist has to make decisions on how to: (a) identify and select potential sample members, (b) contact sampled individuals and collect data from those who are hard to reach (or reluctant to respond), (c) evaluate and test questions, (d) select the mode for posing questions and collecting responses, (e) train and supervise interviewers (if they are involved), (f) check data files for accuracy and internal consistency, and (g) adjust survey estimates to correct for identified errors (Groves et al., 2009).

Although this study could have been undertaken as longitudinal research to establish trend data on food prices, food shortages or food demand and supply, the researcher declined this opportunity because that was not fully suitable to the focus of this study and it could not provide a holistic view of the phenomenon of GFC. Creswell (2003) noted that one of the difficulties of using a quantitative design in a cross-sectional survey lies in trying to disentangle changes over time. Any analysis that seeks to examine food problems in a global context has to consider non-quantifiable data like the impact of bio-fuels policy decisions, shifting land use patterns, environmental degradation, health of US dollar, role played by governments in net exporting countries in balancing domestic political conditions with international demands, and so on. Therefore, straightforward methods (like regression analysis) cannot be fully utilized. Research that has been carried out adopting rigorous methods has dealt with smaller questions, such as the influence of bio-fuel demand on the worldwide price of maize (for more information on such studies, see Mitchell, 2008, and Heady and Fan, 2008).

The Measurement Instrument Design

The measurement instrument (questionnaire) has been specially designed on the basis of system dimensional structure of the phenomenon of GFC in order to obtain information on different constructs of GFC (See, chapters 4 and 5). It consists of 48 questions grouped in six different dimensions that correspond to five critical food crisis factors and GFC. Therefore, there are eight questions in each dimension that adequately cover the domain of that construct. Each question uses a 10-point scaling technique 1[i] on which respondents rate the food situation with respect to a specific food crisis attribute. Open-ended questions[ii] are used to obtain information, classifying subjects, rank items and rate attributes. Out of four levels of measurement, i.e., nominal[iii], ordinal[iv], interval[v] and ratio[vi] scales (Stevens, 1946), nominal (qualitative) and ordinal (ranking) scales have been used in the questionnaire. Nominal measurement is used to classify subjects such as classifying the constructs of GFC. Ordinal measurement is used for ranking items such as relative importance of critical food crisis factors and rating of crisis such as GFC.

There are yet other two types of measurement scales that are available in the market place. The first set of measures used unipolar scales[vii] as the most reliable scales to specially measure a socioeconomic or organisational phenomenon. The second set of measures used 'bipolar' scale[viii], prompts a respondent to balance two opposite attributes in mind, determining the relative proportion of these opposite attributes. It measures the scale as two-ended. The basic notion in this research is that unipolar scales induce participants to think of the presence vs. absence of a particular attribute (e.g., presence vs. absence of positive characteristics) whereas bipolar scales induce participants to think of the relative proportion of two opposite attributes (e.g., relative proportion of positive versus negative attributes). The results are basically opposite in unipolar and bipolar measurement (Locke, 2002). It is worth looking at the works of Norbert Schwarz's (1991) and Gannon & Ostrom (1996) on bipolar vs. unipolar scales to get enlightening insights into the importance of scale construction. The present study uses unipolar scale only. Moreover, bipolar scales do not show the full picture for scales where 'you can have too much of a good thing' (Sparrow and Knight, 2006). Answering survey questions is by itself a cognitive process consisting basically of four tasks: question interpretation, memory retrieval, judgement formation, and response editing. Keeping this in view, the questionnaire has been designed in such a way that the respondents use every bit of information they can infer from it. We have divided our questionnaire in two parts, namely, criteria of question formation and response categories part. Considering the impact of question interpretation on the respondents' answer formation, we have specially designed all questions (manifest variables) of different dimensions of phenomenon, for example, 'The extent to which the global food demand has experienced due to an increase in crop consumption under bio-fuel initiatives, production or 'bio-fuel rush' (corn-based ethanol or soybeans for biodiesel)'.

The fundamental knowledge of the subject of agriculture, food system and global food problems is extremely important in designing the measurement instrument. A first draft of the questionnaire was prepared and subjected to a pre-test. This has been carried out by presenting the questionnaire to several agricultural experts based in different universities and agricultural research organisations. Based on their feedback, the questionnaire was revised, refined, in terms of question wording and questionnaire format to improve its clarity and ensure a collection of the highest quality data possible with good responses. This helps to minimise the measurement error and subjectivity.

There is one possibility of having biased answers from a particular school of agricultural thought. The followers of food demand-supply mismatch approach will rate those constructs very high, the intuitionalists will blame institutional factors and public sector economists will rate high importance to different variables. Despite various deficiencies associated with questionnaire surveys, the application of the SEM methodology as described in Chapter 3 actually reduces some of the possible counterproductive effects by essentially taking into account the correlation/covariance matrix. Table 7.1 shows the expressly designed measurement instrument for obtaining required detailed information pertaining to the six dimensions of food crisis at worldwide level. When designing the measurement instrument, a thorough literature review was conducted and expert opinions incorporated to ensure that the instrument adequately covers the domain of the concepts under study and measures what it is purported to measure. There are various methods available to administrate the questionnaires to obtain information regarding GFC from the target respondents.

Table 7.1   *Measurement Instrument for Global Food Crisis*

Assessment from the respondents under question

Part 1: Global Agricultural and Food System (GAFS)
The extent to which the existing global agricultural and food system

		Not at all						Very much			
Serial Number	Criteria	1	2	3	4	5	6	7	8	9	10
1	Is influenced by the environmental, geo-ecological and natural forces										
2	Is influenced by human capital and technical manpower forces										
3	Is influenced by socio-economic and cultural forces										
4	Is influenced by political and institutional forces										
5	Is dominated by the capitalist maximum profit making corporate culture										

Continue...

6	Is affected by the greater integration of agriculture with manufacturing, inter-national trade and service industries										
7	Has underlying dynamics of technologi-cal dominance										
8	Has inherent systemic risks to cope with shocks and stresses of food safety, quality standards, animal welfare and hygiene										

Part 2: Food Demand-Side Forces (FDSFs)

The extent to which the global food demand has experienced

Serial Number	Criteria	1	2	3	4	5	6	7	8	9	10
1	An increase in crop consumption un-der bio-fuel initiatives, production or 'bio-fuel rush' (corn-based ethanol or soybeans for biodiesel)										
2	An increased demand for a more di-verse diet (dietary changes from grain to more diversified diet like meat and dairy products) due to changes in life-style and consumption patterns										
3	Livestock revolution and an increase in demand for animals feed										
4	An increase due to more larger, pros-perous and urban population and de-clining ratio of food producers to food consumers										
5	An increase in food demand due to global population growth										
6	Sustained food demand from emerg-ing markets and agribusiness in new markets										
7	Panic buying for the purpose of hoard-ing buffer stock										
8	An increase in demand in industrial sector for agricultural raw materials and wage goods										

Part 3: Food Supply-Side Restrictions (FSSRs)
The extent to which the world has experienced

Serial Number	Criteria	Not at all → Very much →									
		1	2	3	4	5	6	7	8	9	10
1	Shortage of food supply due to scarcity of resources (seeds, fertilizers, irrigation facilities, proper knowhow, energy, etc)										
2	Food supply constraints due to land constraints such as inflexibility in total area under cultivation, changing farm structure, serious degradation and loss of arable and fertile soil, and urban-rural land use conflicts										
3	Uncertainty and instability in production due to vagaries of nature and weather shocks such as floods, rain, drought, earthquakes, etc. and ecological constraints on the exploitation of new lands or ocean exploration for sea food										
4	Shocks (low crop outputs) resulting from pests, animal disease (mad cow disease) etc. in key grain regions affecting and afflicting agricultural production										
5	Decline in research expenditure (R&D) affecting new agricultural biotechnology, innovations and higher return farming										
6	Growing costs of factors of production and marketing including fertilisers, water, labour, energy, oil, seeds, credit and storage and transportation costs (food miles)										
7	Food supply conditioned by the biological nature of the production process, rules of the global food market, global geopolitics, global food trade and lack of decoupling agricultural support (government policy to discourage food production)										
8	Food production and supply conditioned by the farmer's access to finance and extended credit facilities										

Part 4: Global Agricultural Markets Failures (GAMFs)

The extent to which the global agricultural markets have experienced

Serial number	Criteria	*Not at all* →				→		*Very much* →		→
		1	2	3	4	5	6	7	8	9	10
1	Trade distortions and emergence of oligopolistic and oligopsonistic structures (multinational agri-business and food giants)										
2	Displacement of natural fibres by synthetic substitutes (e.g., jute by synthetics)										
3	Factor market imperfections in terms of unequal land ownership distribution, imperfect competition in land tenancy market, unequal access to finance, farm and off-farm employment gaps, rural credit market imperfections, and so on.										
4	Markets failures in terms of erosion of crop genetic diversity arising because markets do not reward farmers for their provision of this public good										
5	Negative externalities related to agricultural production and consumption activities										
6	Market failures due to cobweb process of time lag between planting and harvesting and cyclical fluctuations in demand and supply decisions in agricultural markets										
7	Raising expectations and speculations in the agricultural commodity market (the transfer of capital from the stressed US real estate market to the commodities markets which have pushed up prices)										
8	Information asymmetries or gaps due to location, distance, contamination in raw and processed foods, etc. that erode the supply of food safety and result in food-borne illnesses										

Part 5: Public Sector Interventions and Collective Actions Failures (PSICAFs)

The extent to which the agriculture sector has experienced

Serial Number	Criteria	Not at all — Very much									
		1	2	3	4	5	6	7	8	9	10
1	Fiscal policy interventions (indirect tax, lack of tax relief, tariffs, costly strategy grain reserves, etc.) failures by making food products expensive and less accessible for poor consumers										
2	Public sector agricultural and food enterprises failures										
3	State monopoly on food imports and exports										
4	Deterioration of existing infrastructure facilities in rural sector										
5	Inefficient government agricultural and rural development programmes										
6	Collective actions institutions (such as rules and norms, farmers organizations and agricultural cooperatives) failures in achieving desired results										
7	Food health and safety regulations failures										
8	Urban bias in terms of inadequate public investments and access to resources to rural sector										

Part 6: Global Food Crisis (GFC)

The extent to which the global economy has experienced

Serial Number	Criteria	Not at all — Very much									
		1	2	3	4	5	6	7	8	9	10
1	Rise in general food prices										
2	Deficiencies in utilization of food resulting in worsening of food problems (phenomenon of 'luxus consumption')										
3	Changes in environmental sustainability and ecological security affecting global food crisis										

Continue...

225

4	Food insufficiency due to least traded food commodities such as rice										
5	Existence of food paradox (existence of food under-consumption, overcon-sumption and food wastage culture)										
6	Food crisis due to distortions in food distribution system										
7	Obstacles to agricultural development and productivity due to the conflicting food policies of international institu-tions and national governments										
8	Food vulnerability leading to food inse-curity, hunger and malnutrition										

However, since the principals dealing with the food problems are universal, demanding that common aspects must be addressed under each criterion and these changes should be kept to a minimum as radical changes may jeopardise the model's reliability and the chance of getting meaningful and comparable results. To complete the questionnaire, it is necessary only to indicate the extent to which the world has experienced each suggested dimension in a 1 to 10 scale. There are some requirements in terms of the number of questionnaire responses needed to perform the statistical analysis associated with KCGFC model which have been discussed in the next section.

Data Collection and Sample Size

Collection of data using the questionnaire (measurement instrument) is the basic tool to measure GFC against the model. Since each GFC dimension corresponds to a concept that cannot be directly measured due to complex nature of the various indicators of a particular dimension, it must be translated into a set of indicators that are then converted into items of the questionnaire. Data collection from various sources is a small though important part of the sampling process. A reliable data collection involves following a defined sampling process, keeping the data in time order, noting comments and other contextual events, and recording non-responses. Data for this study have been collected at random from agricultural experts and stakeholders in agriculture and food industry from both developed and developing countries, including economists at various agricultural universities and colleges, individual researchers working on food problems, health experts, analysts and experts with leading world institutions such as WTO, World Bank, IMF, FAO, UNO, IFPRI, Bretton Woods Institutions, etc., food policy makers at various agricultural and rural development departments in local and national governments, various independent research centres on food insecurity and farmers, food multinational, wholesalers and retails. Thus, the questionnaires have been administered throughout the whole range of experts and food and agriculture stakeholders covering different dimensions of GFC so that everyone's opinions can be accommodated. Specific questionnaires have been developed for the purpose of getting feedback from the experts who will certainly have a say on how well they think the global agricultural and food system is doing and on what improvements they would like to see.

An alternative method to develop the theory was to perform a qualitative research with focus groups and direct observations in one country at one time for example, food crisis in China. The disadvantage to this approach was that the interview data would be focused on the phenomenon of GFC with respect to one country only. The intent of this work was to derive a research method that could be easily applied to measurable GFC variables in any country at any time. The weakness of using a survey method to study an issue is potentially a low response rate of 10 per cent to 25 per cent. To encourage participation on the KCGFCMS, it was hoped that agricultural scientists, economists, policy makers, bureaucrats, senior level officials in agricultural research teams at international organisations and commitment to making positive change based on the survey results would improve return response rates to between 30 per cent and 50 per cent. A third option to obtaining the data was to use historical trends from existing records. This approach was not taken because of the potential bias that would be introduced into the analysis either because the researcher injected his own opinion or the questions that were relevant over time may be taken out of context.

Data are collected by means of e-mail surveys. Several reasons influenced the decision to use this procedure: (a) the need for a great deal of data from individual researchers; (b) the questionnaire could be self-administrated; (c) face-to-face contact was not possible because of the geographical distance and distribution of respondents; and (d) mail survey is the least expensive form of data collection. Priority was given to clarity of questions so that respondents can provide their responses without any difficulty. The questionnaire is made up of close-ended questions that further aided respondents in providing responses. By providing a reasonable amount of time to respondents to complete the questionnaires, respondents could put in more thought to questions, check records, and consult others, which could improve the accuracy of responses. The survey was conducted by email and postal method during January 2011 and March 2012. A total of 350 questionnaires were administrated across the prospective respondents and 103 responses were received. So, the response rate was 29.43 per cent. As a general rule, it is possible to run the GFCI program with a number of responses between 100 and 250. Data thus collected was analysed without delay in order to identify GFC and closely control the outcomes of the GFC plans and the way they are being perceived by the experts on food problems.

Data Entry

Inputting the questionnaires' responses using Kanji-Chopra GFC software is very simple. All that is needed is the introduction of the data (the questionnaire responses) into the excel spreadsheet (See Table 7.1). Of course, the spreadsheet must follow a structure that fits the questionnaires (See Table 7.2), i.e. have exact number of columns to match the number of manifest variables for each model dimensions.

Table 7.2   *Data Entry Procedure Illustration (First Two Dimensions of Global Food Crisis)*

Global Agricultural and Food System								Food Demand-Side Forces							
4	3	4	2	7	6	5	6	5	3	7	6	4	8	4	6
6	5	4	5	4	7	4	3	2	4	3	5	6	5	5	6
6	5	3	5	9	5	1	2	6	8	2	5	8	2	8	5
9	10	2	6	1	8	6	1	9	2	8	8	9	1	3	8
3	4	8	5	3	9	10	8	4	1	3	9	10	2	6	7

A survey methodology has been applied to measure the GFC and the questionnaires for the measurements are given in Table 7.1. Respondents were asked to evaluate the extent to which each factor is problematic for the occurrence and growth of GFC, with potential answers ranging from 1 (no crisis) to 10 (extremely major crisis).

Data Analysis

Data analysis comprises estimating the various parameters of model and calculating the indices for each criterion as well as the final GFC index. The software automatically calculates all the indices and produces some standard graphics. This software is based on a structural equation modelling technique which produces mean scores, outer and inner path coefficients, relative importance of critical food crisis factors, validity of the model and other indices. Given that all criteria aspects are interrelated, the indices for the different variables of the model are calculated simultaneously according to the whole data set. Through the results provided, the world will know how each criterion impacts on the overall GFC index and where improvement efforts are more likely to have a greater impact. The measurement software uses PLS method in the simultaneous estimation of the weights of the constructs of the model. It calculates these variables in a way that maximises the goodness of fit of the model and, thus, the ability to explain GFC as the ultimate endogenous variable.

Critical Food Crisis Factors Scores

The relationships between the manifest variables and the GFC indices are addressed next. The research questions asked are shown with the appropriate latent variables in Tables 7.3 and 7.4. Table 7.3 shows how the twelve research questions were related to the specific critical food crisis factors (latent variables) of the KCGFC model for the global economy in the empirical study.

Table 7.4 shows the total survey questions for each research question and the link to the latent and manifest variables of the model. Different research questions have different latent and manifest variables attached with them. The research question R1 regarding global agricultural and food system has one latent variable, eight manifest variables and addressed by eight total questions. R2 involves two latent variables, GAFS and FDSFs, and 16 questions and manifest variables. Similarly R10 involves five latent variables, η_1, η_2, η_3, η_4 and η_5 and 40 manifest variables.

Table 7.3   ***Research Questions Associated with Critical Food Crisis Factors***

Research Questions	Label	Critical Food Crisis Factors (Latent Variables)
To what extent do the underlying driving forces of global agricultural and food system interact within the system and explain the phenomenon of global food crisis?	R1	GAFS: Global food governance
How effective are the critical food crisis factors under study in explaining the phenomenon of global food crisis?	R2	Causal connection between GAFS and CFCFs
What is the numerical strength of the relationship between global agricultural and food system and construct of food demand-side forces?	R3	Causal connection between GAFS and FDSFs
To what extent is the global agricultural and food system related to food supply-side dimension?	R4	Causal connection between GAFS and FSSRs
What is the extent of relationship between global agricultural and food system and global agricultural markets failures?	R5	Causal connection between GAFS and GAMFs
To what extent is the GAFS related with public sector interventions and collective actions failures?	R6	Causal connection between GAFS and PSICAFs
To what extent do the food demand-side forces contribute to the global food crisis?	R7	FDSFs: Food Demand Pull Food Crisis
To what extent do the food supply-side restrictions contribute to the global food crisis?	R8	FSSRs: Food Supply Push Food Crisis
To what extent does the construct of global agricultural market failures contribute to the global food crisis?	R9	GAMFs: Markets Failures Driven Food Crisis
To what extent does the dimension of public sector interventions and collective actions failures contribute to the global food crisis?	R10	PSICAFs: Government Failures Driven Food Crisis
What are the significant constituents of the conceptualisation of global food crisis?	R11	GFC: Conceptual foundations
What is the extent of overall severity of global food crisis?	R12	GFC Index: Extent to which humanity facing food crisis

Table 7.4 **Research Questions Related to the Number of Latent and Manifest Variables of KCGFC Model**

Label	Research Questions	Latent Variables	Total Questions	Manifest Variables Label
R1	To what extent do the underlying driving forces of global agricultural and food system interact within the system and explain the phenomenon of global food crisis?	ξ_1	8	x_1 to x_8
R2	How effective are the critical food crisis factors under study in explaining the phenomenon of global food crisis?	$\xi_1, \eta_1, \eta_2, \eta_3, \eta_4$ and η_5	48	x_1 to x_8, y_1 to y_8, y_9 to y_{16}, y_{17} to y_{24}, y_{25} to y_{32}, and y_{33} to y_{40}
R3	What is the numerical strength of the relationship between global agricultural and food system and construct of food demand-side forces?	ξ_1 and η_1	16	x_1 to x_8 and y_1 to y_8
R4	To what extent is the global agricultural and food system related to food supply-side dimension?	ξ_1 and η_2	16	x_1 to x_8 and y_9 to y_{16}
R5	What is the extent of relationship between global agricultural and food system and global agricultural markets failures?	ξ_1 and η_3	16	x_1 to x_8 and y_{17} to y_{24}
R6	To what extent is the GAFS related with public sector interventions and collective actions failures?	η_1 and η_4	16	y_1 to y_8 and y_{25} to y_{32}
R7	To what extent do the food demand-side forces contribute to the global food crisis?	ξ_1, η_2 and η_5	16	x_1 to x_8, y_1 to y_8 and y_{33} to y_{40}
R8	To what extent do the food supply-side restrictions contribute to the global food crisis?	ξ_1, η_3 and η_5	16	x_1 to x_8, y_9 to y_{16} and y_{33} to y_{40}
R9	To what extent does the construct of global agricultural market failures contribute to the global food crisis?	ξ_1, η_4 and η_5	16	x_1 to x_8, y_{17} to y_{24} and y_{33} to y_{40}
R10	To what extent does the dimension of public sector interventions and collective actions failures contribute to the global food crisis?	ξ_1, η_4 and η_5	16	x_1 to x_8, y_{25} to y_{32}, and y_{33} to y_{40}
R11	What are the significant constituents of the conceptualisation of global food crisis?	η_5	8	y_{33} to y_{40}
R12	What is the extent of overall severity of global food crisis?	$\xi_1, \eta_1, \eta_2, \eta_3, \eta_4$ and η_5	48	x_1 to x_8, y_1 to y_8, y_9 to y_{16}, y_{17} to y_{24}, y_{25} to y_{32}, and y_{33} to y_{40}

Multivariate Model Validation, Reliability and Accuracy: Results and Findings

The process of multivariate model validation, testing and estimation involves a two step approach, advocated by the majority of researchers (Garver and Mentzer, 1999) has been followed. First, the measurement model was validated through the examination of the various issues associated with construct validity and reliability in order to ensure that legitimate conclusions are drawn about the nature of construct relationships. As recommended by Hulland (1999), the quality of the measurement model is to be examined looking essentially at (a) individual item reliability, (b) convergent validity of the measures associated with individual constructs, and (c) discriminant validity. Then, the structural coefficients and the latent variable scores were analysed.

Validity of Empirical Measurements

(a) Content Validity : A valid measurement scale is one that does what it is supposed to do and measures that it is supposed to measure (Nunnally, 1978). The assessment of content validity is not a simple matter for complex concepts like GFC because it is difficult, if not impossible, to enumerate all dimensions that compare the essence of concepts being studied. The procedure used to tap the critical dimensions of GFC: (a) carrying out an exhaustive literature review for all possible variables to be included in the scale; (b) soliciting expert opinions on the inclusion of variables and dimensions; (c) a pre-test on pilot run was held to ascertain that all weaknesses in the instrument were identified and dealt with; (d) based on the feedback obtained from the pilot run, questions difficult to understand and questions that did not sufficiently cover the theme of the dimension of GFC were replaced in the final draft of the measurement instrument. Although the procedure may not give complete guarantee of content validity, it does, however, give a reasonable degree of confidence as to its existence. Thus, it is argued that the scales used have content validity.

(b) Construct Validity: The assessment of construct validity involves two aspects. The first aspect is basically theoretical and the second aspect is statistical in nature. Theoretically, the constructs such as global agricultural

and food system, food demand-side forces, food supply-side restrictions, global agricultural markets failures and public sector interventions and collective actions failures, used in KCGFC model have been used and analysed fruitfully in various other studies (Friedmann, 1982 and 2009; Patel, 2007; Praussello, 2011; Giménez and Peabody, 2008; McCullough et al., 2008). Different studies have used different constructs but no study has taken into consideration all these constructs simultaneously. This provides support to the theoretical foundation of the variables under study.

Statistically, there are two types of construct validity: convergent validity and discriminant validity (Campbell and Fiske, 1959). Convergent validity is commonly defined as the degree of association between two maximally different measurements that purport to measure essentially the same concepts. If the measurement scales developed for the model's principles and core concepts are correlated, then the two 'constructs' are said to exhibit convergent validity and, thus, some degree of construct validity. Both independent and dependent latent variables are strongly correlated (Table 7.5) and they provide support to the statistical foundation of the variables under study. Discriminant validity is largely the opposite of convergent validity in that it can be defined as the degree to which the measurement scale may be differentiated from other scales purporting to measure maximally different concepts. Discriminant validity is not performed in the present research as it provides the same information as convergent validity.

(c) Criterion-related Validity: Sometimes called predictive validity or external validity, it is concerned with the extent to which a measurement instrument is related to an independent measure of the relevant criterion. The five measures of food crisis (critical food crisis factors) have criterion-related validity if these measures collectively are highly correlated with GFC.

Statistical Reliability Analysis

Statistical reliability comprises two main issues. One refers to the stability of the measurement over time (test-retest reliability), i.e., administrating the measurement instrument to the same group of subjects on two occasions and the other is concerned with the internal consistency of the measures used (Klime, 2000). The present research is concerned only with internal consistency of the model that was assessed by using the reliability coefficient alpha for both latent variables and manifest variables of the model as suggested in most structural equation applications. The reliability score α for the empirical analysis is presented in Table 7.5 which reveals that the Cronbach-alpha values for all six scales are above 0.7 as recommended by Nunnally (1967). However, Flynn and Saladin (2001) recommend the minimum acceptable level of 0.6. It is considered that any alpha values less than 0.6 would put at risk the meaning of the construct containing manifest variables. The alpha scores for the latent variables of global agriculture and food system (0.823512), food demand-side forces (0.892437), food supply-side restrictions (0.856569), of global agricultural market failures (0.761856), and public sector interventions and collective actions failures (0.782437) indicate that the manifest variables were consistent. The values of the manifest variables from x_1 to x_8 vary between 0.643892 for x_4 and 0.876354 for x_7 and all the values have been found consistent. Moreover, all the values of manifest variables pertaining to the construct of FDSFs. GFC index alpha was 0.80 indicating that each latent variable did fit the model as a positive indicator.

Model Accuracy

The strength of the relationship is a proportion of the regression sum of squares corresponding to latent variables. The coefficient of determination, which is the square of correlation coefficient, can be used to evaluate the accuracy of a structural model. It indicates the amount of variance of a dependent variable that is explained by an independent variable. Table 7.6 indicates the values for the coefficient of determination for the paths leading up to GFC. The values of coefficient of determination can also be thought of as a numerical percentage for each variable. For example, the global agricultural and food system has an $R^2 = 0.897$ or 90% as related to GFC. The higher the value of r^2, the better the model fits the data. The values of r^2 resulted vary between 0.832 and 0.913. The minimum value of at least 0.65 was considered a reasonably high indication of model accuracy. In this case, all of the r^2 values were higher than the cut-off value of 0.65, meaning that the variations in the model explained more than 65% of the variance of dependent variables in the model. Thus, given the positive and higher scores of the model, several good correlations could be deducted from the data results.

Table 7.5:   *Statistical Reliability Analysis of Manifest and Latent Variables of the Model*

Critical Food Crisis Factors and Manifest Variables	Reliability Coefficients –Alpha
Global agricultural and food system (ξ_1)	0.823512
Environmental, geo-ecological and natural forces (x_1)	0.714723
Human capital and technical manpower Forces (x_2)	0.682873
Socio-economic and cultural forces (x_3)	0.738926
Political and institutional forces (x_4)	0.643892
Capitalist maximum profit making corporate culture (x_5)	0.836723
Greater sectoral integration (x_6)	0.663452
Technological dominance (x_7)	0.876354
Systemic risks (x_8)	0.794389
Food demand side forces (η_1)	0.892437
Bio-fuels initiatives (y_1)	0.925647
Increase in dietary diversity (y_2)	0.867391
Livestock revolution and increased demand for animals feed (y_3)	0.667493
Urbanisation and declining ratio of food producers to food consumers (y_4)	0.794357
Global population growth (y_5)	0.746728
Emerging markets (y_6)	0.697621
Panic buying (y_7)	0.698374
Increase in demand for agricultural raw materials and wage goods (y_8)	0.773295
Food supply side restrictions (η_2)	0.856569
Scarcity of resources (y_9)	0.723289
Land constraints (y_{10})	0.718392
Climate and ecological constraints (y_{11})	0.629821
Pests and animal diseases shocks (y_{12})	0.738932
Agricultural research and development expenditure (y_{13})	0.783929
Peculiar nature of costs (y_{14})	0.812833
Biological nature of the production process (y_{15})	0.862372
Access to finance (y_{16})	0.739283

Continue...

Global agricultural market failures (η_3)	0.761856
Emergence of oligopolistic and oligopsonistic structures (y_{17})	0.724736
Social justice and economic equity (y_{18})	0.749821
Factor market imperfections (y_{19})	0.738934
Agricultural commodities trade distortions (y_{20})	0.863543
Externalities related to production and consumption activities (y_{21})	0.658279
Cobweb process (y_{22})	0.876329
Rising expectations and financial speculations (y_{23})	0.838923
Information asymmetries (y_{24})	0.692738
Public sector interventions and collective actions failures (η_4)	0.782437
Fiscal policy interventions failures (y_{25})	0.746378
Public sector agricultural and food enterprises failures (y_{26})	0.728391
State monopoly on food imports and exports (y_{27})	0.837882
Deterioration of existing infrastructure facilities in rural sector (y_{28})	0.878724
Inefficient government rural development programmes (y_{29})	0.632837
Collective actions institutions failures (y_{30})	0.783476
Food health and safety regulations failures (y_{31})	0.762893
Urban-bias investment strategy (y_{32})	0.793784
Global food crisis (η_5)	0.801132
Rising food prices (y_{33})	0.934785
Utilisation of food (y_{34})	0.682342
Environmental sustainability and ecological security (y_{35})	0.745892
Food security and self-sufficiency (y_{36})	0.708374
Phenomenon of overeating and food wastage (y_{37})	0.674592
Social welfare, social justice and economic equity (y_{38})	0.732934
Policies of international institutions and organisations (y_{39})	0.759283
Food vulnerability (y_{40})	0.723843

Note: Cronbach alphas used in this study were a measure of latent variable reliability and were not intended to represent a significance level used in other statistical texts.

Path Analysis: Causal Pathways to Global Food Crisis

Path analysis calculates the strength of the relationships (path coefficients) in the structural equation model using the covariance or the correlation matrix as input. There are two categories of path coefficients: outer coefficients and inner coefficients. Before the values of path coefficients can be obtained, the structural equation model must be specified in such a way that the model is 'identified'. Identifying a model involves fixing the values of some coefficients (fixed parameters) and using data to estimate values of other coefficients (free parameters) that would result in a unique hypothetical population covariance matrix of manifest variables (James, Mulaik and Brett, 1982). The least squares estimation method is used to minimise the sum of squares differences between the elements of sample covariance matrix (S) and the hypothetical population covariance ($\sum_0'$) matrix for manifest variables.

Table 7.6:   *Inner R-Squares of the KCGFC Model*

Path Latent Variables		Coefficient of Determination (r^2)
Global agricultural and food system ➤	Food demand-side forces	0.913
Global agricultural and food system ➤	Food supply side restrictions	0.878
Global agricultural and food system ➤	Global agricultural market failures	0.832
Global agricultural and food system ➤	Public sector intervention and collective actions failures	0.861
Global agricultural and food system ➤	Global Food Crisis Index	0.897

Outer Path Coefficients of KCGFC Model

These outer coefficients show how each question loads into the respective factors in the GFC model. Outer coefficients are those associated with relationships linking manifest variables to latent variables. Analysis of path coefficients begins with the outer path coefficients. For every relationship, all measurement items with values of path coefficients that are less than 0.1 are removed from the model. This is to ensure that only manifest variables that adequately reflect the empirical content of latent variables are retained for further analysis. Usually PLS has to be run several times to remove all manifest variables that are poorly linked to latent variables. The outer coefficients of remaining manifest variables are then used to compute critical GFC factors and GFC indices. Table 7.7 indicates how each variable contributes to the respective factors of the KCGFC model.

Table 7.7: *Outer Path Coefficients of the KCGFC Model*

OUTER COEFFICIENTS					
Global Agricultural and Food System	Food Demand-side Forces	Food Supply-side Restrictions	Global Agricultural Markets Failures	Public Sector Interventions and Collective Actions Failures	Global Food Crisis
0.831173	0	0	0	0	0
0.194166	0	0	0	0	0
-0.045653	0	0	0	0	0
0.484097	0	0	0	0	0
0.880868	0	0	0	0	0
0.048763	0	0	0	0	0
0.093714	0	0	0	0	0
0.474325	0	0	0	0	0
0	0.891653	0	0	0	0
0	0.631313	0	0	0	0
0	0.470485	0	0	0	0
0	0.463753	0	0	0	0
0	0.759317	0	0	0	0
0	-0.008420	0	0	0	0
0	0.099776	0	0	0	0
0	0.073423	0	0	0	0
0	0	0.728493	0	0	0
0	0	0.574071	0	0	0
0	0	0.782374	0	0	0
0	0	-0.162978	0	0	0
0	0	0.107134	0	0	0
0	0	0.667759	0	0	0
0	0	0.057193	0	0	0
0	0	0.411538	0	0	0
0	0	0	0.894542	0	0
0	0	0	0.086793	0	0
0	0	0	0.522123	0	0
0	0	0	-0.174371	0	0
0	0	0	0.619153	0	0

Continue...

0	0	0	0.076784	0	0
0	0	0	0.655447	0	0
0	0	0	0.406873	0	0
0	0	0	0	-0.092684	0
0	0	0	0	0.076139	0
0	0	0	0	0.432823	0
0	0	0	0	0.544483	0
0	0	0	0	0.605593	0
0	0	0	0	0.070574	0
0	0	0	0	0.486235	0
0	0	0	0	0.815174	0
0	0	0	0	0	0.863013
0	0	0	0	0	0.196149
0	0	0	0	0	0.771492
0	0	0	0	0	0.162183
0	0	0	0	0	0.688537
0	0	0	0	0	0.719674
0	0	0	0	0	-0.056821
0	0	0	0	0	0.625428

Inner Path Coefficients of KCGFC Model

Inner coefficients are associated with latent to latent variable relationships. It is expected that the relationship between the various GFC measurements and the path coefficients will be positive, emphasising the nature and the principles of the model. Following the analysis of outer coefficients, the research is then concerned with inner coefficients which represent the amount of change in a dependent variable expressed as multiples of standard deviation when the value of its independent variable is changed by one unit.

Standardised inner coefficients cannot be compared across groups of sample, nor can those that are produced by the same population over time. However, standardisation of data simplifies the computation of path coefficients because correlation matrix of manifest variables is used instead of the covariance matrix. In the PLS method the values of inner coefficients for causal connections that do not involve a single dependent variable can be easily determined by reading their values directly from the correlation matrix. The values of inner coefficients for causal connections that involve a single dependent variable, however, have to be solved from the following equation (Namboodiri et al., 1975):

$$r_{ij} = \sum_{k}^{i} P_{ik}\, r_{kj}$$

where, I = endogenous variable (I > k, j); j = causal variable; and k begins with I-1 and ranges down to 1 (i.e., η_i). All path coefficients in a structural model can be determined using the same equation.

Table 7.8:   *Inner Path Coefficients of KCGFC Model*

	GAFS	FDSFs	FSSRs	GAMFs	PSICAFs	GFCI
Global agricultural and food system (GAFS)	0	0	0	0	0	0
Food demand side factors (FDSFs)	0.9177	0	0	0	0	0
Food supply side factors (FSSRs)	0.8770	0	0	0	0	0
Global agricultural markets failures (GAMFs)	0.7162	0	0	0	0	0
Public sector interventions and Collective action Failures (PSICAFs)	0.6346	0	0	0	0	0
Global Food Crisis Index (GFCI)	0	0.3215	0.2761	0.2352	0.1148	0

Research Question 2 asked, "How effective are the critical food crisis factors under study in explaining the phenomenon of global food crisis?"

The research question 2 has been addressed by the inner structure of the model. Figure 7.3 shows the inner coefficients weights of the relationships and are illustrated by the forward-pointing arrows and the cause and effect links for each latent variable and ultimate dependent variable called GFC. Using Figure 7.3 to view the links of critical food crisis factors to GFC, one can see that the inner path coefficients for FDSFs, FSSRs, GAMFs and PSICAFs ranged from 0.3215 and 0.1148 and are significantly greater than zero. It can be concluded from the non-negative values of inner path coefficients indicate that all latent variables contribute to and explain GFC in varying degrees. The cause and effect strengths between these latent variables and the model are quite strong. However, it is the strongest (0.3215) between FDSFs and GFC and the weakest for PSICAFs and GFC (0.1148). Thus, food demand is the strongest contributor followed by food supply factor, agricultural market failures and government failures.

Based on the information in Table 7.8 and Figure 7.3, two observations can be drawn from the inner coefficients: (a) all of the inner coefficients are non-zero, and (b) the values of the inner coefficients are much larger from the global agricultural and food system to four latent variables of food demand-side factors, food supply-side restrictions, global agricultural markets failures and public sector interventions and collective actions, when compared to the significantly smaller coefficients, ranging from food demand-side forces, food supply-side restrictions, global agricultural markets failures and public sector interventions and collective actions to GFC. Moreover, the positive correlations among the latent constructs indicate that the factors that form KCGFCMS complement each other. If the numbers are different than zero, there is an indication that the strength of the causal relationships among the latent variables is strong. Only a negative number indicates there may be a need for further attention and intervention.

Figure 7.1: *Inner Path Coefficients Weightings through the Latent Variables for each Cause and Effect Link*

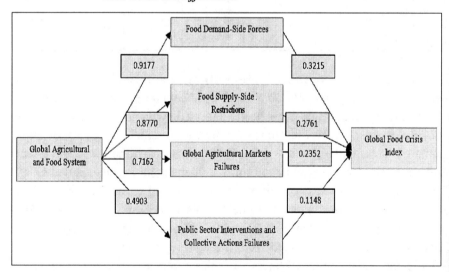

Correlation Analysis

For the purpose of validating the KCGFCM as a whole, score from different manifest variables of the same construct are pooled together to give a single manifest variable of mean scores of the construct, thus reducing the validity and complexity of the test. The mean of each dimension of GFC together with their least significant differences and the t-values, corrected for finite population, are given in Table 7.4 where the Pearson product-moment correlation is given in Table 7.9. As expected, independent and dependent latent variables are strongly correlated (CL = 95%). Because of the causal connections among latent variables in the KCGFC Model, variables are not only connected, but correlated as well. A further examination of the correlation analysis provides answers to research questions 3, 4, 5 and 6. The answer to research question 3, "What is the numerical strength of the relationship between GAFS and the construct of FDSFs?" has the highest correlation coefficient between ξ_1 and η_1 than all other correlation coefficients related to research questions 4, 5 and 6. This means that the degree of integration of global agricultural and food system (GAFS) and food demand-side forces is highest and lowest for GAFS and the construct of public sector interventions and collective actions failures.

Table 7.9:   *Correlation between Conceptually Related Independent and Dependent Variables in the KCGFCM (CL= 95%)*

Independent Latent variable	Dependent Latent variable	Correlation (r)
Global agricultural and food system (ξ_1)	Food demand-side forces (η_1)	0.915
Global agricultural and food system (ξ_1)	Food-supply-side restrictions (η_2)	0.887
Global agricultural and food system (ξ_1)	Global agricultural markets failures (η_3)	0.857
Global agricultural and food system (ξ_1)	Public sector interventions and collective actions failures (η_4)	0.743

Sensitivity Analysis on Research Questions: Detailed Item Analysis and Interpretations

Albeit the inner and outer path coefficients, coefficients of determination and the Cronbach's alpha are all statistically important tools used by the academia for the reliability, validity and accuracy of the model. But they do not mean anything to the men on the street, normal households, farmers, food traders and retailers. Moreover, these measures are not comparable across time or within the same industry. For this reason, mean scores, correlations, weights and indices have been developed to measure GFC. The responses to the research questions have to be addressed, and mean scores and outer coefficients (weights) are analysed to facilitate the interpretation of the results. The survey questions provide insights drilled through the complexity of the phenomenon of GFC by analysis and interpretation of the results. The detailed item analysis assists us to uncover the layers of complexity and complications arise from the dynamics of global agriculture and food system in which the phenomenon of GFC lies. The criterion for making judgement is based on the grading system. The lower index value means low GFC and vice versa. For example, below 25% will provide a good indication of with low GFC, while 25% to 50% will give medium crisis and 50% to 75% will indicate a higher crisis. The value of index above 75% will indicate extremely high food crisis.

Global Agricultural and Food System

Research Question 1 asked, "To what extent do the underlying driving forces of global agricultural and food system interact within the system and explain the phenomenon of global food crisis?"

The question has been addressed by the manifest variables of the GAFS which is an indication of how well the system is working and how it affects the food demand and subsequently the GFC. Table 7.16 shows that global agricultural and food system provides an index of 75.84%, indicating that the there are factors involved in the system that need careful monitoring and controlling as they are contributing to the food crisis the world is facing. The results of a further in-depth investigation into the GAFS have been presented in Table 7.10. The manifest variable x_1 had a fairly strong perception from the respondents as indicated by the outer coefficient value 0.8312 with an average score of 8.21. It reveals that the GAFS is influenced by the environmental, geo-ecological and natural forces. However, x_3 was not a significant contributor to the model at -0.0457. One explanation of negative value of outer coefficient is that there is a disagreement among the respondents about the existing agricultural and food system which is influenced by socio-economic and cultural forces. The main worrying factor is x_5 that has the highest value of outer coefficient 0.8809 which is very strong with an average score of 8.11. It shows that the GAFS is dominated by the capitalist maximum profit making corporate culture. So, there is an urgent need for food policy makers to look into this profit making culture of corporations dealing in food products. The manifest variable x_7 has very low outer coefficient value at 0.0937, therefore, the policy makers and government need not worry about this issue of underlying dynamics of technological dominance. The manifest variable x_6 with mean score 7.01 and week outer coefficient of 0.0488 reveals that the GAFS is insignificant in affecting the GAFS and hence GFC. The other two strong contributing manifest variables are x_3 and x_8 with outer coefficient values of 0.4841 and 0.4743 respectively. This reveals the fact that the political and institutional forces as well as systemic risks are affecting the existing global agricultural and food system. The manifest variable x_2 has a low value of outer coefficient which reveals that the existing GAFS is not influenced by human capital and technical manpower forces.

Food Demand-Side Forces

Research question 7 asked, "To what extent do the food demand-side forces contribute to the global food crisis?" The critical food crisis factors attributed to this question explained the factors affecting GAFS (ξ_1), and, food demand (η_1) and global food crisis (η_5). The portions of survey specially related to this question are x_1 to x_8, y_1 to y_8 and y_{33} to y_{40}.

The results of GAFS have been presented in Table 7.10. The overall food demand-side forces index is 89.23 per cent (Table 7.16) which indicates that there is an extremely high level of demand-side food crisis.

Table 7.10:   ***Results for Global Agriculture and Food System***

Label	Criteria	Average Score	Outer Coefficients
x_1	Is influenced by the environmental, geo-ecological and natural forces	8.21	0.8312
x_2	Is influenced by human capital and technical manpower forces	7.08	0.1942
x_3	Is influenced by socio-economic and cultural forces	8.26	-0.0457
x_4	Is influenced by political and institutional forces	7.08	0.4841
x_5	is dominated by the capitalist maximum profit making corporate culture	8.11	0.8809
x_6	Is affected by the greater integration of agriculture with manufacturing, international trade and service industries	7.01	0.0488
x_7	Has underlying dynamics of technological dominance	8.69	0.0937
x_8	Has inherent systemic risks to cope with shocks and stresses of food safety, quality standards, animal welfare and hygiene	6.74	0.4743

The manifest variables related to this score were y_1 to y_8. These variables are addressing research question 7 as a part of food demand construct. A further closer analysis is required to uncover its complexity. Therefore, it is important to analyse and interpret the results of food demand-side forces as shown in Table 7.11. The manifest variable y_1 has been found to have the strongest outer coefficient or weight with the highest mean score. It means that the food demand has been greatly influenced by an incredible increase in crop consumption under bio-fuel initiatives, production or 'bio-fuel rush' (corn-based ethanol or soybeans for biodiesel). The second manifest variable y_5 has been found to have a very strong outer coefficient (weight) at 0.7593 with mean score of 7.33. This indicates that the food demand has been strongly influenced by a steady increase in global population growth over the decades. Another strong manifest variable has been found to be y_2 with a third strong value of outer coefficient at 0.6313 with average scores of 7.27 which indicates that the food demand has been greatly influenced by an increased demand for a more diverse diet (dietary changes from grain

245

to more diversified diet like meat and dairy products) due to changes in lifestyle and consumption patterns. The manifest variable y_3 has also shown a fourth relatively high value of outer coefficient at 0.4705 with mean score of 8.29 which highlights that the global food demand has been influenced by livestock revolution and an increase in demand for animals feed. A closer look at the factors influencing food demand reveals that the manifest variable y_4 has the fifth highest outer coefficient at 0.4638 with a mean score of 8.29 that indicates that the global food demand is influenced by an increase due to more larger, prosperous and urban population and declining ratio of food producers to food consumers. This phenomenon has been taking place due to migration from rural areas to cities and prosperity of urban middle class population mainly in developing countries. The outer coefficient or weight of -0.0084 indicates that the respondents disagree with the sustained food demand from emerging markets and agribusiness in new markets. The panic buying for the purpose of hoarding buffer stock does not seem to contribute much as indicated by low outer coefficient value of .0998.

Table 7.11:   ***Results for Food Demand-Side Forces***

Label	Criteria	Average Score	Outer Coefficients
y_1	An increase in crop consumption under bio-fuel initiatives, production or 'bio-fuel rush' (corn-based ethanol or soybeans for biodiesel)	8.18	0.8917
y_2	An increased demand for a more diverse diet (dietary changes from grain to more diversified diet like meat and dairy products) due to changes in lifestyle and consumption patterns	7.27	0.6313
y_3	Livestock revolution and an increase in demand for animals feed	6.14	0.4705
y_4	An increase due to more larger, prosperous and urban population and declining ratio of food producers to food consumers	8.29	0.4638
y_5	An increase in food demand due to global population growth	7.33	0.7593
y_6	Sustained food demand from emerging markets and agribusiness in new markets	6.09	-0.0084
y_7	Panic buying for the purpose of hoarding buffer stock	6.29	0.0998
y_8	An increase in demand in industrial sector for agricultural raw materials and wage goods	7.33	0.0734

Further, an increase in demand in industrial sector for agricultural raw materials and wage goods has been found to be not contributing much to food demand and to the overall GFC index and the policy makers need to worry too much to tackle this area in order to mitigate the effects of GFC.

To conclude, the results for research question 7 were strong, but mixed and contributing to GFC. Overall, the manifest variables y_1, y_5, y_2, y_3, and y_4 have been contributing to global food demand and hence, GFC that are the main areas of concern for food policy makers. The underlying forces of global agricultural and food system produce changes in food demand factors which further contribute to GFC as indicated by the forward-pointing arrows in Figure 7.3.

Food Supply-Side Restrictions

Research question 8 asked, "To what extent do the food supply-side restrictions contribute to the global food crisis?". The critical food crisis factors attributed to this question explained the factors affecting GAFS (ξ_1), and, the construct of food supply-side restrictions (η_2) and global food crisis (η_5). The portions of survey specially related to this question are x_1 to x_8, y_9 to y_{16} and y_{33} to y_{40}.

The results of GAFS have been presented in Table 7.10. Table 7.16 reveals the overall index of food supply-side dimensions as 67.81 which is above 50% indicating that there is a high level of supply-side food crisis, but requires an intervention by watching certain factors. Table 7.12 shows the results for food-supply side factors. A further analysis shows that the manifest variable y_{11} reflects the highest value of outer coefficient at 0.7823 along with mean score of 8.57 ascertaining that the food supply is affected by uncertainty and instability in production due to vagaries of nature and weather shocks such as floods, rain, drought, earthquakes, etc., and ecological constraints on the exploitation of new lands or ocean exploration for sea food. The manifest variable y_9 with second highest outer coefficient at 0.7285 and mean score of 7.07 reveals that the shortage of food supply take place due to scarcity of resources (seeds, fertilizers, irrigation facilities, proper knowhow, energy, etc). The growing costs of factors of production and marketing including fertilisers, water, labour, energy, oil, seeds, credit and storage and transportation costs (food miles) has been reported as the third major factor affecting food supply and hence, GFC with its outer coefficient value at 0.6678 with mean score of 8.57. On average 6.24 respondents have reported that the food supply is constrained due to land constraints such as inflexibility in total area under cultivation, changing farm structure, serious degradation and loss of arable and fertile soil, and urban-rural land use conflicts, as revealed by the manifest variable y_{10} with outer coefficient (weight) value at 0.5740. The manifest variable (y_{16}) of food production and supply conditioned by the farmer's access to finance and extended credit facilities has been found to be fifth strongest factor as revealed by the outer coefficient at 0.4115 with an average score of 6.16. Moreover, there has been no agreement among the respondents regarding the shocks (low crop outputs) resulting from pests, animal disease (mad cow disease) etc. in key grain regions affecting and afflicting agricultural production as indicated by the outer coefficient -0.1629. Food supply is not conditioned by the rules of the global food market, global geopolitics and global food trade as indicated by a low value of outer coefficient (.0572). A decline in research expenditure (R&D) affecting new agricultural biotechnology, innovations and higher return farming (.1071) has been found to be insignificant in contributing to food supply and the overall GFC index. Governments and policy makers should worry too much about this manifest variables.

However, the GFC can be significantly reduced by reducing food supply side dimensions index through significantly reducing agricultural costs, increasing investments in rural agricultural and working towards better climate conditions.

Global Agricultural Markets Failures

Research question 9 asked, "To what extent does the construct of global agricultural market failures contribute to the global food crisis?". The critical food crisis factors attributed to this question explained the factors affecting GAFS (ξ_1), and, the construct of global agricultural markets failures (η_3) and global food crisis (η_5). The portions of survey specially related to this question are x_1 to x_8, y_{17} to y_{24} and y_{33} to y_{40}.

On Measuring Global Food Crisis

Table 7.12: *Results for Food Supply-Side Restrictions*

Label	Criteria	Average Score	Outer Coefficients
y_9	Shortage of food supply due to scarcity of resources (seeds, fertilizers, irrigation facilities, proper knowhow, energy, etc)	7.07	0.7285
y_{10}	Food supply constraints due to land constraints such as inflexibility in total area under cultivation, changing farm structure, serious degradation and loss of arable and fertile soil, and urban-rural land use conflicts	6.24	0.5740
y_{11}	Uncertainty and instability in production due to vagaries of nature and weather shocks such as floods, rain, drought, earthquakes, etc., and ecological constraints on the exploitation of new lands or ocean exploration for sea food	8.57	0.7823
y_{12}	Shocks (low crop outputs) resulting from pests, animal disease (mad cow disease) etc. in key grain regions affecting and afflicting agricultural production	4.88	-0.1629
y_{13}	Decline in research expenditure (R&D) affecting new agricultural biotechnology, innovations and higher return farming	5.31	0.1071
y_{14}	Growing costs of factors of production and marketing including fertilisers, water, labour, energy, oil, seeds, credit and storage and transportation costs (food miles)	8.95	0.6678
y_{15}	Food supply conditioned by the biological nature of the production process, rules of the global food market, global geopolitics, global food trade and lack of decoupling agricultural support (government policy to discourage food production)	5.07	0.0572
y_{16}	Food production and supply conditioned by the farmer's access to finance and extended credit facilities	6.16	0.4115

Table 7.10 presented the results of GAFS. The overall global agricultural markets failures index is 63.69 % (Table 7.16) which is above 50% and requires careful further investigation. Table 7.13 shows the results for global agricultural markets failures. A further careful analysis shows that the manifest variable y_{17} reflects the highest value of outer coefficient at 0.8945 with mean score at 8.86 ascertaining that existence of trade distortions in terms of barriers to entry, monopoly power, consolidation, lack of market transparency, integration and emergence of oligopolistic and oligopsonistic structures (multinational agri-business and food giants) in the global agricultural and food system. On average 6.10 respondents have reported that worldwide agricultural markets have failed due to rising expectations

and speculations which have pushed the prices up as revealed by the second highest value of outer coefficient of 0.6554. Negative externalities related to agricultural production and consumption activities is also a matter of concern as reported by third highest value of outer coefficient at 0.6191 with average score of 7.02. The outer coefficient of manifest variable y_{19} indicating factor market imperfections in terms of unequal land ownership distribution, imperfect competition in land tenancy market, unequal access to finance, farm and off-farm employment gaps, rural credit market imperfections, and so on (0.5221) reveals that this manifest variable is the fourth main contributor to the construct of GAMFs and to the overall index and there is a major concern for food policy makers in this regard. Hence, food policy makers should look into these manifest variables very carefully prior in order to mitigate the GFC. However, the outer coefficient of -0.1744 reflects that there is disagreement regarding erosion of crop genetic diversity arising because markets do not reward farmers for their provision of this public good. The outer coefficient of manifest variable y_{19} indicating market failures due to cobweb process of time lag between planting and harvesting and cyclical fluctuations in demand and supply decisions in agricultural markets (.0768) reveals that this manifest variable is the least contributor to the construct of GAMFs and to the overall index and hence, there is no concern for food policy makers in this regard. Similarly, the manifest variable y_{21} with the value of outer coefficient at 0.0868 and mean score of 7.17 reveals that displacement of natural fibres by synthetic substitutes (e.g., jute by synthetics) does not matter much as a market failure for GAMFs and therefore, it does not contribute to the GFC index.

Public Sector Interventions and Collective Actions Failures

Research question 10 asked, "To what extent does the dimension of public sector interventions and collective actions failures contribute to the global food crisis?" The critical food crisis factors attributed to this question explained the factors affecting GAFS (ξ_1), and, the construct of public sector interventions and collective actions failures (η_4) and global food crisis (η_5). The portions of survey specially related to this question are x_1 to x_8, y_{25} to y_{32} and y_{33} to y_{40}.

Table 7.13: **Results for Global Agriculture Markets Failures**

Label	Criteria	Average Score	Outer Coefficients
y_{17}	Trade distortions and emergence of oligopolistic and oligopsonistic structures (multinational agri-business and food giants)	8.86	0.8945
y_{18}	Displacement of natural fibres by synthetic substitutes (e.g., jute by synthetics)	7.17	0.0868
y_{19}	Factor market imperfections in terms of unequal land ownership distribution, imperfect competition in land tenancy market, unequal access to finance, farm and off-farm employment gaps, rural credit market imperfections, and so on.	6.10	0.5221
y_{20}	Markets failures in terms of erosion of crop genetic diversity arising because markets do not reward farmers for their provision of this public good	6.35	-0.1744
y_{21}	Negative externalities related to agricultural production and consumption activities	7.02	0.6191
y_{22}	Market failures due to cobweb process of time lag between planting and harvesting and cyclical fluctuations in demand and supply decisions in agricultural markets	6.19	0.0768
y_{23}	Raising expectations and speculations in the agricultural commodity market (the transfer of capital from the stressed US real estate market to the commodities markets which have pushed up prices)	6.10	0.6554
y_{24}	Information asymmetries or gaps due to location, distance, contamination in raw and processed foods, etc. that erode the supply of food safety and result in food-borne illnesses	6.44	0.4069

The overall public sector interventions and collective actions failures index is 56.36 as shown in Table 7.16. Table 7.14 presents further deeper results on the manifest variables of PSICAFs. The manifest variable y_{32} reveals that there is an urban bias in terms of inadequate public investments and access to resources to rural sector as indicated by the highest outer coefficient value at 0.8152 with average score of 7.17 which is matter of concern. The governments are not spending enough in agriculture sector and are favouring the cities instead. The manifest variable y_{29} with its second highest outer coefficient value at 0.6056 and mean score 7.23 reveals that there has been public sector intervention failure in terms of inefficient government rural development programmes. It reinforces the universal fact that majority of the wealthiest and politically well-connected farmers receive the maximum of the total agricultural support in comparison to the poor small farmers. State monopoly has been identified as another significant variable contributing to the construct of PSICAFs. Food policy makers should be extremely careful about these issues in order to mitigate the effects of GFC. The manifest variable y_{31} with fourth largest outer coefficient value at 0.4862 with average score 5.96 reveals that the factor of food health and safety regulations failures do matter and are contributing to the overall GFC. The manifest variable y_{25} with negative outer coefficient value at -0.0907 with mean score of 7.36 reveals that fiscal policy interventions (indirect tax on oils, subsidies, tax relief, tariffs, costly strategy grain reserves, and so on) has emerged as an area of confusion and lack of agreement among the respondents on this issue. However, the outer coefficient 0.0706 with average score of 5.96 indicates that the issue of ineffectiveness in farm organisations and collective action does not matter much in achieving desired results.

Table 7.14:   ***Results for Public Sector Interventions and Collective Actions Failures***

Label	Criteria	Average Score	Outer Coefficients
y_{25}	Fiscal policy interventions (indirect tax, lack of tax relief, tariffs, costly strategy grain reserves, etc.) failures by making food products expensive and less accessible for poor consumers	7.36	-0.0927
y_{26}	Public sector agricultural and food enterprises failures	6.05	0.0761
y_{27}	State monopoly on food imports and exports	5.26	0.4328
y_{28}	Deterioration of existing infrastructure facilities in rural sector	6.19	0.5445
y_{29}	Inefficient government agricultural and rural development programmes	7.23	0.6056
y_{30}	Collective actions institutions (such as rules and norms, farmers organizations and agricultural cooperatives) failures in achieving desired results	5.09	0.0706
y_{31}	Food health and safety regulations failures	7.96	0.4862
y_{32}	Urban bias in terms of inadequate public investments and access to resources to rural sector	7.17	0.8152

Research question 11 asked, "What are the significant constituents of the conceptualisation of global food crisis?". The critical food crisis factor attributed to this question explained the factors constituting global food crisis (η_5). The portions of survey specially related to this question are y_{33} to y_{40}. The term 'conceptual constituents' is used here in the sense to identify the factors that empirical constitute the phenomenon of GFC. Table 7.15 shows the factor y_{33} has the highest outer coefficient value at 0.86300with mean score of 8.18 indicating a rise in general food prices as the main constituent of GFC. The policy makers and governments need to improve this area in order to improve upon the GFC. The factor food vulnerability leading to food insecurity, hunger and malnutrition has been identified as the second most important constituent included in the domain of phenomenon of GFC with the second highest value of outer coefficient at 0.7254 with average score 7.63. Food crisis due to distortions in food distribution system has been acknowledged as the third important determinant with outer coefficient value at 0.7197 and average score of 7.03. The outer coefficient value of 0.6885 with average score 6.08 reveals the existence of food paradox with the existence of huge overeating and food wastage in households, supermarkets, buffet parties, restaurants which is also contributing to GFC. Food insufficiency due to least traded commodities such as rice (0.5622) has been indentified as another manifest variable indicating GFC. There has been a disagreement among respondents on the issue of obstacles to agricultural development and productivity due to the conflicting food policies of international institutions and national governments as the constituent of GFC as indicated by its negative value. The manifest variable y_{35} indicating changes in environmental sustainability and ecological security affecting GFC does not matter much as indicated by the low value of outer coefficient (0.0715).

The last research question asked, "What is the extent of overall severity of global food crisis?" This question has been explained by taking into consideration all six critical food crisis factors and forty eight manifest variables as indicated in Table 7.2 and all portions of survey have been taken into consideration.

Global Food Crisis Index and Its Decomposition

The GFC index is a means of measuring the extent of food problems and failures of economic forces of food demand, food supply, markets, and

Table 7.15: *Results for Global Food Crisis Index*

Label	Criteria	Average Score	Outer Coefficients
y_{33}	Rise in general food prices	8.18	0.8630
y_{34}	Deficiencies in utilization of food resulting in worsening of food problems (phenomenon of 'luxus consumption')	5.07	0.3961
y_{35}	Changes in environmental sustainability and ecological security affecting global food crisis	4.95	0.7715
y_{36}	Food insufficiency due to least traded food commodities such as rice	5.04	0.1622
y_{37}	Existence of food paradox (existence of food undercon- sumption, overconsumption and food wastage culture)	6.08	0.6885
y_{38}	Food crisis due to distortions in food distribution system	7.03	0.7197
y_{39}	Obstacles to agricultural development and productivity due to the conflicting food policies of international institutions and national governments	5.34	-0.0568
y_{40}	Food vulnerability leading to food insecurity, hunger and malnutrition	7.63	0.6254

government simultaneously within global agricultural and food system in order to obtain a comprehensive evaluation of global food security and the ownership and command over the adequate amount of food. For every critical food crisis factor and GFC, their respective index scores are a function of mean scores of corresponding manifest variables such that higher mean scores give higher index scores. The mean scores reflect crisis level of activities that are being measured. Therefore, a decrease in index would mean decreasing the food problems equivalent to the required decrease in mean scores of latent variables. Here the index can be used in a similar manner to measure how well different dimensions (such as FDSFs, FSSRs, GAMFs, PSICAFs) of the global food security are performing. It has been constructed in such a way so as to allow a direct comparison across each area while at the same time being able to compare the food crisis in different geographical areas. The index also allows the food crisis to be measured over time. The index monitors a number of different areas which are all combined into the final calculations to present a single number between one and 100. It is this single number that represents a food crisis score which makes our comparison of food crisis across countries and overtime so easy. In the measurement of food crisis process a number of different dimensions are measured and each is analysed to produce the index total. In our empirical study the overall GFC index has been found to be 69.17% (Table 7.16) which indicates a very high degree of GFC. Table 7.16 also shows the scores obtained for each criterion of the GFC measurement system. The final GFC will reflect the simultaneous effect of all the relationships estimated in the model.

Table 7.16:   ***Global Food Crisis Indices***

Global Agriculture and Food System	F1	75.84
Food Demand Side Forces	F2	89.23
Food Supply Side Restrictions	F3	67.81
Global Agricultural Markets Failures	F4	63.69
Public Sector Interventions and Collective Actions Failures	F5	56.36
Global Food Crisis Index	F6	69.17

Figure: 7.2   ***Indices of Global Food Crisis***

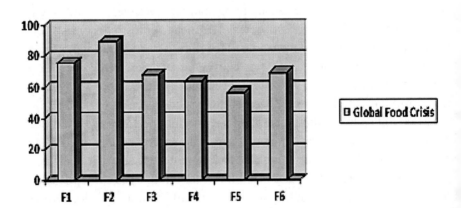

Concluding Remarks

The phenomenon of GFC is exceedingly complex. An analysis of such a latent phenomenon wants a specially designed measurement system that is based on holistic conceptualisation and takes into account all possible relevant driving forces, dimensions and factors therein. The index is produced by using a sophisticated and extremely robust statistical method called latent variable Partial Least Squares (PLSs) method. KCGFC model emerges from conceptually based theory to facts (model-based theory) specifying the food crisis process where a predefined structure is essential in order to be able to analyse interactions and to drive any cause-effect relationships. Further, the food crisis process is based on the conclusions of agricultural experts, and the model is seen as a simplification of the true relationship. Thus, in order to arrive at precision estimates a probabilistic model rather than a deterministic model has been adopted. The model used a simultaneous system approach rather than a partial model approach for the analysis in order to estimate the entire model at once. Hence, the present study had adopted a structural model based on a probabilistic approach using simultaneous equation estimation techniques for the measurement of GFC. The demographics of the survey sample were analysed and determined to be proportional to the groups by means of post-stratification. Cronbach's alpha scores were calculated on the critical food crisis factors which were greater than 0.7, a criteria for reliability mentioned in the previous chapter. All coefficients of determination were positive, which was indicative of goodness of fit of the variables within the model. The research questions provided a framework for grouping and compiling the results from KCGFCMS for GFC. Inner and outer coefficients agreed throughout the analysis and evaluations and provided information on how strongly the terms and constructs were related to global agricultural and food system. Specifically, items that correspond to sufficiently large values of outer coefficients as a whole provide a reliable measure of latent variables are selected by the procedure. Computed indices for critical food crisis factors and GFC with high values are suitable candidates for improvements.

To sum up, KCGFCMS is a single concise and global measurement instrument that would have general applicability for assessing the severity of food problems in any part of the globe at any level, given some modifications in measurement instrument. It is simple in terms of concepts and conceptual framework. It is easy to use in terms of model parameters and output. It is generic so can be applied in different contexts. It is robust as it effectively yields different outputs when its inputs are changed. It is comprehensive as it includes all food crisis factors and utilises a measurement instrument that is flexible, i.e. questionnaire items can be added or removed when and if desired. It is objective in the sense that its results are replicable by other researchers if the same study with the same conditions is performed. Its validity has been statistically proven. Finally, it is able to measure all critical food crisis factors and their contributions towards global food crisis.

Notes

i.   Also acknowledging the impact of response categories (the second section of our questionnaire) can have on the cognitive task of formatting an answer, we have taken 10 point linear scale, 1 to 10, 1 indicates 'not at all' and 10 indicates 'very much'. The main advantages of using ten points scale are as: (1) Using a ten-point scale stops people from choosing the middle value and makes them lean slightly in favour or against a given subject. However, in reality the two middle options of '5' and '6' are treated equally as being undecided. (2) By using a ten point scale also brings the added advantage of being able to treat scale as a continuous piece of data, a requirement of our research methodology. (3) A ten point scale requires only 71.3% of the sample required for 5 point scale (Wittink and Bayer, 1994). (4) The measurement of overall socioeconomic or other phenomenon has to be reliable and valid. (5) If the two measurement scales have the same sample sizes, the 10 point scale provides greater opportunity to detect changes in the overall phenomenon like emotional intelligence, poverty or social capital (Wittink and Bayer, 1994). (6) If the results are used to motivate people to improve their efforts, the more room for the improvement, the greater the scale's sensitivity. (7) 10 point scales minimises the skewness in the distribution of scores (Fornell, 1992).

ii.   Close-ended questions are those which can be answered by a simple "yes" or "no," while open-ended questions are those which require more thought and more than a simple one-word answer

iii.   A nominal category or a nominal group is a group of objects or ideas that can be collectively grouped on the basis of shared, arbitrary characteristic. A nominal group only has members and non-members. For example "race" is a nominal group. A person can be a member of a certain nominal racial group, such as black, white, or Asian, or he cannot. A black person does not have "more race" than a white person, therefore it is impossible to "order" races according to any sort of mathematical logic. Variables assessed on a nominal scale are called categorical variables. The central tendency of a nominal attribute is given by its mode; neither the mean nor the median can be defined.

iv. 4 In ordinal ranking, all items receive distinct ordinal numbers, including items that compare equal. The assignment of distinct ordinal numbers to items that compare equal can be done at random, or arbitrarily, but it is generally preferable to use a system that is arbitrary but consistent, as this gives stable results if the ranking is done multiple times. An example of an arbitrary but consistent system would be to incorporate other attributes into the ranking order (such as alphabetical ordering of the competitor's name) to ensure that no two items exactly match. With this strategy, if A ranks ahead of B and C (which compare equal) which are both ranked ahead of D, then A gets ranking number 1 ("first") and D gets ranking number 4 ("fourth"), and either B gets ranking number 2 ("second") and C gets ranking number 3 ("third") or C gets ranking number 2 ("second") and B gets ranking number 3 ("third").

v. On internal scale of measurement, all quantitative attributes are measureable. The numbers are rank ordered but now contain more information, specifically the difference between the numbers are equivalent. The difference between 3 and 4 can be assumed to be the same as the difference between 4 and 5. For interval-level data, each case has an absolute value associated with it and can be multiplied by any real number to exceed or equal another difference.

vi. The next higher complicated level of measurement is the *ratio scale*. At this level, measurement is the estimation of the ratio between a magnitude of a continuous quantity and a unit magnitude of the same kind (Michell, 1986, 1997, 1999). It has all the characteristics of interval-level measurement, plus there is an absolute zero point. Most measurement in the physical sciences and engineering is done on ratio scales. Scales measured at the ratio level would include height, weight, mass, energy, electric charge, speed, time, and distance.

vii. A unipolar scale starts with the absence of something and increases towards all of something. A unipolar scale prompts a respondent to think of the presence or absence of a quality or attribute: not at all satisfied, slightly satisfied, moderately satisfied, very satisfied or completely satisfied.

viii. 8 A common bipolar scale: Completely dissatisfied, mostly dissatisfied, somewhat dissatisfied, neither satisfied nor dissatisfied, somewhat satisfied, mostly satisfied and completely satisfied. Statisticians often map these answers to a scale with 0 in the middle: -3, -2, -1, 0, 1, 2, 3. So bipolar is having a middle point with amounts that increase in both ways as you move toward the ends.

Chapter 8   Resume, Conclusions and Policy Options

"If people let the government decide what they eat and what medicines they take, their bodies will soon be in as sorry a state as are the souls of those who live under tyranny".
Thomas Jefferson, American Founding Father, the Principal Author of the Declaration of Independence (1776) and the Third President of the United States of America (1801–1809).

Introduction

The idea of allowing government alone to decide what people eat and what medicines they consume had several negative consequences on human body capital in the past and will continue to do so in the future. Similarly the institution of market and the system of market mechanism that have many advantages including the benefit of allowing people to interact with each other for their mutual gains, also experienced various failures in the past and will do so in future in attaining *total food security* due to information asymmetries, externalities, allowing powerful capitalists and supermarkets to capitalise, principle-agent problems, and many other causes. Millions of people suffer from various psycho-socioeconomic pressures due to undemocratic agricultural and food-related decisions, widening economic hiatus between 'haves' and 'haves-not' as well as human contestability failures. As we all know that past cannot be altered, the shape of a better future depends upon us to make which may be achieved by focusing our choices and actions on actual facts and truth of life since human behaviour and reasoning cognitive minds are structured to a greater extent by these objective and verifiable observations. The same is true for the phenomenon of GFC which needs to be addressed, assessed and examined in an integrated perspective in the light of all facts in their totality. For this we need a suitable evaluative structure that allows us to address food problems correctly. Such a framework ought to be based on scientific foundations, statistical, theoretical and empirical reasoning and holism that permit the powerful decision makers to make correct major decisions that affect our lives.

The fact remains that GFC is an outgrowth of a combination of both natural and human behaviour within the boundaries of GAFS and the simultaneous interactions of multifaceted old and new driving forces that are both internal and external to the system. It lies at the heart of these mechanisms and behaviour of GAFS that jointly produce food conflicts, paradoxes and imbalances posing serious challenges for the present and future food security. As an open system it helps us to understand the relationships among its various sub-systems and elements as well as between the system and its environment. Basically, the smooth functioning of such a system will depend on how its components interact with each other than on how they work independently. Since the concept of GFC is holistic, multidimensional, multidisciplinary and complex along with its multifarious inter-linkages and interdependencies of different components that may not allow a clearer understanding of the functioning and behaviour of GAFS, it is, therefore, indispensable to analyse the phenomenon of GFC in a way that allows us to drill through the layers of multiple blending complicated behaviours, interactions and relationships created by various key driving forces that are profoundly entwined with the issues of poverty, food distribution and economic inequality. In nutshell, the primary interest of the present work was to analyse and study the phenomenon of GFC by considering the entire system and by using a new measurement system that, we argue, can provide a rich understanding and profound insights into multiple pathways originating from GAFS and leading to severe food problems.

Resume

In the present study the complexity perspective and systems approach have been wedded together with multivariate modelling approach to conceptualise, analyse and measure the GFC that has been seen as a process of worsening of aggregate exposure or disaster borne out of the functioning, behaviour and interdependence of a range of underlying processes and mechanisms within GAFS that, directly or indirectly, adversely influence food security situation worldwide. It began with identifying the critical food crisis factors (CFCFs) for the subsequent examination of their multiple causal connections. It utilized Kanji-Chopra statistically validated measurement tool based on its previous several other applications in areas such as such as total quality management, business excellence, leadership, poverty, work stress, emotional intelligence, corporate social responsibility, country risk, social capital, environmental health and other phenomena (Kanji, 2002; Kanji-Chopra, 2007; Kanji-Chopra, 2010; Chopra-Kanji; 2011a, Chopra-Kanji, 2011b). The KCGFCMS has been applied to achieve the objectives of identifying and quantifying the problem areas causing GFC and pinpointing the areas in significance order which needed improvements for their effective management. It is a *theory-driven model* based on a validated structure that facilitates the production of GFC and CFCFs indices. In brief, it aimed at managing GFC with its measurement.

By rediscovering the past we might predict the future. Considering this, the exploratory work of the study reviewed the literature to identify the problem areas and obtained an inventory of CFCFs. It is evident that previous studies have addressed various food problems intrinsic in direct or indirect driving forces independently one from the other. The scientific way to understand, analyse and manage the GFC, we argue, is to take into account all CFCFs simultaneously. In descriptive work the list of CFCFs was finalised to construct the conceptual model and then measurement instrument was designed. In empirical work the conceptual model was converted into the operational model that subsequently was further translated into latent variable structural model based on structural equations and latent variables that analysed and measured GFC not by juxtaposing different food crisis types as if they were independent one from the other, but subsequently through weighting systems arriving at a synthetic indicator. In fact, in certain situations one type of food crisis (say food availability crisis) in this measurement system interacted with other food crises types (say food price crisis or food adequacy crisis) in a multiplicative way whilst in others it may interact producing reciprocal compensatory and attenuating effects. Only after an overall estimate of GFC, the model could enable the index to be broken down into various food crisis indices such as food demand-side forces, food supply-side restrictions, global agricultural market failures and public sector interventions and collective actions failures. The KCGFCMS was constructed as a very flexible framework that can be advantageously employed with minor required changes in the measurement instrument both for *measuring* and *managing* food crisis at any level, i.e., global, regional, national, local or household.

In total, forty eight manifest variables and six latent variables were carefully developed to create theoretical constructs and the model to uncover the underlying complex driving forces within certain boundaries of the prevailing GAFS. They represented important aspects of the present research because they involved a synthesis of the general agricultural economics concepts with essential elements of the GAFS and GFC. Thereafter, causal path diagrams were constructed. At the next stage, the manifest variables were used to develop a measurement instrument for the measurement system where each construct was operationalised by a group of manifest variables that corresponded to ten-point multi-item measurement scales. This was performed because it was thought that the constructs cannot be directly understood due to their multifarious nature. Then, the survey data entry and Partial Least Squares were run. The results were then analysed for latent manifest weights, inner coefficients, multiple correlation matrix, mean scores of manifest variables, and standard deviations. The reliability and validity analysis was performed for the KCGFC model by computing inner R squares, coefficient alphas, chi-squares, content, construct and criterion-related validity and summary indices for CFCFs and GFC. Finally, the sensitivity analysis on research questions was carried out and findings summarised. In brief, the symmetrical relationships in the model were analysed for their theoretical rationale before being subjected to an empirical test and a substantial validation. A comparison of the model with perceptions of agricultural experts and food problems researchers concerning relationships among CFCFs showed that the model had a good theoretical rationale.

Main Findings and Conclusions

A systematic investigation was employed by developing a scheme to guide the conduct of the present work at several stages: exploratory work, descriptive work, model developing, empirical work, model testing, validation and application. The emerging conclusions and major findings of the present study can be discussed as follows:

On Measuring Global Food Crisis

1. *Interface between GAFS and GFC:* The present work discussed explicitly and verified the interface and links between GAFS and GFC that was seldom unequivocally mentioned or scientifically measured in literature. Making sense of GAFS is both straightforward and complex. It is straightforward considering the direct connection of adequate, safe and nutritious food with health, well-being, sustaining and growth of human life and indirectly to a number of big issues. It is complex due to mixture of global driving forces and local dynamics. Virtually, GFC can be described as a phenomenon that lies within the boundaries of GAFS, with four different causal pathways. Therefore, the relationship between GAFS and GFC assists us to understand the entire structure and functioning of the food crisis generating mechanism.

2. *Contributions of Critical Food Crisis Factors towards Global Food Crisis:* The quest for CFCFs is the essence of identifying the factors involved in world food problems and establishing the GFC severity level so that an appropriate food policy can lead to the world's resources in the desired direction. The CFCFs approach is believed to be a practical approach for modelling because the stress is on critical factors determining food crisis. On the same line, the present research has identified, analysed and examined the relevant CFCFs. The application of CFCFs approach to the modelling of GFC has a particular strength in producing results that are of high relevant value for food policy makers. This is of particular consideration to the present research because in the past food policy makers had to rely on a set of few agricultural production and other indicators to support their decision making in a complex food retail, consumption, distribution, and production environment. Recognising these difficulties of the food policy makers, the KCGFC model aimed to provide a better framework for understanding the key drivers of food crisis and for bringing a wider set of measures together so that food policy makers have an appropriate range of indicators to use.

The KCGFC model has four paths going through it, each starting from GAFS and ending with GFC (Figure 7.3). As stated in the previous chapter, path coefficients represent the amount of increase in dependent variables as a result of one unit increase in independent variables. It is possible to determine the contribution of each variable towards GFC from the value of path coefficients. For latent variables: FDSFs, FSSRs, GAMFs, and PSICAFs, their unit contributions are equal to the values of path coefficients of their relationships with GFC, i.e., 0.3215, 0.2761, 0.2352 and 0.1148 respectively. Figure 8.1 shows four different pathways to GFC.

Figure 8.1: **The Four Paths through the Global Food Crisis Model**

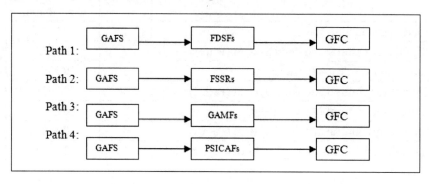

The unit contributions of other variables are obtained by multiplying path coefficients on the variables' paths that join the variables to GFC. For example, it can be seen from Table 7.8 that for every unit change in GAFS, the variable FDSFs increases by 0.9177 units. Furthermore, the contribution of FDSFs to the GFC would be 0.3215 and consequently, the GFC would have increased by 0.9177 X 0.3215 = 0.2950 unit (Path 1) which represents the unit contribution of GAFS towards GFC. The unit contribution of GAFS can also be calculated from the other three paths of the model. This would yield unit contribution of 0.2421 for path 2, 0.1684 for path 3 and 0.0562 for path 4. The highest of the calculated unit contribution is the unit contribution for FDSFs followed by GAFS (0.2950) via FDSFs. Table 8.1 shows the ranking of unit contributions of critical food crisis factors.

Several conclusions can be drawn from the results:

a. The strengths of causal connections between CFCFs are different. There is the highest correlation coefficient (degree of connection) between GAFS and FDSFs and the lowest correlation between GAFS and PSICAFs.

b. The construct of food demand side forces has been found as a main factor contributing highest to the present GFC. It is predominately a demand pull food crisis.

Table 8.1:   *Unit Contributions of Critical Food Crisis Factors to Global Food Crisis*

Critical Food Crisis Factor	Rank	Unit Contribution
Food-Demand Side Forces	1	0.3215
Global Agricultural and Food System (Path 1)	2	0.2950
Food Supply Side Restrictions	3	0.2761
Global Agricultural and Food System (Path 2)	4	0.2421
Global Agricultural Markets Failures	5	0.2352
Global Agricultural and Food System (Path 3)	6	0.1684
Global Agricultural and Food System (Combined Average)	7	0.1904
Public Sector Interventions and Collective Action Failures	8	0.1148
Global Agricultural and Food System (Path 4)	9	0.0562

c. GAFS is contributing to GFC in different magnitudes through different pathways. It reflects systematic failures in how to produce, buy, sell and share food. GAFS is contributing highest via path 1 of food demand in comparison to other three pathways through food supply, market failures and government interventions. Hence, the construct of food demand outweighs other constructs.

d. The pathways from GAFS to the factors located earlier on the paths tend to have higher unit contributions compared to the four variables to GFC because their influences are tempered when path coefficients are multiplied together.

e. The unit contribution can be used by planners and food policy makers for improving food crisis by allowing resources and measures to be concentrated on factors with highest contributions. However, this would depend on the availability of resources and cost of allocating them.

f. The knowledge about unit contributions is useful for the continuous monitoring of GFC in all the key areas of this phenomenon. Since GFC depends on all CFCFs in varying degrees, larger improvements can be made by focusing on the activities or manifest variables related to the CFCFs that have higher unit contributions. For example, the findings indicate that the highest contributor to GFC is the construct of food demand. For practical reasons, the factors (manifest variables) of food demand with the highest outer coefficients and average scores should be improved first and then followed by other factors according to their relative contribution to GFC in order to manage it successfully with limited financial and non-financial resources.

g. The results have revealed the food supply failures as the second prime factor significantly contributing to the global food crisis. The magnitude of their impact is determined by the uncertainty and instability in production, scarcity of resources, the growing costs of factors of production and marketing, the land constraints, and the farmers' access to finance and extended credit facilities. These factors are influencing the food supply which in turn contributes to GFC.

h. The market failures have been found to be present in GFC. Within the construct of GAMF, trade distortions and emergence of oligopolistic and oligopsonistic structures (multinational agri-businesses and food giants) have been identified as the main culprits. The speculations in commodity markets and displacement of natural fibres by synthetic substitutes have also been responsible for agricultural markets failures.

i. There have been colossal government failures contributing to GFC. However, the present study reveals that market failures outweigh government failures. Within PSICAFs, 'urban bias' in terms of inadequate government investments and access of resources to rural sector has been identified as the main factor contributing to public sector failures. Fiscal policy interventions in terms of taxes and farm subsidy are contributing to PSICAFs and GFC.

j. It seems that a generalisation can be made on the significance of GAFS towards GFC by comparing the results and it has been reported to be the most important factor for food problems from inception onwards (Thompson et al., 2007; Ericksen, 2006; Hefferman and Henderickson, 2006; Friedmann, 1987). As far as the values of unit contributions of different pathways are concerned, they have been influenced by the way the model was constructed. The model has been specified with five CFCFs intervening in all paths linking GAFS to GFC. Thus, the influence of GAFS on GFC has to be examined within the context of the intervening variables.

3. Measurement of GFC Indices: The fundamental question is "What does GFC measurement mean for food policy makers?" The indices were computed by using a function that takes into account the strength of causal connections of manifest variables to their corresponding constructs (outer coefficients) and mean scores of manifest variables. Indices representing food problems can be used to make inter and intra-country comparisons and compare past with the present food problems. The basis of determining a mix of CFCFs in food policy options is by using unit contributions of CFCFs that are selected for improvements one at a time in order of their potential contribution and importance from the highest to the lowest. This may, however, mean higher costs to national governments in terms of additional resources such as human resources, investments, time, materials, technology, and so on. Thus, a measure that incorporates the marginal unit contribution will be more appropriate for use as a basis for bringing CFCFs into solution. The GFC index measures the extent of food problems and failures of driving forces of food demand, food supply, markets, and government and collective actions simultaneously within GAFS in order to obtain a comprehensive evaluation of global food security and the ownership and command over the adequate amount of food. The overall GFC index is 69.17 indicating to the food policy makers that the food problems are very acute and need immediate attention and action. The index of food demand is the highest followed by GAFS, FSSRs, GAMFs, and PSICAFs indices in significance of contribution and therefore, the food policy makers should first focus on improving these forces in importance from the highest in order to reduce the overall GFC index. The model has content validity because its constructs are the actual CFCFs of the phenomenon of GFC which have been identified by following a scientific procedure discussed in previous chapters. Thus, the scales used have content validity. The results of the higher degrees of causal correlations among the constructs indicate that the model has construct validity. The results have been found to be reliable for stakeholders and policy makers as indicated by the higher values of Cronbach-alpha values for all the latent and manifest variables.

Resume, Conclusions and Policy Options

4. *Findings on Research Questions:* The results on research questions have brought out old and new driving forces that are jointing affecting and defining the GFC. The following results assist for setting priorities for resource allocation on significance order basis.

The present study concludes that there are many failures and transformations in the global agricultural and food system. Its high index value indicated that the food policy makers need to seriously focus on this construct. It needs to be resilient, properly coordinated and carefully managed for achieving total global food security. Globalisation of the food chain with increasing consolidation and concentration resulted in dominance of multinational companies in the food sector along the value chain. The environmental, geo-ecological and natural forces exert the second highest impact on GFC. The third force of GAFS affecting GFC was the political and institutional forces. The fourth force of GAFS affecting GFC has been inherent systemic risks to cope with shocks and stresses of food safety, quality standards, animal welfare and hygiene. The weakest force influencing GFC was the dynamics of technological dominance and socio-economic and cultural forces.

Global demand for food is growing and resulting in food-demand crisis. In significance order, the first reason was an increase in crop consumption under bio-fuels production. The second reason was global population and income growth. The third cause was an increased demand for more diverse dietary preferences due to changes in lifestyle and consumption patterns and thus switching towards more resource-intensive food. The fourth reason was the livestock revolution and an increase in demand for animals feed. The fifth cause was urbanisation and declining ratio of food producers to food consumers.

The study concludes that the food supply-side restrictions are expected to define the future food production and are third main contributors to the GFC. It revealed that food supply has been affected firstly by uncertainty and instability in production due to vagaries of nature and weather shocks such as floods, rain, drought, earthquakes, tropical storms, etc.; secondly, by the scarcity of resources (seeds, fertilizers, water and irrigation facilities, proper knowhow, energy, etc); thirdly, by the growing costs of factors of production and marketing including fertilisers, water, labour, energy, oil, seeds, credit and storage and transportation costs (food miles); fourthly, by

land constraints such as inflexibility in total area under cultivation, changing farm structure, serious land degradation and loss of arable and fertile
soil, bio-fuel crops and urban-rural land use conflicts, and fifthly, due to
farmer's access to finance and extended credit facilities.

*The study concludes that global agricultural markets have been fail-
ing* firstly due to the emergence of oligopolistic and oligopsonistic structures, multinational agri-businesses and food retail giants, lack of transparency in food markets, existence of unfair competition and rise in the
monopoly power of the global food retail giants resulting in food trade distortions. Secondly, the rising speculations in commodities pushed the food
prices up. Negative externalities related to agricultural production and consumption activities have been identified as the third market failure. The factor market imperfections in terms of unequal land ownership distribution,
imperfect competition in land tenancy market, unequal access to finance,
farm and off-farm employment gaps, rural credit market imperfections have
emerged as the fourth component of market failures. Information asymmetries or gaps due to location and distance that erode the supply of food safety
resulting in food-borne illnesses have been identified as the fifth cause of
market failures.

*Public sector or government interventions and collective actions
exhibited gigantic failures in regulating agricultural and food systems.*
Urban bias has been found as the main manifest variable in the domain of
government failures. This is a manifestation of domestic and international
policy (pricing, investment, development, trade, aid, etc.) environments to
continue discriminating against and neglecting agricultural developments
in developing countries. Another government failure was manifested by the
fiscal policy interventions (indirect tax on oils, subsidies, tax relief, tariffs,
costly strategy grain reserves, and so on) which are failing by making food
products more expensive and less accessible for poor consumers. Across
developing countries the government rural development programmes have
been failing due to various reasons such as corruption, complicated administrative structures, lack of resources, lopsided policies and so on. The study
found state monopoly as another factor contributing to government failures.

*The manifest variables analysis in the construct of GFC concluded
an exorbitant hike in basic food prices as the prime constituent of GFC
which has pushed millions of people in food poverty across the globe.* It

269

further revealed the possibility that food vulnerability will increase more hunger and malnutrition as there may not be enough food for everyone. Distortions in food distribution system and the existence of food paradox with the existence of huge overeating (obesity and overweight) and post production food wastage were also contributing to GFC. The study finally concludes that the extent of overall severity of GFC has been quite severe as indicated by the high value (69.17 %) of GFC index.

Food Policies That Can Work: Putting Evidence into Practice

The intricacy of the global nature of agricultural and food system intertwined with the local factors dynamics demonstrates various types of failures in the ways we grow, process, distribute, exchange, consume, utilise and manage our food. A multidimensional phenomenon such as GFC necessitates a multidisciplinary approach to tackle it holistically. The GFC management strategies should not only include efforts to address current constraints on food production, consumption and distribution, but also address the future threats to food insecurity and vulnerability. The findings of the present study suggest that it is not possible to have food security in one country alone in this globalised world and it therefore calls for a transition from a *'leaderless world'* to a *new improved global governance for total world food security* to fix the broken GAFS by being governed globally and multilaterally. A well-connected, effective and improved co-ordination of international actions, information and transparency is required as a response to various identified failures and to fight against short term and long term effects of GFC. The danger of having too many agencies to deal with food problems is the possibility of burden shifting and lack of total commitment. Instead of having different food governing bodies at different global organisations such as the *Committee on World Food Security* at Food and Agriculture Organisation (FAO), *High Level Task Force on Global Food Security* at United Nations and *Agricultural Market Information System* (AMIS) created in June 2011 in Paris by the G20, dealing with same issues of food security and nutrition, there should be one high powered inter-governmental platform with its headquarters at the United Nations and offices across the world to deal with critical factors of global food crisis generating hunger, malnutrition and obesity.

On Measuring Global Food Crisis

A *new* democratic food-related world order needs to emerge via global partnership among all nations where each and every country is a member with equal say, equal right to vote in decision-making, collective liability, responsibility, obligations (financial contributions) and benefits. All stakeholders of GAFS including local governments, private sector organisations, farmers and civil society must also be allowed to actively participate in global governance forum to have their say in providing support and advice to most vulnerable small farmers, address critical food crisis factors, cope with shocks and stresses and resolve food paradoxes and inequalities. The financial and non-financial resources should be used in accordance with the operating principles and food policy priorities of global food governance by following five fundamental missions: universal implementation of 'rights to food approach'; food and health first and profit afterwards; feeding people before cars; reforms, innovations and substantial investments in agricultural and food-related areas; and community-based and informed agricultural programs to achieve *zero hunger, undernutrition and obesity.* Putting emerging evidence into practice is the key to resolve food crisis at all levels such as global, regional, national, local and household. Moreover, policies and guidelines for *total food security management* should be legally binding on all nations and must filter through all levels within each country by cutting red tape and bureaucracy hurdles and costs so that all humanity is benefitted. A strong global system of checks and balances is required for the successful implementation and monitoring of food policies and guidelines. The repeat offenders or violators of global food policy guidelines that may be governments or corrupt political leaders, global fast food giants, multinational supermarkets, profit-hungry food hoarders and speculators, land grabbers, capitalist farmers exploiting poor agricultural workers, and the like, should be dealt with heavy hands of international laws to bring them to justice. Most importantly the variations across countries and regions with regard to the extent and depth of hunger, malnutrition, obesity and other food problems must be incorporated in the food policies priorities. Various components of new global governance system should be carefully designed so that important issues such as agricultural research, education and innovation, market transparency, coordination among government actions, corporate social responsibility, information sharing, effects of food price volatility, ethical investments and balanced ethical eating and the like

271

are taken care of.

It is evident that neither government nor free markets or private sector alone can achieve total food security. Therefore, it is absolutely vital to have a strong partnership among all stakeholders at different levels. It calls for a non-conflicting *six-dimensional approach* to food policy that puts an ultimate onus on improved global governance involving all stakeholders to implement GFC management strategies in an environmentally and socially sustainable and adaptable manner.

The *first set of food policies* focuses on GAFS in order to make it more resilient and sustainable so that future environmental, socioeconomic and food problems can be avoided. According to the level of significance of manifest variables found in this research, it includes practical solutions: (a) corporate nature of GAFS based on the idea of global sourcing shadows the entity of nations as an organizing principle of the world economy, therefore, a *new global tax system* should be introduced to control the corporate nature of profit hungry food and non-food transnational corporations (TNCs) in their race to the bottom. Surprising the TNCs that are actively operating in food production and processing are also involved in global sourcing of input sites and output markets. The study calls for the development of a *global political organization* to regulate these types of monopolistic activities of the TNC's. They should be legally forced to practice corporate *social responsibility* to act in public interest by producing healthier food, conserve energy and other resources in their operations. (b) working with nature by rejecting the agricultural practices that damage environment and ecological system with less use of pesticides and chemical fertilizers, a by-product of petroleum, by encouraging people to produce as much of their own food as possible by applying low-impact ecological methods, and by using permaculture, harmonized planting and biological techniques. There 'worm bins' should be used to turn waste into horticulture gold. Practically, all waste ought to be recycled. *International action on climate change* needs be addressed by total shift to low energy light bulbs, renewable energy use at household and industrial levels, including solar and wind generated electricity and other methods in order to cut CO_2 emissions; (c) nation-states should build up a more global vision of food system instead of TNCs. Political party in power should put control locally over territory, land grabbing, grazing, water, seeds, livestock and fish populations; reject the privatisation of natural resources through laws, commercial contracts and intellectual property rights regimes; and regulate the impact corporations and financial speculators have on food security; political courage and imagination to invest in a long-term bid to restore their core strength in dealing with food crisis; (d) controlling the systemic risks to cope with shocks and stresses of production and sale of unsafe, unhealthy and junk food. The total implementation of food safety standards is necessary to ensure that we do not have pesticide residues, unacceptable levels of hormones or heavy metals; (e) a basic rethink of agricultural knowledge, science and innovation technology by building skills, knowledge, information systems and other needs of small to medium farmers in diverse ecosystems, and areas with the greatest needs; (f) regulating and stabilising food prices and ensuring food supplies through mechanisms such as establishment of international food corporation, international grain storage in key locations, global food aid, food rationing, effective global food distribution system and the like.

The dominance of political and institutional forces affecting GFC revealed a policy-determined crisis. Most of the countries followed inappropriate policies that originated from *neo-liberal open market-oriented* framework. For example, a policy neglect of agriculture, policy of decline in public investment in agriculture and agricultural research, policy of a shift from 'food crops' to 'cash crops', policy of bio-fuels, reduction in public provision of different inputs for cultivation, and other political-institutional factors contributing to GFC. Therefore, there should be a policy shift in the food policies.

The *second set of food policies* focuses on the food demand-side forces and includes: (a) a 'food-first approach': Feed people before feeding cars. Bio-fuels are increasing world hunger. The *food-fuel conflict* can be resolved by promoting environmentally sustainable higher-generation bio-fuels that do not compete for cropland and water resources. The *bio-fuels factor affects both food demand and food supply*, it is the demand for bio-fuels that created its own supply. It is recommended that the *food-fuel conflict* should be resolved by *second generation bio-fuels* that involve short term adjustment in bio-fuels policies to accommodate both fuel and food and *a shift from crop-based bio-fuel to cellulosic ethanol* that is obtained by converting jutropha oil (a non-edible oilseed), shrubs and even trees to biodiesel fuel. Crops like miscanthus (perennial grasses native to Africa and

Asia) can yield as much as three times ethanol as traditional corn ethanol. Moreover, cellulosic bio-fuel production should be made only from degraded wastelands, marginal land, agricultural waste, fast growing grasses, waste biomass and molasses based bio-fuel productions that are not suitable for agriculture so that there is no conflict with food production. Thus, careful land use management, technological innovations to invent new oil fields, providing subsidies to encourage non-crops bio-fuels, and balanced policy approaches can be recommended to deal with the burning issue of bio-fuels.

(b) The second significant manifest variable contributing to rise in food demand is rapid *population growth*. Both global population and net food quantity have been increasing over the centuries. The *population-food availability relationship* in an area or country becomes more complex with human migration as well as international food trade or aid across borders from a place of plenty to the area of paucity. On one hand, countries like Germany, Japan, Italy, etc. have negative population growth whereas on the other hand, over-populated countries such as China, India, Pakistan, Bangladesh, Afghanistan, etc. demonstrate the social laws and norms that are hindering the global efforts to slow population growth. The national governments of over-populated countries should mobilise public opinion to check population growth. Positive measures such as family planning (birth control measures), cash incentives, female education, and the like should be given more attention to stabilize the world population size (zero population growth) and to establish favourable population-food sufficiency ratios across the countries. This may reduce heavy food import dependence for many countries such as Iran, Egypt, Israel, Yemen etc. and may help to reduce the absolute numbers of undernourished children in the world.

(c) The third manifest variable is dietary diversity. *Diet matters*. People should be encouraged to eat more ethically and ecologically sustainable diet. More and more people should be encouraged to shift to plant-based diets. The recommendations to introduce diet-related changes also subsume the fourth significant manifest variable of *livestock revolution* as it overlaps with *dietary diversity* up to a certain extent. Both of these manifest variables pose major threats to global water, soil, and air quality, the livelihood of smallholders, and public health, if no preventive and mitigating measures are taken in time. As we know that in order to obtain animal protein rich diets, a huge amount of basic foods are utilised to feed industrial livestock production. This is not ecologically sustainable since basic foods are required to feed people directly. The current high level of meat consumption is damaging human health and the planet.

A two sided approach is needed to tackle this situation. First is to tackle the issue of dietary diversity and second is to manage livestock revolution. More community based educational campaigns across the globe are needed to highlight the humanitarian, economic and health benefits of balanced vegetarian diets. A well planned vegetarian diet is much cheaper, nutritious, tasty and healthier than the one with meat. The well documented health benefits may include lower risks of heart disease, type 2 diabetes, obesity, certain types of cancer and lower blood cholesterol levels keeping all other factors constant. The vegetarian diet should include protein, iron, calcium and Vitamins B, B12 and D and provides often a much wider choice of food as compared to diets of meat-eaters. Vegetarian diets should include eating fruits, vegetables and starchy foods such as bread, cereals and potatoes; moderate amounts of alternatives to meat and fish; some dairy foods or alternatives (such as fortified soya milk and yoghurts); and small amounts of foods high in fat, salt and/or sugar. Vegetable oils particularly flaxseed, walnut, rapeseed and soya oils provide Alpha Linolenic Acid (ALA) and our bodies can convert some ALA into two types of Omega-3s, long versions found in oily fish-docosahexaenoic acid (DHA) and eicosapentaenoic acid (EPA). The long Omega-3 fats obtained from fish are particularly good for us and non-fish eaters should consider a supplement made from algae derived DHA. Vegetarians are more likely to consume unrefined carbohydrate foods, salads, fruit, nuts and pulses. Intakes of many nutrients are higher in vegetarians than consumers of more usual western diets: thiamine, folate, vitamin C, carotene, potassium and vitamin E. More importantly, grains and cereals are regarded as crisis crops which can be stored for a long time in the house as emergency food. Thus, an increase in the availability, affordability and consumption of nutrient-dense, wholesome vegetables and pulses is one way in which malnutrition and problems associated with obesity may be substantially reversed.

Recognizing our individual differences and freedom to make their own decisions regarding our eating habits and also acknowledging the economic benefits and contributions of livestock revolution, is a demand-driven phenomenon. While not neglecting the health (fulfilling protein and micronutrient deficiencies for most women and children in developing countries) and, this phenomenon should be managed carefully by enhancing awareness among farmers and general public regarding animal rights, environmental risks and growing health concerns about high intakes of bad cholesterol and saturated fatty acids from some animal and milk products specially in developing countries. A taste shift is needed away from harmful and costly meat products. In a price-responsive global food markets, a substitution of meat and poultry products for low-priced nutritious grain in the human diet is required. The study recommends that modern technology should be used to develop safe and healthy *'in vitro'* meat, also known as laboratory-grown, cultured, hydroponic, test-tube, vat-grown meat or shmeat, as an alternative to animal meats.

(d) Another significant manifest variable is the rapid urbanisation with prosperous population and declining ratio of food producers to food consumers. Even in future, more developing nations will continue to urbanise that will cause serious problems with food distribution and marketing to growing numbers of 'megacities'. Urban and peri-urban (areas immediately surrounding the cities) agriculture have significant role and contribution in food and nutrition security in most low-income nations, although in many cities it is more difficult for the urban poor to get access to the land needed for agriculture. There is a need to set up small urban centres in agricultural areas to provide livelihoods to the poorest of the urban poor. Urban poor should be encouraged to explore their links in rural areas that allow their reincorporation into rural livelihoods. Policies that improve urban incomes, employment, wages and health can also improve nutrition levels of urban households. A shift in employment structure within the food industry towards agriculture sector to cultivate crops is needed instead of more people working in transport, wholesaling, warehousing, packaging, retailing, food processing and vending.

The *third set of food policies* includes recommendations related to food-supply side restrictions: (a) On one hand, there is a need to invest heavily in building local disaster management capacity to respond and manage suitable defences in the areas like East Timor that are most prone to natural disasters of floods, droughts, earthquakes, landslides, tsunamis, tropical storms such as Katina and Sandy and prolonged dry spells. This includes supporting national climate risk assessments, provide *fast track emergency relief* to natural disaster-affected areas, improve soil moisture availability in drought prone areas through watershed programs, develop new technologies and biotechnology tools through research to help protection from drought or floods, heavy investment in agricultural research for developing mitigation and adaptation strategies, and programme implementation. On the other, hand farm households should adopt different coping strategies as safeguards against natural disasters such as a system of early warning and preparedness, crop insurance, crop risk management including careful choice of cropping patterns, rice varieties, planting date, planting method. (b) The second manifest variable is the *scarcity of resources* (seeds, fertilizers, irrigation facilities, proper knowhow, energy etc). Guidelines should be provided to national and local governments to provide subsidised resources to the areas with scarcity of agricultural inputs and resources. The crop intensity and productivity can be increased by the use of high yielding and hybrid varieties of seeds, improved soil health with efficient water management, incentives for labour migration to rural areas with labour shortages, heavy investment in other inputs (fertilizers, pesticides, improved seeds, or technological implements like irrigation systems). This can be achieved by providing assistance in subsidised inputs, subsidised oils, market access and information, infrastructure facilities, credit needs, better and modern technology, government financial subsidy, and small farmers debt forgiveness. There should be effective dissemination of technology by establishing agri-clinics and employing rural knowledge workers.

(c) The issue of *growing costs of factors of production, marketing and transportation costs* (food miles) can be tackled by using three-fold strategy: firstly, 'buying local' slogan should be promoted by highlighting product quality, total quality management, nutritional value, methods of raising food, good effects on environment, freshness of local food, and support for local farming community. Local food with these characteristics may encourage consumers to pay more and may have good impact on economic development, employment, health or environmental quality. Secondly, there should be government food programs and policies to increasingly support local food systems. Thirdly, input costs vary widely among countries and regions reflecting differences in production practices. Agriculture can become more productive only by using cheap capital goods and other inputs. (d) Land makes up of 30 per cent of earth's surface and out of which over 4/5th

of the total land is unsuitable for agriculture because either it is too hot, too cold, too dry, too rocky, too flooded (areas like swamps, marshes and low-lying coastal areas), and damaged through mining or poor farming practices. The manifest variable of *land constraint* can be taken care of by converting unfertile land into arable land, reclaiming lost land to sea, ameliorating the difficulties of poor soil quality and making more land available for agriculture. Regions with underutilized arable land should receive the requisite public investment in physical infrastructure to raise its economic value and land should be given priority in resource management programs. The continuation of colonial tenure systems in certain countries should be abolished and the arable land under government control should be leased among small farmers not to local elites or foreign investors. (e) The limited farmer's access to finance and extended credit facilities can be resolved by providing subsidies to microfinance institutions to give emergency and quick microloans and mesofinance at low cost or no cost within the reach of the small farmers. Simple and low cost farm finance is another powerful instrument for providing credit to small farmers as it reaches the beneficiary directly, builds capacity for self-employment in farms, helps participate in income generating activities, develops entrepreneurial capacity and provides ladder to get out of poverty and thereby allows the beneficiary to mark off from poverty. (f) The agricultural production and food supply can also be boosted by developing nutritious non-grain crops and provision of crisis foods. These crops, particularly cassava, are viewed as 'crisis foods' by poor consumers who may switch to consumption of these cheaper foods when cereal prices rise prohibitively; (g) Improved and cost-effective food preservation, storage and processing technologies, agricultural research and cheap alternative sources to boost agricultural productivity are the key to feeding the ever-growing world population.

The *fourth set of food policies* includes recommendations to manage global agricultural markets failures. Agricultural markets failed as the exchanges between buyers and sellers were impeded, efficiency was compromised and agricultural market activities failed to coordinate. It is evidence from the conclusions of the study that market failures are often mixed. Therefore, the most appropriate policy response for correcting the problem may not be clear cut. Individuals and private organisations unwilling to pay for public goods they enjoy. Therefore, the global governance should have strict guidelines to manage such market failures. Considering this, the study recommends: (a) promote alternatives to oligopolistic and oligopsonic structures which remain as local organization of food such as organic markets, local farmers' markets, community supported/shared agriculture, and other non integrated sources and implement the regulation or rules to control the operations of anti-competitive practices of food giants that are against the public interest, i.e., consumers exploitation and excess profits extraction by food TNCs; (b) delink agricultural and food industry from capital markets as a paradigm shift and limit speculative activity by raising margins, eliminating long contracts, strengthening spot markets and increasing grain reserves since speculation in food commodity markets is evil as it creates artificial food scarcity. Financial activities tax, financial transactions tax, and bank levy should be imposed heavily; (c) factor market imperfections may be addressed adopting policies to reduce inequality in access to land ownership and tenancy, finance, credit, employment and so on; (d) information asymmetries can be tackled by introducing business social networks for farmers so that they can reach out to customers by cutting middlemen out. This can help in filling the communication gaps and allows farmers to get the better and fair prices for their produce. Also, the customers get the fresh produce at cheaper prices by cutting middlemen like TNCs; (e) the monopoly power of state trading enterprises in agriculture based in developed countries should be controlled so that they can play a far broader and perhaps more justifiable role in both developing and developed countries.

When agricultural markets fail, there may, indeed, be justification for some market regulation by government and collective actions by small groups at local level. Therefore, government should also protect small farmers by providing information on market competition, guard them against unfair competition, assisting by providing cheap loans, and teaching them the successful research and development results to improve productivity and save costs. Insufficient information about the characteristics of a good or a service may prevent markets from forming even though, with more complete information, consumers would be willing to buy and manufacturers would be willing to sell. For example, whether food is organically grown is not immediately apparent to consumers. There should be global level agencies to regulate the safety and quality of food products especially all meat and egg products, flour, rice etc. traded across the globe and to develop and implement written sanitation standard operating procedures and to test for the harmful pathogens E. coli and Listeria. Third-party services, assurances or certificates from private firms like SGS and AIB International and many more are available to validate safety procedures, to bolster market differentiation with respect to food safety, and to provide validation of quality attributes and other information provided on package labels is truthful. But branding and third-party certifications are not universal, so consumers' demands for safety may go unmet without government oversight. However, safety claims by the suppliers do influence prices back in the food supply chain. Customers should be protected by strict implementation of regulations aimed to provide science-based nutritional information on food labels, inspections of food safety, standards and certification to increase customers' loyalty and confidence.

Governments should pay the farmers directly to adopt practices to contribute seriously towards preserving farm and grasslands, improving air, water, soil, and wildlife habitat quality, restoring wetlands, contributing to improve environment, protect farm labourers from exposure to pesticides, and reducing the loss of sediment or chemicals to the environment. Another approach to control environmental negative externalities is to introduce international and national regulations such as Global Clean Air Act, Global Clean Water Act, Global Soil Preservation Act, Global Pesticides and Chemicals Control Act, and so on that restrict the use of harmful chemicals and provision for farmers to adopt environmental-friendly practices. These acts should become integral part of global governance for total food security.

The *fifth set of food policies* includes recommendations related to public sector interventions and collective actions failures: (a) government failure in terms of 'urban bias' can be addressed by ethically responsible agricultural investment, and providing resources to farmers and pro-poor growth by focusing on poor first strategy. Like industrial sector, agricultural multiplier's effect on the national and global economy is quite significant. Therefore, targeted investment in agricultural sector and continuous objection to urban bias remain central to growth, poverty reduction, employment generation and rural skills formation in many regions and countries such as sub-Saharan Africa, poorer regions of South and South-East Asia; (b) big push of investment in rural development programmes, rural education, sanitation and health care is recommended; (c) global governance should invest in maintaining rural infrastructure facilities and rural public works such as roads, transport, canals, etc.; (d) government failure in terms of food health and safety regulations should be addressed by developing a system of better implementation and monitoring of food health and safety programmes; (e) public sector grains stockholdings should be properly managed to enhance food security. There is a greater need to control inefficiencies and waste of scarce resources as a result of government interventions. However, governments should increasingly intervene in the agriculture and food sectors by establishing food rationing system, food banks, providing coupons to buy food, and other commodity programs of assisting poor and needy people in food crisis. Last but not the least, the governments should cut down on red tape and unnecessary bureaucracy to implement the above recommendations.

The *sixth set of food policies* includes recommendations related to the impacts of GFC: (a) identifying the true nature and magnitude of hunger, malnutrition and obesity across the globe; (b) developing strategies in maintaining or mitigating the volatility and unpredictability in global food prices; (c) develop funds that respond to climate shocks, such as 'index-linked funds' that provide rapid relief when extreme weather events affect communities, through public-private partnerships based on agreed principles; (d) the achievement of equitable distribution of food among different regions and countries across the globe by developing international public food distribution system under the umbrella of global governance; (e) management and prevention of food wastage as about half of the food grown is either lost converted or wasted "from field to fork" and reducing post-harvest losses; (f) adopting policies to manage the phenomenon of 'luxus consumption' across the globe.

Obesity is increasingly becoming a major health crisis both physical and mental across the nations in varying degrees. People are consuming too much and wrong type of food, i.e., junk food including salted snack foods, chocolates, gum, candy, sweet desserts, fried fast food, and carbonated beverages containing poor nutritional quality with too much sugar or calorie-rich food. Many nations are becoming fatter with their overweight people. This study strongly recommends ten short term and long term measures for every nation and individual to control the ever growing phenomenon of obesity that has severe ramifications in terms of increasing social, economic and health costs. First, there is a need for global governance on obesity crisis. Second, the national governments should impose an urgent ban on attractive advertisements on unhealthy junk fast food. Third, food education as a part of cookery lessons and food technology should remain a priority and a compulsory part of national curriculum in all schools. Fourth is promoting awareness and healthy attitude towards food by encouraging people to consume balanced diet and fruits and green vegetables. Fifth, parents at home should recognise their responsibilities in providing healthy meals to family members. Sixth, daily regular exercise should be promoted. Seventh, junk-food tax should be imposed as a surcharge on packaged and fast foods containing over the limit poor nutritional quality saturated fat, sugar or salt. Eighth, mothers when pregnant or breastfeeding should be encouraged to avoid high-fat, high-sugar junk foods in order to avoid their children becoming more prone to obesity or health problems later in life. Ninth, enhancing body capital via encouraging people to follow weight loss either through cognitive behavioural therapy or healthy nutrition and exercise behaviour program. cut down on red tape and unnecessary bureaucracy not the least, national celebrities such as film stars, TV presenters, singers, sports personalities, communities leaders, clinicians, health and food professionals, support groups, religious or political leaders should act as role models and encourage individuals, families and governments to provide access and take up healthy eating habits with regular physical activities.

The mix and match of the above set of policies can be adopted depending upon the specific food problems of a country or region. Besides this, the global governance should adopt a set of *fast track emergency measures* to cope with the sudden natural disasters and crises and to provide the households with sudden and extra food needs. These measures may include: (a) extra allocation of *food aid* to the most food-deprived countries and communities stricken by food crisis; (b) international organizations, national governments and food giants to provide fixed yearly financial support to community-based food voluntary groups, relief agencies, religious groups and charities such as Red Cross; (c) establishment of *agricultural emergency fund* for poor farmers including herd restocking, provision of fertilizers, improved seeds and other agricultural supplies and equipment in case of natural disaster; (d) create and support social safety nets and other programs for the impoverished and vulnerable families in all countries (for example, cash for food and in-kind transfers, quick small short-term loans, employment guarantee schemes, programs to build resilience, health and nutrition, delivery of education and seeds of quick growing foods in times of famine); (d) establish robust emergency food reserves and financing capacity that can deliver rapid humanitarian responses to vulnerable populations threatened by food crises and unforeseen emergencies all over the globe; (f) establishment of *emergency food banks* in local and remote areas to provide immediate food struggling households across the globe; and (g) form and support platforms for harmonizing and coordinating global donor programmes, policies and activities to improve local nutritional outcomes.

Besides this, vulnerable households and individuals should adopt frugal *food crisis coping strategies* in short run and long run such as: (a) households should store long-life survival food to avoid panic buying in supermarkets in case of food shortage; (b) reduce food intakes by maintaining adequate nutrition level to reduce obesity; (c) shop around for cheaper food and maybe food reaching expiry date soon; (d) households manage the food shortfall by rationing the available food in the household either by cutting portion size or the number of meals, skipping whole days without eating or fasting, favouring certain household members over other members; (e) change in diets (from preferred food to cheaper less preferred food); (f) food sharing with well-off neighbours; (g) going for free food programs in schools, nurseries for kids and pupils; (h) reducing the number of people to be fed by sending some of them elsewhere; (i) strategies that are not sustainable over a long period i.e. borrowing, purchasing on credit, consuming wild foods or even see stocks; (j) adopting short term strategies to increase their food supply by borrowing or purchasing on credit, etc; and (k) longer-term alteration of income earning or food production patterns and one-off responses such as assets sales.

Implications

Different CFCFs lead to widely differing implications for food policy. A lack of clarity about which factors are responsible reinforces policy inaction. Agricultural and food industry employees are the citizens of the community first with common interests in housing, parenting, health, education, the art, leisure, sports and so on. When the suggested recommendations of this study are adopted and put into practice the potential implications will be: (a) agricultural and food industry stakeholders will be in a position to contribute towards the goal of achieving food security for communities that will be healthier, nutritious, food safer and productive. By examining the data and gaining an understanding of the strengths of the causes and effects of relationships, as numerically demonstrated between the latent and the manifest variables, farmers and other stakeholders can focus and prioritize constrained resources of money, time and people. If improvement actions are followed up consistently and honestly, a culture or an environment can be created where poor people are looked after properly by avoiding the problems of malnutrition and obesity. Good agricultural and food system will bring out mutual trust and commitment in people and bad system will breed extreme self-interest; (b) social implications are that society's economic and social well-being is impacted when food products are produced at the lowest environmentally and financially sustainable costs and prices; (c) body capital and human health implications: young children and older people will be free from the irreversible harm of malnutrition and obesity; (d) economic implications: poor households everywhere, including many female-headed households and those with a large proportion of dependents and net food importing countries will feel less economic pressure of food problems; (e) political implications: there will be no fights or riots for food and countries will be political stable; (f) ethical implications and (g) environmental implications. The most important is that GAFS needs to be sustainably modified at every level otherwise the food crisis will become acute.

A Closing Remark

The theory of human needs asserts that food is a basic human necessity and an essential ingredient utilised in the body of an organism to sustain its growth, repair and vital processes, and to provide energy for the perpetuation and development of *body capital*. Every human being has a fundamental universal right to food and should enjoy freedom from hunger, undernutrition and obesity. Global economy is a multifarious living entity where everything is connected with every other thing and the GAFS as a part of it influences and is influenced by the dynamics and forces within this living organism which in turn affects and is affected by a system of food problems. All these three systems namely, global economy, GAFS and system of food problems constantly interact with each other creating patterns of interdependencies in varying degrees with unpredictable outcomes such as GFC whose impact can be felt by hundreds of thousands of people across the global who face the issues of hunger and poverty; rural livelihood, nutrition and human health; and also who work towards the mutual goal of producing, distributing and consuming food products safely, adequately and reliably. Let us take a brief look at how everything is connected with each other with regards to GFC.

World food equation involves many elements. *First element* is the acquirement mechanism and its elements to command over food. Food can be acquired either by growing own food or exchanging or buying in the markets with money (or resources), or by accepting food aid/charity/food sharing in certain circumstances. Thus, the command over food depends upon conditions and factors that administer these exchanges of resources (labour, wages or money) for food. The *second element* is the availability of food. Food problems are governed by command over resources vis-à-vis availability of basic food. Depending upon various conditions, there may be different scenarios. Either the food is accessible (affordable) and available, or it is available but not accessible, or neither available nor accessible, or available and accessible but not utilised properly, or available, accessible and utilised properly. All these situations lie within the prevailing complex GAFS that is highly vulnerable to many shocks and disturbances. For instance, a disturbance in food supply chain just for a few weeks due to any small or big reason such as strike of lorry drivers or farmers, non-availability of oils, political unrest, terrorist attacks, floods, droughts or natural calamities leading to crop failures etc, will make the supermarkets, local shops and farms run out of food and people may be driven by their desperation to extreme situations of riots, starvation and deaths.

The *third element* of world food equation is the driving forces (institutional, administrative, social, political, environmental, geographical and economic forces) that govern and bring changes in GAFS. For example, continuing conflicts between heavily armed superpowers, economic and debt crises in the so-called First World, awakening of Arab world, incredible economic growth in BRIC countries, mergers and acquisitions leading to the centralization of control in the hands of a few global giants, big business of war, unprecedented population growth, conflicting food policy objectives, social unrest, droughts, floods and earthquakes, and so on. All these forces are not only reshaping the world food system, but also affecting the entire food chain, food prices and food security. The *fourth element* that has emerged over the years is the existence and perpetuation food paradoxes. There are six main food paradoxes of different genres that have fundamental link in the world food equation. *The first paradox* is that the farmers and landless rural farm labourers (mainly women in many regions) who spend their lives producing food for others remain poor and go hungry themselves. Their livelihood is tied to the livelihoods of those who consume the food they produce. The *second paradox* is the co-existence of 1.6 billion obese people who overconsume food whereas there are nearly 1 billion people who are undernourished (the lack of enough protein (from meat and other sources) and food that provides energy (measured in calories) which all of the basic food groups provide. The *third paradox* is that the nations who face food shortages are forced to export food to other rich countries. The changing diet habits have triggered the co-existence of food for the animals as well as for humans giving rise to the *fourth paradox* as more and more food grains are needed to feed animals. The fashion and trend of bio-fuels originated from the policies on bio-fuels in Europe and the US have led to the *food-fuel paradox*. Last but not the least *paradox* is the co-existence of massive food wastage and food shortage in both Western world and developing world. The intertwining act of above four actors has divided our one world among the hungry, the obese and a group of people free from hunger, undernutrition and obesity.

GFC is a problem here to stay and the struggle between food and man will continue. The ultimate solution lies in a *new paradigm* of *food-related emotional intelligence* that develops relationships among people based on awareness, participation, care and respect for others, self-respect, trust, transparency and food sharing. Such a paradigm ought to be free from exploitation, conflicts, corruption, self-interest and greed. People should be made aware of what is happening and how food consumption and utilization is affecting their health and pockets. Moreover, positive thinking and public awareness on world hunger, obesity and other food problems should be enhanced through marathons, charity walks, popular concerts, and so on.

Consumers should be courageous enough to boycott the food being sold by profit hungry food giants and TNCs. People food co-operatives should be encouraged with an aim: local food first for local people and no food wastage. Donations, charities and religious groups should help those who cannot afford adequate food. Restaurants, supermarkets and households should avoid food wastage and establish a local network to distribute the over produced or leftover good quality food to needy poor families. The food wastage between food production and consumption ought to be minimized to its lowest level.

We are living in an age of extremes, uncertainties and paradoxes in the sense that we have more collective food production but less food distribution, more global income but less equality and equity, more resources but less nourishment, more possessions but less happiness, more technologies but less emotional intelligence, more information but less common sense, more population but less social capital, more medicines but less health, wider motorways but narrow viewpoints, steep profits but low corporate social responsibility, more fast foods and slow digestion, overweight bodies but not enough physical exercises, more advanced food technology and more food experts, yet more food problems. Therefore, the challenges are enormous. Governments need to put more efforts to create jobs, anti-poverty programmes, pro-poor growth strategies and social inclusion efforts to generate income and resources for both rural and urban poor so that people can establish command over food. A fundamental shift is required in the creation of *basic socioeconomic opportunities* in various areas such as education, healthcare, recreation, sports, agricultural reforms, rural development and so on, to allow people to enjoy economic benefits with equity and justice. Establishment of social safety nets, fast trace emergency relief system, food banks and charity will also contribute immensely. More investments in agricultural education, research, innovations and technologies are essential. Food preservation, storage and processing technologies with minimum food wastage are the key to feeding the ever-growing world population. Bio-fuel is increasing world hunger so its production must be redesigned. Linking agricultural and food policies with obesity and food-related diseases is a must. More reforms are required to allow markets to function smoothly and fairly, and markets failures need to be managed and controlled by careful and determined public sector interventions. The broken public food distribution systems in many countries should be repaired. Government failures can be addressed by the powerful global governance and a system of checks and balances. All countries must endeavour in an integrated fashion to achieve self-sufficiency in food production, achieve equal food distribution at affordable prices, and maintain total food security by all means. The co-ordination among global complexities and local factors dynamics based on adequate information system is an essential pathway to 'zero hunger, undernutrition and obesity'. All religions and communities should encourage a culture of food sharing with no food wastage. To sum up, the phenomenon of global food crisis conceals more than it reveals. Man does not live by bread alone. However, food remains fundamentally important in sustaining body capital. A usual caveat remains: eat to live but never live to eat. Quality of life persists with a simultaneous pursue of three pathways: feed facts to the mind, spirituality to the soul and balanced nutritious diet with regular exercise to the body.

Bibliography

Aaker, D.A. and Bagozzi, R.P. (1979). Unobservable Variables in Structural Equation Models with Application in Industrial Setting. *Journal of Marketing Research*, 16, 147-158.

Abbott, P. C. (2009). *Development Dimensions of High Food Prices*. OECD Food, Agriculture and Fisheries Working Papers 18.

Abbott, P. C. (2010). *Stabilization Policies in Developing Countries after the 2007-08 Food Crisis*. Global Forum on Agriculture. Retrieved October, 22, 2011 from http://www.oecd.org/dataoecd/50/34/46340396.pdf.

Abbott, P.C. (2012). Export Restrictions as Stabilization Responses to Food Crisis. *American Journal of Agricultural Economics*, 94(2), 428-434.

Abbott, P. and de Battisti, A.B. (2011). Recent Global Food Price Shocks: Causes, Consequences and Lessons for African Governments and Donors. *Journal of African Economies*, 20 (supplement 1), i12-i62.

Abbott, P.C., Hurt, C. and Tyner, W.E. (2008). *What's Driving Food Prices?* Issue Report. Farm Foundation.

Abbott, P. and McCalla, A. (2002). Agriculture in the Macroeconomy. In: B.L. Gardner and G. Rausser (Eds.), *Handbook of Agricultural Economics*, Vol. 2A, Amsterdam: Elsevier.

Abdi, H. (2003). Partial Least Squares (PLS) Regression. In: M. Lewis-Beck, A. Bryman and T. Futing (Eds.). *Encyclopedia of Social Sciences Research Methods (pp. 2-3)*. Sage. Thousands Oaks (CA).

Accion, Finca, Grameen Foundation, Opportunity International, Unitus, Women's World Banking (2010). *Measuring the Impact of Microfinance: Our Perspective*. A Paper Responding to a Grameen Foundation Publication: Measuring the Impact of Microfinance – Taking another look.

Ackoff, R.A. (1994). *The Democratic Corporation*. Oxford: Oxford University Press.

Adger, W.N., Brown, K. and Tompkins, E.L. (2005). The Political Economy of Cross-Scale Networks in Resource Co-management. *Ecology and Society*, 10(2), 9.

Ahluwalia, M.S. (1978). Rural Poverty and Agricultural Performance in India. *The Journal of Development Studies*, 14(3), 298-323.

Ahrens, H. (2010). The World Food Crisis: Questions of Economic Theory and Contemporary Practices. Vestnik BSAU, 4.

Aksoy, A. and Isik-Dikmelik, A. (2008). *Are Low Food Prices Pro-Poor? Net Food Buyers and Sellers in Low Income Countries*. Policy Research Working Paper 4642.World Bank, Washington, DC.

Aksoy, M.A. and Ng, F. (2008). *Who are the Net Food Importing Countries?*. Policy Research Working Paper Series No. 4457. The World Bank, Washington DC.

Allen, R.C. and Ó Gráda, C. (1988). On the Road Again with Arthur Young: English, Irish, and French Agriculture During the Industrial Revolution. *Journal of Economic*

History, 48, 93-116.

Amare, Y. (2008). *Urban Food Insecurity and Coping Mechanisms: A Case Study of Lideta Sub-city in Addis Ababa.* FSS Research Report no.5, Forum for Social Studies.

Amato, A. and Dagostino, V. (2011). Economic Issues on Nanotechnology: An International Comparison and Results from Economic and Econometric Analysis. *Economia Internazionale / International Economics,* 64(2), 131-151.

Amine, E. et al. (2012). *Diet, Nutrition and the Prevention of Chronic Diseases: Report of a Joint WHO/FAO Expert Consultation* World Health Organization, Geneva, Switzerland.

Anderson, J.C. and Gerbing, D.W. (1998). Structural Equation Modeling in Practice: A Review and Recommended Two-step Approach. *Psychological Bulletin,* 103(3), 411-423.

Anderson, J.R. (1995). Confronting Uncertainty in Rain Fed Rice Farming: Research Challenges. In: *Fragile Lives in Fragile Ecosystems: Proceedings of the International Rice Research Conference* (101-108), 13-17 February 1995. Manila: International Rice Research Institute.

Anderson, J.R. (2001). *Risk Management in Rural Development: A Review.* Rural Development Strategy Background Paper 7, Washington, D.C.: World Bank.

Anderson, P.W., Arrow, K.J. and Pines, D. (Eds.) (1988). *The Economy as an Evolving Complex System.* Reading, MA: Addison-Wesley.

Anderson, J., Dillon, J. and Hardaker, B. (1977). *Agricultural Decision Analysis.* Ames, IA: Iowa University Press.

Angus, I. (2008). Food Crisis: The Greatest Demonstration of the Historical Failure of the Capitalist Model. *Global Research,* April 28.

Antle, J.M. (1987). Econometric Estimation of Producers' Risk Attitudes. *American Journal of Agricultural Economics,* 69(3), 509-22.

Antle, J.M. (2009). Agriculture and the Food System: Adaptation to Climate Change. *Resources for the Future Report,* June. Retrieved October, 22, 2011 from http://www.rff.org/rff/documents/rff-rpt-adaptation-antle.pdf.

Antle, J.M. et al. (2004). Adaptation, Spatial Heterogeneity, and the Vulnerability of Agricultural Systems to Climate Change and CO2 Fertilization: An Integrated Assessment Approach. *Climatic Change,* 64(3), 289–315.

Ardeni, P.G. and J. Freebairn. (2002). The Macroeconomics of Agriculture. In: B.L. Gardner and G. Rausser (Eds.). *Handbook of Agricultural Economics (pp.1455-1485),* Vol. 2A. Amsterdam: Elsevier.

Armah, P., Archer, A. and Phillips, G.C. (2009). Drivers Leading to Higher Food Prices: Biofuels are Not the Main Factor. In: *Vitro Cellular & Developement Biology – Plant,* 45(3), 330-341.

Arndt, C. et al. (2008). Higher Fuel and Food Prices: Impacts and Responses for Mozambique. *Agricultural Economics,* 39 (Supplement), 497–511.

Arndt, C. et al. (2009). Biofuels, Poverty, and Growth: A Computable General Equilibrium Analysis of Mozambique. In: *Climate Change: Global Risks, Challenges and Decisions.* IOP Publishing IOP Conf. Series: Earth and Environmental Science 6.

Arthur, W.B. (1999). Complexity and the Economy. *Science,* 284(541), 107-109.

Arthur, W.B., Durlauf, S.N. and Lane, D.A. (Eds.) (1997). *The Economy as an Evolving Complex System II.* Proceedings Volume XXVII, Santa Fe Institute Studies in the Science of Complexity. Reading, MA: Addison-Wesley.

On Measuring Global Food Crisis

Asian Development Bank (2008). *Food Prices and Inflation in Developing Asia: Is Poverty Reduction Coming to an End?*. ADB: Manila.

Asian Development Bank (2008). *Soaring Food Prices - Response to the Crisis.* ADB: Manila.

Astyk, S. and Newton, A. (2009). *A Nation of Farmers: Defeating the Food Crisis on American Soil.* Canada: New Society Publishers.

Attanasio, O., Battistin, E. and Ichimura, H. (2004). *What Really Happened to Consumption Inequality in the US?.* NBER Working Paper No. W10338. National Bureau of Economic Research, Cambridge. MA.

Axelrod, R. (1986). An Evolutionary Approach to Norms. *American Political Science Review,* 80(4), 1095-111.

Baffes, J. (2007). Oil Spills on Other Commodities. *Resources Policy,* 32(3), 126-134.

Bak, P. et al. (1993). Aggregate Fluctuations from Independent Sectoral Shocks: Self-Organized Criticality in a Model of Production and Inventory Dynamics. *Ricerche Economiche,* 47(1), 3-30.

Balzli, B. and Hornig, F. (2008). *The Role of Speculators in the Global Food Crisis.* Der Spiegel. Retrieved October, 22, 2011 from http://www.spiegel.de/international/world/0,1518,549187,00.html.

Banerjee, A. (2011). Reviewing the Global Food Crisis: Magnitude, Causes, Impact and Policy Options. In: B.N. Ghosh (Ed.), *Global Food Crisis: Contemporary Issues and Policy Options (pp. 12-46).* Leeds UK: Wisdom House Publications.

Bardhan, P.K. (1982). *Poverty and 'Trickle Down' in Rural India: A Quantitative Analysis.* Berkeley: University of California.

Bardhan, P.K. and Srinivasan (Eds.) (1974). *Poverty and Income Distribution in India.* Calcutta: Statistical Publishing Society.

Barndt, D.J. (2008). Tangled Routes: *Women, Work, and Globalization the Tomato Trail* (2nd Edition). Lanham, Maryland: Rowman & Littlefield Publishers.

Barichello, R. and Patunru, A. (2009). Agriculture in Indonesia: Lagging Performance and Difficult Choices. *Choices- The Magazine of Food, Farm, and Resource Issues.* 24(4). Retrieved March, 22, 2011 from http://www.choicesmagazine.org/magazine/article.php?article=76.

Barrett, C.B. (2002). Food Security and Food Assistance. In: B.L. Gardner and G. Rausser (Eds.). *Handbook of Agricultural Economics.* 2B. Amsterdam: Elsevier.

Bar-Yam, Y. (1997). *Dynamics of Complex Systems.* Perseus Press: New York.

Bassett, T.J. and Winter-Nelson, A. (2010). *The Atlas of World Hunger.* The United States: The University of Chicago Press.

Baviera, M. and Bello, W. (2009). Food Wars. *Monthly Review,* 61(03), July-August, http://monthlyreview.org/2009/07/01/food-wars.

BBC (2008). *Vietnam Next to Cut Exports.* BBC World News, 28 March. Retrieved October, 22, 2011 from http://news.bbc.co.uk/2/hi/business/7317989.stm.

Bellemare, M.F. (2011). Rising Food Prices, Food Price Volatility, and Political Unrest. SSRN. from http://ssrn.com/abstract=1874101.

Bello (2009). *The Food Wars.* London: Verso.

Bennett, D. (2011). *Vilsack: No Correlation Between Food Prices and Ethanol.* Delta Farm Press. from http://deltafarmpress.com/government/vilsack-no-correlation-between-food-prices-and-ethanol.

Bibliography

Bennett, J. (1995). Biotechnology and the Future of Rice Production. *Geo Journal*, 35(3), 335-37.

Benson, T. (2008). *An Assessment of the Likely Impact on Ugandan Households of Rising Global Food Prices: A Secondary Data Analysis.* International Food Policy Research Institute Kampala office, Kampala.

Berazneva, J. and Lee, D.R. (2011). *Explaining the African Food Riots of 2007-2008: An Empirical Analysis.* from http://www.csae.ox.ac.uk/conferences/2011-EDiA/ papers/711-Berazneva.pdf.

Berndt, E.R. (1991). *The Practice of Econometrics: Classical and Contemporary.* Reading, MA, Addison-Wesley.

Bezemer, D.J. and Headey, D. (2008). Agriculture, Development and Urban Bias. *World Development* 36(8), 1342–1364.

Bhalla, G.S. and Chadha, G.K. (1981). *Structural Changes in Income Distribution: A Study of the Impact of the Green Revolution.* New Delhi: JNU.

Black, J.D. (1926). *Introduction to Production Economics.* New York: Henry Holt and Co.

Black, J.D. (1943). *Food Enough.* Lancaster: The Jaques Cattell Press.

Blaikie, P. et al. (1994). *At Risk: Natural Hazards, People's Vulnerability and Disasters.* London: Routledge Publishers.

Blair, D. and Sobal, J. (2006). Luxus Consumption: Wasting Food Resources through Overeating. *Agriculture and Human Values*, 23, 63-74.

Blas, J. (2011). Global Food Prices Hit Record High. *The Financial Times*, January 5. Retrieved March, 22, 2012 from http://www.ft.com/cms/s/0/51241bc0-18b4-11e0-b7ee-00144feab49a.html#axzz29r2eAINZ.

Block, J. (2012). *Rising Food Prices? Can't Blame Ethanol. The Chicago Tribune.* http://articles.chicagotribune.com/2011-03-26/new/sct-oped-0328-biofuel-20110317_1_ ethanol-production-ethanol-industry-corn-gluten.

Blum, A. (2005). Drought Resistance, Water-Use Efficiency and Yield Potential – Are They Compatible, Dissonant or Mutually Exclusive?. *Australian Journal of Agricultural Research*, 56(11), 1159-68.

Blume, L.E. (1997). Population Games. In: W.B. Arthur, S.N. Durlauf and D.A. Lane (Eds.), *The Economy as an Evolving Complex System II(pp. 425-60).* Reading, MA: Addison-Wesley.

Bohrnstedt, G.W. (1970). Reliability and Validity Assessment in Attitude Measurement. In: G. F. Summers (Ed.), *Attitude Measurement (pp.81-99).* Chicago: Rand McNally.

Bohstedt, J. (2010). *The Politics of Provisions: Food Riots, Moral Economy, and Market Transition in England, c. 1550-1850.* Farnham: Ashgate Publishing Company.

Bollen, K.A. (1989). *Structural Equations with Latent Variables.* New York: Wiley.

Borsboom, D., Mellenbergh, G.J., and van Heerden, J. (2003). The Theoretical Status of Latent Variables. *Psychological Review*, 110(2), 203–219.

Boserup, E. (1965). *The Conditions of Agricultural Growth: The Economics of Agrarian Change Under Population Pressure.* London: Allen & Unwin.

Boucher, D.M. (1999). *The Paradox of Plenty: Hunger in a Bountiful World.* Oakland, CA: Food First Books.

Bouet, A. and Corong, E.(2008). *Regional trade cooperation and food prices: an assessment for South Asian Free Trade.* https://www.gtap.agecon.purdue.edu/resources/ download/4508.pdf.

Bounds, A. (2007). OECD *Warns Against Biofuels Subsidies.* http://www.ft.com/cms/s/0/ e780d216-5fd5-11dc-b0fe-0000779fd2ac.html?nclick_check=1.

Boussard, J.M. and Petit, M. (1967). Representation of Farmers' Behaviour under Uncertainty with a Focus Loss Constraint. *Journal of Farm Economics,* 49, 869-880.

Boyce, J.K. (1999). *The Globalization of Market Failure?. International Trade and Sustainable Agriculture.* Political Economy Research Institute, University of Massachusetts: Amherst. Retrieved March, 22, 2012 from http://www.peri.umass. edu/fileadmin/pdf/published_study/PS3.pdf.

Bradsher, K. (2007). *A Drought in Australia, A Global Shortage of Rice.* Retrieved March, 26, 2012 from http://www.nytimes.com/2008/04/17/business/worldbusiness/17warm. html.

Brandt, H. and Otzen, U. (2007). *Poverty Orientated Agricultural and Rural Development.* New York: Routledge.

Breese, G. (1966) (Ed.). *Urbanisation in Newly Developing Countries.* Prentice Hall.

Breimyer, H.F. (1961). *Demand and Prices for Meats.* Tech. Bull., USDA 1253.

Brewster, J.M. (1959). The Impact of Technical Advance and Migration on Agricultural Society and Policy. *Journal of Farm Economics,* 41, 1169-1184.

Brinkman, H.J. and Hendrix, C.S. (2011). *Food Insecurity and Conflict: Applying the WDR Framework.* World Development Report 2011. http://wdr2011.worldbank.org/food.

Brock, W.A. et al. (Eds.) (1995). *Handbook of Statistics 12: Finance.* Amsterdam: North Holland.

Brown, L. (1995). *Who Will Feed China? Wake-up call for a Small Planet.* Worldwatch Institute Books: New York, NY.

Brown, L. and Kane, H. (1994). *Full House: Reassessing the Earth's Population Carrying Capacity.* New York: Norton.

Bruinsma, J. (Ed.) (2003). *World Agriculture: Towards 2015/30, An FAO Perspective.* London: Earthscan and Rome: FAO.

Boulding, K.E. (1981). *Evolutionary Economics,* Beverly Hills and London: Sage Publications.

Buchanan, E. (2008). *Assessing the Global Food Crisis.* http://news.bbc.co.uk/1/hi/7361945. html.

Buchanan, J.M. (1979). *What Should Economists Do?.* Indianapolis: Liberty Press.

Backlund, P. et al. (2008). Introduction. In: *The Effects of Climate Change on Agriculture, Land Resources, Water Resources, and Biodiversity.* Washington, DC: U.S. Climate Change Science Program and the Subcommittee on Global Change Research, 11–20.

Buera, F., Kaboski, J. and Shin, Y. (2011). *The Macroeconomics of Microfinance.* A paper presented at a conference organized by the Consortium on Financial Systems and Poverty at the Bureau for Research and Economic Analysis Development (BREAD) in September.

Buetre, B. et al. (2004). *Agricultural Trade Liberalization: Effects on Developing Countries' Output, Incomes, and Trade.* Australian Bureau of Agricultural and Resource Economics Project 110039. Washington, D.C.

Burby, L.N. (2006). *World Hunger.* San Diego: Lucent Books, Inc.

Bureau of Industry Economics (1995). *Potential Gains to Australia from APEC.* Occasional Paper 29, AGPS, Canberra.

Burt, O.R. (1966). Economic Control of Groundwater Reserves. *Journal of Farm Economics,* 46, 632-647.

Bibliography

Burt, O.R. and Allison, J.R. (1963). Farm Management Decisions with Dynamic Programming. *Journal of Farm Economics,* 45, 121-136.

Burt, O.R. and Cummings, R.G. (1970). Production and Investment in Natural Resource Industries. *American Economic Review,* 60, 576-590.

Bush, R. (2010). Food Riots: Poverty, Power and Protest. *Journal of Agrarian Change,* 10(1), 119–129.

Buzby, J. and Hyman, J. (2012). Total and Per Capita Value of Food Loss in the United States. *Food Policy,* 37 (5), 561–570.

Byers, J. (1979). Of Neo-populist Pipe Dreams: Daedalus in the Third World and the Myth of Urban Bias. *Journal of Peasant Studies,* 6(2), 210-44.

Caballero, R.J., Farhi, E. and Gourinchas, P.-O. (2008). *Financial Crash, Commodity Prices and Global Imbalances.* National Bureau of Economic Research 14521.

Campbell, D.T. and Fiske, D.W. (1959). Convergent and Discriminant Validation by the Multi-trait-Multi-method Matrix. *Psychological Bulletin,* 56, 81-105.

Canning, D. (1988). Increasing Returns in Industry and the Role of Agriculture in Growth. Oxford Economic Papers, 40(3), 463-476.

Cavatassi, R., Hopkins, R.J. and Lipper, L. (2005). *Crop Genetic Diversity, Food Security and Farm Household Well-being During Shocks.* American Agricultural Economics Association annual meeting, Providence, Rhode Island. http://ageconsearch.umn. edu/bitstream/19372/1/sp05ca07.pdf.

Centre for Studies in Food Security (CSFS)(2011). *Food Security Defined.* http://www. ryerson.ca/foodsecurity/index.html.

Chambers, R. (1991). Complexity, Diversity and Competence: Toward Sustainable Livelihood from Farming Systems in the 21st Century. *Journal of the Asian Farming Systems Association,* 1(1), 79-89.

Chen, X. and Khanna, M. (2012). Food vs. Fuel: The Effect of Biofuel Policies. *American Journal of Agricultural Economics,* first published online May 11.

Chatterjee, B. and Mukumba, C. (2011). Food Exporting Restrictions: Balance [sic] importers' and exporters' rights, CUTS/CITEE Working Paper No. 1/2011.

Chatterjee, C.S. (2009). The Global Food Equation: Food Security in an Environment of Increasing Scarcity. Deutsche Bank Research, Deutsche Bank Report. *The Global Food Equation. Biofuels Supplement, 1-40.*

Chau, P. Y. K. (1997). "Reexamining a Model for Evaluating Information Center Success Using a Structural Equation Modeling Approach." *Decision Sciences,* 28 (2), 309-334.

Checkland, P. (1997). *Systems Thinking, Systems Practice.* Chichester: John Wiley & Sons, Ltd.

Chenery, H.B. and Syrquin, M. (1975). *Development, 1950-1970.* Oxford: Oxford University Press.

Chin, W.W. and Gopal, A. (1995). Adoption Intention in GSS: Relative Importance of Beliefs. *DATA BASE for Advances in Information Systems,* 26, (2&3), 42-64.

Chopra, Parvesh K. (1987). *Logic, Scientific Method and Economic Analysis.* Ambala Cantt: India: Chopra Book Agency.

Chopra, Parvesh K. (1989). Economy of Haryana: Two Decades of Development. *Udyog Yug,* 9(10), 30-34.

Chopra, Parvesh K. (1990). Quest for Agricultural Development in Haryana. *Third Concept,* 4(43), 25-29.

Chopra, Parvesh K. (2003). *Political Economy of Rural Poverty Alleviation Measures in India.* Leeds: Wisdom House Publications.

Chopra, Parvesh K. (2008). *Poverty as Human Contestability Failure.* Leeds: Wisdom House Publications.

Chopra, Parvesh K. (2010). Social Capital: Applying Ozay Mehmet's Civil War Conflict Hypothesis with reference to War in Afghanistan. In: B.N. Ghosh (Ed.). *Global Governance, Labour Market Dynamics and Social Change: Essays in Honour of Emeritus Professor Ozay Mehmet.* Leeds: Wisdom House Publications, pp. 189-214.

Chopra, Parvesh K. (2011). A Kanji-Chopra Model of Global Food Crisis. *Journal of Human Development,* 3(2), 197-230.

Chopra, Parvesh K. (2011a). Global Food Crisis: A Systems Modelling Approach to Measurement. In: B.N. Ghosh (Ed.). *Global Food Crisis: Contemporary Issues and Policy Options (pp.47-90).* Leeds: Wisdom House Publications.

Chopra, Parvesh K. (2012). Country Matters: Country Risk Measurement by Causal Pathways. *Economia Internazionale/International Economics,* LXV (2), May, 251-289.

Chopra, Parvesh K. (Ed.) (2012). *Development Macroeconomics, Global Issues and Human Development: Essays in Honour of Professor B.N. Ghosh.* Leeds: Wisdom House Publications.

Chopra, Parvesh K. A Conceptual Model of Global Food Crisis and Its Implications for Forthcoming.

Chopra, Parvesh K. Can Complexity Theory Explain Global Food Crisis? (Forthcoming)

Chopra, Parvesh K. System Dimensional Structure of Global Food Crisis. (Forthcoming)

Chopra, Parvesh K. A Theoretical Model of Global Agricultural and Food System. (Communicated)

Chopra, Parvesh K. and Bhardwaj, S. (1993). Rural Poverty Alleviation and Business Education: A Case Study of TRYSEM in Haryana. In: J.L. Rastogi and Bidhi Chand (Eds.). *Management and Business Education in India.* Jaipur: Rawat Publications, 275-295.

Chopra, Parvesh K. and Kanji, G.K. (2011). Environmental Health: Assessing Risks to Society. *Total Quality Management & Business Excellence,* 22 (4), 461-489.

Chopra, Parvesh K. and Kanji, G.K. (2011). On the Science of Management with Measurement. *Total Quality Management & Business Excellence,* 22(1), 63-81.

Christiaensen, L.J. and Subbarao, K. (2005). Towards an Understanding of Household Vulnerability in Rural Kenya. *Journal of African Economies,* 14, 520-558.

Churchamn, C.W. (1968). *The System Approach.* New York: Delacorte Press.

Ciriacy-Wantrup, S.V. (1952). *Resource Conservation – Economics and Policies.* Berkeley, CA: University of California Press.

Clapp, J. and Helleiner, E. (2010). Troubled Futures? The Global Food Crisis and the Politics of Agricultural Derivatives Regulation. *Review of International Political Economy,* 1-27.

Clements, K.W. and Fry, R. (2006). *Commodity Currencies and Currency Commodities.* CAMA Working Paper Series 19/06.

Clemmitt, M. (2008). Global food crisis. *CQ Researcher, 18,* 553-576. Retrieved March, 22, 2011 from http://library.cqpress.com/cqresearcher/cqresrre2008062700.

Coase, R.H. (1960). The Problem of Social Cost. *The journal of Law and Economics,* 3(1), 1-44.

Bibliography

Cochrane, W.W. (1958). *Farm Prices: Myth and Reality.* Minneapolis: University of Minnesota Press.

Cochrane, W.W. and Runge, C.F. (1992). *Reforming Farm Policy: Toward a National Agenda.* Ames, IA: Iowa State University Press.

Cohen, M. and Garrett J. (2009). *The Food Price Crisis and Urban Food Insecurity. London, UK: IIED.*

Cohen, M.J. and Clapp, J. (2009) (Eds.). *The Global Food Crisis: Governance Challenges and Opportunities.* Centre for International Governance Innovation.

Collins, K. (2008). *The Role of Biofuels and Other Factors in Increasing Farm and Food Prices. A Review of Recent Developments with a Focus on Feed Grain Markets and Market Prospects.* Keith J. Collins LLC. www.foodbeforefuel.org/files/Role%20 of%20Biofuels%206-19-08.pdf .

Conceição, P. and Mendoza, R.U. (2009). Anatomy of the Global Food Crisis. *Third World Quarterly,* 30 (6), 1159-1182.

Congress of the Unites States, Congressional Budget Office (2006). *The Effects of Liberalizing World Agricultural Trade: A Review of Modelling Studies.* http://www. cbo.gov/ftpdocs/73xx/doc7352/06-30-Trade.pdf.

Conway, D. et al. (2005). Rainfall Variability in East Africa: Implications for Natural Resources Management and Livelihoods. *Philosophical Transactions of the Royal Society,* 363, 49–54.

Conway, G. and Toenniessen, G. (2003). Science for African Food Security. *Science,* 299(21), 1187-1188.

Cooke, B. and Robles, M. (2009). *Recent Food Prices Movements: A Time Series Analysis.* IFPRI Discussion Paper 00942.

Cooper, R.N. and Lawrence, R.Z. (1975). The 1972-75 Commodity Boom. *Brookings Papers on Economic Activity,* 3, 671.

Crespi, V. and Lovatelli, A. (2010). *Aquaculture in Desert and Arid Lands: Development Constraints and Opportunities.* FAO Technical Workshop 6–9 July 2010, Hermosillo, Mexico. FAO Fisheries and Aquaculture Proceedings No. 20. Rome.

Creswell, J.W. (2003). *Research Design: Quantitative, Qualitative, and Mixed Methods Approaches.* SAGE. Thousand Oaks. USA.

Cribb, J. (2010). *The Coming Famine .The Global Food Crisis and What We Can Do to Avoid It.* CSIRO Publishing.

Cronbach, L.J. (1951). Coefficient Alpha and the Internal Structure of Tests. *Psychometrika.*16, 297–334.

Crutchfield, J. and Zellner, A. (1962). *Economic Aspects of the Pacific Halibut Industry.* Fishery Industrial Research 1.United States Department of the Interior, Washington, D.C.

Cudjoe, G., Breisinger, C. and Diao, X. (2010). Local Impacts of a Global Crisis: Food Price Transmission and Poverty in Ghana. *Food Policy,* 35(4), 294-302.

Cuhls, K.C. (2006). *Science, Technology and Innovation Drivers,* Short Report to the SCAR Expert Working Group/ EU Commission, Karlsruhe.

Cummings, R.G. and Winkelmann, D.L. (1970). *Water Resource Management in Arid Environs. Water Resources Research,* 6, 1559-1568.

Darley, V.M. and Kauffman, S.A. (1997). Natural Rationality. In: W.B. Arthur, S.N. Durlauf and D.A. Lane (eds), *The Economy as an Evolving Complex System II.* Reading, M.A. Addison-Wesley, pp. 425-60.

Day, R.H. (1963). *Recursive Programming and Production Response*. Amsterdam: North-Holland.

Dawe, D. (2008). *Have Recent Increases in International Cereal Prices Been Transmitted to Domestic Economies? The Experience in Seven Large Asian Countries*. ESA Working Paper No. 08-03.

Dawe, D. (2010). *The Rice Crisis: Markets, Policies and Food Security*. Earthscan: London and Washington, DC.

de Gorter, H. and Just, D.R. (2010).The Social Costs and Benefits of Biofuels: The Intersection of Environmental, Energy and Agricultural Policy. *Applied Economic Perspective and Policy*, 32 (1), 4-32.

De Haen, H. and Heidhues, T. (1973). Recursive Programming Models to Simulate Agricultural Development-Applications in West Germany. Institute for Agricultural Economics, Working Paper 18, Göttingen.

De Schutter, O. and Cordes, K.Y (2011) (Eds.). *Accounting for Hunger: The Right to Food in the Era of Globalisation*. Oxford: Hart Publishing.

Deaton, A.S. and Laroque, G. (1990). *On the Behaviour of Commodity Prices*. NBER Working Paper Series w3439.

Defries, R.S., Asner, G.P. and Houghton, R. (2005). Trade-offs in Land-use Decisions: Towards a Framework for Assessing Multiple Ecosystem Responses to Land Use Change. In: R.S. DeFries, G.P. Asner and R. Houghton (Eds.). *Ecosystems and Land Use Change (pp.1-12)*. American Geophysical Union, Washington, DC.

Delgado, C., Rosegrant, M., Steinfeld, H., Ehui, S. and C. Courbois (1999). *Livestock 2020: The Next Food Revolution*. Discussion Paper 28, International Food Policy Research Center, Washington, D.C.

Delgado, C.L. (2003). Meating and Milking Global Demand: Stakes for Smallscale Farmers in Developing Countries. In: *The Livestock Revolution: A Pathway from Poverty?, A.G. Brown (Ed.), Record of a Conference Conducted by the Academy of Technological Sciences and Engineering Crawford Fund, Parliament House, Canberra, Australia, 13 August 2003, A Festschrift in Honor of Derek E. Tribe*, The ATSE Crawford Fund, Parkville, Victoria, Australia.

Deming, W.E. (1986). *Out of the Crisis*. Centre for Advanced Engineering Study.

Deming, W.E. (1994). *The New Economics for Industry, Government, Education*. Cambridge, MA: MIT Centre for Advanced Engineering Study.

Dercon, S. and Krishnan, P. (2000). *In Sickness and in Health: Risk Sharing within Households in Rural Ethiopia*. CSAE Working Paper Series 1997-12, Centre for the Study of African Economies, University of Oxford.

Destler, I.M. (1978). United States Food Policy 1972–1976: Reconciling Domestic and International Objectives. *International Organization*, 32, 617-653.

Dewbre, J. et al. (2008). High Food Commodity Prices: Will They Stay? Who Will Pay? *Agricultural Economics*, 39, 393.

Dharm, N. (1972). Growth and Imbalance in Indian Agriculture. *JISAS*, June.

Diamond, J. (2005). *Collapse: How societies Choose to Fail or Succeed*. Viking Press: New York.

Dickens, C. (1854). *Hard Times-For These Times*. Bradbury & Evans.

Dillon, J.L. (1971). An Expository Review of Bernoullian Decision Theory in Agriculture: Is Utility Futility? *Review of Marketing and Agricultural Economics*, 39, 3-80.

Bibliography

Dolan, C. and Humphrey, J. (2000). Governance and Trade in Fresh Vegetables: The Impact of UK Supermarkets on the African Horticulture Industry. *Journal of Development Studies*, 37, 147-176.

Dollive, K. (2008). *The Impact of Export Restraints on Higher Grain Prices* (Working Paper). Office of Economics, U.S. International Trade Commission, Washington DC. http://www.usitc.gov/ind_econ_ana/ research_ana/research_work_papers/documents/EC200809A.pdf.

Domanski, D. and Heath, A. (2007). Financial Investors and Commodity Markets. *BIS Quarterly Review*, March, 53–67.

Drèze, J. and Sen, A.K. (1989). Entitlement and Deprivation. In: J. Dreze and A. Sen (Eds.), *Hunger and Public Action (pp.20-34)*, Oxford: Clarendon Press.

Drèze, J. and Sen, A.K. (1989). *Hunger and Public Action*. Oxford: Clarendon Press.

Drèze, J., and Sen, A.K. (1995). Introduction to the Political Economy of Hunger. In: R. Dutt, and K.P.M. Sundaram (Eds.), *Indian Economy (pp.56-72)*. S. Chand and Co, New Delhi.

Drèze, J., Sen, A.K. and Hussain, A. (1989) (Eds.). *The Political Economy of Hunger: Selected Essays*. Oxford: Oxford University Press.

Egbert, A.C. and Heady, E.O. (1961). *Regional Adjustments in Grain Production: A Linear Programming Analysis*. USDA Technical Bulletin 1241.

Ehrlich, P.R. (1968). *The Population Bomb*. Ballantine Books: New York.

Ehrlich, P.R. and Ehrlich, A.H. (1990). *The Population Explosion*. New York: Simon & Schuster.

Ehrlich, P.R., Ehrlich, A.H. and Daily, G.C. (1993). Food Security, *Population and Environment. Population and Development Review*, 19(1), 1-32.

Elliott, K.A. (2009). US Biofuels Policy and the Global *Food Price Crisis: A Survey of the Issues. In: J. Clapp and M. Cohen (Eds.). The Global Food Crisis: Governance Challenges and Opportunities*. Waterloo, ON: Wilfrid Laurier University Press.

Emmanuel, A. (1974). Myths of Development vs. Myths of Underdevelopment. *New Left Review*, 85, May-June.

Engel, E. (1857). Die Productions-und Consumtionsverhaltnisse des Königreichs Sachse. *Zeitschrift des Statistischen Bureaus des Königlich-Sächsischen, Ministerium des Innern*, 8(9), 1-54. It was reprinted as an appendix to *"Die Lebenskosten Belgischer Arbeiter Familien frfther und jetzt,"* Bulletin de l'institut international de statistique, tome IX, premiere livraison, Rome, 1895.

Epstein, G. (2008). Commodities: Who's Behind the Boom?. *Barron's*. 31 March. http://online.barrons.com/article/SB120674485506173053.html#articleTabs_panel_article%3D1%26articleTabs%3Darticle.

Ericksen, P.J. (2006). *Assessing the Vulnerability of Food Systems to Global Environmental Change: A Conceptual and Methodological Review*. GECAFS Working Paper 3.

Ericksen, P.J. (2007). Conceptualizing Food Systems for *Global Environmental Change* Research. Global Environmental Change. http://www.eci.ox.ac.uk/publications/downloads/ericksen07-foodsystems.pdf.

Evans, L.T. (1998). *Feeding the Ten Billion: Plants and Population Growth*. Cambridge: Cambridge University Press.

Ezekiel, M. (1930). *Methods of Correlation Analysis*. New York: Wiley; London: Chapman and Hall.

On Measuring Global Food Crisis

Ezekiel, M. (1938). The Cobweb Theorem. *Quarterly Journal of Economics, 52*(2), 255-280.

Fan, S. et al. (2003). *National and International Agricultural Research and Rural Poverty: The Case of Rice in India and China.* EPTD Discussion Paper No. 109. Washington, D.C.: Environment and Production Technology Division, International Food Policy Research Institute.

FAO (1996). *Report of the World Food Summit,* Nov. 13-17. http://www.fao.org/docrep/003/w3548e/w3548e00.html.

FAO (2001). *Report of the Asia-Pacific Conference on Early Warning, Prevention, and Preparedness and Management of Disasters in Floods and Agriculture,* Chiangmai, Thailand, 12-15 June 2001. RAP Publication No. 2001/14. Bangkok: Regional Office for Asia and the Pacific, Food and Agriculture Organization of the United Nations.

FAO (2007). *Food Balance–Cereals Excluding Beer (2001-2003).* Food and Agriculture Organization of the United Nations, Statistical Yearbook 2005-2006, Volume Two. http://www.fao.org/statistics/yearbook/vol_1_1/site_en.asp?page=consumption.

FAO (2008). *Climate Change: Implications for Food Safety.* Rome: Food and Agriculture Organization of the United Nations. http://www.fao.org/documents.

FAO (2008a). *The State of Food Insecurity in the World. High Food Prices and Food Security-Threats and Opportunity.* http://ftp.fao.org/docrep/fao/011/i0291e/i0291e00a.pdf.

FAO (2008b). *The World Only Needs 30 Billion Dollars a Year to Eradicate the Scourge of Hunger: Time for Talk Over Action Needed.* Newsroom. June 3, 2008. Rome, Italy: FAO. http://www.fao.org/newsroom/en/news/2008/1000853/index.html.

FAO (2008c). *Number of Hungry People Rises to 963 Million.* Food and Agriculture Organization of the United Nations. http://www.fao.org/news/story/en/item/8836/.

FAO (2009). *Hunger Statistics.* http://www.wfp.org/hunger/stats.

FAO (2009a). *The State of Food Insecurity in the World Economic Crises – Impacts and Lessons Learned.* Italy.ftp://ftp.fao.org/docrep/fao/012/i0876e/i0876e.pdf.

FAO (2009b). *Countries by Commodity: Rice, Paddy. Major Food and Agricultural Commodities and Producers, Statistics Division, Food and Agriculture Organization of the United Nations.* http://faostat.fao.org/site/339/default.aspx.

FAO (2010). *The State of Food Insecurity in the World: Addressing Food Insecurity in Protracted Crises.* http://www.fao.org/docrep/013/i1683e/i1683e.pdf.

FAO (2011). *How to Feed the World in 2050.* http://www.fao.org/fileadmin/templates/wsfs/docs/expert_paper/How_to_Feed_the_World_in_2050.pdf.

FAO (2011a). *The State of Food and Agriculture 2010-2011- Women in Agriculture: Closing the Gender Gap for Development.* http://www.fao.org/publications/en/.

FAO (2012). *Global Initiative on Food Loss and Waste Reduction.* http://www.fao.org/save-food/en.

FAO (2012a). The State of Food Insecurity in the World 2012. http://www.fao.org/infographics/pdf/FAO-infographic-SOFI-2012- en.pdf.

Farrell, M.J. (1957). The Measurement of Productive Efficiency. *Journal of the Royal Statistical Society,* Series A, General 125, Part 2, 252-267.

Federico, G. (2008). *Feeding the World: An Economic History of World Agriculture, 1800-2000.* New Jersey: Princeton University Press.

Fischer, G. et al. (2002). *Global Agro-ecological Assessment for Agriculture in the 21st Century: Methodology and Results.* Research Report RR-02-02, International Institute for Applied System Analysis, Austria.

Bibliography

Florkowski, W.J. (2012). Food Policy for Developing Countries: The Role of Government in Global, National, and Local Food Systems. *American Journal of Agricultural Economics, 94(4), 1024-1025.*

Fox, K.A. (1953). A Spatial Equilibrium Model of Livestock-Feed Economy in the United States. *Econometrica,* 21, 547-566.

Folke, C. (2006). Resilience: The Emergence of a Perspective for Social- Ecological Systems Analyses. *Global Environmental Change,* 16(3), 253-267.

Fornell, C. (1992). A National Customer Satisfaction Barometer: The Swedish Experience. *Journal of Marketing, 56(1), 6-21.*

Fornell, C. and Bookstein, F.L. (1982). Two Structural Equation Models: LISREL and PLS Applied to Consumer Exit-voice Theory. *Journal of Marketing Research,* 19, 440–452.

Fornell, C. and Cha, J. (1994). Partial Least Squares. In: R.P. Bagozzi (Ed.), *Advanced Methods of Marketing Research* (pp. 52–78). Cambridge, England: Blackwell.

Fornell, C. and Larcker, D.F. (1981). Evaluating Structural Equation Models with Unobservable Variables and Measurement Error. *Journal of Marketing Research,* 18, 39-50.

Fortson, D. (2012). Blighted Crops to Spark Food Riots. *The Sunday Times,* 12th August, 7.

Fox, J. (1984*). Linear Statistical Models and Related Methods:* With Applications to Social Research. New York: Wiley.

Frankel, J. (2008). The Effect of Monetary Policy on Real Commodity Prices. In: J. Campbell (Ed). *Asset Prices and Monetary Policy (pp. 291 - 333).* Chicago: University of Chicago Press.

Fraser, E.D.G. and Rimas, A. (2010). *Empires of Food: Feast, Famine, and the Rise and Fall of Civilizations.* New York: Free Press.

Fraser, E.D.G. and Rimas, A. (2011). The Psychology of Food Riots: When Do Price Spikes Lead to Unrest?. *Foreign Affairs,* January 30. http://www.foreignaffairs.com/articles/67338/evan-fraser-and-andrew-rimas/the-psychology-of-food-riots.

Friedmann, H. (1982). The Political Economy of Food: The Rise and Fall of the Postwar International Food Order, *American Journal of Sociology,* 88 (Supplement): S248-286.

Friedmann, H. (2009). Discussion: Moving Food regimes forward- Reflections on Symposium Essays, *Agricultural and Human Values,* 26(4), 335-344.

Fuglie, K.O. (2008). Is a Slowdown in Agricultural Productivity Growth Contributing to the Rise in Commodity Prices?. *Agricultural Economics,* 39 (2008 supplement), 431–441.

Galbraith, J.K. (1959). John D. Black: A Portrait. In: J.P. Cavin (Ed.). *Economics for Agriculture.* Cambridge, MA: Harvard University Press.

Gale, F. and Henneberry, S. (2009). Markets Adapt to China's Changing Diet. *Choices – The Magazine of Food Farm and Resource Issues,* 2nd Quarter, 24(2). http://www.choicesmagazine.org/magazine/article.php?article=75.

Gannon, K.M. and Ostrom, T.M. (1996). How Meaning is Given to Rating Scales: The Effects of Response Language on Category Activation. *Journal of Experimental Social Psychology,* 32, 337-360.fsparrow

Garver, M.S. and Mentzer, J.T. (1999). Logistics Research Methods: Employing Structural Equation Modeling to Test for Construct Validity. *Journal of Business Logistics,* 20(1), 33-48.

Gaster, L. (1995). *Quality in Public Services: Managers' Choices.* Buckingham: Open University Press.

Geo, G. (2012). World Food Demand. *American Journal of Agricultural Economics,* 94(1), 25-51.

George, S. (1977). *How The Other Half Dies: The Real Reasons for World Hunger.* Montclair, NJ: Allenheld, Osmun and Co.

Georgescu–Roegen, N. (1966). *Analytical Economics: Issues and Problems.* Cambridge, Mass.: Harvard University Press.

Georgescu-Roegen, N. (1960). Economic Theory and Agrarian Economics. *Oxford Economic* Papers, 12, 1-40.

Griliches, Z. (1957). Hybrid Corn: An Exploration in the Economics of Technological Change. *Econometrica,* 25(4), 501-522.

Ghosh, B.N. (1977). *Disguised Unemployment in Underdeveloped Countries, with special reference to India.* New Delhi: Heritage Publishers.

Ghosh, B.N. (1988). A Note on Agricultural Taxation and Rural Poverty in India. *Asian Economic Review,* December, 421-432.

Ghosh, B.N. (1990). *Political Economy of Rural Poverty in India: Lipton Thesis Revisited.* New Delhi: Deep and Deep Publications.

Ghosh, B.N. (2001). *From Market Failure o Government Failure: A Handbook of Public Sector Economics.* Leeds: Wisdom House Publications.

Ghosh, B.N. (2002). Gandhian Political Economy: The Methodological Structuration. *Humanomics, 18(1), 9-28.*

Ghosh, B.N. (Ed.) (2011). Global Food Crisis: *Contemporary Issues and Policy Options.* Leeds UK: Wisdom House Publications.

Ghosh, S. (1991). *Economic Development in India: Urban Bias or Rural Bias?.* New Delhi: Deep and Deep Publications.

Gilbert, C.L. and Morgan, C.W. (2010). Food Price Volatility. *Philosophical Transactions of the Royal Society,* 365, 2023.

Gilbert, G.L. (2010). How to Understand High Food Prices. *Journal of Agricultural Economics,* 61, 398.

Giménez, E. and Peabody, L. (2008). *From Food Rebellions to Food Sovereignty: Urgent Call to Fix a Broken Food System.* Institute for Food and Development Policy.

Glauber, J.W. (2004). Crop Insurance Reconsidered. *American Journal of Agricultural Economics,* 86(5), 1179-95.

Goldenberg, S. (2012). *US Drought Could Trigger Repeat of Global Food Crisis.* http://www.guardian.co.uk/environment/2012/jul/23/us-drought-global-food-crisis#start-of-comments.

Goodall, J. (2008). *Biofuel Crops Hurt Rain Forests. Reuters,* April 29.

Goodland, R. (1997). Environmental Sustainability in Agriculture: Diet Matters. *Ecological Economics,* 23,189–200.

Gorst, J. (2000). *Modelling Customer Satisfaction in Service Industries.* PhD Thesis, Sheffield Hallam University, UK.

Goss, J. and Burch, D. (2001). From Agricultural Modernisation to Agri-Food Globalisation: The Waning of National Development in Thailand. *Third World Quarterly,* 22(6), 969-986.

Gray, A. and Kleih, U. (1997). The Potential for Selected Indian Horticultural Products on the European Market. *Marketing Series,* 11, Natural Resources Institute, Chatham, UK.

Bibliography

Gray, L.C. (1922). *Introduction to Agricultural Economics.* New York: Macmillan.

Gray, L.C. (1933). *History of Agriculture in the Southern United States to 1860.* Contributions to American Economic History, 2 Vols., Washington: Carnegie Institution of Washington.

Green, D.H., Barclay, D.W. and Ryan, A.B. (1995). Entry Strategy and Long Term Performance: Conceptualization and Empirical Examination. *Journal of Marketing,* 59, 1-17.

Grescoe, T. (2008). *Bottomfeeder: How to Eat Ethically in a World of Vanishing Seafood.* Bloomsbury USA.

Griffiths, T.L. and Tenenbaum, J.B. (2005). Structure and Strength in Causal Induction, *Cognitive Psychology,* 51, 334–384.

Griliches, Z. (1957). Hybrid Corn: An Exploration in the Economics of Technical Change. *Econometrica,* 25(4), 501–522.

Groves, R.M. et al. (2009). *Survey Methodology.* New Jersey: John Wiley & Sons.

Gustafson, R.L. (1958). Implications of Recent Research on Optimal Storage Rules. *Journal of Farm Economics,* 40, 290-300.

Gulati, A. and Dutta, M. (2009). *Rice Policies in India in the Context of Global Rice Price Spike.* Paper presented at the Food and Agriculture Organization of the United Nations workshop "Rice Policies in Asia—What Have We Learned from the Rice Price Crisis and Can We Avoid Another One?". February 10–12, Chiang Mai, Thailand.

Gulati, A., Landes, M.R. and Ganguly, K. (2009). Indian Agriculture: Managing Growth with Equity. *Choices – The Magazine of Food Farm and Resource Issues,* 2nd Quarter, 24(2). http://www.choicesmagazine.org/magazine/article.php?article=77.

Gunderson, L.H., Holling, C.S. and Light, S.S. (1995). Barriers Broken and Bridges Built: A Synthesis. In. L.H. Gunderson (Ed.), *Barriers and Bridges to the Renewal of Ecosystems and Institutions (pp. 489-532).* NY: Columbia University Press.

Gürkan, A.A., Balcombe, K. and Prakash, A. (2003). Food Import Bills: Experiences, Factors Underpinning Changes and Policy Implications for Food Security of Least Developed and Net Food-Importing Developing Countries. *In FAO. Commodity Market Review 2003-2004,* 19-38, Rome.

Haavelmo, T. (1943). The Statistical Implications of a System of Simultaneous Equations. *Econometrica,* 11, 1-12.

Hackl, P. and Westlund, A.H. (2000). On Structural Equation Modelling for Customer Satisfaction Measurement. *Total Quality Management,* 11(4-6), 820-825.

Haddad, L. and Gillespie, S. (2001). *Effective Food and Nutrition Policy Responses to HIV/AIDS: What We Know and What We Need to Know.* FCND Discussion Papers. IFPRI, Washington, DC.

Haddad, L. et al. (1996). *Food Security and Nutrition Implications of Intra-household Bias: A Review of the Literature.* Discussion Paper 19. Washington, D.C.: International Food Policy Research Institute.

Haggblade, S., Hazell, P. and Reardon, T. (2007) (Eds.). *Transforming the Rural Non-farm Economy: Opportunities and Threats in the Developing Countries.* Baltimore, MD: Johns Hopkins University Press.

Hair, J.F., Jr., Anderson, R.E., Tatham, R.L. and Black, W.C. (1998). *Multivariate Data Analysis with Readings.* 5th Edition. Englewood Cliffs, NJ: Prentice Hall.

Hall, T. (2006). *Changing the Face of Hunger.* Tennessee: W Publishing Group.

Hallett, G. (1981). The Economics of Agricultural Policy. New York: Wiley.

Hanley, C.J. (2011). *It's Costly to Keep Egypt's Daily Bread Cheap.* Associated Press. http://www.msnbc.msn.com/id/42303838/ns/business-world_business/t/its-costly-keep-egypts-daily-bread-cheap/.

Hansen, J.W. (2002). Realizing the Potential Benefits of Climate Prediction to Agriculture: Issues, Approaches and Challenges. *Agricultural Systems,* 74, 309-30.

Harmon, D. et al. (2010). Predicting Economic Market Crises using Measures of Collective Panic. *arXiv,* 1102.2620v1.

Harmon, D. Stacey, B. and Bar-Yam, Y. (2010a). Networks of Economic Market Interdependence and Systemic Risk. *arXiv* 1011.3707v2.

Harrison, R.W. (2009). The Food versus Fuel Debate: Implications for Consumers. Journal of *Agricultural and Applied Economics,* 41(2), 493–500.

Hassan, Z.A. and Katz, L. (1975). The Demand for Meat in Canada. *Canadian Journal of Agricultural Economics,* 23, 53.

Hatfield, J. et al. (2008). Agriculture. In: M. Walsh (Ed.) *The Effects of Climate Change on Agriculture, Land Resources, Water Resources, and Biodiversity (pp. 21–74).* Washington, DC: U.S. Climate Change Science Program and the Subcommittee on Global Change Research.

Hawkes, C., Friel, S. Lobstein, T. and Lang, T. (2012). Linking Agricultural Policies with Obesity and Non-communicable Diseases: A New Perspective for a Globalising World. *Food Policy,* 37(3), 343–353.

Hayami, Y. and Ruttan, V.W. (1971). *Agricultural Development: An International Perspective.* Baltimore: Johns Hopkins University Press.

Hazell, P.B.A. (1971). A Linear Alternative to Quadratic and Semivariance Programming for Farm Planning under Uncertainty. *American Journal of Agricultural Economics,* 53, 53-62.

Hazell, P. B.R., Pomerada, C. and Valdes, A. (1986). *Crop Insurance for Agricultural Development: Issues and Experience.* Baltimore, MD: Johns Hopkins University Press.

Headey, D. (2010). *Rethinking the Global Food Crisis: The Role of Trade Shocks.* Discussion Paper 00958. Washington, D.C.: International Food Policy Research Institute.

Headey, D. and Fan, S. (2008). Anatomy of a Crisis: The Causes and Consequences of Surging Food Prices. *Agricultural Economics,* 39 (supplement), 375-391.

Headey, D. and Fan, S. (2010). *Reflections on the Global Food Crisis.* Research Monograph 165, International Food Policy Research Institute, Washington DC.

Heady, E.O. (1951). A Production Function and Marginal Rates of Substitution in the Utilization of Feed Resources by Dairy Cows. *Journal of Farm Economics,* 33, 485-498.

Heady, E.O. (1957). An Econometrics Investigation of the Technology of Agricultural Production Functions. *Econometrica,* 25(2), 249-268.

Heady, E.O. and Candler, W. (1958). *Linear Programming Methods.* Ames, IA: Iowa State University Press.

Heady, E.O. and Dillon, J.L. (1961). *Agricultural Production Functions.* Ames, Iowa: Iowa State University Press.

Healy, B. and Munckton, S. (2008). Global Food Crisis: Biofuels Threaten Hunger. *Green Left.* http://www.greenleft.org.au/node/39360.

Bibliography

Heidhues, T. (1966). A Recursive Programming Model of Farm Growth in Northern Germany. *Journal of Farm Economics*, 48,668-684.

Helbling, T., Mercer-Blackman, V. and Cheng, K. (2008). Commodities Boom: Riding a Wave. *Finance and Development*, 45 (1), 10–15.

Henderson, J.M. (1959). The Utilization of Agricultural Land: A Theoretical and Empirical Inquiry. *Reviews of Economics and Statistics*, 41, 242-259.

Hendrickson, R.F. (1943). *Food "Crisis"*. New York: Doubleday, Doran and Company, Inc.

Hendrickson, M., Heffernan, W., Howard, P. and Heffernan, J. (2001). *Consolidation in Food Retailing and Dairying: Implications for Farmers and Consumers in a Global Food System*. Aurora, Illinois: National Farmers Union.

Henn, M. (2011). Evidence on the Impact of Commodity Speculation by Scientists, Analysts and Public Institutions. *World Economy, Ecology, and Development* (WEED). http://www.makefinancework.org/IMG/pdf/evidence_on_impact_of_commodity_speculation.pdf.

Henry, C.T. (1928). Research in Agricultural Economics. *American Journal of Agricultural. Economics*, 10(1), 33-41.

Hermann, M. (2006). *Agricultural Support Measures of Advanced Countries and Food Insecurity in Developing Countries*. United Nations University, Research Paper No. 141.

Hertel, T.W. (1997). *Global Trade Analysis Modeling and Applications*. New York: Cambridge University Press.

Hertel, T.W. (2011). The Global Supply and Demand for Agricultural Land in 2050: A Perfect Storm in the Making? *American Journal of Agricultural Economics*. 93(2): 259-275.

Hibbard, B.H. (1948). *Agricultural Economics*. New York: McGraw Hill.

Hicks, J. R. (1932). *The Theory of Wages*. London: Macmillan.

Hicks, J.R. (1939). *Value and Capital: An Inquiry into Some Fundamental Principles of Economic Theory. Oxford:* Clarendon Press.

Hildreth, C. (1957). Problems of Uncertainty in Farm Planning. *Journal of Farm Economics*, 39, 1430-1441.

Hildreth, H. and Houck, J. (1968). Some Estimators for a Linear Model with Random Coefficients. *Journal of the American Statistical Association*, 63(322), 584–595.

Himmelgreen, D. and Kedia, S. (2010). *The Global Food Crisis: New Insights into an Age-old Problem*. NAPA Bulletin, 32,

Hirway, I. (2001). Vicious Circle of Droughts and Scarcity Works: Why not Break It?. *Indian Journal of Agricultural Economics*, 56(4), 708-21.

Hochman, G., Sexton, S.E. and Zilberman, D.D. (2008). The Economics of Biofuel Policy and Biotechnology. *Journal of Agricultural and Food Industrial Organization*, 6, 8.

Hodgson, G.M. (2002). *Reconstructing Institutional Economics*. Unpublished Manuscript, UK.

Hoekman, B. and Ataman, A.M. (2010). *Food Prices and Poverty: Rethinking Conventional Wisdom*. World Bank. Centre for Economic Policy Research.

Hofer, C.W. and Schendel, D.E. (1978). *Strategic Management: A new View of Business Policy and Planning*. Boston: Little, Brown and Co.

Holt-Giménez, E. and Leahy, E. (2008). Biofuels and Food Prices. *Inter-Press Service News Agency*.

Holt-Giménez, E., Patel, R. and Shattuck, A. (2009). *Food Rebellions: Crisis and the Hunger for Justice.* Oakland: Food First Books.

Hopper, W.D. (1965). Allocative Efficiency in a Traditional Indian Agriculture. *Journal of Farm Economics,* 47(61), 16-24.

Hossain, M. (1996). Recent Developments in the Asian Rice Economy: Challenges for Rice Research. In: R.R. Evenson, R.W. Herdt and M. Hossain (Eds.), *Rice Research in Asia: Progress and Priorities (pp. 17-33).* Wallingford, UK: CAB International.

Hotelling, H. (1931). The Economics of Exhaustible Resources. *Journal of Political Economy,* 39,137-175.

Hoyle, R. (1995). *Structural Equation Modeling: Concepts, Issues and Applications.* Thousand Oaks, CA: Sage Publications.

Huang, J. et al. (2012). Biofuels and the Poor: Global Impact Pathways of Biofuels on Agricultural Markets. *Food Policy,* 37(4), 439-451.

Huberman, B.A. and Glance, N.S. (1993). The Dynamics of Collective Action. *Computational Economics,* 8(1), 27-46.

Huberman, M. et al. (1997). Role of Ethylene biosynthesis and Auxin content and transport in high temperature induced Abscission of Pepper Reproductive Organs. *Journal of Plant Growth Regulators,* 16(3), 129-135.

Hulland, J.S. (1999). Use of Partial Least Squares (PLS) in Strategic Management Research: A Review of Four Recent Studies. *Strategic Management Journal,* 20, 195-204.

Humphrey, J. and Schmitz, H. (1999). *Governance and Upgrading: Linking Research on Industrial Districts and Global Value Chains.* Institute of Development Studies, Brighton: Wiley-Blackwell.

IFAD (International Fund for Agricultural development) (2012). *The Future of World Food and Nutrition Security.* http://www.ifad.org/pub/factsheet/food/foodsecurity_e.pdf

IFPRI (International Food Policy Research Institute) (2012). *Hunger in Times of Land, Water and Energy Pressures.* October 11, http://www.ifpri.org/pressrelease/hunger-times-land-water-and-energy-pressures.

IFPRI (International Food Policy Research Institute) (2012a). *2012 Global Hunger Index – Background Facts and Key Findings.* http://www.ifpri.org/publication/2012-global-hunger-index-background-facts-and-key-findings.

Igbaria, M., Livari, J. and Maragah, H. (1995). Why do Individuals Use Computer Technology? A Finnish Case Study. *Information and Management,* 5, 227-238.

Igbaria, M, Guimaraes, T., and Davis, G.B. (1995). Testing the Determinants of Microcomputer Usage via a Structural Equation Model. *Journal of Management Information Systems,* Vol.11, No. 4, 87-114.

IMF (2008). *Food and Fuel Prices – Recent Developments, Macroeconomic Impact and Policy Responses. An Update.* http://www.imf.org/external/np/pp/eng/2008/091908.pdf.

IMF (2012). *Commodity Prices Rebound on Supply Shortfalls.* October 12, http://www.imf.org/external/pubs/ft/survey/so/2012/res101212a.htm

Innman, P. (2011). *Food Price Rises Pushing Millions into Extreme Poverty, World Bank Warns.* http://www.guardian.co.uk/business/2011/apr/14/food-price-inflation-world-bank-warning.

Ioannides, Y.M. (1997). Evolution of Trading Structures. In: W.B. Arthur, S.N. Durlauf and D.A. Lane (Eds.), *The Economy as an Evolving Complex System II (pp. 129-67).*

Bibliography

Reading, MA: Addison-Wesley.

IRRI (2008). *The Rice Crisis: What Needs to be Done?*. http://solutions.irri.org/images/the_rice_crisis.pdf.

Irwin, S.H. and Sander, D.R. (2010). *The Impact of Index and Swap Funds on Commodity Futures Markets*. OECD Food, Agriculture and Fisheries Working Papers 27.

Ison, R.L., Maiteny, P.T. and Carr, S. (1997). Systems Methodologies for Sustainable Natural Resources Research and Development. *Agricultural Systems*, 55, 257–272.

Ivanic, M. and Martin, W. (2008). Implications of Higher Global Food Prices for Poverty in Low-income Countries. *Agricultural Economics*, 39(s1), 405-16.

Jackson, P. (1995). Reflections on Performance Measurement in Public Service Organisations. In: P.M. Jackson (Ed.), *Measures of Success in the Public Sector: A Public Finance Foundation Reader*. CIPFA.

James, H.S. (2006). Sustainable Agriculture and Free Market Economics: Finding Common Ground in Adam Smith. *Agriculture and Human Values*, 23(4), 427-438.

James, L.R., Mulaik, S.A. and Brett, J.M. (1982). *Causal Analysis. Assumptions, Models, and Data*. Beverly Hills, CA: Sage Publications.

Jayne, T.S. et al. (2003). Smallholder Income and Land Distribution in Africa: Implications for Poverty Reduction Strategies. *Food Policy*, 28(3), 253-275.

Jin, H.J. and Kim, T. (2012). Structural Changes in the Time Series of Food Prices and Volatility Measurement. *American Journal of Agricultural Economics*, 94(4), 929-944.

Johnson, D.G. (1975). World Agriculture, Commodity Policy, and Price Variability. *American Journal of Agricultural Economics*, 57, 823–828.

Johnson, D.G. (1977). Post- war Policies Relating to Trade in Agricultural Products. In: L.R. Martin (Ed.), *A Survey of Agricultural Economics Literature (pp.34-67)*. Minneapolis: University of Minnesota Press.

Johnson, R.A. and Wichern, D.W. (1992). *Applied Multivariate Statistical Analysis*. 3rd ed. Englewood Cliffs N.J.: Prentice Hall, Inc.

Johnston, B.F. and Mellor, J.W. (1961). The Role of Agriculture in Economic Development. *The American Economic Review*, 51(4), 566-593.

Joreskog, K.G. (1970) A General Method for Analysis of Covariance Structures. *Biometrika*, 57, 239-251.

Jouzier, É. (1911). *Économie Rural*. (In French). Paris : Baillière.

Kahlon, A.S. and Tyagi, D.S. (1980). Inter-Sectoral Terms of Trade. *Economic and Political Weekly*, 27, 133-140.

Kaldor, N. (1934). The Cobweb Theorem. *Quarterly Journal of Economics*, 52(2), 255–280.

Kamanou, G. and Morduch, J. (2002). *Measuring Vulnerability to Poverty*. Discussion Paper 2002/58. Helsinki: World Institute for Development Economics Research (WIDER), United Nations University.

Kanji, G.K. (2002). *Measuring Business Excellence*. London: Routledge.

Kanji, G.K. and Alfred, W.S. (2002). *Supply Management Excellence*. Chichester, UK: Kingsham Press.

Kanji, G.K. and Chopra, P.K. (2007). Poverty as a System: Human contestability Approach to Poverty Measurement. *Journal of Applied Statistics*, 34(9), 1135-1158.

Kanji, G.K. and Chopra, P. (2010). Corporate Social Responsibility in a Global Economy. *Total Quality Management & Business Excellence*, 21(2),119-143.

Kao, C.H.C., Anschel, K. R. and Eicher, C. K. (1964). Disguised Unemployment in Agriculture: A Survey. In: C.K. Eicher and L. Witt (Eds.), *Agriculture in Economic Development (pp. 129-43).* New York: Karnikova, Ludmila.

Kaplan, D. (2000). *Structural Equation Modelling: Foundations and Extensions.* Thousand Oaks, CA: Sage Publications.

Karim, M. (2011). *Measures Taken to Control Food Prices.* http://www.bdnews24.com/details.php?cid=2&id=188224.

Kauffman, S. (1995). *At Home in the Universe: The Search for the Laws of Self-organisation and Complexity.* New York: Oxford University Press.

Kaufman, F. (2010). The Food Bubble: How Wall Street Starved Millions and Got Away with It? *Harper's Magazine,* 27.

Kavi Kumar, K. S. and Parikh, J. (2001). Socio-Economic Impacts of Climate Change on Indian Agriculture. *International Review for Environmental Strategies,* 2(2), 277-93.

Kenadjian, B. (1957). *Disguised Unemployment in Underdeveloped Countries.* Unpublished Thesis. Harvard University, Cambridge: Massachusetts.

Kennedy, G., Nantel, G. and Shetty, P. (2004). Globalization of Food Systems in Developing Countries: A Synthesis of Country Case Studies. In: FAO (Ed.), *Globalization of Food Systems in Developing Countries: Impact on Food Security and Nutrition (pp.13-24).* FAO, Rome.

Kerr, J., Pangare, G. and Pangare, L.P. (2002). *Watershed Development Projects in India: An Evaluation.* Research Report 127. Washington, D.C.: International Food Policy Research Institute.

Kherallah, M. et al. *(2002). Reforming Agricultural Markets in Africa.* Johns Hopkins University Press: Baltimore, MD, USA.

Khosla, V. (2008). Biofuels: Clarifying Assumptions. *Science,* 322, 371.

Khusro, A.M. (1961). Inter-Sectoral Terms of Trade and Price Policy. *Economic Weekly,* 13(4/6), 289-291.

Kingombe, C.K.M. (2011*). Mapping the New Infrastructure Financing Landscape.* London: Overseas Development Institute.

Kirman, A.P. (1997). The Economy as an Interactive System. In: W.B. Arthur, S.N. Durlauf and D.A. Lane (Eds.), *The Economy as an Evolving Complex System II (pp. 491-531),* Reading, MA: Addison-Wesley.

Klime, P. (2000). *A Psychometrics Primer.* London: Free Association Books.

Kline, R.B. (2005). *Principles and Practice of Structural Equation Modeling.* 2nd Edition. New York: Guilford Press.

Kollman, K., Miller, J.H. and Page, S. (1997). Computational Political Economy. In: W.B. Arthur, S.N. Durlauf and D.A. Lane (Eds.), *The Economy as an Evolving Complex System II (pp. 461-86),* Reading, MA: Addison-Wesley.

Kong, D. (2012). Does Corporate Social Responsibility Matter in the Food Industry? Evidence from a Nature Experiment in China. *Food Policy,* 37 (3), 323–334.

Krebs, D. and Hoffmeyer-Zlotnik, J.H.P (2009). *Bipolar versus Unipolar Scale Format in Fully versus Endpoint Verbalized Scales.* European Survey Research Association. Retrieved March, 22, 2011 http://surveymethodology.eu/conferences/warsaw-2009/presentation/163.

Krugman, P. (2011). *Signatures of Speculation.* New York Times Blog. http://krugman.blogs.nytimes.com/2011/02/07/signatures-of-speculation/.

Bibliography

Kudlow, L. (2011). Food Riots: Is Bernanke Partially to Blame?. *Money and Politics.* http://www.cnbc.com/id/41317486/Food_Riots_Is_Bernanke_Partially_to_Blame.

Kulshreshtha, S.N. (1979). Functional form Specification in the Quarterly Demand for Red Meats in Canada. *Western Journal of Agricultural Economics,* 4, 89.

Kulshreshtha, S.N. (2008). Linear versus Log-linear Unit-root Specification: An Application of Misspecification Encompassing. *Oxford Bulletin of Economics and Statistics,* 70, 829.

Krueger, A.O. (1990). *Government Failures in Development.* National Bureau of Economic Research Working Paper Series No 3340, Cambridge, MA 02138, April.

Krueger, A.O., Schiff, M. and Valdes, A. (1991-1994). *The Political Economy of Agricultural Policy.* 4 Volumes. Baltimore: Johns Hopkins University Press.

Kuchler, M. and Linnér, B. (2012). Challenging the Food vs. Fuel Dilemma: Genealogical Analysis of the Biofuel Discourse Pursued by International Organizations. *Food Policy,* 37(5), 581–588.

Lagi, M., Bertrand, Bar-Yam, Y., K.Z. and Bar-Yam, Y. (2011). Food Crises: A Quantitative Model of Food Prices Including Speculators and Ethanol. *arXiv:1109.4859.*

Lagi, M., Bertrand, Bar-Yam, Y., K.Z. and Bar-Yam, Y. (2012). *Economics of Food Prices and Crisis.* New England Complex Systems Institute.

Lane, D.A. and Maxfield, R. (1997). Foresight, Complexity, and Strategy. In: W.B. Arthur, S.N. Durlauf and D.A. Lane (Eds.), *The Economy as an Evolving Complex System II (pp. 169-98),* Reading, MA: Addison-Wesley.

Lang, T., D. Barling, D. and Caraher,M.(2009). *Food Policy.* Oxford: Oxford University Press.

Lappe, F.M. et al. (1998). *World Hunger: 12 Myths.* New York: Grove Press.

Larkin, J.H. and Simon, H.A. (1987). Why a Diagram is (Sometimes) Worth Ten Thousand Words. *Cognitive Science,* 11(1), 65–100.

Lee, S.Y. (2007). *Structural Equation Modelling: A Bayesian Approach.* New York: Wiley.

Leibenstein, H. (1957). The Theory of Underemployment in Backward Countries. *Journal of Political Economy,* 65(2), 91-103.

Leidecker, J.K. and Bruno, A.V. (1984). Identifying and Using Critical Success Factors. *Long Range Planning,* 17(1), 23-32.

Leijonhufvud, A. (1997). Macroeconomics and Complexity: Inflation Theory. In: W.B. Arthur, S.N. Durlauf and D.A. Lane (Eds.), *The Economy as an Evolving Complex System II (pp. 321-35).* Reading, MA: Addison-Wesley.

Leontief, W.W. (1971). Theoretical Assumptions and Non-observed Facts. *American Economic Review,* 61, 1-7.

Lerner, R.L. (2000). *The Mechanics of the Commodity Futures Markets: What They Are and How They Function.* Mount Locus Management Corporation.

Lewis, W.A. (1954). Economic Development with Unlimited Supplies of Labor. *Manchester School,* 22, 139-191.

Leyna, H.G. (2009). *Food Insecurity: Associated Factors, Nutritional and Health-related Outcomes in Rural Kilimanjaro, Tanzania.* Oslo: Faculty of Medicine, University of Oslo.

Li, Eric A.L. (2011). Examining Food Security in China. In: B.N. Ghosh (Ed.). *Global Food Crisis: Contemporary Issues and Policy Options.* (pp.209-230). Leeds: Wisdom House Publications.

Liefert, W. and Swinnen, J. (2002). *Changes in Agricultural Markets in Transition Economies.* Agricultural Economics Reports 33945, United States Department of Agriculture, Economic Research Service.

Liefert, W.M., Liefert, O. and Serova, E. (2009). Russia's Transition to Major Player in World Agricultural Markets. *Choices – The Magazine of Food Farm and Resource Issues,* 2nd Quarter, 24(2). http://www.choicesmagazine.org/magazine/article.php?article=78.

Lindgren, K. et al. (Eds.) (1991). Evolution as a Theme in Artificial Life: The Genesis/ Tracker system. In *Artificial Life II (pp. 549-577),* Reading, MA: Addison-Wesley.

Lipsky, J. (2008). *Commodity Prices and Global Inflation.* http://www.imf.org/external/np/speeches/2008/050808.htm

Lipton, M. (1969). The Transfer of Resource from Agriculture to Non-Agriculture Activities: The Case of India. *IDS Communication,* Series No. 109.

Lipton, M. (1977). *Why Poor People Stay Poor: Urban Bias in World Development.* London: Temple Smith.

Lo, Y.T. et al. (2009). Health and Nutrition Economics: Diet Costs are Associated with Diet Quality. *Asia Pacific Journal of Clinic Nutritious,* 18, 598.

Locke, K.D. (2002). Are Descriptions of the Self More Complex than Descriptions of Others?. *Personality and Social Psychology Bulletin,* 28(8), 1094-1105.

Loehlin, J.C. (1998). *Latent Variable Models: An Introduction to Factor, Path and Structural Analysis.* 3rd ed. Mahwah, NJ: Lawrence Erlbaum Associates.

Lohmoller, J.B. (1989). *Latent Variables Path Modeling with Partial Least Squares.* Physica-Verlag, Heildelberg.

Lucas, R.B. and Papaneck, G. (1988). *The Indian Economy: Recent Development and Future Prospect.* Oxford: Oxford University Press.

Lusk, J.L. (2012). The Political Ideology of Food. *Food Policy,* 37(5), 530–542.

Lustig, N. (2008). *Thought for Food: The Causes and Consequences of Soaring Food Prices.* Shapiro Lecture. http://elliott.gwu.edu/news/transcripts/shapiro/lustig_shapiro.cfm.

Macan-Markar, M. (2011). *Food Price Hike Worsens Poverty in Asia IPS.* http://ipsnews.net/news.asp?idnews=55445.

MacKenzie, D. (2011). Can Complexity Theory Explain Egypt's Crisis?. *New Scientist.* http://www.newscientist.com/article/dn20082-   can-complexity-theory-explain-egypts-crisis.html.

Maddala, G.S., V.K. Srivastava and H. Li, (1995). Shrinkage Estimators for the Estimation of Short-run and Long-run Parameters from Panel Data Models, Working Paper (Ohio State University, Ohio).

Magdoff, F. and Tokar, B. (Eds.). (2010). *Agriculture and Food in Crisis: Conflict, Resistance and Renewal.* New York: Monthly Review Press.

Malthus, T. (1798). *An Essay on the Principle of Population.* London: J. Johnson.

Mardia, K.V., Kent, J.T. and Bibby, J.M. (1979). *Multivariate Analysis.* San Diego, San Francisco, New York, Boston, London, Sydney, Tokyo: Academic Press.

Marei, S. (1977). *The World Food Crisis.* Harlow, Essex: Longman Group Ltd.

Markelova, H. and Meinzen-Dick, R. (2006). *Collective Action and Market Access for Smallholders: A Summary of Findings.* Research Workshop on Collective Action and Market Access for Smallholders. Cali, Colombia.

Marimon, R., McGrattan, E. and Sargent, J.T. (1990). Money as a Medium of Exchange in an Economy with Artificially Intelligent Agents. *Journal of Economic Dynamics*

Bibliography

and Control, 14, 329-373.

Marsden, T. and Wrigley, N. (1996). Retailing, the Food System and the Regulatory State. In: T. Wrigley and N. Lowe (Eds.), Retailing, Consumption and Capital: *Towards the New Retail Geography (pp.33-47)*, Harlo Longman.

Marsden, T. et al. (2009). *The New Regulation and Governance of Food: Beyond the Food Crisis?*. New York/London: Routledge.

Marshall, A. (1920). *Principles of Economics* (Revised Edition). London: Macmillan.

Martin, M.A. (2010). First Generation Biofuels Compete. *New Biotechnology*, 27, 596.

Martin, W. and Anderson, K. (2011). Export Restrictions and Price Insulation during Commodity Price Booms. *American Journal of Agricultural Economics*, 94(1), 25-45.

Maruyama, G.M. (1998). *Basics of Structural Equation Modeling.* Thousand Oaks, CA: Sage Publications.

Marx, H.L. (1975). *The World Food Crisis.* New York: H. W. Wilson.

Mathur, A. (1964). An Anatomy of Disguised Unemployment. *Oxford Economic Papers*, 16, 163-193.

Maxwell, S. (2001). The Evolution of Thinking about Food Security. In: S. Devereux and S. Maxwell (Eds.), *Food Security in Sub- Saharan Africa (pp.68-93).* ITDG, London.

Maxwell, S. and Slater, R. (Eds.) (2003). Food Policy- Old and New. *Development Policy Review*, 21 (5/6), 531-553.

Mazumdar, D. (1959). The Marginal Productivity Theory of Wages and Disguised Employment. *The Review of Economic Studies*, 26(3), 190-197.

McCann, S. (2011). *America and the Middle East Food Riots. American Thinker.* http://www.americanthinker.com/2011/01/america_and_the_middle_east_fo.html.

McClelland, D. (1969). *Motivating Economic Achievement.* New York: Free Press.

McCarl, B.A. (2008). U.S. *Agriculture in the Climate Change Squeeze: Part 1: Sectoral Sensitivity and Vulnerability. Report to the National Environmental Trust.* http://agecon2.tamu.edu/people/faculty/mccarlbruce.

McCullough, E.B., Pingali, P.L. and Stamoulis, K.G. (Eds.) (2008). *The Transformation of Agri-food Systems: Globalization, Supply Chains and Smallholder Farmers.* Food and Agriculture Organisation.

McKeon, N. (2009). *The United Nations and Civil Society: Legitimizing Global Governance-Whose Voice?.* London: Zed.

McKeon, N. (2011). *Global Governance for World Food Security: A Scorecard Four Years After the Eruption of the "Food Crisis".* Heinrich-Böll-Stiftung, Berlin, October. http://www.boell.de/downloads/Global-Governance-for-World-Food-Security.pdf.

McMichael, P. (2009). The World Food Crisis in Historical Perspective. *Monthly Review*, 61(03), 15-23 http://monthlyreview.org/2009/07/01/the-world-food-crisis-in-historical-perspective.

McMichael, P. (2009). *A Food Regime Genealogy, Journal of Peasant Studies*, 36 (1), 139–169.

McMichael, P. (2009). Contemporary Contradictions of the Global Development Project: Geopolitics, Global Ecology and the 'Development Climate, *Third World Quarterly*, XXX, 1, 251–66.

Meade J.E. (1952). External Economies and Diseconomies in a Competitive Situation. *The Economic Journal*, 62(245), 54-67.

Meade, J.E. (1973). *The Theory of Economic Externalities.* A.W. Sijthoff, Leiden and Institut Unversitaire de Hautes Etudes Internationales, Genève (Collection d'EconomieInternationale – 2/ International Economics Series – 2), 92.

Meadows, D.H., Meadows, D.L. and Randers, R. (1992). Beyond the Limits: *Confronting Global Collapse, Envisioning a Sustainable Future.* White River Junction, VT: Chelsea Green.

Meijerink, G.W. (2010). Panic as an Explanation for the Food Crisis of 2007-08? *Strategy & Policy Brief,* 15.

Meinzen-Dick, R. Markelova, H., Hellin, J., and Dohrn, S. (2009). Collective Action for Smallholder Market Access. *Food Policy.* 34 (1), 1-118.

Meller, J.W. (1963). The Use and Productivity of Farm Family Labor in Early Stages of Agricultural Development. *Journal of Farm Economics,* 45, 517-534.

Mellor, J.W. (1966). *The Economics of Agricultural Production.* Ithaca: Cornell University Press.

Mellor, J.W. and Desai, G. (1985). *Agricultural Change and Rural Poverty.* Baltimore: Johns Hopkins University Press.

Michell, J. (1986). Measurement Scales and Statistics: A Clash of Paradigms. *Psychological Bulletin,* 3, 398–407.

Michell, J. (1997). Quantitative Science and the Definition of Measurement in Psychology. *British Journal of Psychology,* 88, 355–383.

Michell, J. (1999). *Measurement in Psychology – A Critical History of a Methodological Concept.* Cambridge: Cambridge University Press.

Miehlbradt, A.O. and McVay, M. (2005). *From BDS to Making Markets Work for the Poor.* International Labour Organization, Geneva, Switzerland.

Miranda, M.J. and Glauber, J.W. (1997). Systematic Risk, Reinsurance, and the Failure of Crop Insurance Markets. *American Journal of Agricultural Economics,* 79, 206-215.

Mitchell, D. (2008). *A Note on Rising Food Prices.* World Bank Development Economics Group 4682.

Mitra, A. (1977). *Terms of Trade and Class Relations.* London: Frank Cass.

Mitra, S. and Josling, T. (2009). *Agricultural Export Restrictions: Welfare Implications and Trade Disciplines.* Rome: International Food and Agricultural Trade Policy Council.

Mittal, A. (2006). Food Security: Empty Promises of Technological Solutions. *Development,* 49(4), 33–38.

Mondi, A., Koo, C.M. and Kim, W.J. (2010). *Oil Shocks and the World Rice Market Puzzle: A Structural Var Analysis.* Tech. rep., Kangwon National University, Department of Economics. http://www.apeaweb.org/confer/hk10/papers/mondi_alberto.pdf.

Moore, M. (1984). Political Economy and the Rural-Urban Divide. *Journal of Peasant Studies,* 24(1-2), 226-250.

Morduch, J. (1994). Poverty and Vulnerability. *American Economic Review,* 84 (2), 221-25.

Morgan, D. (1980). *Merchants of Grain.* New York: Viking.

Morin, E. (2008). *On Complexity.* Cresskill, NJ: Hampton Press.

Murphy, J. and Levidow, L. (2006). *Governing the Transatlantic Conflict over Agricultural Biotechnology: Contending Coalitions, Trade Liberalisation and Standard Setting.* London: Routledge.

Myers, R. J. (1989). Econometric Testing for Risk Averse Behaviour in Agriculture. *Applied Economics,* 21, 542-552.

Bibliography

Nair, M.S. (2010). Globalisation and its Impact on Agriculture: A Case Study of Kerala. In: B.N. Ghosh (Ed.), *Global Governance, Labour Market Dynamics and Social Change: Essays in Honour of Emeritus Professor Ozay Mehmet (pp.241-264),* Leeds: Wisdom House Publications.

Namboodiri, N.K., Carter, L.F. and Blalock, H. M. (1975). *Applied Multivariate Analysis and Experimental Designs.* New York: McGraw-Hill.

Naylor, R.L. et al. (2007). The Ripple Effect: Biofuels, Food Security and the Environment. *Environment Magazine,* 49, 30–43.

Naylor, R.L. and Falcon, W.P. (2010). Food Security in an Era of Economic Volatility. *Population and Development Review,* 36, 693.

Nedergaard, P. (2006). Market Failures and Government Failures: A Theoretical Model of the Common Agricultural Policy. *Public Choice,* 127 (3/4), 393-413.

Nellemann, C. et al. (Eds.). (2009). *The Environmental Food Crisis –* The Environment's Role in Averting Future Food Crises. A UNEP Rapid Response Assessment. United Nations Environment Programme, GRID-Arendal.

Nene, Y.L. (2002). Modern Agronomic Concepts and Practices Evident in Kautilya's Arthasastra (c.300 BC). *Asian Agri-History,* 6(3), 231-242.

Nerlove, M. (1958). *The Dynamics of Supply: Estimation of Farmers Response to Price.* Baltimore: Johns Hopkins University Press.

Ness, I. (2009) (ed.). *The International Encyclopedia of Revolution and Protest.* New York: Blackwell.

Newbury, D.M.G. and Stiglitz, J.E. (1981). *The Theory of Commodity Stabilization- A Study in the Economics of Risk.* Oxford: Claredon.

Nord, M. (2009). *Food Spending Declined and Food Insecurity Increased for Middle-income and Low-income Households from 2000-2007.* United States, Department of Agriculture.

Norgaard, R.B., 1984. Co-evolutionary Agricultural Development. *Economic Development and Cultural Change,* 32(3),525-546.

North, D.C. (1997). Some Fundamental Puzzles in Economic History/Development. Complexity Vision and the Teaching of Economics. In: W.B. Arthur, S.N. Durlauf and D.A. Lane (Eds.), *The Economy as an Evolving Complex System II (pp. 223-37),* Reading, MA: Addison-Wesley.

Nunnally, J. C. (1978). *Psychometric Theory* (2nd ed.). New York: McGraw Hill

Nunnally, J. and Bernstein, I. (1994). *Psychometry Theory* (3rd edition). New York: McGraw Hill.

Olson, M. (1965). *The Logic of Collective Action: Public Goods and the Theory of Groups.* Cambridge, Mass.: Harvard University Press.

Orden, D. (2010). Recent Macroeconomic Dynamics and Agriculture in Historical Perspective. *Journal of Agricultural and Applied Economics,* 42, 467.

Oshima, H. (1958). Underemployment in Backward Economies: An Empirical Comment. *Journal of Political Economy,* 66, 259-263.

Otter, C. (2010). *Feast and Famine: The Global Food Crisis.* http://ehistory.osu.edu/osu/origins/article.cfm?articleid=38.

Parry, M.L. et al. (Eds.) (2007). *Climate Change 2007: Impacts, Adaptation and Vulnerability. Contribution of Working Group II to the Fourth Assessment Report of the Intergovernmental Panel on Climate Change.* Cambridge, UK.

Passaorio, J.C. and Wodon, Q. (2008). *Impact of Higher Food Prices on Cost of Living: Assessing Multiplier Effects Using Social Accounting Matrices.* Washington, D.C.: World Bank.

Patel, R. (2009). *Stuffed and Starved: Markets, Power and the Hidden Battle for the World's Food System.* London: Portobello.

Patel, R. (2010). *Mozambique's Food Riots – The True Face of Global Warming. The Observer.* http://www.guardian.co.uk/commentisfree/2010/sep/05/mozambique-food-riots-patel.

Patel, R., Holt-Giménez, E. and Shattuck, A. (2009). Ending Africa's Hunger. *The Nation.* September 21.

Patnaik, U. (1996). Export-oriented Agriculture and Food Security in Developing Countries and India. *Economic and Political Weekly,* 31, 35–37.

Patnaik, U. (2009). Origins of the Food Crisis in India and Developing Countries. *Monthly Review,* 61(03), 25-36. http://monthlyreview.org/2009/07/01/origins-of-the-food-crisis-in-india-and-developing-countries.

Pelletier, D.L. (2002). *Toward a Common Understanding of Malnutrition. Assessing the Contribution of the UNICEF Framework.* Background Paper. World Bank/United Nations Children's Emergency Fund (UNICEF) Nutrition Assessment, September 2002, 2–24.

Pender, J. (2009). *The World Food Crisis, Land Degradation and Sustainable Land Management: Linkages, Opportunities and Constraints.* International Food Policy Research Institute, Washington, D.C. Photocopy.

Per Pinstrup-Anderson, P. (2008). *High Food Prices and Food Riots: Is the Global Food Crisis Here to Stay?.* Cornell University, CIIFAD Seminar.

Per Pinstrup-Andersen, P. (2009). *Food security:* definition and measurement. Food Security, 1, 5–7.

Perry, G.M. et al. (2009). *Bio-fuels Production and Consumption in the United States: Some Facts and Answers to Common Questions.* Technical Report, Oregon State University, Agricultural & Resource Economics.

Peters, M., Langley, S. and Westcott, P. (2009). Agricultural Commodity Price Spikes in the 1970s and 1990s: Valuable Lessons for Today. *Amber Waves,* 7(1), 16-23.

Piesse, J. and Thirtle, C. (2009).Three Bubbles and a Panic: An Explanatory Review of Recent Food Commodity Price Event. *Food Policy,* 34, 119.

Pilcher, J.M. (2006). *Food in World History.* New York: Routledge.

Pingali, P. (2007). Westernization of Asian Diets and the Transformation of Food Systems: Implications for Research and Policy. *Food Policy,* 32(3), 281-298.

Pingali, P.L. and Binswanger, H. (1988). Population Density and Farming Systems: The Changing Locus of Innovations and Technical Change. In: R. Lee (Ed.) *Population, Food and Rural Development (123-140).* Oxford: Clarendon Press.

Pollan, M. (2006). *The Omnivore's Dilemma: A Natural History of Four Meals.* Penguin Press: New York.

Pollan, M. (2008). *In Defence of Food.* New York: Penguin Press.

Poole, N. (1997). *Change and Research in the Food Industry: A European Perspective.* University of Connecticut, Food Marketing Policy Center, Storrs, CT.

Popkin, B.M. (2003). The Nutrition Transition in the Developing World. *Development Policy Review,* 21(5-6), 581-597.

Bibliography

Porter, M. (1990). *The Competitive Advantage of Nations*. London: Macmillan.

Postel, S.L. (2000). *Entering an Era of Water Scarcity: The Challenges Ahead. Ecological Applications*, 10, 941–948. http://www.bioone.org/doi/abs/10.1899/08-178.1.

Praussello, F. (2011). The Impact of Policy and Institutional Factors. In: B.N. Ghosh (Ed.), Global Food Crisis: *Contemporary Issues and Policy Options (pp. 280-298)*, Leeds UK: Wisdom House Publications.

Pritchard, B. and Burch, D. (2003). *Agro-food Globalisation in Perspective. International Restructuring in the Processing Tomato Industry*. Aldershot: Ashgate.

Pyzdek, T. (1999a). Why Six Sigma is Not Enough. *Quality Digest, 19(11), 26*.

Quesnay, F. (1759).*Tableau Economique, 3rd Edition. Herausgegeben*.

Quisumbing, A., Meinzen-Dick, R. and Bassett, L. (2008). *Helping Women Respond to the Global Food Price Crisis*. International Food Policy Research Institute.

Rae, A.N. (1998). The Effects of Expenditure Growth and Urbanization on Food Consumption in East Asia: A Note on Animal Products. *Agricultural Economics*, 18(3), 291-299.

Ragan, H., and P. Kenkel (2007). The Impact of Biofuel Production on Crop Production in the Southern Plains, Mobile, AL: Southern Agriculture Economics Association Conference. (http://ageconsearch.umn.edu/bitstream/34883/1/sp07ra01.pdf).

Rahman, R.I. (1985). The Relevance of Urban Bias Theory for Bangladesh. *Bangladesh Development Studies*, March, 36-51.

Raikes, P. and Gibbon, P. (2000). Globalisation and African Export Crop Agriculture. *The Journal of Peasant Studies*, 27(2), 50–93.

Rajagopal, D. et al. (2011). *Quantifying the Role of Biofuels in the Global Food Crisis.* http://deepak.berkeley.edu/WB%20food.pdf.

Rajcaniova, M. and Pokrivca, J. (2010). *What is the Real Relationship between Biofuels and Agricultural commodities?*. http://www.pulib.sk/elpub2/FM/Kotulic13/pdf_doc/08.pdf.

Randall, A. (1985). Methodology, Ideology, and Economics of Policy. *American Journal of Agricultural Economics*, 67(5), 1022-1029.

Rao, C.H.H. (1978). Urban vs Rural, Or Rich vs Poor. *Economic and Political Weekly*, 40, Oct. 7, 45-68.

Rao, V.K.R.V. (1980). Urban Bias and Rural Development. *Indian Economic Review*, Jan-March, 23-31.

Ravallion, M. (1990). Rural Welfare Effects of Food Price Changes under Induced Wage Rate Responses: Theory and Evidence for Bangladesh. *Oxford Economic Papers*, 42(3), 574-85.

Reardon, T., Timmer, C. P., Barrett, C. B. and Berdegue, J. (2003). The Rise of Supermarkets in Africa, Asia and Latin America, *American Journal of Agricultural Economics*, LXXXV, 5, 1140–46.

Reilly, J. et al. (2003). U.S. Agriculture and Climate Change: New Results. *Climatic Change*, 57, 43–69.

Reisinger, Y. and Turner, L. (1999). Structural Equation Modelling with LISREL Application in Tourism. *Tourism Management*, 20, 71-80.

Retherford, R.D. and Choe, M.K. (1993). *Statistical Methods for Causal Analysis*. New York: Wiley.

Ricardo, D. (1815). *An Essay on the Influence of a Low Price of Corn on the Profits of Stock*. London: John Murray.

Ricardo, D. (1921). *The Principles of Political Economy and Taxation.* London: Dent & Sons.

Richmond, B. (1993). *Systems Thinking: Critical Thinking Skills for the 1990s and Beyond. System Dynamics Review,* 9(2), 113-133.

Roberts, P. (2008). *The End of Food.* Boston: Houghton Mifflin Harcourt.

Robinson, K.L. (1989). *Farm and Food Policies and Their Consequences.* New Jersey: Prentice Hall.

Robinson, S. (2012). *Fear Grows as Food Prices Rise.* http://www.foodworldnews.com/articles/1917/20120802/food-price-rise-us-drought-dollar.htm.

Robles, M., Torero, M. and von Braun, J. (2009). *When Speculation Matters.* International Food Policy Research Institute, 57.

Rocha, C. (2006). *Food Insecurity as Market Failure: A Contribution from Economics.* Mimeo, School of Nutrition and Centre for Studies in Food Security, Ryerson University.

Roll, E. (1938). *A History of Economic Thought.* London; New York: Faber and Faber; Prentice-Hall.

Rosegrant, M.W. et al. (2008). *The Impact of Bio-fuel Production on World Cereal Prices.* International Food Policy Research Institute, Washington, D.C.

Rosegrant, M.W., Tokgos, S. and Bhandary, P. (2012). The New Normal? A Tighter Global Agricultural Supply and Demand Relation and its Implications for Food Security. *American Journal of Agricultural Economics,* published on line on May 24.

Rosen, S. and Shapouri, S. (2008). Rising Food Prices Intensify Food Insecurity in Developing Countries. *Amber Waves* 6 (1), 16–21.

Rosenstein-Rodan, P.N. (1957). Disguised Unemployment and Underemployment in Agriculture. *Monthly Bulletin of Agricultural Economics and Statistics,* 6, 1-7.

Rosin, C., Stock, P. and Campbell, H. (2011). *Food Systems Failure: The Global Food Crisis and the Future of Agriculture.* Earthscan, London.

Rostow, W.W. (1980). *Why the Poor Get Richer and the Rich Slow Down.* Austin: University of Taxes Press.

Roumasset, J. (1976). Rice and Risk: Decision Making Among Low Income Farmers. Amsterdam: Elsevier.

Rozelle, S. and Swinnen, J. (2004). Success and Failure of Reform: Insights from the Transition of Agriculture. *Journal of Economic Literature,* 42, 404-456.

Ruel, M.T. (2003). Operationalizing Dietary Diversity: A Review of Measurement Issues and Research Priorities. *The American Society for Nutritional Sciences, Journal of Nutrition,* 133 (11), 3911S-3926S.

Ruigrok, W. and van Tulder, R. (1995). *The Logic of International Restructuring,* London: Routledge.

Runge, C.F. et al. (2003). *Ending Hunger in Our Lifetime: Food Security and Globalization.* Baltimore, MD: Johns Hopkins University Press.

Runge, C.F. (2006). *Agricultural Economics: A Brief Intellectual History.* Working Paper WP06-1, University of Minnesota, Department of Applied Economics.

Runge, C.F. and Myers, R.F. (1985). Shifting Foundations of Agricultural Policy Analysis: Welfare Economics when Risk Markets are Incomplete. *American Journal of Agricultural Economics,* 67(5), 1010-1016.

Rutten, M.M., Chant, L.J. and Meijerink, G.W. (2011). *Sit Down at the Ballgame: How*

Bibliography

Trade Barriers Make the World Less Food Secure. 14th Annual Conference on Global Economic Analysis "Governing Global Challenges: Climate Change, Trade, Finance and Development". http://papers.ssrn.com/sol3/papers.cfm?abstract_id=1769745.

Sachs, J. (2005). *The End of Poverty: Economic Possibilities for Our Time.* New York: Penguin Press.

Sachs, J. (2008). Surging Food Prices Mean Global Instability. *Scientific American,* June, 35-49.

Saghaian, S.H. (2010). The Impact of the Oil Sector on Commodity Prices: Correlation or Causation?. *Journal of Agricultural and Applied Economics,* 42, 477.

Sakurai, T. (2002). *Quantitative analysis of collective action: Methodology and challenges.* Paper presented at the CAPRI Workshop on Collective Action, Nairobi, 25-28 February 2002. Retrieved February, 22, 2012 from www.capri.cgiar.org/pdf/ca_sakurai.pdf.

Salifu, A., G.N. Francesconi, S. Kolavalli. (2010). *A Review of Collective Action in Rural Ghana.* IFPRI Discussion Paper 00998, Washington DC.

Samuelson, P. (1947). *Foundations of Economic Analysis.* Cambridge, MA: Harvard University Press.

Sanders D.R., Irwin, S.H. and Merrin, R.P. (2008). *The Adequacy of Speculation in Agricultural Futures Markets: Too Much of a Good Thing?.* University of Illinois at Urbana-Champaign, Marketing and Outlook Research Report 2008-02.

Sanderson, I. (1994). *The Public Sector Management Handbook.* London: Longman.

Sargent, T.J. (1993). *Bounded Rationality in Macroeconomics.* Oxford: Clarendon Press.

Sarris, A. (2009). *Evolving Structure of World Agricultural Trade and Requirements for New World Trade Rules. Expert Meeting on How to Feed the World in 2050.* http://ftp.fao.org/docrep/fao/012/ak979e/ak979e00.pdf.

Saruchera, M. and Matsungo, O. (2003). *Understanding Local Perspectives: Participation of Resource Poor Farmers in Biotechnology – The Case of Wedza District of Zimbabwe.* Background Paper, IDS Biotechnology and the Policy Process in Developing Countries Project.

Satterthwaite, D., McGranahan, G. and Tacoli, C. (2010). Urbanization and Its Implications for Food and Farming. *Philosophical Transactions of the Royal Society,* B, 365, 2809–2820.

Scaife, M. and Rogers, Y. (1996). External Cognition: How do Graphical Representations Work?. *International Journal of Human-Computer Studies,* 45, 185-213.

Schmidhuber, J. (2006). *Impact of an Increased Biomass Use on Agricultural Markets, Prices and Food Security: A Longer-term Perspective.* Paper presented at a conference organized by Notre Europe, Paris.

Schnepf, R. (2008). *High Agricultural Commodity Prices: What Are the Issues?.* CRS Report for Congress. Congressional Research Service.

Schlosser, E. (2001). *Fast Food Nation.* New York: Houghton Mifflin Co.

Schoderbek, P.P., Schoderbek, C.G. and Kefalas, A.G. (1990). *Management Systems: Conceptual Considerations.* (4th ed.) Boston: R.D. Irwin Inc.

Schreiber, M. (2011). *Japan's Food Crisis Goes Beyond Recent Panic Buying.* http://www.japantimes.co.jp/text/fd20110417bj.html.

Schuh, G.E. (1974). The Exchange Rate and U.S. Agriculture. *American Journal of Agricultural Economics,* 56, 1-13.

Schuh, G.E. (1976). The New Macroeconomics of Agriculture. *American Journal of Agricultural Economics*, 58, 802-811.

Schuh, G.E. (1983). The World Food Situation: Changing Trends in World Food Production and Trade. *AEA Papers and Proceedings*, 73(2), 235–238.

Schultz, T.W. (1945). *Agriculture in an Unstable Economy*. McGraw-Hill: New York.

Schultz, T.W. (1953). *The Economic Organisation of Agriculture*. Bombay: TMM.

Schultz, T.W. (1956). Reflections on Agricultural Production, Output and Supply. *Journal of Farm Economics*, 38(3), 748–762.

Schultz, T.W. (1964). *Transforming Traditional Agriculture*. New Haven, CT: Yale University Press.

Schultz, T.W. (1968). *Economic Growth and Agriculture*. New York: MacGraw-Hill.

Schultz, T.W. (1971). *Investment in Human Capital*. New York: Free Press.

Schumacker, R. and Lomax, R. (1996). *A Beginner's Guide to Structural Equation Modeling*. Mahwah, NJ: Lawrence Erlbaum Associates.

Schwarz, N. (1991). Rating Scales: Numeric Values may Change the Meaning of Scale Labels. *Public Opinion Quarterly*, 55(4), 570-582.

Scott, A. (1955). The Fishery: The Objectives of Sole Ownership. *Journal of Political Economy*, 63, 116-124.

Scaramozzino, P. (2006). *Measuring Vulnerability to Food Insecurity*. ESA Working Paper No. 06-12, October, Agricultural and Development Economics Division, The Food and Agriculture Organization of the United Nations, www.fao.org/es/esa.

Seers, D. (1977). *Indian Bias in Urban Bias: Seers Vs Lipton*. Discussion Paper, Institute of Development Studies, University of Sussex, England.

Seers, D. and Joy, L. (1971) *(Eds.)*. *Development in a Divided World*. Harmondsworth: Penguin Books.

Segerson, K. (1988). Uncertainty and Incentives for Nonpoint Pollution Control. *Journal of Environmental Economics and Management*, 15(1), 87-98.

Sen, A.K. (1960). *Choice of Techniques*. Oxford: Basil Blackwell.

Sen, A.K. (1966). Peasants and Dualism With or Without Surplus Labour. *The Journal of Political Economy*, LXXIV (5), 425-450.

Sen, A.K. (1973). Poverty, Inequality and Unemployment: Some Conceptual Issues in Measurement. *Economic and Political Weekly*, August, 8, 31-33.

Sen, A.K. (1981). *Poverty and Famines: An Essay on Entitlement and Deprivation*. Clarendon Press, Oxford.

Sen, A.K. (1982). *Choice, Welfare and Measurement*. Oxford: Blackwell; Cambridge, Mass: MIT Press.

Sen, A.K. (1999). *Development as Freedom*. Oxford: Oxford University Press.

Senauer, B. and Venturini, L. (2005). *The Globalization of Food Systems: A Conceptual Framework and Empirical Patterns*. The Food Industry Center, University of Minnesota.

Senge, P. (1993). *The Fifth Discipline: The Art and Practice of the Learning Organization*. New York: Doubleday.

Sexton, R. (1990). Imperfect Competition in Agricultural Markets and the Role of Cooperatives: A Spatial Analysis. *American Journal of Agricultural Economics*, 72, 709-720.

Sexton, R. and Lavoie, N. (2002). Food Processing and Distribution: An Industrial Organization Approach. In: B.L. Gardner and G.C.

Bibliography

Rausser (Eds.). *Handbook of Agricultural Economics* (pp.156-175), Vol. 2B. Amsterdam: Elsevier.

Shackle, G. (1949). *Expectation in Economics*. Cambridge: Cambridge University Press.

Sharma, R. (2011). *Food Export Restrictions: Review of the 2007-2010 Experience and Considerations for Disciplining Restrictive Measures*. FAO Commodity and Trade Policy Research Working Paper, No. 32, May.

Shaw, D.J. (2007). *World Food Security: A History Since 1945*. London: Palgrave-Macmillan.

Shaw, D.J. (2008). *Global Food and Agricultural Institutions*. London: Routledge.

Shergill, H.S. (1988). Growing Imbalance in Agricultural Sector. *Mainstream*, 5 March, 25-38.

Shutes, K. and Meijerink, G.W. (2012). *Food Prices and Agricultural Futures Markets: A Literature Review*. Wageningen School of Social Sciences, The Netherlands, Working Paper No. 3. http://www.wass.wur.nl.

Shubik, M. (1997). Time and Money. In: W.B. Arthur, S.N. Durlauf and D.A. Lane (Eds.), *The Economy as an Evolving Complex System II* (pp. 263-83), Reading, MA: Addison-Wesley.

Simon, J.L. (1998). *The Ultimate Resource 2*. Princeton, NJ: Princeton University Press.

Skoet, J. and Stamoulis, K. (2006). *The State of Food Insecurity in the World 2006: Eradicating World Hunger*. Rome: Food and Agricultural Organization of the United Nations.

Skoufias, E., Tiwari, S. and Zaman, H. (2011). *Can We Rely on Cash Transfers to Protect Dietary Diversity during Food Crises? Estimates from Indonesia*. World Bank Policy Research Working Paper.

Smil, V. (2002). Eating Meat: Evolution, Patterns, and Consequences. *Population and Development Review*. 28,599-639.

Smit, J., Ratta, A. and Nasr, J. (1996). *Urban Agriculture: Food, Jobs and Sustainable Cities*. New York: UNDP.

Smith, A. (1776). *An Enquiry into the Nature and Causes of the Wealth of Nations*. London: W. Strahan and T. Cadell, London.

Smith, D.W. (1998). Urban Food Systems and the Poor in Developing Countries. *Transactions of the Institute of British Geographers*, 23, 207–219.

Smith, K., Lawrence, G. and Richards, C. (2010). Supermarkets' Governance of the Agri-food Supply Chain: Is the 'Corporate-Environmental' Food Regime Evident in Australia?, *International Journal of Sociology of Agriculture & Food, 17(2), 140-161*.

Smith, T.G. (2012). Obesity and the Economics of Prevention: Fit Not Fat. *American Journal of Agricultural Economics, 94(3), 815-817*.

Stage, J. (2010). Is Urbanization Contributing to Higher Food Prices? *Environment & Urbanization*, 22(1), 199-215.

Standford, C. (2007). *World Hunger*. Bronx, N.Y.: H.W. Wilson Co.

Steinbeck, J. (1939). *The Grapes of Wrath*. The Viking Press.

Stevens, S.S. (1946). On the Theory of Scales of Measurement. *Science,* 103 (2684), 677–680. http://www.mpopa.ro/statistica_licenta/Stevens_Measurement.pdf.

Stewart, S. and Waldie, P. (2008). *Who is Responsible for the Global Food Crisis?*. http://www.theglobeandmail.com/report-on-business/who-is-responsible-for-the-global-food-crisis/article688931/.

Stone, P., Haugerud, A. and Little, P. (Eds.) (2004). *Rethinking Commodities: Anthropological Views of the Global Marketplace,* Boulder, CO: Rowman & Littlefield.

Stover, L.E. (1987). *Robert A. Heinlein.* New York: Twayne.

Streeten, P. (1987). *What Price Food: Agricultural Price Policies in Developing Countries.* Ithaca, N.Y.: Cornell University Press.

Stringer, R. (2001). Food Security in Developing Countries. In: B.N. Ghosh (Ed.), *Contemporary Issues in Development Economics (pp.124-145).* London and New York: Routledge.

Sukhdev, P. (2008). *The Economics of Ecosystems and Biodiversity European Communities.* http://www.bmu.de/naturschutz_biologische_vielfalt/unkonferenz_2008/dokumente/doc/41607.php.

Tainter, J. (1988). *The Collapse of Complex Societies.* Cambridge University Press: Cambridge, UK.

Taylor, H.C. (1905). *An Introduction to the Study of Agricultural Economics.* New York: MacMillan.

Taylor, H.C. (1928). Research in Agricultural Economics. *Journal of Farm Economics,* 10(1), 33-41.

Tenenbaum, D.J. (2008). Food vs. fuel: Diversion of Crops Could Cause More Hunger. *Environmental Health Perspectives,* 116.

Tesfatsion, L. (1997). How Economists Can Get A Life. In: W.B. Arthur, S.N. Durlauf and D.A. Lane (Eds.), *The Economy as an Evolving Complex System II (pp. 533-64),* Reading, MA: Addison-Wesley.

The Economist (2012). *Artificial Meat: Hamburger Junction.* February 25th, Vancouver. http://www.economist.com/node/21548147

Thompson, J. (2003). Feeding the Future? Agri-food Systems and the Millenium Development Goals. In: David Satterthwaite(Ed.), *The Millennium Development Goals and Local Processes. Hitting the target or missing the point? (pp.93-102),* IIED.

Thompson, J. et al. (2007). *Agri-food System Dynamics: Pathways to Sustainability in an Era of Uncertainty,* STEPS Working Paper 4, Brighton: STEPS Centre.

Thorbecke, E. (Ed.) (1970). *The Role of Agriculture in Economic Development.* UMI.

Thrupp, L.A. (1995). *Bittersweet Harvests for Global Supermarkets: Challenges in Latin America's Agricultural Export Boom,* Washington, DC: World Resources Institute.

Thurow, R. and Kilman, S. (2009). *Enough: Why the World's Poor Starve in an Age of Plenty.* New York: Public Affairs.

Timmer, C.P. (1989). Food Price Policy: The Rationale for Government Intervention. *Food Policy,* 14, 17.

Timmer, C.P. (1995). Getting Agriculture Moving: Do Markets Provide the Right Signals?. *Food Policy,* 20, 455.

Timmer, C.P. (2000). The Macro Dimensions of Food Security: Economic Growth, Equitable Distribution, and Food Price Stability. *Food Policy,* 25, 283.

Timmer, C.P. (2008). Causes of High Food Prices. *Asian Development Bank,* Economics Working Paper SeriesNo. 128, October.

Timmer, C.P. (2009). *Rice Price Formation in the Short Run and the Long Run: The Role of Market Structure in Explaining Volatility.* Center for Global Development, Working Paper Series 172.

Timmer, C.P. (2010). Reactions on Food Crises Past. *Food Policy,* 35, 1.

Timmer, C.P. (2011). *Managing Price Volatility: Approaches at the Global, National, and Household Levels.* Center on Food Security and the Environment, May 26. Retrieved

Bibliography

February, 22, 2012 from http://foodsecurity.stanford.edu/publications/managing_
price_volatility_approaches_at_the_global_national_and_household_levels/

Timmer, C.P., Falcon, W.P. and Pearson, S.R. (1983). *Food Policy Analysis*. Baltimore: Johns Hopkins University Press.

Timmer, C.R. (2002). Agriculture and Economic Development. In: B.L. Gardner and G.C. Rausser (Eds.), *Handbook of Agricultural Economics* (pp. 245-270), Vol. 2 A. Amsterdam: Elsevier.

Tisdell, C.A. (2005). *Economics of Environmental Conservation*. Cheltenham: Edward Elgar Publishing.

Tobias, R. D. (1997). *An Introduction to Partial Least Squares Regression*. Cary, NC: SAS Institute.

Todaro, M.P. (1977). *Economic Development in the Third World*. London: Longman.

Tolossa D. (2010). Some Realities of Urban Poor and their Food Security Situations: A Case Study at Berta Gibi and Gemachi Safar in Addis Ababa City, Ethiopia. *Environment Urban*, 22, 179–198.

Trostle, R. (2008). Fluctuating Food Commodity Prices: A Complex Issue With No Easy Answers. *Amber Waves*, 6(5), 10-17.

Trostle, R. (2008). *Global Agricultural Supply and Demand: Factors Contributing to the Recent Increase in Food Commodity Prices*. Washington, D.C.: United States Department of Agriculture.

Tsioumanis, A. and Mattas, K. (2009). The Not-so-modern Consumer, Considerations on Food Prices, Food Security, New Technologies and Market Distortions. *European Association of Agricultural Economists*. http://ageconsearch.umn.edu/bitstream/58151/2/Tsioumanis.pdf.

Tyner, W.E. (2010). The Integration of Energy and Agricultural Markets. *Agricultural Economics, 41, 193*.

Tyner, W.E. (2010).What Drives Changes in Commodity Prices? Is it biofuels?. *Biofuels, 1, 535*.

UNCTAD (2008). *Addressing the Global Food Crisis: Key Trade, Investment and Commodity Policies in Ensuring Sustainable Food Security and Alleviating Poverty*. http://unctad.org/en/docs/osg20081_en.pdf.

UNCTAD (2008). *Tackling the Global Food Crisis* (Policy Brief 2). http://www.unctad.org/en/docs/presspb20081_en.pdf.

United Nations World Food Programme (2006). *World Hunger Series 2006: Hunger and Learning*. http://www.wfp.org/content/world-hunger-series-2006-hunger-and-learning/.

United Nations (2011). *Action Plan on Food Price Volatility and Agriculture*. http://www.un.org/issues/food/taskforce/.

United Nations (2012). FAO Food Price Index. http://www.fao.org/worldfood situation/wfs-home/foodpricesindex/en/

USDA (2008). *Food Security Assessment, 2007*. http://www.ers.usda.gov/media/205647/gfa19fm_1_.pdf

Valdes, C., Lopes, I.V. and Lopes, M.R. (2009). Brazil's Changing Food Demand Challenges the Farm Sector. *Choices – The Magazine of Food Farm and Resource Issues*, 2nd Quarter, 24(2), http://www.choicesmagazine.org/magazine/article.php?article=79.

Valero-Gil, J. and Valero, M. (2008). The Effects of Rising Food Prices on Poverty in Mexico. *Agricultural Economics*, 39 (Supplement), 485–496.

Vanhaute, E. (2011). From Famine to Food Crisis: What History can Teach Us About Local and Global Subsistence Crises', *Journal of Peasant Studies*, 38(1), 47-65.

Veblen, T.B. (1893). The Food Supply and the Price of Wheat. *Journal of Political Economy*, 1(3), 365-379.

Veblen, T.B. (1990). The Preconceptions of Economic Science. *Quarterly Journal of Economics*, 14, 240-69.

Veneroso, F. (2008). Commodity Comment. Global Strategic Outlook. *Veneroso's View*, April 1.

Vernon, J. (2007). Hunger: *A Modern History*. Cambridge, MA: The Belknap Press.

Viner, J. (1964). *Some Reflections on the Concept of Disguised Unemployment. Contribucoes a Analise do Desenvolvimento Economico*. Oxford: Oxford University Press.

von Braun, J. et al. (1993). *Urban Food Insecurity and Malnutrition in Developing Countries: Trends, Policies and Research Implications*. Washington D.C.: International Food Policy research Institute.

von Braun von, J. (2007). *The World Food Situation: New Driving Forces and Required Actions*. International Food Policy Research Institute, Washington

von Braun, J. (2008). *High and Rising Food Prices: Why are They Rising, Who is Affected, how are They Affected, and What Should be Done?*. Paper presented.at the USAID conference Addressing the Challenges of a Changing World Food Situation: Preventing Crisis and Leveraging Opportunity. April 11,Washington, D.C. http://www.ifpri.org/presentations/20080411jvbfoodprices.pdf.

von Braun, J., Ruel, M. and Gulati, A. (2008). *Accelerating Progress toward Reducing Childhood Malnutrition in India: A Concept for Action*. Washington DC: International Food Policy Research Institute.

von Braun, J. and Meinzen-Dick, R.S. (2009). *Land Grabbing by Foreign Investors in Developing Countries: Risks and Opportunities*. Policy briefs 13, International Food Policy Research Institute (IFPRI). http://www.eldis.org/go/topics/resource-guides/agriculture/land-grabbing&id=43603&type=Document.

von Grebmer, K. et al. (2008). *The Challenge of Hunger 2008: Global Hunger Index*. Bonn, Washington DC and Dublin: Deutsche Welthungerhilfe, International Food Policy Research Institute and Concern.

von Grebmer, K. et al. (2011). *Global Hunger Index*. International Food Policy Research Institute (IFPRI) Report. Concern Worldwide, and Welt- hungerhilfe.

von Thünen, J.H. (1828). *The Isolated State*. Translated to English (1966). Oxford: Oxford University Press.

Vu, L. and Glewwe, P. (2009). *Impacts of Rising Food Prices on Poverty and Welfare in Vietnam*. Development and Policies Research Center Working Paper 13, University of Minnesota, St Paul.

Wahl, P. (2008). Food Speculation: the Main Cause of the Price Bubble in 2008. *World Economy, Ecology, and Development*, Berlin. http://www2.weed-online.org/uploads/weed_food_speculation.pdf.

Waite, W.C. (1929). The Economics of Consumption as a Field for Research in Agricultural Economics. *Journal of Farm Economics*, 11(4), 565-573.

Walker, B. and Steffen, W. (1997). An Overview of the Implications of Global Change for Natural and Managed Terrestrial Ecosystems. *Conservation Ecology*, 1(2), 2. http://www.consecol.org/vol1/iss2/art2.

Bibliography

Walker, B.H. et al. (2004). Resilience, Adaptability, and Transformability. *Ecology and Society,* 9(2), 5. http://www.ecologyandsociety.org/vol9/iss2/art5/.

Walsh, B. (2011). *Why Biofuels Help Push Up World Food Prices.* http://www.time.com/time/health/article/0,8599,2048885,00.html.

Walton, J.K. and Seddon, D. (Eds.) (1995). *Free Markets and Food Riots: The Politics of Global Adjustment (Studies in Urban and Social Change).* Oxford UK& Cambridge USA: Blackwell.

Wansink, B. (2007). *Mindless Eating: Why We Eat More Than We Think.* New York: Bantam-Dell

Warr, S., Rodriguez, G. and Penm, J. (2008). *Changing Food Consumption and Imports in Malaysia: Opportunities for Australian Agricultural Exports.* Canberra: Australian Bureau of Resource and Agricultural Economics. Washington DC.

Watts, J. (2007). Riots and Hunger Feared as Demand for Grain Sends Food Costs Soaring, *The Guardian,* December 4.

Waugh, F.V. (1928). Quality Factors Influencing Vegetable Prices. *Journal of Farm Economics,* 10(2), 185-196.

Williams, J.C. and Wright, B.D. (1991). *Storage and Commodity Markets.* Cambridge University Press: Cambridge, UK.

Wilson, G.A. (2008). *Multifunctional Agriculture: A Transition Theory Perspective.* CAB International: Oxfordshire (UK) and Cambridge (USA).

Wittink, D.R. and Bayer, L.R. (1994). The Measurement Imperative. *Marketing Research,* 6, 14-22.

Wodon, Q. and Zaman, H. (2010). Higher Food Prices in Sub-Saharan Africa: Poverty Impact and Policy Responses. *World Bank Research Observer,* 25(1), 157-76.

Wold, H. (1954). Causality and Econometrics. *Econometrics,* 22, 162-177.

Wolf, C. Jr (1987). Market and Non-Market Failure. *Journal of Public Policy,* 7, 43-70.

Wonnacott, P. (1962). Disguised and Overt Unemployment in Underdeveloped Economies. *The Quarterly Journal of Economics,* 76(2), 279-297.

Wood, S. et al. (2005). *Food, Ecosystems and Human Well-being: Current State and Trends.* Washington, DC: Island Press.

Working, E.J. (1927). What Do Statistical 'Demand Curves' Show?. *Quarterly Journal of Economics,* 41, 212-35.

Working, H. (1922). *Factors Determining the Price of Potatoes in St. Paul and Minneapolis.* University of Minnesota Agricultural Experiment Station Technical Bulletin 10, October.

Working, H. (1949). The Theory of Price of Storage. *American Economic Review,* 39, 1254.

World Bank (2005). *Managing Food Price Risks and Instability in an Environment of Market Liberalization.* Agriculture and Rural Development Department Report 32727-GLB.

World Bank (2005a). *Managing the Livestock Revolution: Policy and Technology to Address the Negative Impacts of a Fast-Growing Sector.* Agriculture and Rural Development Department, Report No. 32725-GLB.

World Bank (2006). *Repositioning Nutrition as Central to Development: A Strategy for Large Scale Action.* Washington, DC: The World Bank.

World Bank (2007). *World Development Report 2008:* Agriculture for Development. Washington, D.C.: World Bank.

World Bank (2008). *Rising Global Prices: The World Bank's Latin American and Caribbean Region Position Paper.* First Draft for Discussion March 24, 2008. Washington, DC, United States: World Bank.

World Bank (2008a). *World Development Report, 2008, Agricultural for Development, Overview.* http://siteresources.worldbank.org/INTWDR2008/Resources/2795087-1192111580172/WDROver2008-ENG.pdf.

World Bank (2008b). *Rising Food Prices: Policy Options and World Bank Response.* http://siteresources.worldbank.org/NEWS/Resources/risingfoodprices_backgroundnote_apr08.pdf.

World Bank (2008c). *Bio-fuels: The Promise and the Risks.* World Development Report - 2008.

World Bank (2008d). *Food Price Crisis Imperils 100 Million in Poor Countries, Zoellick Says.* http://web.worldbank.org.

World Bank (2008e). *World Development Indicators 2008.* Washington, D.C.: World Bank.

World Bank (2011). *Food Price Watch, Poverty Reduction and Equity Group, Poverty Reduction.* http://siteresources.worldbank.org/INTPOVERTY/News%20and%20Events/22982478/Food-Price-Watch-August-2011.htm

World Bank (2012). *Global Agriculture and Food Security Program Announces New Round of Grants to Fight Hunger and Poverty.* http://web.worldbank.org/WBSITE/EXTERNAL/NEWS.

World Bank (2012a). *The Global Food Crisis Response: A Quick Response, But Long-Term Solutions.* April. web.worldbank.org.

World Food Programme (2012). *Safety Nets to Catch World's Hungry.* http://www.wfp.org/.

World Health Organisation (2010). *Food security.* http://www.who.int/trade/glossary/story028/en/.

World Health Organisation (2012). *Child Malnutrition: A Hidden Crisis Which Threatens the Global Economy.* http://www.who.int/pmnch/media/news/2012/20120215_stc_pr_children_malnutrition/en/.

World Health Organisation (2012a). *Response to the Food and Health Crisis in the Sahel.* http://www.who.int/hac/sahel_donor_alert_21june2012update.pdf

World Hunger Notes (2012). *2012 World Hunger and Poverty Facts and Statistics.* http://www.worldhunger.org/articles/Learn/world%20hunger%20facts%202002.html.

Wright, B. (2009). *A Note on International Grain Reserves and Other Instruments to Address Volatility in Grain Markets.* Policy Research Working Paper 5028, Washington, DC: World Bank.

Wright, B. and Cafiero, C. (2010). *Grain Reserves and Food Security in MENA Countries.* Tech. rep., World Bank http://siteresources.worldbank.org/DEC/Resources/84797-1288208580656/7508096128820861960 3/Wright_Grain_Reserves_and_Food_Security_in_MENA_Countries_PAPER.pdf.

Wright, S. (1921). Correlation and Causation. *Journal of Agricultural Research,* 20, 557-585.

Wright, S. (1934). The Method of Path Coefficients. *Annals of Mathematical Statistics,* 5, 161- 215.

Wunderlich, G.S. (2006). *Food Insecurity and Hunger in the United States: An Assessment of the Measure.* Washington, DC: The National Academies Press.

Young, P.H. (1993). The Evolution of Conventions. *Econometrica,* 61.

Young, A. (1767). *The Farmer's Letters to the People of England.* W. Nicoll, London.

Bibliography

Young, H. (2001). Nutrition and Intervention Strategies. In: S. Devereux and S. Maxwell, (Eds.). *Food Security in Sub-Saharan Africa.* ITDG, London.

Zezza, A. et al. (2008). *The Impact of Rising Food Prices on the Poor.* ESA Working Paper 08-07. Rome: Agricultural and Development Economics Division, Food and Agriculture Organization of the United Nations.

Zhang, K. et al. (2007). Land Use Change and Land Degradation in China from 1991 to 2001. *Land Degradation & Development,* 18(2), 209–19.

Zilberman, D. (1999). *Externalities, Market Failure, and Government Policy.* Spring Semester, Department of Agricultural and Resource Economics, University of California at Berkeley. http://are.berkeley.edu/courses/EEP101/Detail%20Notes%20PDF/Cha03,%20Externalitites.pdf.

Zilberman, D. et al. (2012). The Impact of Biofuels on Commodity Food Prices: Assessment of Findings. *American Journal of Agricultural Economics, first published online June 7.*

Ziska, L.H. et al. (2009). An Evaluation of Cassava, Sweet Potato and Field Corn as Potential Carbohydrate Sources for Bioethanol Production in Alabama and Maryland. *Biomass and Bioenergy,* 33, 1503-1508. http://www.cabi.org/Uploads/File/GlobalSummit/Lewis%20Ziska%20final%20paper.pdf.

Index

Index

Index

Index

Index

Index